FRANCE

TOP SIGHTS, AUTHENTIC EXPERIENCES

THIS EDITION WRITTEN AND RESEARCHED BY

Nicola Williams,
Alexis Averbuck, Oliver Berry, Jean-Bernard Carrillet,
Kerry Christiani, Catherine Le Nevez, Hugh McNaughtan,
Christopher Pitts, Daniel Robinson, Regis St Louis

Contents

Panthéon towering over Paris (p60)
BRUNO DE HOGUES/GETTY IMAGES ©

Plan Your Trip
France's Top 12

MAZIARZ / SHUTTERSTOCK ©

Paris

Romance and culture in the City of Light

Possibly claiming more famous landmarks than any other city in the world, the French capital evokes all sorts of expectations – and more than lives up to the promise. Think grand vistas across tree-shaded boulevards, romance along the Seine, world-class art museums, magnificent monuments evoking glorious histories, buzzing cafe pavement terraces and a bevy of city bistros. Allow yourself plenty of time to absorb, embrace and enjoy. Left: Parisian street; Right: Eiffel Tower (p38)

BODY PHILIPPE / GETTY IMAGES ©

NAUGHTYNUT / SHUTTERSTOCK ©

Loire Valley

Fabulous châteaux, medieval to Renaissance

If it's aristocratic pomp and architectural splendour you're after, this regal valley west of Paris is the place to linger. The Loire is one of France's last *fleuves sauvages* (wild rivers) and its banks provide a 1000-year snapshot of French high society. The valley is riddled with beautiful châteaux sporting glittering ballrooms and lavish cupolas. Hopeless romantics seeking the perfect fairy-tale castle, head for moat-ringed Azay-le-Rideau or supremely graceful Chenonceau.

Top: Château d'Azay-le-Rideau (p90); Bottom: Château de Chenonceau (p88)

2

ESPERANZA33 / GETTY IMAGES ©

Champagne
The heart and soul of French bubbly

Nothing quite fulfils the French dream like easy day hikes through neat rows of vineyards, exquisite picture-postcard villages and a gold-stone riverside hamlet. This is Champagne, the land of French bubbly where everyone – from world-famous Champagne houses in Reims and Épernay to passionate, small-scale vignerons (wine-growers) in drop-dead gorgeous villages along the exquisite Marne driving routes – lives, breathes and dreams the region's fizzy liquid gold. Do the same. Champagne vineyards and village in the Marne region

3

Nice

Riviera high life for savvy urbanites

There is no better city for soaking up the glitz, glamour and hedonist lifestyle of the legendary French Riviera. Undisputed queen of this Mediterranean kingdom of shimmering seas, idyllic beaches and lush hills, Nice is one of France's smartest urban hang-outs. Its old town is gorgeous, its street markets buzz and it knows how to party. Take the dramatic trio of coastal roads, impossible to drive without conjuring up the glitz of Riviera high life.

Right: Villefranche-sur-Mer (p219)

Provence

Slow touring around lazy lunches

Sip pastis over *pétanque* (boules) on the village square, mingle over buckets of herbs and tangy olives at the weekly market, hunt for truffles, taste Côtes de Provence rosé and congratulate yourself on arriving in Provence. At home in France's hot, sultry south, this region is a place that calls for slow touring around lazy lunches – be it motoring past scented lavender fields and chestnut forests, cycling through apple-green vineyards or hopping between hilltop villages.

AGAETA / GETTY IMAGES ©

Brittany

Outdoor capers with cider and crêpes

With its wild coastline, islands stitched together with craggy coastal paths, medieval towns and thick forests laced in Celtic lore and legend, this is a land for explorers. Pedalling past open fields dotted with megaliths gives a poignant reminder of Brittany's ancient human inhabitants, while the enthralling city of St-Malo promises visitors pure drama. Throw back a cider, bite into a sweet crêpe, rev up your sense of Breton adventure and tuck in. St-Malo (p140)

BONCHAN / GETTY IMAGES ©

Lyon

Gastronomic capital of France

No city in France excites taste buds quite like Lyon, the country's second-largest city, commandeering the vineyard-laced Rhône Valley in eastern France. The red-and-white checked tablecloths could be anywhere in France, but it's the extraordinary piggy-parts cuisine and quaint culinary customs that make Lyonnais dining so unique. Fabulous street markets, a stunning old town and fascinating silk-weaving heritage complete the ensemble. *Andouillette* (pig-intestine sausage)

7

Normandy

Emotional histories in northern France

This coastal chunk of northern France is a pastoral land of butter and soft cheeses, a kingdom where creamy Camembert, cider, fiery apple brandy and super-fresh seafood entice and inspire. Seductive is its coastline, a wind-buffeted ribbon of chalk-white cliff and dune-lined beach, climaxing with the mysterious, iconic, tide-splashed island-abbey of Mont St-Michel and D-Day landing beaches of 1944. In a small town called Bayeux meanwhile, history buffs relive the Norman invasion of England in 1066 with the world-famous Bayeux Tapestry. Right: Mont St-Michel (p108)

MOIRENC CAMILLE / AGE FOTOSTOCK ©

KYREN / SHUTTERSTOCK ©

MATT MUNRO / LONELY PLANET ©

Marseille
Two millennia of Mediterranean heritage

The Greeks loved it and so will you after a while: hot, sultry Marseille grows on visitors with its unique history, fusion of cultures, souk-like markets, millennia-old port and hair-raising corniches (coastal roads) chicaning around spectacular rocky inlets, surprise coves and glistening sun-baked beaches. The icing on the cake: the striking Musée des Civilisations de l'Europe et de la Méditerranée (MuCEM), a state-of-the-art museum showcasing Mediterranean history and mind-blowing panoramas across one of the Med's most bewitching cities. Far left: MuCEM (p248); Left: Le Panier (p250)

JUSTIN FOULKES/LONELY PLANET ©

Bordeaux

Fine wine and gourmet dines in southwest France

Bordeaux is a name synonymous with some of France's finest wine. Little wonder then that this elegant, architecturally rich city on the Garonne River oozes tasteful splendour from every historic crevice. A feast of gourmet dining awaits foodies and wine-tasting opportunities are outstanding, kicking off with the groundbreaking La Cité du Vin. Top: Winery in the Bordeaux region (p272); Above left: Locally produced wine; Above right: Assorted cheeses

10

RITTHA HUANG / GETTY IMAGES ©

French Alps

Mountain-and-lake outdoor action

Crowned by Mont Blanc (4810m), the French Alps show no mercy in their outdoor-action overload. At the heart of these big mountains is the iconic ski resort of Chamonix, birthplace of mountaineering and winter playground to the rich, famous and not-so-famous. Hop aboard the Aiguille du Midi cable car for the ride of a lifetime above 3800m. For foodies, fondue is the tip of the culinary iceberg in this region where cow's milk goes into dozens of cheeses.

11

CHRISTIAN MUELLER / SHUTTERSTOCK ©

St-Tropez

Sexy Riviera fishing port with bags of glamour

Sizzling St-Tropez is the French Riviera's hang-out of choice on the Med for celebrities and star-spangled party aficionados in summer, but the Riviera town is strangely quiet the rest of the year. Sit for hours in a bottleneck to arrive in August and curse the old fishing port; arrive by boat on the shimmering Mediterranean and love it forever. Indisputable assets: bewitching light, brilliant sandy beaches, fabulous market, chic bars, nightlife on the sand.

12

Plan Your Trip
Need to Know

When to Go

Brittany & Normandy
GO Apr–Sep

Paris
GO May & Jun

French Alps
GO late Dec–
early Apr (skiing) or
Jun & Jul (hiking)

French Riviera
GO Apr–Jun,
Sep & Oct

Corsica
GO Apr–Jun,
Sep & Oct

Warm to hot summers, mild winters
Warm to hot summers, cold winters
Mild year-round
Mild summers, cold winters
Alpine climate

High Season (Jul & Aug)

○ Queues at big sights and on the road, especially August.

○ Late December to March is high season in ski resorts.

○ Book accommodation and tables in the best restaurants well in advance.

Shoulder (Apr–Jun & Sep)

○ Accommodation rates drop.

○ Spring brings warm weather, flowers, local produce.

○ The *vendange* (grape harvest) is reason to visit in autumn.

Low Season (Oct–Mar)

○ Prices up to 50% less than high season.

○ Sights and restaurants open fewer days and hours.

○ Hotels and restaurants in quieter rural regions (such as the Dordogne) are closed.

Currency
Euro (€)

Language
French

Visas
Generally not required for stays of up to 90 days (or at all for EU nationals); some nationalities need a Schengen visa.

Money
ATMs at every airport, most train stations and on every second street corner in towns and cities. Visa, Master-Card and Amex widely accepted.

Mobile Phones
European and Australian phones work, but only American cells with 900 and 1800 MHz networks are compatible; check with your provider before leaving home. Use a French SIM card to call with a cheaper French number.

Time
Central European Time (GMT/UTC plus one hour)

Daily Costs

Budget: Less than €130

- Dorm bed: €18–30
- Double room in a budget hotel: €90
- Admission to many attractions first Sunday of month: free
- Lunch *menus* (set meals): less than €20

Midrange: €130–220

- Double room in a midrange hotel: €90–190
- Lunch *menus* in gourmet restaurants: €20–40

Top End: Over €220

- Double room in a top-end hotel: €190–350
- Top restaurant dinner: *menu* €65, à la carte €100–150

Useful Websites

France.fr (www.france.fr) Official country website.

France 24 (www.france24.com/en/france) French news in English.

Paris by Mouth (www.parisbymouth.com) Dining and drinking; one-stop site for where and how to eat in the capital with plenty of the latest openings.

French Word-a-Day (http://french-word-a-day.typepad.com) Fun language learning.

Lonely Planet (www.lonelyplanet.com/france) Destination information, hotel bookings, traveller forum and more.

Opening Hours

Opening hours vary throughout the year. We list high-season opening hours, but remember that longer summer hours often decrease in shoulder and low seasons.

Banks 9am to noon and 2pm to 5pm Monday to Friday or Tuesday to Saturday

Restaurants Noon to 2.30pm and 7pm to 11pm six days a week

Cafes 7am to 11pm

Bars 7pm to 1am

Clubs 10pm to 3am, 4am or 5am Thursday to Saturday

Shops 10am to noon and 2pm to 7pm Monday to Saturday

Arriving in France

Aéroport de Charles de Gaulle (p75) Trains, buses and RER suburban trains run to Paris' city centre every 15 to 30 minutes between 5am and 11pm, after which night buses kick in (12.30am to 5.30am).

Aéroport d'Orly (p75) Linked to central Paris by Orlyval rail then RER or bus every 15 minutes between 5am and 11pm. Or T7 tram to Villejuif-Louis Aragon then metro to the centre.

Getting Around

Transport in France is comfortable, quick, usually reliable and reasonably priced.

Train Run by the state-owned SNCF (p346), France's rail network is truly first class, with extensive coverage of the country and frequent departures.

Car Meander away from cities and large towns (where a car is hard to park), and a car comes into its own. Cars can be hired at airports and train stations. Drive on the right. Be aware of France's potentially hazardous 'priority to the right' rule.

Bus Cheaper and slower than trains. Useful for more remote villages that aren't serviced by trains.

Bicycle Certain regions – the Loire Valley, Brittany, the Lubéron in Provence – beg to be explored by two wheels and have dedicated cycling paths, some along canal towpaths or between fruit orchards and vineyards.

For more on **getting around**, see p341

Plan Your Trip
Hot Spots For...

French Cuisine

Gourmet appetites know no bounds in France, paradise for food lovers with its varied regional cuisines, open-air markets overflowing with seasonal produce and local gusto for dining well. Bon appétit!

ROMRODPHOTO / SHUTTERSTOCK ©

Art & Architecture

Literature, music, painting, cinema: France's vast artistic heritage is the essence of French art de vivre (art of living).

RASTI SEDLAK / SHUTTERSTOCK ©

Great Outdoors

From Alpine glaciers and canyons to the snowy dome of Mont Blanc – not to mention 3200km of coastline lacing both the Atlantic and the Med – France's dramatically varied landscapes beg outdoor action.

VICTORPALYCH / SHUTTERSTOCK ©

Wine Tasting

Viticulture in France is an ancient art and tradition. Be it tasting in cellars, watching grape harvests or sleeping au château, French wine culture demands immediate road-testing.

PAUL TRIDON/500PX ©

Lyonnais Bouchons (p172) No city enjoys such a gargantuan reputation for its cuisine and culinary culture as Lyon, France's gastronomic capital.	**Best Dish** A feisty *andouillette* (pig-intestine sausage) at Le Poêlon d'Or (p183).
Marseillais Bouillabaisse (p260) Originally cooked by fishers from the scraps of their catch, Marseille's iconic fish soup requires know-how and etiquette to eat.	**By the Sea** Eaten al fresco in the fishing village of Vallon des Auffes (p260).
Provençal Markets (p196) Fresh fish on the quayside in Marseille, plump melons and cherries, marinated olives; shopping at the *marché* is la belle France at her foodie best.	**Best Buy** Aromatic black truffles in season on Friday morning in Carpentras (p198).
Paris' Art Museums (p40, p59 & p62) *Mona Lisa,* impressionist masters at the Musée d'Orsay, Monet's famous water lilies; the capital's art collection is world class.	**Picasso Canvases** The world's finest collection in the Musée National Picasso (p60).
Belle Époque Nice (p210) From beach-side art deco palace to belle époque folly, iconic seaside town Nice oozes old-world architectural opulence.	**Photo Op** Seaside strolls and sunset watching along Promenade des Anglais (p220).
Signac's St-Tropez (p234) The legendary light of the Côte d'Azur comes into its own in this fishing port which is bathed in a golden light quite unlike anywhere else.	**Modern Art** Pointillist, Fauvist and cubist art at the Musée de l'Annonciade (p232).
Chamonix Ski Action (p290) In the French Alps, the birthplace of mountaineering and winter playground to the rich and famous, is heaven on earth for adrenaline junkies.	**Daredevil Run** The legendary Vallée Blanche with an off-piste guide (p291).
Kayaking Les Calanques (p252) Bijou rocky coves lace the shore east of Marseille and kayaking is the only proper way to enjoy these natural works of art up close.	**Lunch Break** Seafood lunch at Nautic Bar (p253), Calanque de Morgiou.
Climbing Dune du Pilat (p274) Stunning coastal panorama from Europe's largest sand dune. Nearby beaches have some of the Atlantic coast's best surf.	**Best Moment** Guided walks on the dune at sunset run by the Espace Accueil (p275).
Champagne Routes (p158) These gourmet driving itineraries are slow, scenic journeys wrapped around beautiful villages, vineyards and cellars packed with bubbly.	**Prettiest Village** Study up on Champagne at Le Mesnil-sur-Oger (p160).
Bordeaux Wine Tasting (p272) Bordeaux has the perfect climate for producing well-balanced reds. *Dégustation* (tasting) is the key to understanding local culture.	**Best Tasting** Exploratory tours and smart tasting at La Cité du Vin (p270).
Parisian Wine Bars (p71) Nowhere is wine culture so strong as in the capital, where Parisians mingle in atmospheric *bars à vin* over a glass of wine and tasty morsels.	**Black Book Address** A glass of wine around barrels at Le Baron Rouge (p73).

Plan Your Trip
Local Life

JOHNBRAID / SHUTTERSTOCK ©

Activities

Most French wouldn't be seen dead walking down the street in trainers and tracksuits. But contrary to appearances, they love sport. Shaved-leg cyclists toil up Mont Ventoux in Provence, football fans fill stadiums and anyone who can flits off for the weekend to ski or snowboard. Don't be shy in joining in.

Spring and autumn are the best seasons for walking and cycling in Provence and on the French Riviera, which swelter in summer.

Shopping

Paris is the bee's knees for luxury goods like *haute couture*, high-quality fashion accessories, lingerie, perfume and cosmetics. Lovely as they are, they most probably aren't any cheaper to buy in France than at home.

Non-EU residents can claim a VAT refund on same-day purchases over €175, providing the goods are for personal consumption and are being personally transported home; retailers have details.

Take along your own bag or basket when shopping for fresh fruit, vegetables and other edible goodies at the local weekly market. Ditto for supermarkets.

With the exception of the odd haggle at the market, little bargaining goes on in France.

Entertainment

Catching a performance in Paris is a treat. French and international opera, ballet and theatre companies and cabaret dancers take to the stage in fabled venues, and a flurry of young, passionate, highly creative musicians, thespians and artists make the city's fascinating fringe art scene what it is.

Paris' two top listings guides *Pariscope* (€0.70) and *L'Officiel des Spectacles* (www. offi.fr; €0.70), both in French but easy to navigate, are available from newsstands on Wednesday, and are crammed with everything that's on in the city.

Away from the capital, most large cities have an opera house, theatres and cinemas showing French-language films; the occasional movie house screens films in their original language (including English) with

BOTOND HORVATH / SHUTTERSTOCK ©

French subtitles – look for films labelled 'VO' *(version originale)*.

Eating

Adopting the local culinary pace is key to savouring every last exquisite moment of the delicious French day. Breakfast is a *tartine* (slice of baguette smeared with unsalted butter and jam) and *un café* (espresso), long milky *café au lait* or – especially kids – hot chocolate. Croissants (eaten straight, never with butter or jam) are a weekend treat. *Déjeuner* (lunch) translates as an *entrée* (starter) and *plat* (main course) with wine, followed by an espresso. Dinner, generally with wine and often ending with cheese and/ or dessert, is a longer, more languid affair.

A *menu* in French is a two- or three-course meal at a fixed price – by far the best-value dining.

Drinking & Nightlife

For the French, drinking and eating are best friends and the line between a cafe, *salon de thé* (tearoom), bistro, brasserie, bar and *bar*

★ Best Cafe Terraces

L'Ebouillanté (p72)

Le Petit Fer à Cheval (p73)

Grand Café des Négociants (p184)

Le Café (p241)

Bar de la Marine (p263)

Utopia (p281)

à vin (wine bar) is blurred. The line between drinking and clubbing is often nonexistent – a cafe that's quiet mid-afternoon might have DJ sets in the evening and dancing later on. One thing is certain though: from traditional neighbourhood cafe to cutting-edge cocktail bar, drinking options abound.

The *apéro* (aperitif; predinner drink) is sacred in France. Cafes and bars get packed out from around 5pm as locals relax over a chit-chat-fuelled *kir* (white wine sweetened with blackcurrant syrup), glass of red or beer.

From left: Al fresco dining in Nice (p224); Interior of Galeries Lafayette (p63)

Plan Your Trip
Month by Month

January

With New Year festivities done and dusted, head to the Alps. Crowds on the slopes thin out once school's back, but January remains busy. On the Mediterranean, mild winters are wonderfully serene in a part of France that's madly busy the rest of the year.

✿ Vive le Ski!

Grab your skis, hit the slopes. Most resorts in the Alps open mid- to late December, but January is the start of the ski season in earnest.

✿ Truffle Season

No culinary product is more aromatic or decadent than black truffles. Hunt them in Provence – the season runs late December to March, but January is the prime month.

February

Crisp cold weather in the mountains – lots of china-blue skies now – translates as ski season in top gear. Alpine resorts get mobbed by families during the February

school holidays and accommodation is at its priciest.

✿ Nice Carnival

Nice makes the most of its mild climate with this crazy Lenten carnival (www.nicecarnival.com). As well as parade and costume shenanigans, merrymakers pelt each other with blooms during the legendary flower battles.

April

Dedicated ski fiends can carve glaciers in the highest French ski resorts until mid-April or later at highest altitudes. Then it's off with the ski boots and on with the hiking gear as peach and almond trees flower pink against a backdrop of snow-capped peaks.

✿ Fête de la Transhumance

During the ancient Fête de la Transhumance in April or May, shepherds walk their flocks of sheep up to green summer pastures; St-Rémy de Provence's fest is the best known.

ANITASSTUDIO / SHUTTERSTOCK ©

May

There is no lovelier month to travel in France, as the first melons ripen in Provence and outdoor markets burst with new-found colour. Spring is always in.

✿ May Day

No one works on 1 May, a national holiday that incites summer buzz, with *muguets* (lilies of the valley) sold at roadside stalls and given to friends for good luck.

☆ Monaco Grand Prix

How fitting that Formula One's most glamorous rip around the streets of one of the world's most glam countries at Monaco's F1 Grand Prix (www.grand-prix-monaco.com).

June

As midsummer approaches, the festival pace quickens alongside a rising temperature gauge, which tempts the first bathers into the sea.

★ Best Festivals

Nice Carnival, February

Monaco Grand Prix, May

Festival d'Avignon, July

Route du Champagne en Fête, August

Fête des Lumières, December

☆ Fête de la Musique

Orchestras, crooners, buskers and bands fill streets with free music during France's vibrant nationwide celebration of music on 21 June (www.fetedelamusique.culture.fr).

✿ Paris Jazz Festival

No festival better evokes the brilliance of Paris' interwar jazz age than this annual fest (http://parisjazzfestival.paris.fr) in the Parc de Floral.

From left: Black truffles; Nice Carnival

July

If lavender's your French love, now is the time to catch it flowering in Provence. But you won't be the only one. School's out for the summer, showering the country with teems of tourists, traffic and too many *complet* (full) signs strung in hotel windows.

☆ Tour de France

The world's most prestigious cycling race ends on Paris' av des Champs-Élysées on the third or fourth Sunday of July, but you can catch it for two weeks before all over France – the route changes each year but the French Alps are a hot spot.

✥ Bastille Day

Join the French in celebrating the storming of the Bastille on 14 July 1789 – country-wide there are firework displays, balls, processions, parades and lots of hoo-ha all round.

✥ Festival d'Avignon

Rouse your inner thespian with Avignon's legendary performing-arts festival. Street acts in its fringe fest are as inspired as those on official stages.

August

It's that crazy summer month when the French join everyone else on holiday. Paris, Lyon and other big cities empty; traffic jams at motorway toll booths test the patience of a saint; and temperatures soar. Avoid. Or don your party hat and join the crowd!

✥ Festival Interceltique de Lorient

Celtic culture is the focus of this festival when hundreds of thousands of Celts from Brittany and abroad flock to Lorient to celebrate just that.

☗ Route du Champagne en Fête

There's no better excuse for a flute or three of bubbly than during the first weekend in August when Champagne toasts its vines and vintages with the Route du Champagne en Fête. Free tastings, cellar visits, music and dancing.

September

As sun-plump grapes hang heavy on dark-ened vines and that August madness drops off as abruptly as it began, a welcome tran-quillity falls across autumnal France. This is the start of France's *vendange* (grape harvest).

☆ Rutting Season

Nothing beats getting up at dawn to watch mating stags, boar and red deer at play. Observatory towers are hidden in woods around Château de Chambord (p84).

October

The days become shorter, the last grapes are harvested and the first sweet chestnuts fall from trees. With the changing of the clocks on the last Sunday of the month, there's no denying that winter is coming.

☆ Nuit Blanche

In one last-ditch attempt to stretch out what's left of summer, Paris museums, monuments, cultural spaces, bars and clubs rock around the clock during Paris' so-called White Night, aka one fabulous long all-nighter!

December

Days are short and it's cold everywhere bar the south of France. But there are Christmas school holidays and festive cele-brations to bolster sun-deprived souls, not to mention some season-opening winter skiing in the highest-altitude Alpine resorts from mid-December.

☆ Fête des Lumières

France's biggest and best light show, on and around 8 December, transforms the streets and squares of Lyon into an open stage.

Plan Your Trip
Get Inspired

Read

A Year in the Merde (Stephen Clarke; 2004) Expat Brit's rant on dog poo, bureaucracy and more.

A Moveable Feast (Ernest Hemingway; 1964) Beautiful evocation of 1920s Paris.

Everybody Was So Young (Amanda Vaill; 1995) The French Riviera in the roaring twenties.

Me Talk Pretty One Day (David Sedaris; 2000) Caustic take on moving to France.

Paris (Edward Rutherford; 2013) Eight centuries of Parisian history.

The Hundred Foot Journey (Richard C Morais; 2010) Culinary warfare in a remote French village between two restaurant owners: a boy from Mumbai and a famous chef!

Watch

Cyrano de Bergerac (1990) Glossy version of the classic, with Gérard Depardieu.

Marseille (2016) Comedy about just that, starring French-Algerian actor and filmmaker Kad Merad.

Bienvenue Chez Les Ch'tis (2008) Satirical comedy about France's north–south divide.

Midnight in Paris (2011) Woody Allen tale about a family in Paris, with dream scenes set in the 1920s.

The Artist (2011) Most awarded French film in history; romantic comedy with charismatic actor Jean Dujardin.

La Môme (La Vie en Rose; 2007) Story of singer Édith Piaf starring French actress Marion Cotillard.

Listen

Eternelle (Édith Piaf; 2002) Excellent intro to the sparrow chanteuse.

Histoire de Melody Nelson (Serge Gainsbourg; 1971) France's most-loved crooner.

L'Absente (Yann Tiersen; 2001) Raw, emotional music from a multitalented Breton.

Scarifications (Abd al Malik; 2015) Rap music by Franco-Congolese rapper and slam-poet.

L'Anomalie (Louise Attaque; 2016) Newest album after a 10-year break from one of France's most beloved rock bands.

Amour Massif (Nosfell; 2014) Powerful love lyrics by one of France's most creative and intense musicians.

Above: Vieux Port (p254), Marseille

Plan Your Trip
Five-Day Itineraries

Cross Channel

Snug on the English Channel (La Manche to the French), the wind-buffeted, dramatic coastline of northern France welcomes visitors with fierce regional pride and passion (not to mention cider, seafood and a whole host of intriguing coastal sights and capers).

1 Rouen (p123)
Explore the stunning Gothic cathedral in one of Normandy's best destinations.
🚗 1–2 hrs to Bayeux

2 Bayeux (p120)
Learn about the history of the Bayeux Tapestry and experience the D-Day landing beaches.
🚗 1½ hrs to Mont St-Michel

4 Carnac (p146)
Get off the beaten track with wild Breton coastline, historic towns and mystical prehistoric relics.

3 Mont St-Michel (p108)
Marvel at sea-splashed Mont St-Michel and go back in time in the abbey.
🚗 2 hrs to Carnac

French Allure

Be it a long weekend or a short break, France's capital city is a hot date any time of year. What makes it even more wonderful is the green and oh-so-non-urban journey of elegant Champagne houses and Renaissance châteaux that unfurls within an hour of the city.

1 Paris (p34)
Play the romantic for a day atop the Eiffel Tower, sail down the Seine or dine at a bistro.
🚌 1¼–2¾ hrs to Épernay

2 Épernay (p166)
Spend two days touring cellars and tasting bubbly in some of the world's most celebrated Champagne houses.
🚌 1½ hrs to Blois

3 Blois (p94)
Flit west to romance, Renaissance-style, in beautiful châteaux befitting of the best fairy tale.

FROM LEFT: VLADONE/GETTY IMAGES ©; VLADONE/GETTY IMAGES ©

Plan Your Trip
10-Day Itinerary

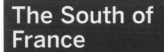

The South of France

Cutting-edge museums, world-class modern art, outstanding food and a fascinating historical heritage – everything on offer in France's sun-baked south exceeds expectations. For outdoor enthusiasts, its picture-postcard landscapes – fields of lavender, vineyards, mountains and dazzling azure sea – demand action.

3 Roussillon (p194) Duck inland to spend four days exploring hilltop villages, hiking red rock and dining exceedingly well in the Lubéron.

FROM LEFT: GUILLAUME CHANSON/GETTY IMAGES ©

1 Nice (p210) Meet the queen of the French Riviera as she unfurls in a pageant of belle époque palaces and iconic sands along the coast.
🚗 1¾ hrs to St-Tropez

2 St-Tropez (p230) Day five move to this mythical fishing port where millionaire yachts jostle for space with street artists.
🚗 2½ hrs to Roussillon

Plan Your Trip
Two-Week Itinerary

Foodie Fortnight

Indulging in France's extraordinary wealth of gastronomic pleasures is reason alone to travel here. Cruising around the country's tastiest destinations inspires hunger, culinary adventure and much mingling with food-passionate locals. Spring and early summer, when markets burst with fresh produce, are brilliant seasons to visit.

1 Paris (p34) Pepper sightseeing with tasty breaks: quintessential bistro dinners, patisserie shopping, market strolls...
🚐 2 hrs to Lyon

3 French Alps (p284) Burn calories hiking and biking. Feast on high-altitude mountain panoramas and hearty cheesy specialities.
🚐 7 hrs to Avignon

2 Lyon (p168) Head south to France's gastronomic capital. Don't miss its food markets and the city's unique *bouchon* culture. 🚐 4½ hrs to Chamonix

4 Avignon (p202) Few regions are as food-driven or as resplendent with lush melons, cherries, homegrown olives, etc as Provence.
🚐 6 hrs to Bordeaux

5 Bordeaux (p266) An essential for wine lovers, this city promises unique tasting opportunities, a fantastic wine museum and ample visits to wine-producing châteaux.

Plan Your Trip
Family Travel

BRUNO DE HOGUES/GETTY IMAGES ©

Be it the kid-friendly extraordinaire capital or rural hinterland, France spoils families with its rich mix of cultural sights, activities and entertainment. To get the most out of travelling en famille, plan ahead.

Savvy parents can find kid-appeal in most sights in France, must-sees included: skip the formal guided tour of Mont St-Michel and hook up with a walking guide to lead you and the children barefoot across the sand to the abbey; trade the daytime queues at the Eiffel Tower for a tour after dark with teens; don't dismiss wine tasting in Provence outright – rent bicycles and turn it into a family bike ride instead. The opportunities are endless.

Museums & Monuments

Many Paris museums organise creative *ateliers* (workshops) for children, parent-accompanied or solo (aged seven to 14 years). Workshops are themed, require booking, last 1½ to two hours and cost €5 to €20 per child.

Countrywide, when buying tickets at museums and monuments, ask about children's activity sheets. Another winner is to arm your gadget-mad child (from six years) with an audioguide. Older children can check out what apps a museum or monument might have for smartphones and tablets.

Many museums and monuments are free to under 18 years. In general, under fives don't pay. Some museums offer money-saving family tickets, worth buying once you count two adults and two children or more.

Entertainment

Tourist offices can tell you what's on – and the repertoire is impressive: puppet shows al fresco, children's theatres, street buskers, illuminated monuments after dark, an abundance of music festivals and so on. A sure winner are the *son et lumière* (sound and light) shows projected on some Renaissance châteaux in the Loire Valley; the papal palace in Avignon; and the cathedral façade in Rouen.

OKSANA SHUFRYCH / SHUTTERSTOCK ©

Dining Out

Classic French mains loved by children include *gratin dauphinois* (sliced potatoes oven-baked in cream), *escalope de veau* (breaded pan-fried veal) and *bœuf bourguignon* (beef stew). In the French Alps fondue and *raclette* (melted cheese served with potatoes and cold meats) become favourites from about five years.

Children's *menus* (fixed meals at a set price) are common, although the ubiquitous spaghetti bolognaise or *saucisse* (sausage), or *steak haché* (beef burger) and *frites* (fries) followed by ice cream can tire. Don't be shy in asking for a half-portion of an adult main.

Bread accompanies every meal and in restaurants is brought to the table before or immediately after you've ordered – watch the battle ensue over who gets the *quignon* (the baguette's knobbly end bit, a hit with teething babies!).

Drinks

Buy a fizzy drink for every child sitting at the table and the bill soars. Opt instead for

★ Best Museums

Cité des Sciences (p60)

Musée des Confluences (p179)

Musée Océanographique (p228)

Ludo (p200)

La Cité du Vin (p270)

a free *carafe d'eau* (jug of tap water) with meals and *un sirop* (flavoured fruit syrup) in between – jazzed up with *des glaçons* (some ice cubes) and *une paille* (a straw). Every self-respecting cafe and bar in France has dozens of syrup flavours to choose from: pomegranate-fuelled grenadine and pea-green *menthe* (mint) are French-kid favourites, but there are peach, raspberry, cherry, lemon and a rainbow of others too. Syrup is served diluted with water and, best up, costs a good €2 less than a coke. Expect to pay around €1.50 a glass.

From left: Ferris wheel on place de la Concorde Paris (p37); *Gratin dauphinois*

Stroll through Paris'
lush green parks (p57)

Cité des Sciences (p60), designed by the architect Adrien Fainsilber and engineer Peter Rice

Arriving in Paris

Aéroport Charles de Gaulle Trains (RER), buses and night buses to the city centre €6 to €17.50; taxi €50 to €55.

Aéroport d'Orly Trains (Orlyval then RER), buses and night buses to the city centre €7.50 to €12.50; T7 tram to Ville-juif-Louis Aragon then metro to centre (€3.60); taxi €30 to €35.

Gare du Nord Train Station Within central Paris; served by metro (€1.80).

Sleeping

Paris has a wealth of accommodation for all budgets, but it's often *complet* (full). Advance reservations are recommended year-round and essential during the warmer months (April to October) and all holidays.

Parisian hotel rooms tend to be small by international standards. Breakfast is rarely included in hotel rates.

See Where to Stay (p79) for a low-down on which Parisian neighbourhood suits you best.

JAN OTTO / GETTY IMAGES ©

Eiffel Tower

No one could imagine Paris today without it. But Gustave Eiffel only constructed this 320m-tall spire as a temporary exhibit for the 1889 World Fair. Climb it to admire Paris laid out at your feet.

Great For...

☑ Don't Miss

A glass of bubbly in the top-floor champagne bar (open noon to 10pm).

It took 300 workers, 2.5 million rivets and two years of nonstop labour to assemble the Eiffel Tower, named after its designer Gustave Eiffel. Upon completion the tower became the tallest human-made structure in the world (324m or 1063ft) – a record held until the completion of New York's Chrysler Building (1930). A symbol of the modern age, it faced massive opposition from Paris' artistic and literary elite, and was originally slated to be torn down in 1909. It was spared only because it proved an ideal platform for the transmitting antennas needed for the newfangled science of radiotelegraphy.

1st Floor

Of the tower's three floors, the 1st (57m) has the most space but the least impressive views. The glass-enclosed **Pavillon Ferrié** houses an immersion film along with a cafe

❶ Need to Know

Map p58; ☑08 92 70 12 39; www.tour-eiffel.
fr; Champ de Mars, 5 av Anatole France, 7e;
adult/youth/child lift to top €17/14.50/8, lift
to 2nd fl €11/8.50/4, stairs to 2nd fl €7/5/3,
lift 2nd fl to top €6; ⏰lifts & stairs 9am-
12.45am mid Jun–Aug, lifts 9.30am–11.45pm,
stairs 9.30am-6.30pm Sep–mid-Jun; Ⓜ Bir
Hakeim or RER Champ de Mars–Tour Eiffel

✕ Take a Break

Dine quintessential-brasserie style at
58 Tour Eiffel (☑01 45 55 20 04; www.
restaurants-toureiffel.com; 2-/3-course
lunch menu €22.50/27, dinner menu €70/80;
⏰11.30am-4.30pm & 6.30-11pm), on the
tower's 1st floor.

★ Top Tip

Cut queues by buying lift tickets
ahead online; print or display on a
smart phone.

and souvenir shop, while the outer walkway features a discovery circuit to help visitors learn more about the tower's ingenious design. Check out the sections of glass flooring that proffer a dizzying view of the ant-like people walking on the ground far below.

2nd Floor

Views from the 2nd floor (115m) are the best – impressively high but still close enough to see the details of the city below. Telescopes and panoramic maps placed around the tower pinpoint locations in Paris and beyond. Story windows give an overview of the lifts' mechanics, and the vision allows you to gaze through glass panels to the ground.

Top Floor

Views from the wind-buffeted top floor (276m) stretch up to 60km on a clear day,

though at this height the panoramas are more sweeping than detailed. Afterwards peep into Gustave Eiffel's restored top-level office where lifelike wax models of Eiffel and his daughter Claire greet Thomas Edison.

To access the top floor, take a separate lift on the 2nd floor (closed during heavy winds).

Nightly Sparkles

Every hour on the hour, the entire tower sparkles for five minutes with 20,000 6-watt lights. They were first installed for Paris' millennium celebration in 2000 – it took 25 mountain climbers five months to install the current bulbs and 40km of electrical cords. For the best view of the light show, head across the Seine to the Jardins du Trocadéro.

NEALE CLARK / ROBERTHARDING ©

Musée du Louvre

Few art galleries are as prized or daunting as the Musée du Louvre, Paris' pièce de résistance. One of the world's largest and most diverse museums, it showcases an unbelievable 35,000-odd works of art.

Great For...

☑ Don't Miss

Da Vinci's bewitching *Mona Lisa;* the Mesopotamian and Egyptian collections.

The Louvre today rambles over four floors and through three wings: the **Sully Wing** creates the four sides of the Cour Carrée (literally 'Square Courtyard') at the eastern end of the complex; the **Denon Wing** stretches 800m along the Seine to the south; and the northern **Richelieu Wing** skirts rue de Rivoli. The building started life as a fortress built by Philippe-Auguste in the 12th century – medieval remnants are still visible on the lower ground floor (Sully). In the 16th century it became a royal residence and after the Revolution, in 1793, it was turned into a national museum.

Priceless Antiquities

Don't rush by the Louvre's astonishing cache of treasures from antiquity: both **Mesopotamia** (ground floor, Richelieu) and **Egypt** (ground and 1st floors, Sully) are well represented, as seen in the *Code of Hammu-*

Canova's *Psyche Revived by Cupid's Kiss*

PETER BARRITT / GETTY IMAGES ©

[Map showing Palais Royal – Musée du Louvre, Jardin des Tuileries, Pl du Carrousel, R de Rivoli, R St-Honoré, Louvre, Louvre Rivoli, Pont du Carrousel, Q du Louvre, Seine]

❶ Need to Know

Map p58; ☏01 40 20 53 17; www.louvre.fr; rue de Rivoli & quai des Tuileries, 1er; adult/child €15/free; ⊘9am-6pm Mon, Thu, Sat & Sun, to 9.45pm Wed & Fri; Ⓜ Palais Royal–Musée du Louvre

✕ Take a Break

Picnic in the Jardin des Tuileries (p57) or enjoy fine wine and cuisine at **Racines 2** (Map p68; ☏01 42 60 77 34; www.racinesparis.com, 39 rue de l'Arbre Sec, 1er; 2-/3-course lunch menu €28/32, mains €24-31; ⊘noon-2.30pm Mon-Fri, 7.30-10.30pm Mon-Sat; Ⓜ Louvre Rivoli).

★ Top Tip

The longest queues are outside the Grande Pyramide – use the Carrousel du Louvre or Porte de Lions entrances.

rabi (Room 3, ground floor, Richelieu) and the *Seated Scribe* (Room 22, 1st floor, Sully). Room 12a (ground floor, Sully) holds impressive friezes and an enormous **two-headed-bull column** from the Darius Palace in ancient Iran, while an enormous seated statue of Pharaoh Ramesses II highlights the temple room (Room 12, ground floor, Sully).

French & Italian Masterpieces

The 1st floor of the Denon Wing, where the *Mona Lisa* is found, is easily the most popular part of the Louvre – and with good reason. Rooms 75 through 77 are hung with monumental French paintings, many iconic: look for the *Consecration of the Emperor Napoleon I* (David), *The Raft of the Medusa* (Géricault) and *Grande Odalisque* (Ingres).

Rooms 1, 3, 5 and 8 are also must-visits. Filled with classic works by **Renaissance** masters – Raphael, Titian, Uccello, Botticini

– this area culminates with the crowds around the *Mona Lisa*. But you'll find plenty else to contemplate, from Botticelli's graceful frescoes (Room 1) to the superbly detailed *Wedding Feast at Cana* (Room 6). On the ground floor of the Denon Wing, take time for the Italian sculptures, including Michelangelo's *The Dying Slave* and Canova's *Psyche and Cupid* (Room 4).

Mona Lisa

Easily the Louvre's most famous painting, Leonardo da Vinci's *La Joconde* (in French) is the lady with that enigmatic smile known as *Mona Lisa* (Room 6, 1st floor, Denon). For centuries admirers speculated on everything from the possibility that the subject was mourning the death of a loved one to the possibility that she might have been in love or in bed with her portraitist.

The Louvre

A HALF-DAY TOUR

Successfully visiting the Louvre is a fine art. Its complex labyrinth of galleries and staircases spiralling three wings and four floors renders discovery a snakes-and-ladders experience. Initiate yourself with this three-hour itinerary – a playful mix of Mona Lisa obvious and up-to-the-minute unexpected.

Arriving in the newly renovated **Hall Napoléon ❶** beneath IM Pei's glass pyramid, pick up colour-coded floor plans at an information stand, then ride the escalator up to the Sully Wing and swap passport or credit card for multimedia guide (there are limited descriptions in the galleries) at the wing entrance.

The Louvre is as much about spectacular architecture as masterly art. To appreciate this zip up and down Sully's Escalier Henri II to admire **Venus de Milo ❷**, then up parallel Escalier Henri IV to the palatial displays in **Cour Khorsabad ❸**. Cross Room 1 to find the escalator up to the 1st floor and the opulent **Napoleon III apartments ❹**. Next traverse 25 consecutive galleries (thank you, floor plan!) to flip conventional contemplation on its head with Cy Twombly's **The Ceiling ❺**, and the hypnotic **Winged Victory of Samothrace sculpture ❻**, which brazenly insists on being admired from all angles. End with the impossibly famous **The Raft of the Medusa ❼**, **Mona Lisa ❽** and **Virgin & Child ❾**.

TOP TIPS

» **Floor Plans** Don't even consider entering the Louvre's maze of galleries without a Plan/Information Louvre brochure, free from the information desk in the Hall Napoléon

» **Crowd dodgers** The Denon Wing is always packed; visit on late nights Wednesday or Friday or trade Denon in for the notably quieter Richelieu Wing

» **2nd floor** Not for first-timers: save its more specialist works for subsequent visits

BRIAN KINNEY/SHUTTERSTOCK ©

Napoleon III Apartments
1st Floor, Richelieu
Napoleon III's gorgeous gilt apartments were built from 1854 to 1861, featuring an over-the-top decor of gold leaf, stucco and crystal chandeliers that reaches a dizzying climax in the Grand Salon and State Dining Room.

Jardin du Carrousel

Galerie du Carrousel Entrances

Porte des Lions Entrance

MISSION MONA LISA

If you just want to venerate the Louvre's most famous lady, use the Porte des Lions entrance (closed Wednesday and Friday), from where it's a five-minute walk. Go up one flight of stairs and through Rooms 26, 14 and 13 to the Grande Galerie and adjoining room 6.

Mona Lisa
Room 6, 1st Floor, Denon
No smile is as enigmatic or bewitching as hers. Da Vinci's diminutive *La Joconde* hangs opposite the largest painting in the Louvre – sumptuous, fellow Italian Renaissance artwork *The Wedding at Cana.*

The Raft of the Medusa
Room 77, 1st Floor, Denon
Decipher the politics behind French romanticism in Théodore Géricault's *Raft of the Medusa*.

Cour Khorsabad
Ground Floor, Richelieu
Time travel with a pair of winged human-headed bulls to view some of the world's oldest Mesopotamian art. DETOUR» Night-lit statues in Cour Puget.

PRYZMAT/SHUTTERSTOCK ©

The Ceiling
Room 32, 1st Floor, Sully
Admire the blue shock of Cy Twombly's 400-sq-metre contemporary ceiling fresco – the Louvre's latest, daring commission. DETOUR» *The Braque Ceiling*, Room 33.

Rue de Rivoli Entrance

Cour Khorsabad

③

Cour Puget

Cour Marly

④

SULLY WING

RICHELIEU WING

Cour Carrée

Cour Napoléon

①

⑤

②

Pyramid Main Entrance

Inverted Pyramid

⑥

Cour Visconti

⑦ ⑧

⑨

DENON WING

Pont des Arts

Pont du Carrousel

PRYZMAT/SHUTTERSTOCK ©

Winged Victory of Samothrace
Escalier Daru, 1st Floor, Sully
Draw breath at the aggressive dynamism of this headless, handless Hellenistic goddess. DETOUR» The razzle-dazzle of the Apollo Gallery's crown jewels.

Virgin & Child
Grande Galerie, 1st Floor, Denon
In the spirit of artistic devotion save the Louvre's most famous gallery for last: a feast of Virgin-and-child paintings by Da Vinci, Raphael, Domenico Ghirlandaio, Giovanni Bellini and Francesco Botticini.

Venus de Milo
Room 16, Ground Floor, Sully
No one knows who sculpted this seductively realistic goddess from Greek antiquity. Naked to the hips, she is a Hellenistic masterpiece.

TUTTI FRUTTI/SHUTTERSTOCK ©

Cathédrale Notre Dame de Paris

Paris' mighty cathedral is a masterpiece of French Gothic architecture. Highlights include its spectacular rose windows, treasury and spectacular city views from the top of its gargoyled bell towers.

Notre Dame was begun in 1163 and largely completed by the early 14th century. The cathedral was badly damaged during the Revolution, prompting architect Eugène Emmanuel Viollet-le-Duc to oversee extensive renovations between 1845 and 1864. Enter the magnificent forest of ornate **flying buttresses** that encircle the cathedral chancel and support its walls and roof.

Rose Windows

The cathedral's grand dimensions are immediately evident: the interior is 127m long, 48m wide and can accommodate some 6000 worshippers. Its most spectacular interior features are three rose windows, particularly the 10m-wide window over the western façade above the organ – one of the largest in the world, with 7800 pipes – and the window on the northern side of the transept, virtually unchanged since the 13th century.

Great For...

☑ Don't Miss

An evening concert at the cathedral (October to June); program online at www. musique-sacree-notredameparis.fr.

Bell Towers

A constant queue marks the entrance
to the **Tours de Notre Dame**. Climb the
400-odd spiralling steps to the top of
the western façade of the North Tower to
find yourself on the rooftop **Galerie des
Chimères** (Chimera Gallery), face-to-face
with frightening and fantastic gargoyles.
These grotesque statues divert rainwater
from the roof to prevent masonry damage
(with the water exiting through the elongated, open mouth) and, purportedly, ward
off evil spirits. From the rooftop there's a
spectacular view over Paris.

Bible of the Poor

The statues above the three main portals
were once brightly coloured to make them
more effective as a Biblia pauperum – a 'Bible
of the poor' – to help the illiterate faithful understand Old Testament stories, the Passion
of the Christ and the lives of the saints.

Treasury

In the southeastern transept, the *trésor*
(treasury) contains artwork, liturgical
objects and first-class relics; pay a small
fee to enter. Among its religious jewels and
gems is the **Ste-Couronne** (Holy Crown),
purportedly the wreath of thorns placed on
Jesus' head before he was crucified.

Easier to admire is the treasury's wonderful collection, **Les Camées des Papes**
(Papal cameos). Sculpted with incredible
finesse in shell and framed in silver, the
268-piece collection depicts every pope in
miniature from St Pierre to the present day,
ending with Pope Benoit XVI.

Notre Dame

TIMELINE

1160 Maurice de Sully becomes bishop of Paris. Mission: to grace growing Paris with a lofty new cathedral.

1182–90 The **choir with double ambulatory ❶** is finished and work starts on the nave and side chapels.

1200–50 The **west façade ❷**, with rose window, three portals and two soaring towers, goes up. Everyone is stunned.

1345 Some 180 years after the foundation stone was laid, the Cathédrale de Notre Dame is complete. It is dedicated to notre dame (our lady), the Virgin Mary.

1789 Revolutionaries smash the original **Gallery of Kings ❸**, pillage the cathedral and melt all its bells except the great bell Emmanuel. The cathedral becomes a Temple of Reason then a warehouse.

1831 Victor Hugo's novel *The Hunchback of Notre Dame* inspires new interest in the half-ruined Gothic cathedral.

1845–64 Architect Viollet-le-Duc undertakes its restoration. Twenty-eight new kings are sculpted for the west façade. The heavily decorated **portals ❹** and **spire ❺** are reconstructed. The neo-Gothic **treasury ❻** is built.

1860 The area in front of Notre Dame is cleared to create the parvis, an al fresco classroom where Parisians can learn a catechism illustrated on sculpted stone portals.

1935 A rooster bearing part of the relics of the Crown of Thorns, St Denis and Ste Geneviève is put on top of the cathedral spire to protect those who pray inside.

1991 The architectural masterpiece of Notre Dame and its Seine-side riverbanks become a Unesco World Heritage Site.

2013 Notre Dame celebrates 850 years since construction began with a bevy of new bells and restoration works.

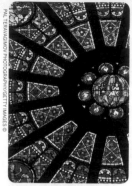

Virgin & Child
Spot all 37 artworks representing the Virgin Mary. Pilgrims have revered the pearly-cream sculpture of her in the sanctuary since the 14th century. Light a devotional candle and write some words to the *Livre de Vie* (Book of Life).

North Rose Window
See prophets, judges, kings and priests venerate Mary in vivid blue and violet glass, one of three beautiful rose blooms (1225–70), each almost 10m in diameter.

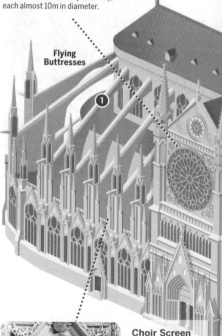

Flying Buttresses

❶

Choir Screen
No part of the cathedral weaves biblical tales more evocatively than these ornate wooden panels, carved in the 14th century after the Black Death killed half the country's population. The faintly gaudy colours were restored in the 1960s.

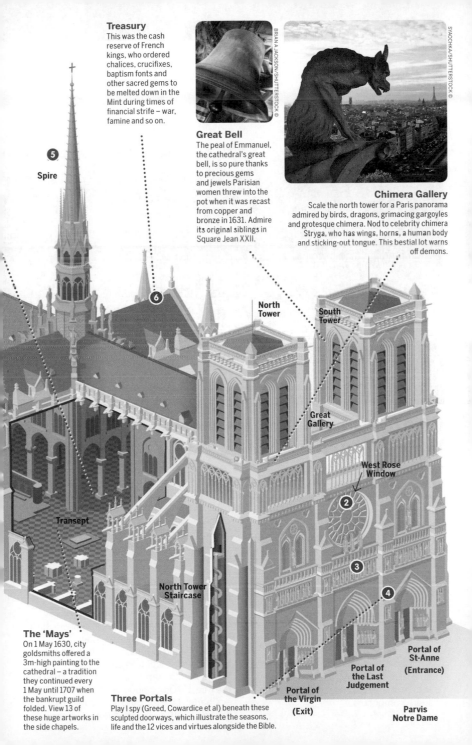

Treasury
This was the cash reserve of French kings, who ordered chalices, crucifixes, baptism fonts and other sacred gems to be melted down in the Mint during times of financial strife – war, famine and so on.

Great Bell
The peal of Emmanuel, the cathedral's great bell, is so pure thanks to precious gems and jewels Parisian women threw into the pot when it was recast from copper and bronze in 1631. Admire its original siblings in Square Jean XXII.

Chimera Gallery
Scale the north tower for a Paris panorama admired by birds, dragons, grimacing gargoyles and grotesque chimera. Nod to celebrity chimera Stryga, who has wings, horns, a human body and sticking-out tongue. This bestial lot warns off demons.

⑤ Spire

⑥

North Tower

South Tower

Great Gallery

West Rose Window
②

③

④

Transept

North Tower Staircase

The 'Mays'
On 1 May 1630, city goldsmiths offered a 3m-high painting to the cathedral – a tradition they continued every 1 May until 1707 when the bankrupt guild folded. View 13 of these huge artworks in the side chapels.

Three Portals
Play I spy (Greed, Cowardice et al) beneath these sculpted doorways, which illustrate the seasons, life and the 12 vices and virtues alongside the Bible.

Portal of the Virgin (Exit)

Portal of the Last Judgement

Portal of St-Anne (Entrance)

Parvis Notre Dame

BRIAN A JACKSON/SHUTTERSTOCK ©

SYAOCHKA/SHUTTERSTOCK ©

SIMON TAM / GETTY IMAGES ©

Château de Versailles

This monumental, 700-room palace and sprawling estate – with its gardens, fountains, ponds and canals – is a Unesco World Heritage-listed wonder situated an easy 40-minute train ride from central Paris.

Great For...

☑ Don't Miss

Summertime 'dancing water' displays set to music by baroque- and classical-era composers.

Amid magnificently landscaped formal gardens, this splendid and enormous palace was built in the mid-17th century during the reign of Louis XIV – the Roi Soleil (Sun King) – to project the absolute power of the French monarchy, which was then at the height of its glory. The château has undergone relatively few alterations since its construction, though almost all the interior furnishings disappeared during the Revolution and many of the rooms were rebuilt by Louis-Philippe (r 1830–48).

Some 30,000 workers and soldiers toiled on the structure, the bills for which all but emptied the kingdom's coffers.

Work began in 1661 under the guidance of architect Louis Le Vau (Jules Hardouin-Mansart took over from Le Vau in the mid-1670s); painter and interior designer Charles Le Brun; and landscape artist André Le Nôtre, whose workers flattened

ⓘ Need to Know

☎01 30 83 78 00; www.chateauversailles.
fr; place d'Armes; adult/child passport ticket
incl estate-wide access €18/free, with musical
events €25/free, palace €15/free, ⏰9am-
6.30pm Tue-Sun Apr-Oct, to 5.30pm Tue-Sun
Nov-Mar; 𝕄RER Versailles-Château-Rive
Gauche

✕ Take a Break

Nearby rue de Satory is lined with restaurants and cafes.

★ Top Tip

Arrive early morning and avoid Tuesday, Saturday and Sunday, Versailles'
busiest days.

hills, drained marshes and relocated forests
as they laid out the seemingly endless
gardens (free except during musical events;
⏰gardens 8am-8.30pm Apr-Oct, to 6pm Nov-Mar,
park 7am-8.30pm Apr-Oct, 8am-6pm Nov-Mar),
ponds and fountains.

Le Brun and his hundreds of artisans
decorated every moulding, cornice, ceiling
and door of the interior with the most luxurious and ostentatious of appointments:
frescoes, marble, gilt and woodcarvings,
many with themes and symbols drawn
from Greek and Roman mythology. The
King's Suite of the Grands Appartements
du Roi et de la Reine (King's and Queen's
State Apartments), for example, includes
rooms dedicated to Hercules, Venus, Diana,
Mars and Mercury. The opulence reaches
its peak in the Galerie des Glaces (Hall of
Mirrors), a 75m-long ballroom with 17 huge

mirrors on one side and, on the other, an
equal number of windows looking out over
the gardens and the setting sun.

To access areas that are otherwise off
limits and to learn more about Versailles'
history, prebook a 90-minute guided **tour**
(☎01 30 83 77 88; €7, plus palace entry; ⏰Eng-
lish-language tours 9.30am Tue-Sun) of the
Private Apartments of Louis XV and Louis
XVI and the Opera House or Royal Chapel.
Tours also cover the most famous parts of
the palace.

The current €400 million restoration
program is the most ambitious yet, and until it's completed in 2020, at least a part of
the palace is likely to be clad in scaffolding
when you visit.

The château is situated in the leafy,
bourgeois suburb of Versailles, about
22km southwest of central Paris. Take the
frequent RER C5 (€4.20) from Paris' Left
Bank RER stations to Versailles-Château-
Rive Gauche station.

Versailles

A DAY IN COURT

Visiting Versailles – even just the State Apartments – may seem overwhelming at first, but think of it as a house where people ate, drank, worked, slept and conspired and you'll be on the right path.

Some two decades into his long reign, Louis XIV began turning his father's hunting lodge into a palace large enough to house his entire court (to keep closer tabs on the 6000-strong army of courtiers). Sparing no expense, the Sun King employed the greatest artists and craftspeople of the day and by 1682 he'd created the most extravagant dormitory in history.

The royal schedule was as accurate and predictable as a Swiss watch. By following this itinerary of rooms you can recreate the king's day, starting with the **King's Bedchamber** ❶ and the **Queen's Bedchamber** ❷, where the royal couple was roused at about the same time. The royal procession then leads through the **Hall of Mirrors** ❸ to the **Royal Chapel** ❹ for morning Mass and returns to the **Council Chamber** ❺ for late-morning meetings with ministers. After lunch the king might ride or hunt or visit the **King's Library** ❻. Later he could join courtesans for an 'apartment evening' starting from the **Hercules Drawing Room** ❼ or play billiards in the **Diana Drawing Room** ❽ before supping at 10pm.

VERSAILLES BY NUMBERS

- ➡ **Rooms** 700 (11 hectares of roof)
- ➡ **Windows** 2153
- ➡ **Staircases** 67
- ➡ **Gardens and parks** 800 hectares
- ➡ **Trees** 200,000
- ➡ **Fountains** 50 (with 620 nozzles)
- ➡ **Paintings** 6300 (measuring 11km laid end to end)
- ➡ **Statues and sculptures** 2100
- ➡ **Objets d'art and furnishings** 5000
- ➡ **Visitors** 5.3 million per year

Queen's Bedchamber
Chambre de la Reine
The queen's life was on constant public display and even the births of her children were watched by crowds of spectators in her own bedchamber. **DETOUR »** The Guardroom, with a dozen armed men at the ready.

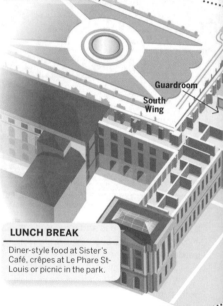

Guardroom
South Wing

LUNCH BREAK

Diner-style food at Sister's Café, crêpes at Le Phare St-Louis or picnic in the park.

Hercules Drawing Room
Salon d'Hercule
This salon, with its stunning ceiling fresco of the strong man, gave way to the State Apartments, which were open to courtiers three nights a week. **DETOUR»** Apollo Drawing Room, used for formal audiences and as a throne room.

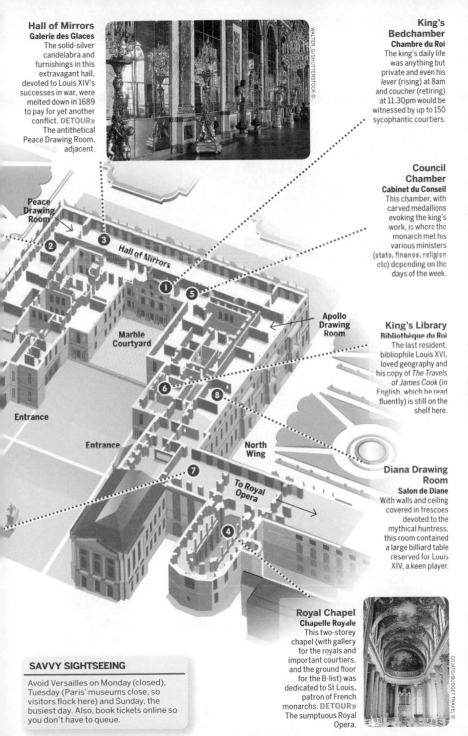

Hall of Mirrors
Galerie des Glaces
The solid-silver candelabra and furnishings in this extravagant hall, devoted to Louis XIV's successes in war, were melted down in 1689 to pay for yet another conflict. DETOUR» The antithetical Peace Drawing Room, adjacent.

WALTER.G/SHUTTERSTOCK ©

King's Bedchamber
Chambre du Roi
The king's daily life was anything but private and even his *lever* (rising) at 8am and *coucher* (retiring) at 11.30pm would be witnessed by up to 150 sycophantic courtiers.

Council Chamber
Cabinet du Conseil
This chamber, with carved medallions evoking the king's work, is where the monarch met his various ministers (state, finance, religion etc) depending on the days of the week.

King's Library
Bibliothèque du Roi
The last resident, bibliophile Louis XVI, loved geography and his copy of *The Travels of James Cook* (in English, which he read fluently) is still on the shelf here.

Diana Drawing Room
Salon de Diane
With walls and ceiling covered in frescoes devoted to the mythical huntress, this room contained a large billiard table reserved for Louis XIV, a keen player.

Royal Chapel
Chapelle Royale
This two-storey chapel (with gallery for the royals and important courtiers, and the ground floor for the B-list) was dedicated to St Louis, patron of French monarchs. DETOUR» The sumptuous Royal Opera.

COJATO/BUDGET TRAVEL ©

Peace Drawing Room

Hall of Mirrors

Marble Courtyard

Entrance

Entrance

Apollo Drawing Room

North Wing

To Royal Opera

SAVVY SIGHTSEEING

Avoid Versailles on Monday (closed), Tuesday (Paris' museums close, so visitors flock here) and Sunday, the busiest day. Also, book tickets online so you don't have to queue.

Montmartre Art Attack

This walk takes you through the heart of hilltop Montmartre, where artists lived, worked and partied hard in the 19th century. With its ivy-clad buildings, steep narrow lanes and celebrity cafe terraces used as film sets, this is cinematic Paris at its best.

Start Ⓜ Abbesses
Distance 1km
Duration 1 hour

5 Watch a man pop out of a stone wall on place Marcel Aymé. The statue portrays Dutilleul, hero of Marcel Aymé's short story **Le Passe-Muraille** (The Walker through Walls).

4 In 1876 one of two surviving windmills, the **Moulin Blute Fin** on rue Lepic, became an open-air dance hall, immortalised by Renoir in *Bal du Moulin de la Galette*.

3 On place Émile Goudeau see where artists Max Jacob, Amedeo Modigliani and Pablo Picasso – who painted his seminal *Les Demoiselles d'Avignon* (1907) here – had art studios at **Le Bateau Lavoir**.

1 Admire Hector Guimard's iconic art nouveau metro entrance (1900) on **place des Abbesses**. Deep underground, beneath a maze of gypsum mines, is one of Paris' deepest metro stations.

6 A mural of a rabbit jumping out of a cooking pot by caricaturist André Gill decorates the façade of celebrated cabaret **Au Lapin Agile** (p74).

7 Uphill, Montmartre's oldest building – a 17th-century manor house and one-time home to painters Renoir, Utrillo and Raoul Dufy – is now the **Musée de Montmartre** (Map p66; www.museedemontmartre.fr; 12 rue Cortot, 18e; adult/child €9.50/5.50; ⊙10am-6pm).

8 In 1534 the 12th-century church **Église St-Pierre de Montmartre** (www.saintpierredemontmartre.net; 2 rue du Mont Cenis, 18e; ⊙8.30am-7pm) witnessed the founding of the Jesuits, who met in the crypt under the guidance of Ignatius of Loyola.

Take a Break... Hardware Société (p73) is great for coffee, breakfast or lunch.

R Cortot

R des Saules

R du Mont Cenis

R Norvins

Pl du Tertre

9

FINISH

8

7

6

Basilique du Sacré Cœur

R Lamarck

2 Learn how to say 'I love you' in another language or 10 with **Le Mur des je t'aime** (p60), a work of art hidden in tiny gated park, Sq Jehan Rictus.

9 Lap up Montmartre's local life on main square **place du Tertre**, packed with buskers, portrait artists, cafe terraces and crowds of tourists.

Ⓝ 0 ———— 100 m
0 ———— 0.05 miles

Marais Mansions

While Henri IV was busy having place Royale (today's place des Vosges) built, aristocrats were commissioning gold-brick *hôtels particuliers* – the city's most beautiful Renaissance mansions that lend Le Marais a particular architectural harmony.

Start Ⓜ St-Paul
Distance 2km
Duration 1½ hours

5 Dip into the **Musée Cognacq-Jay** (www.cognacq-jay.paris.fr; 8 rue Elzévir, 3e; ☉10am-6pm Tue-Sun), inside Hôtel de Donon, to ogle at artistic treasures collected by Ernest Cognacq (1839–1928) and his wife.

R Barbette

R des Francs Bourgeois

R Elzévir

R Payenne

5

LE MARAIS

R Pavée

4

R Malher

4 Stride along rue Pavée, Paris' first cobbled road, where Diane de France (1538–1619), Henri II's legitimised daughter, lived in late Renaissance mansion **Hôtel Lamoignon** at No 24.

St-Paul
4E START Ⓜ
R François Miron

R de Rivoli

R Pavée

R du Prévôt

1 At 7 rue de Jouy, admire majestic **Hôtel d'Aumont,** built around 1650 for a financier.

1

R des Nonnains d'Hyères

R du Figuier

R Charlemagne

R des Jardins de St-Paul

3

2

R de l'Ave Maria

Q des Célestins

Seine

2 Snap geometric gardens and a neo-Gothic turret at **Hôtel de Sens** (1 rue du Figuier), built around 1475 for the lucky archbishops of Sens.

6 One of Paris' most beloved art collections is showcased inside the mid-17th-century Hôtel Salé, now the **Musée National Picasso** (p60).

Classic Photo of place des Vosges – no square in Paris demands to be photographed quite like it.

R de Thorigny

R du Parc Royal

Sq G Cain

R de Sévigné

R St-Gilles

3E

R de Turenne

7 Flop on a bench or on the grassy lawns of Paris' oldest city square, **place des Vosges**, and contemplate the exquisite symmetry of its architecture.

Pl des Vosges

Sq Louis XIII

7

Pl des Vosges

R St-Paul

R de Birague

8

8 At No 6 learn about one of the city's most celebrated novelists and poets at the **Maison de Victor Hugo** (www.musee-hugo.paris.fr; ⊘10am-6pm Tue-Sun).

9
FINISH

R St-Antoine

9 Duck beneath the arch in the southwest corner of place des Vosges and fall instantly in love with **Hôtel de Sully's** beautifully decorated Renaissance courtyards.

3 Mingle in the cobbled alleys of **Village St-Paul**, a set of five vintage courtyards, refashioned in the 1970s from the 14th-century walled gardens of King Charles V.

Ⓝ 0 200 m
    0 0.1 miles

⊙ SIGHTS

⊙ Eiffel Tower & Western Paris

Musée du Quai Branly Museum

(Map p58; 📞01 56 61 70 00; www.quaibranly.
fr; 37 quai Branly, 7e; adult/child €9/free;
⊙11am-7pm Tue, Wed & Sun, 11am-9pm Thu-Sat;
MAlma Marceau or RER Pont de l'Alma) No other
museum in Paris so inspires travellers,
armchair anthropologists and those who
simply appreciate the beauty of traditional
craftsmanship. A tribute to the diversity
of human culture, Musée du Quai Branly
presents an overview of indigenous and folk
art. Its four main sections focus on Ocean-
ia, Asia, Africa and the Americas.

An impressive array of masks, carvings,
weapons, jewellery and more make up the
body of the rich collection, displayed in a
refreshingly unique interior without rooms
or high walls.

**Cité de l'Architecture
et du Patrimoine** Museum

(Map p58; www.citechaillot.fr; 1 place du Trocadéro et du 11 Novembre, 16e; adult/child €8/
free; ⊙11am-7pm Wed & Fri-Mon, to 9pm Thu;

MTrocadéro) This mammoth 23,000-sq-
metre space is an ode on three floors to
French architecture. The highlight is the
light-filled ground floor with a beautiful
collection of plaster and wood *moulages*
(casts) of cathedral portals, columns and
gargoyles; replicas of murals and stained
glass originally created for the 1878 Exposition Universelle are on display on the upper
floors. Views of the Eiffel Tower are equally
monumental.

**Musée Marmottan
Monet** Art Museum

(📞01 44 96 50 33; www.marmottan.fr; 2 rue
Louis Boilly, 16e; adult/child €11/6.50; ⊙10am-
6pm Tue-Sun, to 9pm Thu; MLa Muette) This
museum showcases the world's largest
collection of works by impressionist painter
Claude Monet (1840–1926) – about 100 –
as well as paintings by Gauguin, Sisley,
Pissarro, Renoir, Degas, Manet and Berthe
Morisot. It also contains an important
collection of French, English, Italian and
Flemish illuminations from the 13th to the
16th centuries.

Arc de Triomphe

⊙ Champs-Élysées & Grands Boulevards

Arc de Triomphe — Landmark

(Map p58; www.monuments-nationaux.fr; place Charles de Gaulle, 8e; adult/child €12/free; ⊙10am-11pm Apr-Sep, to 10.30pm Oct-Mar; MCharles de Gaulle–Étoile) If anything rivals the Eiffel Tower as the symbol of Paris, it's this magnificent 1836 monument to Napoléon's victory at Austerlitz (1805), which he commissioned the following year. The intricately sculpted triumphal arch stands sentinel in the centre of the Étoile ('Star') roundabout. From the viewing platform on top of the arch (50m up via 284 steps and well worth the climb) you can see the dozen avenues.

Palais Garnier — Opera House

(Map p58; ☎08 25 05 44 05; www.operade paris.fr; cnr rues Scribe & Auber, 9e; adult/child unguided tours €11/7, guided tours €15.50/11; ⊙unguided tours 10am-5pm, to 1pm on matinee performance days, guided tours by reservation; MOpéra) The fabled 'phantom of the opera' lurked in this opulent opera house designed in 1860 by Charles Garnier (then an unknown 35-year-old architect). Reserve a spot on an English-language guided tour or take an unguided tour of the attached museum, with posters, costumes, backdrops, original scores and other memorabilia, which includes a behind-the-scenes peek (except during matinees and rehearsals). Highlights include the Grand Staircase and horseshoe-shaped, gilded auditorium with red velvet seats, a massive chandelier and Chagall's gorgeous ceiling mural.

Grand Palais — Art Museum

(Map p58; ☎01 44 13 17 17; www.grandpalais. fr; 3 av du Général Eisenhower, 8e; adult/child €15/1; ⊙10am-8pm Sun, Mon & Thu, to 10pm Wed, Fri & Sat; MChamps-Élysées–Clemenceau) Erected for the 1900 Exposition Universelle (World's Fair), the Grand Palais today houses several exhibition spaces beneath its huge 8.5-tonne art nouveau glass roof. Some of Paris' biggest shows (Renoir, Chagall, Turner) are held in the Galeries

 ### Parisian Parks

Explore the city's lush green parks where Parisians stroll in style, admire art, lounge around fountains on sun chairs, bust out cheese and wine...

Jardin du Luxembourg (Map p61; www. senat.fr/visite/jardin; numerous entrances; ⊙hours vary; MMabillon, St-Sulpice, Rennes, Notre Dame des Champs or RER Luxembourg) Napoléon dedicated the 23 gracefully laid-out hectares of formal terraces, chestnut groves and lush lawns here to the children of Paris. Prod 1920s wooden sailboats (Map p61; Jardin du Luxembourg, 30/60min €2/3.30, ⊙Apr-Oct; MNotre Dame des Champs or RER Luxembourg) with long sticks on the octagonal **Grand Bassin** pond; watch puppet shows.

Jardin des Tuileries (Map p58; ⊙7am-11pm Jun-Aug, shorter hours Sep-May; 🚼; MTuileries, Concorde) Filled with fountains and sculptures, these formal, 28-hectare gardens were laid out in 1664 by André Le Nôtre. They soon became the most fashionable spot in Paris for parading in one's finery; it's now part of the Banks of the Seine Unesco World Heritage Site.

Jardin du Palais Royal (Map p58; 2 place Colette, 1er; ⊙7am-10.15pm Apr-May, to 11pm Jun-Aug, shorter hours Sep-Mar; 🚼; MPalais Royal–Musée du Louvre) Sit, contemplate and picnic between boxed hedges, or shop in the trio of arcades that frame this garden so beautifully: the **Galerie de Valois** (east), **Galerie de Montpensier** (west) and **Galerie Beaujolais**. Don't miss sculptor Daniel Buren's 260 black-and-white striped columns.

Nationales, lasting three to four months. Hours, prices and exhibition dates vary significantly for all galleries. Those listed here generally apply to the Galeries Nationales, but always check the website for exact

Western Paris, Champs-Élysées, St-Germain & Les Invalides

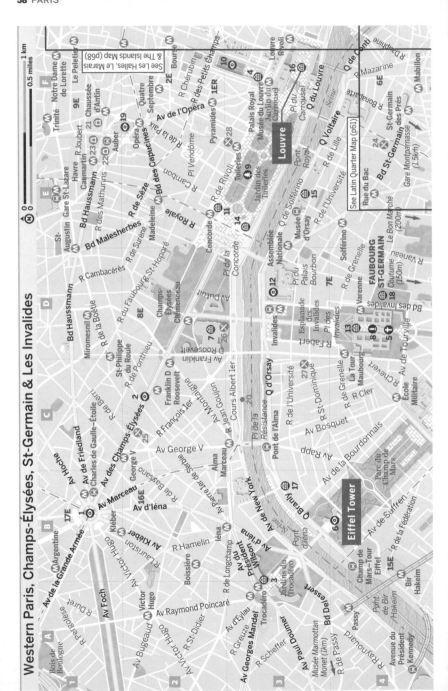

See Les Halles, Le Marais & The Islands Map (p68)

See Latin Quarter Map (p61)

0   0.5 miles

0   1 km

Western Paris, Champs-Élysées, St-Germain & Les Invalides

details. Reserving a ticket online for any show is strongly advised.

⊙ Louvre & Les Halles

Centre Pompidou Museum

(Map p68; ☎01 44 78 12 33; www.centre pompidou.fr; place Georges Pompidou, 4e; museum, exhibitions & panorama adult/child €14/free; ⏱11am-10pm Wed-Mon; Ⓜ Rambuteau) The Centre Pompidou has amazed and delighted visitors ever since it opened in 1977, not just for its outstanding collection of modern art – the largest in Europe – but also for its radical architectural statement. The dynamic and vibrant arts centre delights with its irresistible cocktail of galleries and cutting-edge exhibitions, hands-on workshops, dance performances, cinemas and other entertainment venues. The exterior, with its street performers and fanciful fountains (place Igor Stravinsky), is a fun place to linger.

Musée de l'Orangerie Museum

(Map p58; ☎01 44 77 80 07; www.musee-orangerie.fr; Jardin des Tuileries, 1er; adult/child €9/free; ⏱9am-6pm Wed-Mon; Ⓜ Concorde) Located in the southwestern corner of the Jardin des Tuileries, this museum, with the **Jeu de Paume** (Map p58; ☎01 47 03 12 50; www.jeudepaume.org; 1 place de la Concorde, 8e; adult/child €10/free; ⏱11am-9pm Tue, to 7pm Wed-Sun; Ⓜ Concorde), is all that remains of the former Palais des Tuileries, which was razed during the Paris Commune in 1871. It exhibits important impressionist works, including a series of Monet's *Decorations des Nymphéas* (Water Lilies) in two huge oval rooms purpose-built in 1927 on the artist's instructions, as well as works by Cézanne, Matisse, Picasso, Renoir, Sisley, Soutine and Utrillo. An audioguide costs €5.

⊙ Montmartre & Northern Paris

Basilique du Sacré-Cœur Basilica

(Map p66; ☎01 53 41 89 00; www.sacre-coeur-montmartre.com; place du Parvis du Sacré-Cœur; dome adult/child €6/4, cash only; ⏱6am-10.30pm, dome 8.30am-8pm May-Sep, to 5pm Oct-Apr; Ⓜ Anvers) Although some may poke fun at Sacré-Cœur's unsubtle design, the view from its parvis is one of those perfect Paris postcards. More than just a basilica, Sacré-Cœur is a veritable experience, from the musicians performing on the steps to the groups of friends picnicking on the hillside park. Touristy, yes. But beneath it all, Sacré-Cœur's heart is gold.

Le Mur des je t'aime — Public Art

(Map p66; www.lesjetaime.com; Sq Jehan Rictus, place des Abbesses 18e; ⊙8am-8.30pm Mon-Fri, 9am-8.30pm Sat & Sun May-Aug, to 7.30pm Sep-Apr; MAbbesses) Few visitors to Paris can resist a selfie in front of Montmartre's 'I Love You' wall, a public artwork created in a small city-square park by artists Frédéric Baron and Claire Kito in the year 2000. The striking wall mural made from dark-blue enamel tiles features the immortal phrase 'I love you!' 311 times in 250 different languages. Find a bench beneath a maple tree and brush up your language skills romantic Paris-style.

Cité des Sciences — Science Museum

(☑01 56 43 20 20; www.cite-sciences.fr; 30 av Corentin Cariou, 19e, Parc de la Villette; adult/child €9/7, La Géode €12/9; ⊙10am-6pm Tue-Sat, to 7pm Sun, La Géode 10.30am-8.30pm Tue-Sun; 🚼; MPorte de la Villette) This is the city's top museum for kids, with three floors of hands-on exhibits for children aged two and up, special-effect cinema **La Géode**, a planetarium and a retired submarine. Each exhibit has a separate admission fee (combined tickets exist), so research online beforehand to work out what's most appropriate. Be sure to reserve tickets in advance for both weekend and school-holiday visits, plus for the fabulous **Cité des Enfants** educative play sessions (1½ hours, ages two to seven years or five to 12 years) year-round.

◉ Le Marais

Musée National Picasso — Art Museum

(Map p68; ☑01 85 56 00 36; www.musee picassoparis.fr; 5 rue de Thorigny, 3e; adult/child €12.50/free; ⊙11.30am-6pm Tue-Fri, 9.30am-6pm Sat & Sun; MSt-Paul, Chemin Vert) One of Paris' most beloved art collections is showcased inside the mid-17th-century Hôtel Salé, an exquisite private mansion owned by the city since 1964. Inside is the Musée National Picasso, a staggering art museum devoted to the eccentric Spanish artist, Pablo Picasso (1881–1973), who spent much of his life living and working in Paris. The collection includes more than 5000 drawings, engravings, paintings, ceramic works and sculptures by the *grand maître* (great master), although they're not all displayed at the same time.

Cimetière du Père Lachaise — Cemetery

(Map p68; ☑01 55 25 82 10; www.pere-lachaise. com; 16 rue du Repos & 8 bd de Ménilmontant, 20e; ⊙8am-6pm Mon-Fri, 8.30am-6pm Sat, 9am-6pm Sun, shorter hours winter; MPère Lachaise, Gambetta) The world's most visited cemetery, Père Lachaise, opened in 1804. Its 70,000 ornate, even ostentatious, tombs of the rich and/or famous form a verdant, 44-hectare sculpture garden. The most visited are those of 1960s rock star Jim Morrison (division 6) and Oscar Wilde (division 89). Pick up cemetery maps at the **conservation office** (Bureaux de la Conservation; ☑01 55 25 82 10; 16 rue du Repos, 20e; ⊙8.30am-12.30pm & 2-5pm Mon-Fri; MPère Lachaise) near the main bd de Ménilmontant entrance. Other notables buried here include composer Chopin; playwright Molière; poet Apollinaire; and writers Balzac, Proust, Gertrude Stein and Colette.

◉ Latin Quarter

Panthéon — Mausoleum

(Map p61; www.monum.fr; place du Panthéon, 5e; adult/child €8.50/free; ⊙10am-6.30pm Apr-Sep, to 6pm Oct-Mar; MMaubert-Mutualité or RER Luxembourg) Overlooking the city from its Left Bank perch, the Panthéon's stately neoclassical dome stands out as one of the most recognisable icons on the Parisian skyline. An architectural masterpiece, the interior is impressively vast. Originally a church and now a mausoleum, it has served since 1791 as the resting place of some of France's greatest thinkers, including Voltaire, Rousseau, Braille and Hugo. Its four newest 'residents' are Resistance fighters Germaine Tillion, Genèvieve de Gaulle-Anthonioz, Pierre Brossolette and Jean Zay.

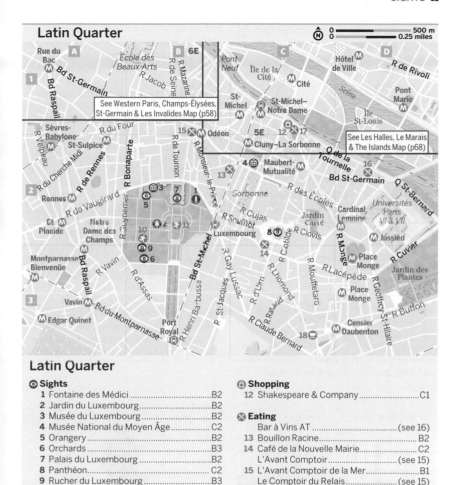

Latin Quarter

◉ Sights

◔ Activities, Courses & Tours

◓ Shopping

◈ Eating

◔ Drinking & Nightlife

Musée National du Moyen Âge
Museum

(Map p61; www.musee-moyenage.fr; 6 place Paul Painlevé, 5e; adult/child €8/free, during temporary exhibitions €9/free; ◔9.15am-5.45pm Wed-Mon; ⓂCluny–La Sorbonne) The National Museum of the Middle Ages holds a series of sublime treasures, from medieval statuary, stained glass and objets d'art to its celebrated series of tapestries, *The Lady with the Unicorn* (1500). Throw in the extant architecture – an ornate 15th-century mansion (the Hôtel de Cluny), and the *frigidarium* (cold room) of an enormous Roman-era bathhouse – and you have one of Paris' top small museums. Outside, four medieval gardens grace the northeastern corner; more bathhouse remains are to the west.

◉ St-Germain & Les Invalides

Musée d'Orsay   Museum

(Map p58; www.musee-orsay.fr; 62 rue de Lille, 7e; adult/child €12/free; ⊙9.30am-6pm Tue, Wed & Fri-Sun, to 9.45pm Thu; ⓂAssemblée Nationale or RER Musée d'Orsay) The home of France's national collection from the impressionist, postimpressionist and art nouveau movements spanning the 1840s and 1914 is the glorious former Gare d'Orsay railway station – itself an art nouveau showpiece – where a roll call of masters and their world-famous works are on display.

Top of every visitor's must-see list is the museum's painting collections, centred on the world's largest collection of impressionist and postimpressionist art.

Musée Rodin   Museum, Garden

(Map p58; www.musee-rodin.fr; 79 rue de Varenne, 7e; adult/child museum incl garden €10/7, garden only €4/2; ⊙10am-5.45pm Tue & Thu-Sun, to 8.45pm Wed; ⓂVarenne) Sculptor, painter, sketcher, engraver and collector Auguste Rodin donated his entire collection to the French state in 1908 on the proviso that they dedicate his former workshop and showroom, the beautiful 1730 Hôtel Biron, to displaying his works. They're now installed not only in the magnificently restored mansion itself, but in its rose-filled garden – one of the most peaceful places in central Paris and a wonderful spot to contemplate his famous work *The Thinker*.

Prepurchase tickets online to avoid queuing.

Hôtel des Invalides   Monument, Museum

(Map p58; www.musee-armee.fr; 129 rue de Grenelle, 7e; adult/child €11/free; ⊙10am-6pm Apr-Oct, to 5pm Nov-Mar, hours can vary; ⓂVarenne) Flanked by the 500m-long Esplanade des Invalides lawns, the Hôtel des Invalides was built in the 1670s by Louis XIV to house 4000 *invalides* (disabled war veterans). On 14 July 1789, a mob broke into the building and seized 32,000 rifles before heading on to the prison at Bastille and the start of the French Revolution.

Admission includes entry to all Hôtel des Invalides sights. Hours for individual sites often vary – check the website for updates.

From left: Musée d'Orsay clock; *The Thinker*, Musée Rodin; Jardin des Tuileries (p57)

SHAUN EGAN / GETTY IMAGES ©

MUNTZ / GETTY IMAGES ©

🎯 ACTIVITIES

Bateaux-Mouches Boat Tour

(Map p58; ☏01 42 25 96 10; www.bateaux
mouches.com; Port de la Conférence, 8e; adult/
child €13.50/6; Ⓜ Alma Marceau) The largest
river cruise company in Paris and a favourite with tour groups. Cruises (70 minutes)
run regularly from 10.15am to 10.30pm
April to September and 13 times a day
between 11am and 9.20pm the rest of the
year. Commentary is in French and English.
It's located on the Right Bank, just east of
the Pont de l'Alma.

🛍 SHOPPING

Galeries Lafayette Department Store

(Map p58; http://haussmann.galeries
lafayette.com; 40 bd Haussmann, 9e; ⊙9.30am-
8pm Mon-Sat, to 9pm Thu; 🛜; Ⓜ Chaussée d'An-
tin or RER Auber) *Grande dame* department
store Galeries Lafayette is spread across
the main store (whose magnificent stained-
glass dome is over a century old), men's
store and homewares store, and includes a
gourmet emporium.

Catch modern art in the **gallery** (www.
galeriedesgaleries.com; 1st fl; ⊙11am-7pm Tue-
Sat) **FREE**, take in a **fashion show** (☏book-
ings 01 42 82 30 25; ⊙3pm Fri Mar-Jun & Sep-Dec
by reservation), ascend to a free, windswept
rooftop panorama, or take a break at one of
its 24 restaurants and cafes.

Le Bon Marché Department Store

(www.bonmarche.com; 24 rue de Sèvres, 7e;
⊙10am-8pm Mon-Wed & Sat, to 9pm Thu & Fri;
Ⓜ Sèvres-Babylone) Built by Gustave Eiffel
as Paris' first department store in 1852,
Le Bon Marché is the epitome of style,
with a superb concentration of men's and
women's fashions, beautiful homewares,
stationery, books and toys as well as chic
dining options.

The icing on the cake is its glorious food
hall, **La Grande Épicerie de Paris** (www.
lagrandeepicerie.com; 36 rue de Sèvres, 7e;
⊙8.30am-9pm Mon-Sat; Ⓜ Sèvres-Babylone).

Merci Concept Store

(Map p68; ☏01 42 77 00 33; www.merci-merci.
com; 111 bd Beaumarchais, 3e; ⊙10am-7pm
Mon-Sat; Ⓜ St-Sébastien-Froissart) A Fiat
Cinquecento marks the entrance to this

Marché aux Puces St-Ouen

A vast flea market, the **Marché aux Puces de St-Ouen** (www.marcheaux puces-saintouen.com; rue des Rosiers; ⊘variable; ⓜPorte de Clignancourt) was founded in the late 19th century. It's said to be Europe's largest market, and has more than 2500 stalls grouped into 15 *marchés* (market areas), each with its own speciality (eg Paul Bert for 17th-century furniture, Malik for clothing, Biron for Asian art). There are miles upon miles of 'freelance' stalls; come prepared to spend some time.

Parisian postcards

unique concept store, which donates all its profits to a children's charity in Madagascar. Shop for fashion, accessories, linens, lamps and nifty designs for the home; and complete the experience with a coffee in its hybrid used-book-shop-cafe or lunch in its stylish basement **La Cantine de Merci** (Map p68; ☑01 42 77 79 28; www.merci-merci. com; 111 bd Beaumarchais, 3e; soups €8-10, salads & tarts €10-17; ⊘noon-6pm Mon-Sat; ⓜSt-Sébastien-Froissart).

 EATING

Eiffel Tower & Western Paris

Hugo Desnoyer   Modern French €€€
(☑01 46 47 83 00; www.hugodesnoyer.fr; 28 rue du Docteur Blanche, 16e; mains from €28; ⊘restaurant 11.30am-3.30pm Tue-Sat, 8-11pm Wed; ⓜJasmin) Hugo Desnoyer is Paris' most famous butcher and the trip to his shop in

the 16e is well worth it. Arrive by noon or reserve to snag a table and settle down to a *table d'hôte* feast of homemade terrines, quiches, foie gras and cold cuts followed by the finest meat in Paris – cooked to perfection *naturellement.*

A more convenient branch, **Steak Point** (Map p58; Lafayette Gourmet, bd Haussmann, 9e; mains €14-26; ⊘noon-7.30pm Mon-Sat; ⓜHavre Caumartin or RER Auber), is located in the basement of Galeries Lafeyette Gourmet.

Champs-Élysées & Grands Boulevards

Ladurée   Patisserie €
(Map p58; www.laduree.com; 75 av des Champs-Élysées, 8e; pastries from €1.50; ⊘7.30am-11.30pm Mon-Fri, 8.30am-12.30am Sat, 8.30am-11.30pm Sun; ⓜGeorge V) One of the oldest patisseries in Paris, Ladurée has been around since 1862 and was the original creator of the lighter-than-air macaron. Its tearoom is the classiest spot to indulge on the Champs. Alternatively, pick up some pastries to go – from croissants to its trademark macarons, it's all quite heavenly.

Richer   Neobistro €€
(Map p68; www.lericher.com; 2 rue Richer, 9e; mains €19-20; ⊘8am-midnight; ⓜPoissonière, Bonne Nouvelle) Run by the same team as across-the-street neighbour **L'Office** (Map p68; ☑01 47 70 67 31; 3 rue Richer, 9e; 2-/3-course lunch menus €22/28, dinner menus €27/34; ⊘noon-2.30pm & 7.30-10.30pm Mon-Fri; ⓜPoissonière, Bonne Nouvelle), Richer's pared-back, exposed-brick decor is a smart setting for genius creations like trout tartare with cauliflower and tomato and citrus mousse, and quince and lime cheesecake for dessert. It doesn't take reservations, but it serves up snacks, Chinese tea and has a full bar outside meal times. Fantastic value.

Louvre & Les Halles

Uma   Fusion €€
(Map p58; ☑01 40 15 08 15; www.uma-restaurant.fr; 7 rue du 29 Juillet, 1er; 2-/3-course lunch €25/29, mains €23-25; ⊘12.30-2.30pm & 7.30-10.30pm Tue-Sat; ⓜTuileries) Embark

Cyclists passing booksellers

on a culinary voyage at Uma, where chef Lucas Felzine infuses contemporary French sensibilities with Nikkei: Peruvian-Japanese fusion food. The lunch menu comes with two exquisitely prepared starters (think ceviche with daikon radish or smoked duck with lychees and huacatay); grab a table upstairs to spy on the open kitchen. Mezcal, pisco and vodka cocktails are served until 1.30am. Reserve.

Frenchie   Bistro €€€

(Map p68; ☎01 40 39 96 19; www.frenchie-restaurant.com; 5-6 rue du Nil, 2e; prix-fixe menu €68; ☻7-11pm Mon-Fri; ⓂSentier) Tucked down an alley you wouldn't venture down otherwise, this bijou bistro with wooden tables and old stone walls is iconic. Frenchie is always packed and for good reason: excellent value dishes are modern, market-driven and prepared with just the right dose of unpretentious creative flair by French chef Gregory Marchand.

The only hiccup is snagging a table: reserve well in advance, arrive at 6.30pm and pray for a cancellation (it does happen)

or – failing that – share tapas-style small plates with friends across the street at **Frenchie Bar à Vins** (Map p68; 6 rue du Nil. 2e; dishes €9-23; ☻7-11pm Mon-Fri; ⓂSentier). No reservations at the latter – write your name on the sheet of paper strung outside, loiter in the alley and wait for your name to be called.

✖ Montmartre & Northern Paris

Du Pain et des Idées   Boulangerie €
(Map p68; www.dupainetdesidees.com; 34 rue Yves Toudic, 10e; pastries from €1.50; ☻6.45am-8pm Mon-Fri; ⓂJacques Bonsergent) This traditional bakery with exquisite interior from 1889 is famed for its naturally leavened bread, orange-blossom brioche and decadent *escargots* ('snails', like cinnamon rolls) in four sweet flavours. Its mini savoury *pavés* (breads) flavoured with Reblochon cheese and fig, or goat's cheese, sesame and honey make for the perfect lunch on the hoof. Top marks for the wooden picnic table on the pavement outside.

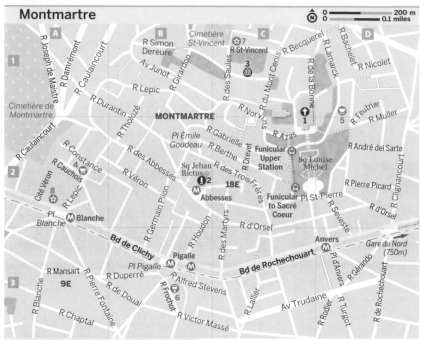

Montmartre

52 Faubourg St-Denis
Modern French €

(Map p68; www.faubourgstdenis.com; 52 rue du Faubourg St-Denis, 10e; mains €16-20; ⊙8am-midnight, kitchen noon-2.30pm & 7-11pm; 🛜; Ⓜ Château d'Eau) This thoroughly contemporary, neighbourhood cafe-restaurant is simply a brilliant space to hang out in at any time of day. Be it for breakfast, coffee, a zingy fresh-sage infusion, dinner or drinks, 52 Faubourg, as locals call it, gets it just right. Cuisine is modern and creative, and the chef is not shy in mixing veg with fruit in every course – including dessert. No reservations.

Holybelly
International €

(Map p68; www.holybel.ly; 19 rue Lucien Sampaix, 10e; breakfast €5-11.50, lunch mains €13.50-16.50; ⊙9am-6pm Thu, Fri & Mon, from 10am Sat & Sun; Ⓜ Jacques Bonsergent) This outstanding barista-run coffee shop and kitchen is always crammed with a buoyant crowd, who never tire of Holybelly's exceptional service, Belleville-roasted coffee and cuisine. Sarah's breakfast pancakes served with egg, bacon, homemade bourbon butter and maple syrup are legendary, while her lunch menu features everything from traditional braised veal shank to squid *à la plancha*.

Le Verre Volé
Bistro €€

(Map p68; ☎01 48 03 17 34; http://leverre vole.fr; 67 rue de Lancry, 10e; mains €15-25; ⊙bistro 12.30-2pm & 7.30-10.30pm, wine cellar

9am-1am; M Jacques Bonsergent) The tiny 'Stolen Glass' – a wine shop with a few tables – is just about the most perfect wine-bar-restaurant in Paris, with top wines and expert advice. Unpretentious and hearty *plats du jour* (dishes of the day) are excellent. Reserve well in advance for meals, or stop by to pick up a bottle.

Le Marais

Breizh Café Crêperie €

(Map p68; www.breizhcafe.com; 109 rue Vieille du Temple, 3e; crêpes & galettes €6.50-18; ⏰11.30am-11pm Wed-Sat, to 10pm Sun; M St-Sébastien-Froissart) It is a well-known fact among Parisians: everything at the Breton Café (*breizh* is 'Breton' in Breton) is 100% authentic, rendering it the top spot in the city for authentic crêpes. Be it the Cancale oysters, 20 types of cider or the buttery organic-flour crêpes, everything here is cooked to perfection. If you fail to snag a table, try **L'Épicerie** (Map p68; www. breizhcafe.com; 111 rue Vieille du Temple, 3e; crêpes & galettes €6.50-17.80; ⏰11.30am-9pm; M St-Sébastien-Froissart) next door.

Chez Alain Miam Miam Sandwiches, Crêperie €

(Map p68; www.facebook.com/ChezAlainMiam Miam; 39 rue de Bretagne & 33bis rue Charlot, 3e, Marché des Enfants Rouges; sandwiches €8; ⏰9am-3.30pm Wed-Fri, to 5.30pm Sat, to 3pm Sun; M Filles du Calvaire) Weave your way through the makeshift kitchens inside **Marché des Enfants Rouges** (Map p68; 39 rue de Bretagne & 33bis rue Charlot, 3e; ⏰8.30am-1pm & 4-7.30pm Tue-Fri, 4-8pm Sat, 8.30am-2pm Sun; M Filles du Calvaire) to find Alain, a retired baker with grey surfer locks and T-shirt with attitude. Watch him prepare you a monster sandwich or *galette* (savoury pancake) on a sizzling crêpe griddle from a bespoke combo of fresh, organic ingredients – grated fennel, smoked air-dried beef, avocado, sesame salt and carefully curated honeys.

Jacques Genin Patisserie €

(Map p68; ✆01 45 77 29 01; 133 rue de Turenne, 3e; pastry €9; ⏰11am-7pm Tue-Sun; M Ober-

💬 Paris with Locals

See Paris through local eyes with two- to three-hour city tours with **Parisien d'un Jour – Paris Greeters** (www.greeters. paris; by donation). Volunteers – mainly knowledgeable Parisians passionate about their city – lead groups (maximum six people) to their favourite spots. Minimum two weeks' notice is needed.

kampf) Wildly creative *chocolatier* Jacques Genin is famed for his flavoured caramels, *pâtes de fruits* (fruit jellies) and exquisitely embossed *bonbons de chocolat* (chocolate sweets). But what completely steals the show at his elegant chocolate showroom is the *salon de dégustation* (aka tearoom), where you can order a pot of outrageously thick hot chocolate and legendary Genin millefeuille, assembled to order.

Au Passage Bistro €€

(Map p68; ✆01 73 20 23 23; www.restaurant-aupassage.fr; 1bis passage St-Sébastien, 11e; small plates €7-14, meats to share €18-70; ⏰7-11.30pm Mon-Sat; M St-Sébastien-Frois-sart) Spawned by talented Australian chef James Henry, who went on to open Bones then Parisian bistro Belon in Hong Kong, this *petit bar de quartier* (neighbourhood bar) is still raved about. Pick from a good-value, uncomplicated choice selection of *petites assiettes* (small plates designed to be shared) featuring various market produce – cold meats, raw or cooked fish, vegetables and so on. Advance reservations essential.

Le Clown Bar Modern French €€

(Map p68; ✆01 43 55 87 35; www.clown-bar-paris.fr; 114 rue Amelot, 11e; mains €25-30; ⏰noon-2.30pm & 7-10.30pm Wed-Sun; M Filles du Calvaire) A historic monument next to the city's winter circus, the Cirque d'Hiver (1852), this unique address is practically a museum with its ceramics, mosaics, original zinc bar and purist art deco style.

Les Halles, Le Marais & The Islands

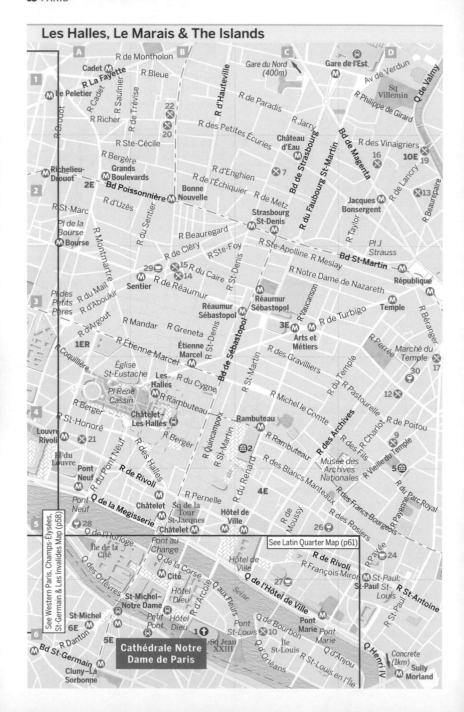

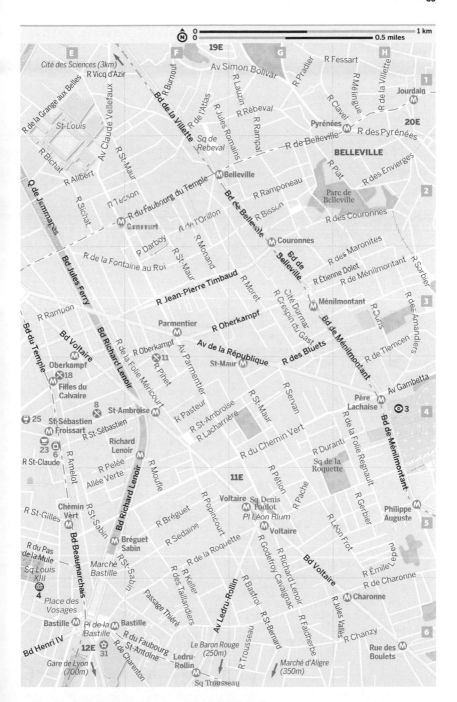

Les Halles, Le Marais & The Islands

A restaurant for decades, this mythical address now serves up fabulous modern French cuisine and excellent natural wines for a jovial crowd. Its pavement terrace gets packed out on sunny days.

Latin Quarter

Shakespeare & Company Café   Cafe €

(Map p61; www.shakespeareandcompany.com; 2 rue St-Julien le Pauvre, 5e; dishes €4-9.50; ⊙10am-6.30pm Mon-Fri, to 7.30pm Sat & Sun; 🛜📶♿; Ⓜ St-Michel) ✐ Instant history was made when this light-filled, literary-inspired cafe opened in 2015 adjacent to magical bookshop **Shakespeare & Company** (Map p61; ☑01 43 25 40 93; www.shakespeareandcompany.com; 37 rue de la Bûcherie, 5e; ⊙10am-11pm; Ⓜ St-Michel), designed from long-lost sketches to fulfil a dream of late bookshop founder George Whitman from the 1960s. Its primarily vegetarian menu (with vegan and gluten-free dishes available) includes homemade bagels, rye bread, soups, salads and pastries, plus Parisian-roasted Café Lomi coffee.

Café de la Nouvelle Mairie   Cafe €€

(Map p61; ☑01 44 07 04 41; 19 rue des Fossés St-Jacques, 5e; mains €12-32; ⊙kitchen 8am-midnight Mon-Fri; Ⓜ Cardinal Lemoine) Shhhh... just around the corner from the Panthéon but hidden away on a small, fountained square, this narrow wine bar is a neighbourhood secret, serving blackboard-chalked natural wines by the glass and delicious seasonal bistro fare from oysters and ribs (*à la française*) to grilled lamb sausage over lentils. It takes reservations for dinner but not lunch – arrive early.

Restaurant AT   Gastronomic €€€

(Map p61; ☑01 56 81 94 08; www.atsushi tanaka.com; 4 rue du Cardinal Lemoine, 5e; 4-/6-course lunch menus €35/55, 12-course dinner tasting menu €95; ⊙12.15-2pm & 8-9.30pm Tue-Sat; Ⓜ Cardinal Lemoine) Trained by some of the biggest names in gastronomy (Pierre Gagnaire included), chef Atsushi Tanaka showcases abstract artlike masterpieces incorporating rare ingredients (charred bamboo, kohlrabi turnip cabbage, juniper berry powder, wild purple fennel, Nepalese Timut pepper) in a blank-canvas-style dining space on stunning outsized plates. Just off the entrance, steps lead to his cellar wine bar, **Bar à Vins AT** (Map p61; dishes €12-16; ☉7pm-2am Tue-Sun).

St-Germain & Les Invalides

L'Avant Comptoir de la Mer
Seafood Tapas €

(Map p61; www.hotel-paris-relais-saint-germain. com; 3 Carrefour de l'Odéon, 6e; tapas €4-30; ☉noon-11pm; MOdéon) The latest in Yves Camdeborde's stunning line-up of Carrefour de l'Odéon eateries, alongside **Le Comptoir** (Map p61; ☑01 44 27 07 97, 9 Carrefour de l'Odéon, 6e; mains €14-39, dinner menu €60; ☉noon-6pm & 8.30-11.30pm Mon-Fri, noon-11pm Sat & Sun; MOdéon) and **L'Avant Comptoir** (Map p61; 3 Carrefour de l'Odéon, 6e; tapas €5-10; ☉noon-midnight; MOdéon), serves succulent oysters (Bloody Mary–style or with chipolata sausages), herring tartine, cauliflower and trout roe, blood-orange razor clams, lobster with almond milk foam, roasted scallops and salmon croquettes, complemented by its bar's artisan bread, flavoured butters, sea salt and Kalamata olives.

Bouillon Racine
Brasserie €€

(Map p61; ☑01 73 20 21 12; www.bouillon racine.com; 3 rue Racine, 6e; weekday lunch menu €16, menus €31-42; ☉noon-11pm; 🐾; MCluny-La Sorbonne) Inconspicuously situated in a quiet street, this heritage-listed 1906 art nouveau 'soup kitchen', with mirrored walls, floral motifs and ceramic tiling, was built in 1906 to feed market workers. Despite the magnificent interior, the food – inspired by age-old recipes – is no afterthought but superbly executed (stuffed, spit-roasted suckling pig, pork shank in Rodenbach red beer, scallops and shrimps with lobster coulis).

Clover
Neobistro €€

(Map p58; ☑01 75 50 00 05; www.clover-paris. com; 5 rue Perronet, 7e; 2-/3-course lunch menus €28/42, 3-/5-course dinner menus €58/73; ☉12.30-2pm & 7.30-10pm Tue-Sat; MSt-Germain des Prés) Dining at hot-shot chef Jean-François Piège's casual bistro is like attend-

Gluten-free Greatness

In a city known for its bakeries, it's only right there's **Chambelland** (Map p68; ☑01 43 55 07 30; www.chambelland.com; 14 rue Ternaux, 11e; lunch menu €12; ☉9am-8pm Tue-Sun; MParmentier) – a 100% gluten-free bakery with serious breads to die for. Using rice and buckwheat flour milled at the bakery's very own mill in southern France, this pioneering bakery creates exquisite cakes and pastries as well as sourdough loaves and brioches (sweet breads) peppered with nuts, seeds, chocolate and fruit.

ing a private party: the galley-style open kitchen adjoining the 20 seats (reserve ahead!) is part of the dining-room decor, putting customers front and centre of the culinary action. Light, luscious dishes span quinoa chips with aubergine and black sesame to cabbage leaves with smoked herring *crème* and chestnuts.

Restaurant David Toutain
Gastronomic €€€

(Map p58; ☑01 45 51 11 10; www.davidtoutain. com; 29 rue Surcouf, 7e; 9-/15-course tasting menus €80/110; ☉noon-2pm & 8-10pm Mon-Fri; MInvalides) Prepare to be wowed: David Toutain pushes the envelope at his eponymous Michelin-starred restaurant with some of the most creative high-end cooking in Paris. Mystery *dégustation* (tasting) courses include unlikely combinations such as smoked eel in green-apple-and-black-sesame mousse, cauliflower, white chocolate and coconut truffles, or candied celery and truffled rice pudding with artichoke praline (stunning wine pairings available).

DRINKING & NIGHTLIFE

Le Verre à Pied
Cafe

(Map p61; http://leverreapied.fr; 118bis rue Mouffetard, 5e; ☉9am-9pm Tue-Sat, 9.30am-4pm Sun; MCensier Daubenton) This *café-tabac* is a pearl of a place where little has changed since 1870. Its nicotine-hued mirrored wall, moulded cornices and original bar make it part of a dying breed, but it epitomises the charm, glamour and romance of an old Paris everyone loves, including stallholders from the rue Mouffetard market who yo-yo in and out.

L'Ebouillanté   Cafe

(Map p68; http://ebouillante.pagesperso-orange.fr; 6 rue des Barres, 4e; ◷noon-10pm summer, to 7pm winter; ⓜHôtel de Ville) On sunny days there is no prettier cafe terrace. Enjoying a privileged position on a pedestrian, stone-flagged street just footsteps from the Seine, L'Ebouillanté buzzes with savvy Parisians sipping refreshing glasses of homemade *citronnade* (ginger lemonade), hibiscus-flower cordial and herbal teas. Delicious cakes, jumbo salads, savoury crêpes and Sunday brunch (€21) complement the long drinks menu.

> *the resting place of some of France's greatest thinkers*

Panthéon (p60)

Wild & the Moon   Juice Bar

(Map p68; www.wildandthemoon.com; 55 rue Charlot, 3e; ◷8am-7pm Mon-Fri, 10am-7pm Sat, 11am-5pm Sun; ⓜFilles du Calvaire) A beautiful crowd hobnobs over nut milks, vitality shots, smoothies, cold-pressed juices and raw food in this sleek new juice bar in the fashionable Haut Marais. Ingredients are fresh, seasonal and organic, and it is one of the few places in town where you can have moon porridge or avocado slices on almond and rosemary crackers for breakfast.

Le Mary Céleste   Cocktail Bar

(Map p68; www.lemaryceleste.com; 1 rue Commines, 3e; ◷6pm-1.30am; ⓜFilles du Calvaire) Predictably there's a distinct nautical feel to this fashionable, ubercool cocktail bar in the Marais. Snag a stool at the central circular bar or play savvy and reserve one of a handful of tables (in advance online). Cocktails (€12 to €13) are creative and the perfect partner to a dozen oysters or your pick of tapas-style 'small plates' designed to be shared (€8 to €15).

Lulu White
Cocktail Bar

(Map p66; www.luluwhite.bar; 12 rue Frochot, 9e; ⏰7pm-3am Mon-Sat; ⓂPigalle) Sip absinthe-based cocktails in Prohibition-era New Orleans surrounds at this elegant, serious and supremely busy cocktail bar on rue Frochot; several more line the same street, making for a fabulous evening out. Should you be wondering, Lulu White was an infamous African American brothel owner in early-20th-century New Orleans.

Les Jardins du Pont-Neuf
Cocktail Bar

(Map p68; www.jdp9.com; quai de l'Horloge, 1er; ⏰7pm-2am Tue-Sat; 🍴; ⓂPont Neuf) Island life became more glamorous with the opening of this ultra-chic floating cocktail bar aboard a barge moored by the Pont Neuf. Decked out with art nouveau-inspired decor including rattan furniture and hanging plants, its two vast terraces overlook the Seine. There's also a dance floor; check the website for upcoming soirées.

Le Baron Rouge
Wine Bar

(📞01 43 43 14 32; 1 rue Théophile Roussel, 12e; ⏰10am-2pm & 5-10pm Tue-Fri, 10am-10pm Sat, 10am-4pm Sun; ⓂLedru-Rollin) Just about the ultimate Parisian wine-bar experience, this place has barrels stacked against the bottle-lined walls. As unpretentious as you'll find, it's a local meeting place where everyone is welcome and it's especially busy on Sunday after the **Marché d'Aligre** (http://marchedaligre.free.fr; rue d'Aligre, 12e; ⏰8am-1pm Tue-Sun; ⓂLedru-Rollin) wraps up. All the usual suspects – cheese, charcuterie and oysters – will keep your belly full.

Le Petit Fer à Cheval
Bar

(Map p68; www.cafeine.com/petit-fer-a-cheval; 30 rue Vieille du Temple, 4e; ⏰9am-2am; ⓂHôtel de Ville, St-Paul) A Marais institution, the Little Horseshoe is a minute cafe-bar with an original horseshoe-shaped zinc bar from 1903. The place overflows with regulars from dawn to dark. Great *apéro* (predinner drink) spot and great WC – stainless-steel toilet stalls straight out of a Flash Gordon film (actually inspired by the interior of the

Best Coffee

Boot Café (Map p68; 19 rue du Pont aux Choux, 3e; ⏰10am-6pm; ⓂSt-Sébastien-Froissart) The charm of this three-table ode to good coffee is its façade – an old cobbler's shop – which must win a prize for 'most photographed'. Excellent coffee, roasted in Paris, to boot.

Lockwood (Map p68; 📞01 77 32 97 21, 73 rue d'Aboukir, 2e; ⏰8am-2am Mon-Sat, 10am-4pm Sun; ⓂSentier) Savour beans from Paris' Belleville Brûlerie during the day, brunch on weekends and well-mixed cocktails in the subterranean candle-lit *cave* at night.

Hardware Société (Map p66; 📞01 42 51 69 03; 10 rue Lamarck, 18e; ⏰9am-4.30pm Thu-Mon, kitchen 9am-3.30pm Thu-Mon; 🍴; ⓂChâteau Rouge, Lamarck-Caulaincourt) With black-and-white floor, Christian Lacroix butterflies fluttering across one wall and perfect love-heart-embossed cappuccinos, there's no finer spot around Montmartre's Sacré-Cœur to linger over superb barista-crafted coffee. Feisty breakfasts and brunches too.

Coutume (www.coutumecafe.com; 47 rue de Babylone, 7e; ⏰8am-7pm Mon-Fri, 10am-7pm Sat & Sun; 🍴; ⓂSt-François Xavier) The flagship cafe of this artisan roaster of premium beans is ground zero for innovative preparation methods including cold extraction and siphon brews. Fabulous organic fare and pastries.

 Life is a Cabaret

Whirling lines of feather-boa-clad, high-kicking dancers at grand-scale cabarets like the cancan creator, the Moulin Rouge, are a quintessential fixture on Paris' entertainment scene – for everyone but Parisians. Still, the dazzling sets, costumes and dancing guarantee an entertaining evening (or matinee).

Moulin Rouge (Map p66; ☎01 53 09 82 82; www.moulinrouge.fr; 82 bd de Clichy, 18e; show €105-130, dinner show from €190; ⊙shows 9pm & 11pm summer, 9pm Sun-Thu, 9pm & 11pm Fri & Sat winter; ⓂBlanche) Immortalised in the posters of Toulouse-Lautrec and later on screen by Baz Luhrmann, Paris' mythical cabaret club twinkles beneath a 1925 replica of its original red windmill. From the opening bars of music to the last high cancan-girl kick, it's a whirl of fantastical costumes, sets, choreography and Champagne.

Au Lapin Agile (Map p66; ☎01 46 06 85 87; www.au-lapin-agile.com; 22 rue des Saules, 18e; adult €28, student except Sat €20; ⊙9pm-1am Tue-Sun; ⓂLamarck-Caulaincourt) This rustic cabaret venue was favoured by artists and intellectuals in the early 20th century and traditional *chansons* are still performed here.

Moulin Rouge
MAXOZEROV / GETTY IMAGES ©

Nautilus submarine in Jules Verne's *20,000 Leagues under the Sea*).

Concrete Club
(www.concreteparis.fr; 60 Port de la Rapée, 12e; ⊙10pm-7am; ⓂGare de Lyon) This hugely popular, wild-child club with different dance floors lures a young international set to a boat on the Seine, firmly moored by Gare de Lyon. Notorious for introducing an 'after-hours' element to Paris' somewhat staid clubbing scene, Concrete is the trendy place to party all night until sunrise and beyond. Watch for all-weekend events aka electronic dance music around the clock.

Le Batofar Club
(www.batofar.org; opposite 11 quai François Mauriac, 13e; ⊙bar noon-midnight, club 11.30pm-6am; ⓂQuai de la Gare, Bibliothèque) This much-loved, red-metal tugboat has a rooftop bar that's terrific in summer, and a respected restaurant, while the club underneath provides memorable underwater acoustics between its metal walls and portholes. Le Batofar is known for its edgy, experimental music policy and live performances from 7pm, mostly electro-oriented but also incorporating hip-hop, new wave, rock, punk or jazz.

⭐ ENTERTAINMENT

Opéra Bastille Opera, Classical Music
(Map p68; ☎01 40 01 19 70, 08 92 89 90 90; www.operadeparis.fr; 2-6 place de la Bastille, 12e; guided tours €15; ⊙box office 2.30-6.30pm Mon-Sat; ⓂBastille) This 3400-seat venue is the city's main opera hall; it also stages ballet and classical concerts. Tickets go on sale online up to two weeks before they're available by telephone or at the box office. Standing-only tickets (*places débouts;* €5) are available 90 minutes before performances begin. By day, explore the opera house with a 90-minute guided tour backstage; check hours online.

Palais Garnier Opera, Ballet
(Map p58; ☎08 92 89 90 90; www.operadeparis.fr; place de l'Opéra, 9e; ⓂOpéra) The

city's original opera house is smaller than its Bastille counterpart, but has perfect acoustics. Due to its odd shape, some seats have limited or no visibility – book carefully. Ticket prices and conditions (including last-minute discounts) are available from the **box office** (Map p58; cnr rues Scribe & Auber; ⊘11am-6.30pm Mon-Sat; ⓂOpéra).

ℹ️ INFORMATION

MEDICAL SERVICES

American Hospital of Paris (☑01 46 41 25 25; www.american-hospital.org; 63 bd Victor Hugo, Neuilly-sur-Seine; ⓂPont de Levallois) Private hospital with emergency 24-hour medical and dental care.

Hôpital Hôtel Dieu (☑01 42 34 82 34; www.aphp.fr; 1 place du Parvis Notre Dame, 4e; ⓂCité) One of the city's main government-run public hospitals; after 8pm use the emergency entrance on rue de la Cité.

Pharmacie Les Champs (☑01 45 62 02 41; Galerie des Champs-Élysées, 84 av des Champs-Élysées, 8e; ⊘24hrs; ⓂGeorge V)

TOURIST INFORMATION

Paris Convention & Visitors Bureau (Office du Tourisme et des Congrès de Paris; www.parisinfo.com; 27 rue des Pyramides, 1er; ⊘7am-7pm May-Oct, 10am-7pm Nov-Apr; ⓂPyramides) The main branch is 500m northwest of the Louvre. It sells tickets for tours and several attractions, plus museum and transport passes. Also books accommodation.

ℹ️ GETTING THERE & AWAY

AIR

Aéroport de Charles de Gaulle (CDG; ☑01 70 36 39 50, www.aeroportsdeparis.fr) Most international airlines fly to Aéroport de Charles de Gaulle, 28km northeast of central Paris. (In French the airport is commonly called 'Roissy' after the suburb in which it is located.)

Aéroport d'Orly (ORY; ☑01 70 36 39 50; www.aeroportsdeparis.fr) Aéroport d'Orly is located 19km south of central Paris but, despite being closer to the centre than CDG, it is not as frequently used by international airlines and public transportation options aren't quite as straightforward.

Al fresco diners

From left: Macarons; Cheese for sale at a local market; Left Bank of the Seine

TRAIN

Paris has six major train stations. For mainline train information visit the SNCF (www.voyages-sncf.com) website.

Gare du Nord (rue de Dunkerque, 10e; MGare du Nord) Trains to/from the UK, Belgium, northern Germany, Scandinavia and Moscow (terminus of the high-speed Thalys trains to/from Amsterdam, Brussels, Cologne and Geneva, and the Eurostar to London); trains to the northern suburbs of Paris and northern France.

Gare de Lyon (bd Diderot, 12e; MGare de Lyon) Gare de Lyon, in eastern Paris, is the terminus for trains from Provence, the Alps, the Riviera and Italy. Also serves Geneva, Switzerland.

Gare de l'Est (bd de Strasbourg, 10e; MGare de l'Est) For trains to/from Luxembourg, parts of Switzerland, southern Germany and points further east; regular and TGV Est trains to areas of France east of Paris including Champagne.

Gare St-Lazare (esplanade de la Gare St-Lazare, 8e; MSt-Lazare) Terminus for trains from Normandy.

Gare Montparnasse (av du Maine & bd de Vaugirard, 15e; MMontparnasse Bienvenüe) Gare Montparnasse is the terminus for trains from the southwest and west, including services from Brittany, the Loire and Bordeaux, and Spain and Portugal.

Gare d'Austerlitz (bd de l'Hôpital, 13e; MGare d'Austerlitz) Gare d'Austerlitz is the terminus for a handful of trains from the south, including services from Orléans. High-speed trains to/from Barcelona and Madrid also use Austerlitz.

❶ GETTING AROUND

TO/FROM THE AIRPORT

Getting into town is straightforward and inexpensive thanks to a fleet of public transport options; the most expedient are listed here. Bus drivers sell tickets.

AÉROPORT CHARLES DE GAULLE

CDG is served by the RER B line (€9.75, approximately 50 minutes, every 10 to 20 minutes), which connects with the Gare du Nord, Châtelet–Les Halles and St-Michel–Notre Dame stations in the city centre. Trains run from 5am to 11pm; there are fewer trains on weekends.

There are six main bus lines:

Les Cars Air France line 2 (€17, 1hr, every 20min, 6am-11pm) Links the airport with the Arc de Triomphe. Children aged 2 to 11 pay half price.

Les Cars Air France line 4 (€17.50, 50-55min, every 30min, 6am-10pm) Links the airport with Gare de Lyon in eastern Paris and Gare Montparnasse in southern Paris. Children aged 2 to 11 pay half price.

Noctilien bus 140 & 143 (€8 or 4 metro tickets, line 140 1¼hrs, line 143 2hr, every 30min, 6am-10pm) Part of the RATP night service, Noctilien has two buses that go to CDG: bus 140 from Gare de l'Est, and 143 from Gare de l'Est and Gare du Nord.

RATP bus 350 (€6, 70min, every 30min, 5.30am-11pm) Links the airport with Gare de l'Est in northern Paris.

RATP bus 351 (€6, 70min, every 30min, 5.30am-11pm) Links the airport with place de la Nation in eastern Paris.

Roissybus (€11, 1hr, from CDG every 15min 5.30am-10pm & every 30min, 10pm &11pm; from Paris every 15min 5.15am-10pm & every 30min 10pm-12.30am) Links the airport with the Opéra.

A taxi to the city centre takes 40 minutes. From 2016, fares have been standardised to a flat rate: €50 to the Right Bank and €55 to the Left Bank. The fare increases by 15% between 5pm and 10am and on Sundays.

AÉROPORT D'ORLY

The **RER B** (€12.05, 35min, every 4 to 12min) train line connects Orly with the St-Michel–Notre Dame, Châtelet–Les Halles and Gare du Nord stations in the city centre. In order to get from Orly to the RER station (Antony), you must first take the Orlyval automatic train. The service runs from 6am to 11pm (less frequently on weekends). You only need one ticket to take the two trains.

Les Cars Air France line 1 (€12.50, 1hr, every 20min, 6am to 11.40pm from Orly, 5am to 10.40pm from Invalides) buses run to/from the Gare Montparnasse (35 minutes) in southern Paris, Invalides in the 7e, and the Arc de Triomphe. Children aged two to 11 pay half price.

Orlybus (€7.50, 30min, every 15min, 6am to 12.30pm from Orly, 5.35am to midnight from Paris) runs to/from the metro station Denfert Rochereau in southern Paris, making several stops en route.

Tourist Passes

The Mobilis and Paris Visite passes are valid on the metro, RER, SNCF's suburban lines, buses, night buses, trams and Montmartre funicular railway. Buy them at the airports and larger metro and RER stations.

Mobilis Allows unlimited travel for one day and costs €7 (two zones) to €16.60 (five zones). Depending on how many times you plan to hop on/off the metro in a day, a *carnet* might work out cheaper.

Paris Visite Allows unlimited travel as well as discounted entry to certain museums and other discounts and bonuses. The 'Paris+Suburbs+Airports' pass includes transport to/from the airports and costs €23.50/35.70/50.05/61.25 for one/two/three/five days. The cheaper 'Paris Centre' pass, valid for zones 1 to 3, costs €11.15/18.15/24.80/35.70 for one/two/three/five days. Children aged four to 11 years pay half price.

Tramway T7 (€1.80, every 6min, 40min, 5.30am to 12.30am) links Orly with Villejuif-Louis Aragon metro station in southern Paris; buy tickets from the machine at the tram stop as no tickets are sold on board.

A taxi to the city centre takes roughly 30 minutes. Standardised flat-rate fares are €30 to the Left Bank and €35 to the Right Bank.

BICYCLE

Paris is increasingly bike-friendly. The **Vélib'** (☏01 30 79 79 30; www.velib.paris.fr; day/week subscription €1.70/8, bike hire up to 30/60/90/120min free/€1/2/4) bike share scheme puts 23,600 bikes at the disposal of Parisians and visitors for getting around the city. There are some 1800 stations throughout the city, accessible around the clock.

BOAT

Batobus (www.batobus.com; adult/child 1-day pass €17/10, 2-day pass €19/10; ⊙10am-9.30pm Apr-Aug, to 7pm Sep-Mar) runs glassed-in trimarans that dock every 20 to 25 minutes at nine small piers along the Seine: Beaugrenelle, Eiffel Tower, Musée d'Orsay, St-Germain des Prés, Notre Dame, Jardin des Plantes/Cité de la Mode et du Design, Hôtel de Ville, Musée du Louvre and Champs-Élysées.

Buy tickets online, at ferry stops or tourist offices.

PUBLIC TRANSPORT

Paris' underground network is run by RATP and consists of two separate but linked systems: the metro and the Réseau Express Régional (RER) suburban train line. The metro has 14 numbered lines; the RER has five main lines (but you'll probably only need to use A, B and C). When buying tickets consider how many zones your journey will cover; there are five concentric transport zones rippling out from Paris (Zone 5 being the furthest); if you travel from Charles de Gaulle airport to Paris, for instance, buy a zone 1–5 ticket.

The same RATP tickets are valid on the metro, the RER (for travel within the city limits), buses, trams and the Montmartre funicular. A ticket – white in colour and called Le Ticket t+ – costs €1.80 (half price for children aged four to nine years) if bought individually and €14.10 for adults for a *carnet* (book) of 10.

For information on the metro, RER and bus systems, visit www.ratp.fr.

Sleeping

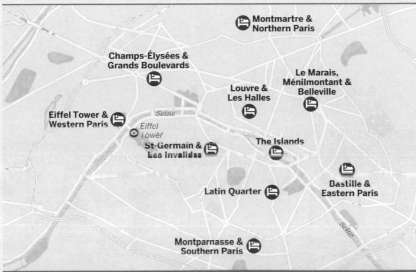

Neighbourhood	Atmosphere
Eiffel Tower & Western Paris	Close to Paris' iconic tower and museums. Upmarket area with quiet residential streets. Short on budget and midrange accommodation. Limited nightlife.
Champs-Élysées & Grands Boulevards	Luxury hotels, famous boutiques and department stores, gastronomic restaurants, great nightlife. Some areas pricey.
Louvre & Les Halles	Epicentral location, excellent transport links, major museums, shopping galore. Not many bargains. Noise can be an issue.
Montmartre & Northern Paris	Village atmosphere; views across Paris. Hilly streets, further out than some areas, some parts very touristy. Pigalle's red-light district, although well lit and safe, won't appeal to all travellers.
Le Marais, Ménilmontant & Belleville	Buzzing nightlife, hip shopping, fantastic eating options. Excellent museums. Lively gay and lesbian scene. Very central. Can be noisy in areas where bars and clubs are concentrated.
Bastille & Eastern Paris	Few tourists, allowing you to see the 'real' Paris up close. Markets, loads of nightlife options. Some areas slightly out of the way.
The Islands	Accommodation centred on the peaceful, romantic Île St-Louis. No metro station on the Île St-Louis. Limited self-catering shops.
Latin Quarter	Energetic student area, stacks of eating and drinking options, late-opening bookshops. Rooms hardest to find during conferences and seminars from March to June and in October.
St-Germain & Les Invalides	Stylish, central location, superb shopping, sophisticated dining, close to the Jardin du Luxembourg. Limited budget accommodation.
Montparnasse & Southern Paris	Good value, few tourists, excellent links to both major airports. Some areas out of the way and/or not well served by metro.

LOIRE VALLEY

Loire Valley at a Glance...

If it's French splendour, style and gastronomy you seek, the Loire Valley will exceed your expectations, no matter how great. Poised on the crucial frontier between northern and southern France, the region was once of immense strategic importance. Kings, queens, dukes and nobles established feudal castles here and, later on, sumptuous pleasure palaces – that's why this fertile river valley cocoons hundreds of France's most extravagant fortresses. With crenellated towers, soaring cupolas and glittering banquet halls, these châteaux, and the villages and vineyards that surround them, attest to a thousand years of rich architectural, artistic and agrarian creativity. The Loire Valley – an enormous Unesco World Heritage Site – is also known for its out-standing wines and lively, sophisticated cities.

Loire Valley in Two Days

Limber up with **Château de Cheverny** (p96) and its morning Soupe des Chiens before heading to **Chambord** (p84) for lunch and some serious château action. Head to Blois for an early-evening **old-city** (p94) stroll, dinner and an after-dark *son et lumière* show. Second day, visit **Chenonceau** (p88), lunch in Saché 40 minutes west by car, then continue to **Azay-le-Rideau** (p90) or **Villandry** (p92).

Loire Valley in Four Days

Change the pace with some languid meandering around elegant Amboise and its royal **château** (p97). Buy a picnic lunch at its morning **food market** (p97) or dine local at **La Fourchette** (p98). Devote the afternoon to *Mona Lisa's* maker at **Le Clos Lucé** (p97). Day four, rent some wheels and pedal your way along the river.

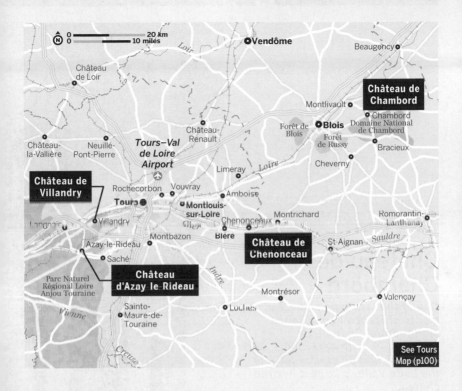

Arriving in the Loire Valley

Tours–Val de Loire Airport Major car-rental agencies; taxi to Tours town centre €15 to €30.

St-Pierre-des-Corps Main Loire Valley rail hub near Tours with TGV connections to/from Paris and other French cities; regional trains from Tours-Centre station include to/from Amboise, Blois, Chenonceaux and Azay-le-Rideau.

Sleeping

Be it hostel, 18th-century mansion or Renaissance château, the Loire Valley has a fabulous selection of places to stay. Rural *chambres d'hôte* (B&Bs) have particular appeal for those who are exploring the region by car or bicycle. For hotels and B&Bs in town, the small, handsome cities of Blois and Amboise make excellent bases – with reasonably priced accommodation. Larger Tours is another option.

Château de Chambord

One of the crowning achievements of French Renaissance architecture, Château de Chambord – with 440 rooms, 365 fireplaces and 84 staircases – is the Loire Valley's largest, visited château.

Great For...

❶ Need to Know

📱 info 02 54 50 40 00, tour & show reservations 02 54 50 50 40; www.chambord.org; adult/child €11/9, parking near/distant €6/4; ⊙9am-5pm or 6pm; ♿

★ **Top Tip**
DIY tour with audioguide (€5) or a Histopad tablet (€8) with treasure hunt for kids.

VALERY ROKHIN / SHUTTERSTOCK ©

Begun in 1519 by François I (r 1515–47) as a weekend hunting lodge, Château de Chambord quickly grew into one of the most ambitious – and expensive – architectural projects ever attempted by a French monarch.

Construction was repeatedly halted by financial problems, design setbacks and military commitments (not to mention the kidnapping of the king's two sons in Spain). Ironically, when Chambord was finally finished after 30-odd years of work, François found his elaborate palace too draughty, preferring instead the royal apartments in Amboise and Blois. In the end he stayed here for just 42 days during his entire reign!

Royal Quarters

Inside the château's main building, an interesting film (in five languages) relates the

history of the castle's construction. The 1st floor is where you'll find the most interesting rooms, including the king's and queen's chambers, complete with interconnecting passages to enable late-night high jinks. Rising through the centre of the structure, the world-famous double-helix staircase – reputedly designed by the king's chum Leonardo da Vinci – ascends to the great lantern tower and the rooftop, where you can marvel at a veritable skyline of cupolas, domes, turrets, chimneys and lightning rods, and gaze out across the vast grounds.

First Modern Building

The quintessential French Renaissance château is a mix of classical components and decorative motifs (columns, tunnel vaults, round arches, domes, etc) with the rich decoration of Flamboyant Gothic. It

Inside the royal quarters

ultimately showcased wealth, ancestry and refinement. Defensive towers (a historical seigneurial symbol) were incorporated into a new decorative architecture, typified by its three-dimensional use of pilasters and arcaded loggias, terraces, balconies, exterior staircases, turrets and gabled chimneys. Heraldic symbols were sculpted on soft stone façades, above doorways and fireplaces, and across coffered ceilings. Symmetrical floor plans broke new ground and heralded a different style of living: Château de Chambord contained 40 self-contained apartments, arranged on five floors around a central axis. This ensured easy circulation in a vast edifice that many rank as the first modern building in France.

Domaine National de Chambord

The 54-sq-km hunting reserve around the Château de Chambord – the largest walled park in Europe – is reserved for the exclusive use of very high-ranking French government officials (though it's difficult to imagine François Hollande astride a galloping stallion). About 10 sq km of the park, north and northwest of the château, is open to the public, with trails for walkers, cyclists and horse riders.

Outdoor Action

Hire bikes, pedal carts, electric golf carts, rowing boats and electric boats at a **rental kiosk** (☏02 54 50 40 00; www.chambord.org; hire bicycle 1/4hr €6/15, rowing boat 1hr €12, golf cart 45min €25; ☺10am-7pm late Mar-early Nov), near the *embarcadère* (dock) midway between the château and its Halle d'Accueil (entrance pavilion).

The park is a great place for wildlife-spotting, especially during the **rutting season** in September and October when you can watch deer 'at play'. Observation towers dot the perimeter of the park; set out at dawn or dusk to maximise your chances of spotting stags, boars and red deer. Or jump aboard a **Land Rover Safari tour** (☏02 54 50 50 40; www.chambord.org; adult/child €18/12; ☺often 11am-5pm year-round) conducted by a French-speaking guide.

> ☑ **Don't Miss**
>
> Summertime equestrian shows (adult/child €14.50/11) with well-dressed riders in medieval garb and birds of prey. Shows are outdoors, last 45 minutes and run April to September.

NETPHOTOGRAPHER / SHUTTERSTOCK ©

> ✕ **Take a Break**
>
> Dine in the château cafe or drive to downtown Blois for toasted bruschetta or a meal-sized salad on a pretty terrace at Les Planches (p95).

VIACHESLAV LOPATIN / SHUTTERSTOCK ©

Château de Chenonceau

Spanning the languid Cher River atop a supremely graceful arched bridge, Chenonceau is one of France's most elegant châteaux. Its formal gardens, glorious setting and stylised architecture are the embodiment of French romance.

Great For...

☑ **Don't Miss**

A romantic **Promenade Nocturne** on summer nights when the grounds are beautifully illuminated.

Girl Power

This extraordinary complex is largely the work of several remarkable women, hence its nickname, Château des Dames. Construction started in 1515 for Thomas Bohier, a court minister of King Charles VIII, although much of the work and design was overseen by his wife, Katherine Briçonnet.

The distinctive arches and the eastern formal garden were added by Diane de Poitiers, mistress of King Henri II. Following Henri's death Catherine de Médicis, the king's scheming widow, forced Diane (her second cousin) to exchange Chenonceau for the rather less grand Château de Chaumont. Catherine completed the château's construction and added the yew-tree maze and the western rose garden. Louise of Lorraine's most singular contribution was her black-walled mourning room on the

Diane de Poitiers' bedroom

Château de Chenonceau

ℹ Need to Know

☏ 02 47 23 90 07; www.chenonceau.com; adult/child €13/10, incl audioguide €17.50/14; ⏰ 9am-7pm or later Apr-Sep, to 5pm or 6pm Oct-Mar

✕ Take a Break

March to mid-November, lunch in gastronomic French restaurant L'Orangerie, in the castle grounds.

★ Top Tip

Grab an audioguide, plus the excellent kid's iPod version for seven to 12 years.

top floor, to which she retreated when her husband, Henri III, was assassinated in 1589. Macabre illustrations of bones, skulls and teardrops adorn the dark walls.

Chenonceau had an 18th-century heyday under the aristocratic Madame Dupin, who made the château a centre of fashionable society. During the Revolution, at the age of 83, she was able to save the château from destruction at the hands of angry mobs thanks to quick thinking and some strategic concessions.

Grande Galerie

The château's pièce de résistance is the 60m-long, chequerboard-floored Grande Galerie over the Cher. Used as a military hospital during WWI, from 1940 to 1942 it served as an escape route for résistants, Jews and other refugees fleeing from the German-occupied zone (north of the Cher) to the Vichy-controlled zone (south of the river) in WWII. The upper level of the gallery, the Galerie Médicis, has a well-presented exhibition on the château's colourful history and the women who moulded it.

Artworks

Rare furnishings and a fabulous art collection that includes works by Tintoretto, Correggio, Rubens, Murillo, Van Dyck and Ribera decorate its otherworldly interior. Don't miss the portrait of Les Trois Graces (The Three Graces) by Van Loo, which hangs next to the Renaissance chimney in François I's bedroom.

Getting There & Away

The château is 33km east of Tours, 13km southeast of Amboise and 40km southwest of Blois. From the town of Chenonceaux (spelt with an 'x'), just outside the château grounds, trains go to Tours (€7, 25 minutes, nine to 12 daily).

VLADIMIR SAZONOV / SHUTTERSTOCK ©

Château d'Azay-le-Rideau

Famed for its elegant turrets, delicate stonework and steep slate roofs, moat-ringed Azay-le-Rideau is one of the Loire's most elegant and harmonious castles. It sits on an island on the Indre River.

Great For...

☑ **Don't Miss**

The reflection of the château in the water on sunny days.

Water Mirror

Visit on a sunny day when the reflection of Azay's pearly white façade – adorned with decorative fortifications and turrets indicating the rank of the owners – shimmers like a mirage in the surrounding lily-pricked waters. This *mirroir d'eau* was only created in the 1950s when one branch of the river was extended in order for the water to lick the château walls.

The château's other famous feature is the open, Italian-style loggia staircase overlooking the central courtyard and decorated with the salamanders and ermines of François I and Queen Claude.

Azay the Burnt

The fate of the old Gallo-Roman settlement of Azay has been inextricably linked to that of its château, ever since the first defensive

Salon de Biencourt

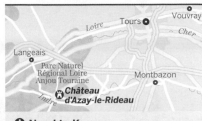

❶ Need to Know

☑ 02 47 45 42 04; www.azay-le-rideau.fr; adult/child €8.50/free, audioguide €4.50; ⊙ 9.30am-6pm Apr-Sep, to 7pm Jul & Aug, 10am-5.15pm Oct-Mar

✕ Take a Break

Enjoy gastronomic French on an idyllic terrace at **Auberge du XIIe Siècle**, 7km east in Saché.

★ Top Tip

Watch for *son et lumière* (sound and light) shows projected on the castle wall in summer.

---

edifice was razed here in the Middle Ages. The bloodiest incident in its history occurred in 1418 when the crown prince (later Charles VII) was insulted by a Burgundian guard during a visit to Azay's fortified castle. Enraged, the future king had the town burned to the ground and executed 350 soldiers and officers. For a period the town became known as Azay-le-Brûlé (Azay the Burnt).

Pleasure Palace

The present château (1518–23) – built very much as a pleasure palace rather than defensive fortress as was typical of the early Renaissance – was begun by Giles Berthelot, one of François I's less-than-selfless financiers. When the prospect of being audited and hanged drew near, Berthelot fled abroad. The finishing touch-

es were not added until the 19th century. A colony of rare greater mouse-eared bats lives in the château attic.

The English-style **park** was restored in 2015 and replanted with plants used in the 1820s: American tulip trees, sequoias, atlas cedars and bald cypress trees.

Interior

The interior decor is mostly 19th century, created by the Marquis Charles de Biencourt (who bought the château after the Revolution) and his heirs. The **Salon de Biencourt** was given historically coherent furnishings – plucked from the extensive collection of the French government – and comprehensively restored to its 19th-century glory in 2016; other interiors will follow suit in 2017.

Getting There & Away

Azay-le-Rideau is 26km southwest of Tours. The train station, 2.5km west of the château, is linked to Tours (€5.90, 30/60 minutes by train/bus, five to 11 daily).

LOSKUTNIKOV / SHUTTERSTOCK ©

Château de Villandry

Villandry's glorious landscaped gardens are among France's finest, with over six hectares of cascading flowers, ornamental vines, razor-sharp box hedges and tinkling fountains. Think 52km of landscaped plant rows and 1016 perfectly pruned linden trees.

Great For...

☑ Don't Miss

Gardening workshops during September's two-day garden festival, Journées du Potager.

Gardens

The original gardens and château were built by Jean le Breton, who served François I as finance minister and ambassador to Italy (and supervised the construction of Chambord). During his time as ambassador, le Breton became enamoured with the art of Italian Renaissance gardening, later creating his own ornamental masterpiece at newly constructed Villandry. His ornamental gardens were returned to their Renaissance glory – as you see today – from 1906 (when Spanish-born Nobel Prize winner Joachim Carvallo bought the château).

Courtly romance played a key role in the Renaissance ornamental garden. Every twist and turn of a box hedge, flower bed or yew tree was loaded with romantic symbolism. Lyres, lutes and harps were hidden in the intricate patterns carved from green foliage.

Ceiling in the Oriental Drawing Room

EVGENY SHMULEV / SHUTTERSTOCK ©

ℹ️ Need to Know

📞02 47 50 02 09; www.chateauvillandry.com; 3 rue Principale; chateau & gardens adult/child €10.50/6.50, gardens only €6.50/4.50, audioguides €4; ⏰9am btwn 5pm & 7pm year-round, château interior closed mid-Nov–mid-Dec & early Jan–early Feb

✖️ Take a Break

Local seasonal produce and Val de Loire wines on the estate at cafe La Doulce Terrasse.

★ Top Tip

Visit between April and October when the gardens are blooming; midsummer is most spectacular.

and carrots are laid out to create nine geometrical, colour-coordinated squares.

Wandering the pebbled walkways, admire the classical **Jardin d'Eau** (Water Garden) designed around a swan-filled lake shaped like a Louis XV mirror; get lost in the hornbeam **Labyrinthe de Charmille** (a maze); and rediscover love in the **Jardin d'Ornement**. The latter, designed to create the impression of being an extension of the château interior, comprises intricate, geometrically pruned hedges and flower beds loaded with romantic symbolism so abstract that you can happily tour the entire garden without comprehending its true meaning: tender, tragic, fickle and passionate love are all to be found amid the manicured hedges, yew trees and rose bushes.

The **Jardin du Soleil** (Sun Garden) is a looser array of gorgeous multicoloured and multiscented perennials. Then there's the 16th-century-style **Jardin des Simples** (Kitchen Garden), where cabbages, leeks

Interior

The château itself, completed in 1536, is something of a letdown after the gardens. It was the last of the Loire Valley châteaux to be built during the Renaissance. Interior highlights include the **Oriental Drawing Room**, with a gilded Moorish ceiling taken from a 15th-century palace in Toledo, and a gallery of Spanish and Flemish art. Best of all are the bird's-eye views across the gardens and the nearby Loire and Cher Rivers from the top of the **donjon** (the only remnant of the original medieval château) and the **belvédère** (panoramic viewpoint).

Getting There & Away

The château is 11km northeast of Azay-le-Rideau. Trains link Savonnières, 4km northeast of Villandry, with Tours (€3.50, 13 minutes, two or three daily).

Blois

The city of Blois makes an excellent base for visits to the châteaux, villages and towns of the central Loire Valley.

◎ SIGHTS

Old City   Historic Site

Blois' medieval and Renaissance old town is well worth a stroll, especially around 17th-century **Cathédrale St-Louis** (place St-Louis; ⊘9am or 10am-6pm or 7pm), whose lovely multistorey bell tower is dramatically floodlit after dark. Most of the stained glass inside was installed by Dutch artist Jan Dibberts in 2000.

Across the square, the façade of **Maison des Acrobates** (3bis place St-Louis) – one of Blois' few surviving 15th-century houses – is decorated with wooden sculptures of figures from medieval farces. Another 15th-century townhouse, 50m from the cathedral's portal, is the **Hôtel de Villebrême** (13 rue Pierre de Blois).

Château Royal de Blois   Chateau

(☑02 54 90 33 33; www.chateaudeblois.fr; place du Château; adult/child €10/5, audioguide €4/3; ⊘9am-6pm or 7pm Apr-Oct, 9am-noon & 1.30-5.30pm Nov-Mar) Seven French kings lived in Blois' royal château, whose four grand wings were built during four distinct periods in French architecture: Gothic (13th century), Flamboyant Gothic (1498–1501), early Renaissance (1515–20) and classical (1630s). You can easily spend a half day immersing yourself in the château's dramatic and bloody history and its extraordinary architecture. In July and August there are free tours in English.

The richly furnished complex's most famous Gothic feature is the richly painted **Hall of the States-General**, from the 13th century. In the **Renaissance wing**, the most extraordinary feature is the spiral **loggia staircase**, decorated with fierce salamanders and curly Fs, heraldic symbols of François I. Other château highlights include the **Queen's Chamber**, in which Catherine de Médicis (Henri II's Machiavellian wife) died in 1589. According to Alexandre

Cathédrale St-Louis, Blois

VIACHESLAV LOPATIN / SHUTTERSTOCK ©

Dumas, the queen stashed her poisons in the adjacent **studiolo** in secret cupboards behind the elaborate wall panels (from the 1520s).

The 2nd-floor **King's Bedchamber** was the setting for one of the bloodiest episodes in the château's history. In 1588 Henri III had his arch-rival, Duke Henri I de Guise, murdered by royal bodyguards (the king is said to have hidden behind a tapestry while the dastardly deed was done). He had the duke's brother, the Cardinal de Guise, killed the next day. The bloodletting of the Wars of Religion continued when Henri III himself was murdered just eight months later by a vengeful monk. Dramatic and very graphic oil paintings illustrate these gruesome events next door in the **Council Room**.

The **Musée des Beaux-Arts** (Fine Arts Museum), in the Louis XII wing (look for his heraldic emblem, the porcupine), displays 300 16th- to 19th-century paintings, sculptures and tapestries.

✕ EATING

Les Planches   Italian €
(☎02 54 55 08 00; 5 rue Grenier à Sel; mains €10.50-15; ☺noon-2pm & 7-10pm Mon-Sat; ✎) Hidden away on a tiny square near lots of other dining options, Les Planches is a Blois favourite for its toasted bruschettas (open-faced Italian sandwiches) and meal-sized salads. Romantic, with a purple light on each table.

Les Banquettes
Rouges   Modern French €€
(☎02 54 78 74 92; www.lesbanquettesrouges. com; 16 rue des Trois Marchands; lunch/dinner menus from €17.50/27.50; ☺noon-1.30pm & 7-9.30pm Tue-Sat) In the St-Nicolas quarter below the château, this restaurant – easy to spot thanks to its bright-red façade – serves French *semi-gastronomique* cuisine. Favourites often available here include pan-fried veal liver with morello cherry and bitter-orange gravy, and *fondant au chocolat*.

Pedal
Power

Funded by 65 Loire municipalities, **Châteaux à Vélo** (www.chateauxavelo. co.uk) maintains 400km of marked bike routes to and around Blois, Chambord and Cheverny among others. Get route maps, a useful mobile app and the latest weather reports from the website, or pick up brochures at local tourist offices.

Detours de Loire (☎02 54 56 07 73; www.detoursdeloire.com; 39 av Dr Jean Laigret; per half-day/day/week €10/15/60), part of a valley-wide bike-rental network, rents bikes a block from Blois train station and also in Tours. In Amboise, head to **Détours de Loire** (☎02 47 30 00 55; www.detoursdeloire.com; quai du Général de Gaulle; half-day/day/week €10/15/60; ☺Jun-Sep), along the river, or **Cycles Richard** (☎02 47 57 01 79; 2 rue de Nazelles), directly across the river from the town centre.

Cycling to Château de Chambord (p84)

L'Orangerie
du Château   Gastronomic €€€
(☎02 54 78 05 36; www.orangerie-du-cha-teau.fr; 1 av Dr Jean Laigret; menus €38-84; ☺noon-1.45pm & 7-9.15pm Tue-Sat; P) This Michelin-starred restaurant serves *cuisine gastronomique inventive* inspired by both French tradition and culinary ideas from faraway lands. The wine list comes on a tablet computer. For dessert try the speciality, soufflé.

Château de Cheverny

Perhaps the Loire's most elegantly proportioned château, **Château de Cheverny** (02 54 79 96 29; www.chateau-cheverny.fr; av du Château; château & gardens adult/child €10.50/7.50; ☉9.15am-7pm Apr-Sep, 10am-5.30pm Oct-Mar), **14km** southeast of Blois and 18km southwest of Chambord, represents the zenith of French classical architecture: the perfect blend of symmetry, geometry and aesthetic order. Inside are some of the most sumptuous and elegantly furnished rooms anywhere in the Loire Valley, virtually unchanged for generations because the Hurault family has lived here, almost continuously, ever since the château's construction in the early 1600s by Jacques Hurault, an intendant to Louis XII.

In the grounds, the 18th-century **Orangerie** is now a tearoom (open April to November) and the **kennels** house about 100 hunting dogs. A cross between Poitevins and English foxhounds, the spectacular **Soupe des Chiens**, aka feeding time, is a sight to behold (daily at 11.30am April to September and on Monday, Wednesday, Thursday and Friday October to March).

Fans of Tintin might find Château de Cheverny's façade oddly familiar: Hérgé used it as a model (minus the two end towers) for Moulinsart (Marlinspike) Hall, the ancestral home of Tintin's irascible sidekick, Captain Haddock. Diehard devotees might enjoy Les Secrets de Moulinsart, which explores the world of Tintin with recreated scenes, thunder and other special effects.

ENTERTAINMENT

Son et Lumière   Light Show
(Sound & Light Show; ☑02 54 90 33 33; adult/child €8.50/5; ☉10pm late Mar-May & Sep, 10.30pm Jun-Aug) In spring and summer, a nightly *son et lumière* show brings Blois'

château's history and architecture to life with dramatic lighting and narration. Tickets are sold at the château.

ⓘ INFORMATION

Tourist Office (02 54 90 41 41; www.blois-chambord.co.uk; 23 place du Château; ☉9am-7pm Easter-Sep, 10am-5pm Oct-Easter) Has maps of town and sells châteaux combo and concert tickets. Download its smartphone app via the website. Situated across the square from the château.

ⓘ GETTING THERE & AWAY

BUS

The tourist office has a brochure detailing public-transport options to nearby châteaux.

TRAIN

The **Blois-Chambord train station** (av Dr Jean Laigret) is 600m west (up the hill) from Blois' château.

Amboise €7.20, 15 minutes, 16 to 25 daily.

Paris Gare d'Austerlitz €29.40, 1½ hours, five direct daily.

Tours €11.20, 40 minutes, 14 to 22 daily.

ⓘ GETTING AROUND

In and around Blois city centre, all-day parking costs €5 in green parking zones. For free parking, head to quai Maréchal de Lattre de Tassigny (promenade Pierre Mendès-France), on the river 400m northeast of the D956 bridge; or promenade Edmond Mounin, on the river 1km southwest of the bridge.

Amboise

Elegant Amboise, childhood home of Charles VIII and final resting place of the incomparable Leonardo da Vinci, is gorgeously situated on the southern bank of the Loire, guarded by a towering château. With some seriously posh hotels, fine dining and one of France's most colourful weekly markets (on Sunday morning),

Interior of the Château Royal d'Amboise

Amboise is a convivial base for exploring the Loire countryside and nearby châteaux by car or bicycle.

◎ SIGHTS

Château Royal d'Amboise　Chateau

(☑02 47 57 00 98; www.chateau-amboise.com; place Michel Debré; adult/child €11.20/7.50, incl audioguide €15.20/10.50; ☺9am-6pm or 7.30pm Mar–mid-Nov, 9am-12.30pm & 2-5.15pm mid-Nov–Feb) Perched on a rocky escarpment above town, Amboise's castle was a favoured retreat for all of France's Valois and Bourbon kings. Only a few of the château's original structures survive, but you can still visit the furnished Logis (Lodge) – Gothic except for the top half of one wing, which is Renaissance – and the Flamboyant Gothic Chapelle St-Hubert (1493), where Leonardo da Vinci's presumed remains have been buried since 1863. The ramparts afford thrilling views of the town and river.

Le Clos Lucé　Historic Building

(☑02 47 57 00 73; www.vinci-closluce.com; 2 rue du Clos Lucé; adult/child €15/10.50; ☺9am-7pm or 8pm Feb-Oct, 9am or 10am-5pm or 6pm Nov-Jan; ⚑) It was on the invitation of François I that Leonardo da Vinci (1452–1519), aged 64, took up residence at this grand manor house (built 1471). An admirer of the Italian Renaissance, the French monarch named Da Vinci 'first painter, engineer and king's architect', and the Italian spent his time here sketching, tinkering and dreaming up ingenious contraptions. Fascinating models of his many inventions are on display inside the home and around its lovely 7-hectare gardens.

◎ EATING

Market　Food Market €

(quai du Général de Gaulle; ☺8am-1pm Sun) Voted France's *marché préféré* (favourite market) in 2015, this riverfront extravaganza, 400m southwest of the château, draws 200 to 300 stalls selling both edibles and durables. Worth timing your visit around.

Bigot　Patisserie €

(☑02 47 57 04 46; www.maisonbigot-amboise. com; cnr rue Nationale & place du Château;

Bigot (p97), Amboise

breakfast €13, lunch menu €16; ⏰8.30am or 9am-7pm or 7.30pm Tue-Sun, to 8pm & open Mon Easter-Oct; 🛜🅿️) Founded by Madame Bigot's grandfather in 1913, this *salon de thé*, *pâtisserie* and *chocolaterie* is known for its *tarte Tatin* (€9), chocolates, homemade ice cream and light meals (omelettes, quiches, meal-size salads). Perfect for a sweet or savoury break.

La Fourchette   French €€

(📱06 11 78 16 98; 9 rue Malebranche; lunch/dinner menus €17/30; ⏰noon-1.30pm Tue-Sat, 7-8.30pm Fri & Sat, plus Tue & Wed evenings summer) Hidden away in a back alley off rue Nationale, this is Amboise's favourite address for family-style French cooking – chef Christine will make you feel as though you've been invited to her house for lunch. The menu has just two starters, two mains and two desserts. It's small, so reserve ahead.

DRINKING & NIGHTLIFE

Le Shaker   Bar

(📱02 47 23 24 26; 3 quai François Tissard, Île d'Or; ⏰6pm-2am Sun, Tue-Thu, to 4am Fri &

Sat) The big draw at this friendly bar on Amboise's mid-Loire island: supremely romantic views of the château. Serves beer (€3.50) and light meals, but the speciality is cocktails.

ℹ️ INFORMATION

Tourist Office (📱02 47 57 09 28; www.amboise-valdeloire.co.uk; cnr quai du Général de Gaulle & allée du Sergent Turpin; internet access per 30min €4; ⏰9am or 10am-6pm or 7pm Mon-Sat, 10am-12.30pm Sun Apr-Oct, 10am-12.30pm & 2-5pm Mon-Sat Nov-Mar; 🛜) Has interesting walking-tour brochures and sells cycling maps and discount combo tickets for nine area châteaux. Its free app, called 'Val d'Amboise Tour', can be downloaded via the website. Situated across the street from the riverfront.

ℹ️ GETTING THERE & AWAY

BUS

Run by **Touraine Fil Vert** (p102), bus line C links Amboise's Théâtre with Tours' Halte Routière (bus station; €2.40, 50 minutes, eight daily Monday to

Saturday) and Chenonceau (€2.40, 18 minutes, one or two daily Monday to Saturday).

TRAIN

Amboise's **train station** (bd Gambetta) is 1.5km north of the château, on the opposite side of the Loire.

Blois €7.20, 15 minutes, 16 to 25 daily.

Paris' Gare d'Austerlitz €33.20, 1¾ hours, four direct daily.

Tours €5.70, 17 minutes, 13 to 23 daily.

Tours

Bustling Tours is a smart and vivacious city, with an impressive medieval quarter, fine museums, well-tended parks and a university of some 25,000 students. Combining the sophisticated style of Paris with the conservative sturdiness of central France, Tours makes an ideal staging post for exploring Touraine or 'the Garden of France' – aka the château-laced region of which it's capital.

If you're touring without your own wheels (two or four), Tours is the best place in the Loire Valley for organised château tours and public-transport options.

⊙ SIGHTS

Tours' focal point is grand, semicircular **place Jean Jaurès**, adorned with fountains, formal gardens and imposing public buildings (the town hall and the courthouse). **Vieux Tours** (the old city) occupies the narrow streets around place Plumereau (locally known as place Plum), about 400m west of boutique- and shop-lined **rue Nationale**.

Musée du
Compagnonnage   Museum
(📞02 47 21 62 20; www.museecompagnonnage. fr; 8 rue Nationale & 1 square Prosper Merimée; adult/child €5.50/3.80; ☺9am-12.30pm & 2-6pm, closed Tue mid-Sep–mid-Jun) A highlight of a visit to Tours, this museum spotlights France's renowned *compagnonnages,* guild organisations of skilled craftspeople who

Wine in the Loire Valley

Splendid scenery and densely packed vineyards make the Loire Valley an outstanding wine-touring destination, with a range of excellent reds, rosés, whites, sweet wines and *crémants* (sparkling wines). Equipped with *Sur la Route des Vins de Loire* (On the Loire Wine Route), a free map from the winegrowers association (www.vinsvaldeloire.fr, in French; www.loirevalleywine.com, in English), or the *Loire Valley Vineyards* booklet, available at area tourist offices and *maisons des vins* (wine visitor centres), you can put together a web of wonderful wine-tasting itineraries, drawing from over 320 wine cellars.

The predominant red is cabernet franc, though you'll also find cabernet sauvignon, pinot noir and others. Appellations (AOCs) include Anjou, Saumur-Champigny, Bourgueil and Chinon.

For whites, Vouvray's chenin blancs are excellent, and Sancerre and the appellation across the Loire River, Pouilly-Fumé, produce great sauvignon blancs. Cour-Cheverny is made from the lesser-known Romorantin grape. Savennières, near Angers, has both a dry and a sweet chenin blanc.

The bubbly appellation Crémant de Loire spans many communities, but you can easily find it around Montrichard (eg Château Monmousseau); other bubblies include Saumur Brut and Vouvray.

Decorated wine press, Vouvray

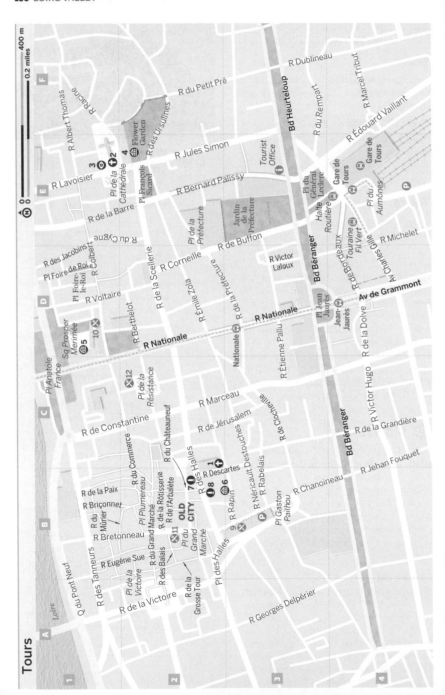

Tours

Tours

have been responsible for everything from medieval cathedrals to the Statue of Liberty. Dozens of professions – from carpentry to saddle-making to locksmithery – are celebrated here with items handcrafted from wood, wrought iron, bronze, stone, brick, clay and leather; standouts include exquisite wooden architectural models. During nearby construction the entrance will be around the back, via the path opposite 23 rue Colbert.

Musée des Beaux-Arts Art Museum
(⎙02 47 05 68 82; www.mba.tours.fr; 18 place François Sicard; adult/child €6/3; ⊙9am-12.45pm & 2-6pm Wed-Mon) This superb fine-arts museum, in a gorgeous 18th-century archbishop's palace, features paintings, sculpture, furniture and *objets d'art* from the 14th to 20th centuries. Highlights include paintings by Delacroix, Degas and Monet, a rare Rembrandt miniature and a Rubens *Madonna and Child*. Next to the flowery gardens is a massive cedar of Lebanon planted in 1804.

Cathédrale St-Gatien Church
(place de la Cathédrale; ⊙9am-7pm) With its flying buttresses, gargoyles and twin Renaissance-style towers (70m) – and, inside, Gothic vaulting, dazzling stained glass and a huge Baroque organ – this cathedral cuts a striking figure. Near the entrance you can pick up an English brochure on its architecture and history; English signs in the choir explain the intricate stained glass. On the north side is **Cloître de la Psalette** (place de la Cathédrale; adult/child €3/free; ⊙9.30am-12.30pm & 2-5pm or 6pm, closed Sun morning, also closed Mon & Tue Sep-Mar), built from 1442 to 1524.

Basilique St-Martin Church
(www.basiliquesaintmartin.fr; rue Descartes; ⊙7.30am-7pm, to 9pm Jul & Aug) In the Middle Ages Tours was an important pilgrimage city thanks to the relics of soldier-turned-evangelist St Martin (c 317–97). In the 5th century a basilica was constructed above his tomb; in the 13th century it was replaced by an enormous Romanesque church, of which only **Tour Charlemagne** and **Tour de l'Horloge** (Clock Tower) remain. Modern-day Basilique St-Martin, a domed, neo-Byzantine structure, was built from 1886 to 1925. The 1700th anniversary of St Martin's birth will be celebrated in 2017.

Down the block, the small **Musée St-Martin** (⎙02 47 64 48 87; www.tours.fr; 3 rue Rapin; adult/child €2/1; ⊙10am-1pm & 2-5.30pm Wed-Sun mid-Mar–mid-Nov) displays artefacts relating to the lost churches and the life of the saint.

TOURS

Lots of château tours begin in Tours – for details, contact the tourist office (p102), which runs **guided city walks** (in French; adult/child €6/free, at night €9) and can supply you with a brochure for a self-guided walking tour.

✗ EATING

Tours has two main dining zones, **Vieux Tours** and **rue Colbert**. Some of Tours' best restaurants are at north–south-oriented **place du Grand Marché** (place du Monstre), but quality varies right around **place Plumereau** and adjacent, east–west-oriented rue du Grand Marché.

🍽 Picnic Perfect

Halles de Tours (www.halles-de-tours.com; place Gaston Pailhou; ⏰7am-7.30pm Mon-Sat, 8am-1pm Sun; 🅿) market stalls – 38 of them – sell everything you could want for a picnic, including cheese, wine and prepared dishes.

Cheese stall
STUNNEDMULLET / SHUTTERSTOCK ©

About 1km east, rue Colbert has a selection of moderately priced restaurants serving international cuisines (eg Lebanese, Indian, Japanese).

Tartines & Co   Sandwiches €
(📞02 47 20 50 60; 6 rue des Fusillés; sandwiches €7.90-14.40, lunch menus €10.50-15.50; ⏰noon-3.30pm & 7.15-10pm Mon-Sat; 🅿) This snazzy little cafe serves *tartines* (toasted or cold open-face sandwiches), made with scrumptious *pain* Poilâne (artisanal bread), amid jazz and friendly chatter. Toppings include smoked duck breast, tomato and red-pepper compote, beef carpaccio and foie gras with artichokes. Also has meal-size salads.

Le Zinc   French €€
(📞02 47 20 29 00; lezinc37@gmail.com; 27 place du Grand Marché; menus €20.90-25.90; ⏰noon-2pm Tue & Thu-Sat, 7.30-10pm Mon-Thu, to 11pm Fri & Sat; 📶🅿) This intimate restaurant, with just a dozen tables, garners rave reviews for its outstanding traditional French cuisine, prepared *à l'ancienne* (in the old style, like grandmother would have). Each dish – saltwater fish, duck breast, steak, rice pudding with caramel sauce – is prepared

with exemplary finesse using market-fresh ingredients from the nearby Halles. Excellent value.

L'Arôme   Modern French €€
(📞02 47 05 99 81; www.restaurant-l-arome-tours. com; 26 rue Colbert; lunch menus €12.60-14.95, 2/3/4-course dinner menus €24/29/33; ⏰noon-1.30pm & 7.30-9.30pm Tue-Sat) A vivacious modern ambience, market-fresh products and creative dishes, some of them not only original but surprising, make this place ever popular. Has a great wine selection too.

ℹ INFORMATION

Tourist Office (📞02 47 70 37 37; www. tours-tourisme.fr; 78-82 rue Bernard Palissy; ⏰8.30am-7pm Mon-Sat, 10am-12.30pm & 2.30-5pm Sun Apr-Sep, 9am-12.30pm & 1.30-6pm Mon-Sat, 10am-1pm Sun Oct-Mar) Abundant info in English on cultural events and the Loire Valley; sells slightly reduced château tickets.

ℹ GETTING THERE & AROUND

AIR

Tours–Val de Loire Airport (TUF; 📞02 47 49 37 00; www.tours.aeroport.fr), 6km northeast of the centre, is linked to London's Stansted and Dublin (Ireland) by Ryanair.

BICYCLE

For bicycle hire, try **Détours de Loire** (📞02 47 61 22 23; www.detoursdeloire.com; classic bike per day/week €15/60, additional day €5, tandem €45/140, electric €30/150).

BUS

Touraine Fil Vert (📞02 47 31 14 00; www. tourainefilvert.com) operates buses to destinations around the Indre-et-Loire *département* from Tours' **Halte Routière** (bus station; place du Général Leclerc; ⏰office 7am-7pm Mon-Fri, to 6.30pm Sat). Destinations include Amboise (40 minutes, seven daily Monday to Saturday) and Chenonceau (1¼ hours, one or two daily Monday to Saturday), both served by line C. All fares are €2.40.

Shops on place Plumereau, Tours

CAR

Tours' perplexing one-way streets make driving a headache. To park your car for more than two hours, use an underground garage; the one below the **Halles de Tours** (place Gaston Pailhou; per 1/24hr €1.80/12) also has some free spots at street level.

Avis (☏02 47 20 53 27; www.avis.com) and other rental companies have offices at Tours' train station, the St-Pierre-des-Corps TGV station and the airport (by reservation).

TRAIN

Tours is the Loire Valley's main rail hub. Regular trains and a few TGVs use the city-centre train station, **Tours-Centre** (place du Général Leclerc), while most TGV trains stop only at **St-Pierre-des-Corps**, 3km east and linked to Tours-Centre by frequent shuttle trains. Some destinations, including Paris, Angers and Orléans, are served by both stations.

Bicycles can be taken aboard almost all trains, so you can train it out and pedal back or vice versa.

Direct services from Tours-Centre:

Amboise €5.70, 17 minutes, 13 to 23 daily.

Azay-le-Rideau €5.90, 60 minutes by train, five to 11 daily.

Blois €11.20, 40 minutes, 12 to 23 daily.

Chenonceaux €7, 25 minutes, nine to 12 daily.

Paris' Gare d'Austerlitz €36.20, 2¼ hours, four non-TGV daily.

Paris' Gare Montparnasse €53 to €69, 1¼ hours, six or seven TGVs daily.

NORMANDY

Normandy at a Glance

From the Norman invasion of England in 1066 to the D-Day landings of 1944, Normandy has long played an out-sized role in European history. This rich and often brutal past is brought vividly to life by the spectacular island monastery of Mont St-Michel; the Bayeux Tapestry, world-famous for its cartoon scenes of 11th-century life; and the cemeteries and memorials along the D-Day beaches. Lower-profile charms include a variety of dramatic coastal landscapes, lots of pebbly beaches, quiet pastoral villages and architectural gems, including Rouen's medieval old city. Camembert, apples, cider, cream-rich cuisine and the very freshest fish and seafood provide further reasons to visit this accessible and beautiful region of France.

Normandy in Two Days

Depending where you are staying, head to the morning market to buy a picnic – a round of Camembert and bottle of cider included – then to **Mont St-Michel** (p108) for the day. Day two, begin with Caen's **Le Mémorial** (p119) or Bayeux' **Musée Mémorial** (p121), then on to the D-Day beaches (p114).

Normandy in Four Days

With four days at hand, you have time to linger longer in Caen or Bayeux on day two, and then hit the beaches on day three instead. Fourth day, trip it to Étretat, followed by lunch in Honfleur and an afternoon in Rouen with its wonderful **cathedral** (p124).

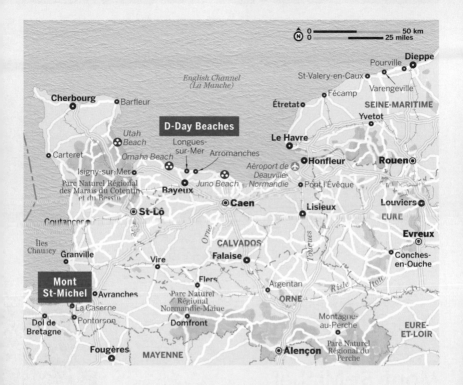

Arriving in Normandy

Boat Car ferries link the port town Le Havre (also Dieppe, Cherbourg and Ouistreham) with several English and Irish ports.

Rouen train station Just 70 minutes from Paris' Gare St-Lazare (€24.10, 1¼ hours, up to 25 daily). Most major towns also accessible by rail.

Aéroport de Deauville-Normandie 7km east of Trouville. Ryanair links with London Stansted Airport.

Sleeping

Normandy has a wide range of accommodation options, from inexpensive budget guesthouses with shared facilities to plush hotels with fine sea views. You'll find the widest variety in Rouen, but smaller flowery Bayeux is closer to both the D-Day beaches and Mont St-Michel.

Mont St-Michel

It's one of France's most iconic images: the slender spires, stout ramparts and rocky slopes of Mont St-Michel rising dramatically from the sea – or towering over sands laid bare by the receding tide. Despite huge numbers of tourists, both the abbey and the labyrinth of narrow alleys below still manage to transport visitors back to the Middle Ages.

Great For...

ⓘ Need to Know

02 33 89 80 00; www.monuments-nationaux.fr; adult/child incl guided tour €9/free; 9am-7pm, last entry 1hr before closing

★ **Top Tip**
Walk the eastern section of the Mont's ramparts for spectacular views of the bay.

The Mont's star attraction is the stunning architectural ensemble high up on top: the abbey. Most areas can be visited without a guide, but it's well worth taking the one-hour tour included in the ticket price.

History

Bishop Aubert of Avranches is said to have built a devotional chapel on the summit of the island in 708, following his vision of the Archangel Michael, whose gilded figure, perched on the vanquished dragon, crowns the tip of the abbey's spire. In 966 Richard I, Duke of Normandy, gave Mont St-Michel to the Benedictines, who turned it into a centre of learning and, in the 11th century, into something of an ecclesiastical fortress, with a military garrison at the disposal of both abbot and king.

In the 15th century, during the Hundred Years War, the English blockaded and besieged Mont St-Michel three times. The fortified abbey withstood these assaults and was the only place in western and northern France not to fall into English hands. After the Revolution, Mont St-Michel was turned into a prison. In 1966 the abbey was symbolically returned to the Benedictines as part of the celebrations marking its millennium. Mont St-Michel and the bay became a Unesco World Heritage Site in 1979.

Église Abbatiale

Built on the rocky tip of the mountain cone, the transept rests on solid rock, while the nave, choir and transept arms are supported by the rooms below. This church is famous for its mix of architectural styles: the nave and south transept (11th and 12th

Room in La Merveille

centuries) are solid Norman Romanesque, while the choir (late 15th century) is Flamboyant Gothic.

La Merveille

The buildings on the northern side of the Mont are known as 'The Marvel'. The famous **cloître** (cloister) is surrounded by a double row of delicately carved arches resting on granite pillars. The early-13th-century, barrel-roofed **réfectoire** (dining hall) is illuminated by a wall of recessed windows – remarkable given that the sheer drop precluded the use of flying buttresses. The Gothic **Salle des Hôtes** (Guest Hall), dating from 1213, has two enormous fireplaces.

Other features to look out for include the **promenoir** (ambulatory), with one of the oldest ribbed vaulted ceilings in Europe, and the **Chapelle de Notre Dame sous Terre** (Underground Chapel of Our Lady), one of the abbey's oldest rooms, rediscovered in 1903.

Tidal Variations

The bay around Mont St-Michel is famed for having Europe's highest tidal variations; the difference between low and high tides – only about six hours apart – can reach an astonishing 15m. The Mont is only completely surrounded by the sea every month or two, when the tidal coefficient is above 100 and high tide is above 14m. Regardless of the time of year, the waters sweep in at an astonishing clip, said to be as fast as a galloping horse.

Guided Tours

When the tide is out (the tourist office has tide tables), you can walk all the way around Mont St-Michel, a distance of about 1km, with a guide (doing so on your own is very risky). Straying too far from the Mont can be dangerous: you could get stuck in wet sand – from which Norman soldiers are depicted being rescued in one scene of the Bayeux Tapestry – or be overtaken either by the incoming tide or by water gushing from the new dam's eight sluice gates.

Experienced outfits offering guided walks into – or even across – are based across the bay from Mont St-Michel in Genêts.

> ☑ **Don't Miss**
>
> Illuminated *nocturnes* (night-time visits) with live chamber music, 7pm to midnight, July and August.

DOZER MARC / GETTY IMAGES ©

> ✕ **Take a Break**
>
> Enjoy bistro classics at Les Terrasses Poulard (www.terrasses-poulard.fr) on main street Grand Rue.

Mont St-Michel

TIMELINE

708 Inspired by a vision of **St Michael ❶**, Bishop Aubert is inspired to 'build here and build high'.

966 Richard I, Duke of Normandy, gives the Mont to the Benedictines. The three levels of the **abbey ❷** reflect their monastic hierarchy.

1017 Development of the abbey begins. Pilgrims arrive to honour the cult of St Michael. They walk barefoot across the mudflats and up the **Grande Rue ❸** to be received in the almonry (now the bookshop).

1203 The monastery is burnt by the troops of Philip Augustus, who later donates money for its restoration and the Gothic 'miracle', **La Merveille ❹**, is constructed.

1434 The Mont's **ramparts ❺** and fortifications ensure it withstands the English assault during the Hundred Years War. It is the only place in northern France not to fall.

1789 After the Revolution, Monasticism is abolished and the Mont is turned into a prison. During this period the **treadmill ❻** is built to lift up supplies.

1878 The Mont is linked to the mainland by a **causeway ❼**.

1979 The Mont is declared a Unesco World Heritage Site.

2014 The causeway is replaced by a bridge.

TOP TIPS

➡ Pick up a picnic lunch at the supermarket in La Caserne to avoid the Mont's overpriced fast food.

➡ Allow 45 minutes to an hour to get from the parking lot in La Caserne to the Mont.

➡ If you step off the island pay close attention to the tides - they can be dangerous.

➡ Don't forget to pick up the Abbey's excellent audioguide – it tells some great stories.

MOR65_MAURO PICCARDY/SHUTTERSTOCK ©

Abbey
The abbey's three levels reflect the monastic order: monks lived isolated in church and cloister, the abbot entertained noble guests at the middle level, and lowly pilgrims were received in the basement. Tip: night visits run from mid-July to August.

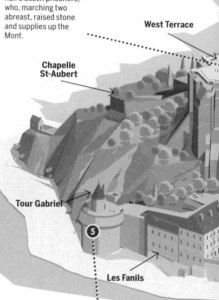

Treadmill
The giant treadmill was powered hamsterlike by half a dozen prisoners, who, marching two abreast, raised stone and supplies up the Mont.

West Terrace

Chapelle St-Aubert

Tour Gabriel

❺

Les Fanils

JULIA KUZNETSOVA/SHUTTERSTOCK ©

Ramparts
The Mont was also a military garrison surrounded by machi-colated and turreted walls, dating from the 13th to 15th centuries. The single entrance, Porte de l'Avancée, ensured its security in the Hundred Years War. Tip: Tour du Nord (North Tower) has the best views.

BEST VIEWS

The view from the Jardin des Plantes in nearby Avranches is unique, as are the panoramas from Pointe du Grouin du Sud near the village of St-Léonard.

St Michael Statue & Bell Tower

A golden statue of the winged St Michael looks ready to leap heavenward from the bell tower. He is the patron of the Mont, having inspired St Aubert's original devotional chapel.

La Merveille

The highlights of La Merveille are the vast refectory hall lit through embrasured windows, the Knights Hall with its elegant ribbed vaulting, and the cloister (above), which is one of the purest examples of 13th-century architecture to survive here.

ÎLOT DE TOMBELAINE

Occupied by the English during the Hundred Years War, this islet is now a bird reserve. From April to July it teems with exceptional birdlife.

Gardens

Tour du Nord

Église St-Pierre

Cemetery

Chemin des Remparts

Toilets

Tour de l'Arcade

Tour du Roi

Porte des Fanils

Tourist Office

Porte de l'Avancée (Entrance)

① ② ③ ④ ⑥ ⑦

Grande Rue

The main thoroughfare of the small village below the abbey, Grande Rue has its charm despite its rampant commercialism. Don't miss the famous Mère Poulard shop here, for souvenir cookies.

New Bridge

In 2014, the Mont's 136-year-old causeway was replaced by a bridge designed to allow seawater to circulate and thus save the island from turning into a peninsula.

D-Day ruins, Omaha Beach

D-Day Beaches

Code-named 'Operation Overlord', the D-Day landings were the largest seaborne invasion in history. Early on 6 June 1944, swarms of landing craft – part of an armada of more than 6000 ships and boats – hit the beaches of northern Normandy. Most of the 135,000 Allied troops who stormed ashore arrived along 80km of beaches north of Bayeux code named Utah, Omaha, Gold, Juno and Sword.

Great For...

❶ Need to Know

Information and reservations for guided minibus tours: Bayeux **tourist office** (📞02 31 51 28 28; www.bayeux-bessin-tour-isme.com; pont St-Jean; ⏰9.30am-12.30pm & 2-6pm).

★ **Top Tip**
Caen's Le Mémorial (p119) and Bayeux' Musée Mémorial (p121) provide a comprehensive overview of the events of D-Day.

The landings on D-Day – known as 'Jour J' in French – were followed by the 76-day Battle of Normandy, during which the Allies suffered 210,000 casualties, including 37,000 troops killed. German casualties are believed to have been around 200,000; another 200,000 German soldiers were taken prisoner. About 14,000 French civilians also died.

Omaha Beach

D-Day's most brutal fighting took place on the 7km stretch of coastline around Vierville-sur-Mer, St-Laurent-sur-Mer and Colleville-sur-Mer, 15km northwest of Bayeux (known as 'Bloody Omaha' to US veterans). Seven decades on, little evidence of the carnage unleashed here on 6 June 1944 remains, except for the American cemetery and German bunkers; at very low tide spot remnants of the Mulberry harbour (p118).

These days Omaha is a peaceful place, a beautiful stretch of fine golden sand partly lined with dunes and summer homes. **Circuit de la Plage d'Omaha**, trail-marked with a yellow stripe, is a self-guided tour along the beach.

White marble crosses and Stars of David stretch off in seemingly endless rows at the **Normandy American Cemetery** (📋02 31 51 62 00; www.abmc.gov; Colleville-sur-Mer; ⏱9am-6pm mid-Apr–mid-Sep, to 5pm mid-Sep–mid-Apr), situated 17km northwest of Bayeux on a now-serene bluff overlooking the bitterly contested sands of Omaha Beach. Featured in the opening scenes of Steven Spielberg's *Saving Private Ryan,* this place of pilgrimage is one of the largest American war cemeteries in Europe. It contains the graves of 9387 American soldiers, including 33 pairs of brothers who are buried side by

Normandy American Cemetery

side (another 12 pairs of brothers are buried separately or memorialised here). Only about 40% of American war dead from the fighting in Normandy are interred in this cemetery – the rest were repatriated at the request of their families.

The visitor centre has an excellent multimedia presentation on the D-Day landings, told in part through the stories of individuals' courage and sacrifice.

Pointe du Hoc

At 7.10am on 6 June 1944, 225 US Army Rangers under the command of Lieutenant Colonel James Earl Rudder scaled the impossibly steep, 30m-high cliffs of Pointe du Hoc, 14km from Utah. Their objective was to disable five 155mm German artillery guns perfectly placed to rain shells onto the beaches of Utah and Omaha. Unbeknownst to Rudder and his team, the guns had been transferred inland shortly before, but they nevertheless managed to locate the massive artillery pieces and put them out of action.

By the time the Rangers were finally relieved on 8 June – after repelling fierce German counter-attacks for two days – 81 of the rangers had been killed and 58 more had been wounded.

Today the **memorial site** (☏02 31 51 90 70; www.abmc.gov; ☺9am–6pm mid-Apr–mid-Sep, to 5pm rest of year) **FREE**, which France turned over to the US government in 1979, looks much as it did right after the battle, with the earth still pitted with huge bomb craters. The German command post (topped by a dagger-shaped memorial) and several concrete bunkers and casemates, scarred by bullet holes and blackened by flame-throwers, can be explored.

Juno Beach

Dune-lined Juno Beach, around Courseulles-sur-Mer, was stormed by Canadian troops on D-Day. A Cross of Lorraine marks the spot where General Charles de Gaulle came ashore after the landings. He was followed by Winston Churchill on 12 June and King George VI on 16 June. Juno Beach's only specifically Canadian museum, the **Juno Beach Centre** (☏02 31 37 32 17; www.junobeach.org; voie des Français Libres, Courseulles-sur-Mer; adult/child €7/5.50, incl guided tour of Juno Beach €11/9; ☺9.30am–7pm Apr-Sep, 10am-5pm Oct-Dec, Feb & Mar, closed Jan), has multimedia exhibits on Canada's role in the landings.

> ☑ **Don't Miss**
>
> English-language tours of the Normandy American Cemetery, daily at 2pm and, mid-April to mid-September, 11am.

FERESANZ / SHUTTERSTOCK ©

> ✕ **Take a Break**
>
> Lunch with locals in Bayeux at Alchimie (p122) or enjoy afternoon tea at La Reine Mathilde (p121).

Arromanches-les-Bains

In order to unload the vast quantities of cargo needed by the invasion forces without having to capture – intact! – one of the heavily defended Channel ports (a lesson of the 1942 Dieppe Raid), the Allies set up prefabricated marinas, code named **Mulberry harbours**, off two of the landing beaches. A total of 146 massive cement caissons were towed over from England and sunk to form two semicircular breakwaters in which floating bridge spans were moored. In the three months after D-Day, the Mulberries facilitated the unloading of 2.5 million men, 4 million tonnes of equipment and 500,000 vehicles.

The harbour established at Omaha was destroyed by a ferocious gale just two weeks after D-Day, but the impressive remains of three dozen caissons belonging to the second, **Port Winston** (named after Churchill), can still be seen off Arromanches-les-Bains, 10km northeast of Bayeux. At low tide you can walk out to one of the caissons from the beach.

The best view of Port Winston and nearby **Gold Beach** is from the hill east of town, site of **Arromanches 360° Circular Cinema** (02 31 06 06 44; www.arromanches360. com; chemin du Calvaire; admission €5.50; 10am-btwn 5.30pm & 7pm, closed 3 weeks in Jan & Mon mid-Nov–mid-Feb), which screens archival footage of the Battle of Normandy.

Down in Arromanches itself, right on the beach, the **Musée du Débarquement** (Landing Museum; 02 31 22 34 31; www.musee-arromanches.fr; place du 6 Juin; adult/child €7.90/5.80; 9am-12.30pm & 1.30-6pm Apr-Sep, 10am-12.30pm & 1.30-5pm Oct-Dec, Feb & Mar, closed Jan) makes for a very informative stop before visiting the beaches. Dioramas, models and two films explain the logistics and importance of Port Winston.

Longues-sur-Mer

Part of the Nazis' Atlantic Wall, the massive casemates and 150mm German guns near Longues-sur-Mer were designed to hit targets 20km away, including Gold Beach (east) and Omaha Beach (west). Over seven decades later, the mammoth artillery pieces are still in their colossal concrete emplacements. Contact the on-site **Longues tourist office** (02 31 21 46 87; www.bayeux-bessin-tourisme.com; Site de la Batterie; 10am-1pm & 2-6pm, closed Nov-Mar) for tour details. The site itself is always open.

Utah Beach

Midway between Bayeux and Cherbourg, this beach – the Allies' right (western) flank on D-Day – stretches for 5km near the village of La Madeleine. It was taken with only light resistance by the US 4th Infantry Division. Don't miss the impressive **Musée du Débarquement de Utah Beach** (Utah Beach Landing Museum; 02 33 71 53 35; www.utah-beach.com; adult/child €8/4; 9.30am-7pm Jun-Sep, 10am-6pm Oct-May, closed Jan), a few kilometres inland in Ste-Marie du Mont.

Musée du Débarquement de Utah Beach

Caen

Founded by William the Conqueror in the 11th century, Caen – capital of the Basse Normandie region – was 80% destroyed during the 1944 Battle of Normandy. Rebuilt in the 1950s and '60s in the utilitarian style in vogue at the time, modern-day Caen nevertheless offers visitors a walled medieval château, two ancient abbeys and excellent museums, including **Le Mémorial – Un Musée pour La Paix** (Memorial – A Museum for Peace; ☑02 31 06 06 44; www.memorial-caen.fr; esplanade Général Eisenhower; adult/child €20/17; ⊙9am-7pm early Feb-early Nov, 9.30am-6.30pm Tue-Sun early Nov-early Feb, closed 3 weeks in Jan).

With a special focus on the Battle of Normandy, this war and peace museum is among Europe's premier WWII museums. It's a hugely impressive affair, using film, animation and audio testimony to graphically evoke the realities of war, the trials of occupation and the joy of liberation. It is situated 3km northwest of the city centre, reachable by bus 2 from place Courtonne; by car follow the signs marked 'Le Mémorial'.

★ Resources

Several excellent websites have details on D-Day and its context, including www.normandiememoire.com, www.6juin1944.com and www.normandie44lamemoire.com.

★ Motoring Trails

Follow the D514 along the D-Day coast or signposted circuits around the battle sites – look for 'D-Day–Le Choc' signs in the American sectors, 'Overlord-L'Assaut' signs in the British and Canadian sectors.

Bayeux

Bayeux was the first French town to be liberated (on the morning of 7 June 1944) and is one of the few places in Calvados to have survived WWII practically unscathed. It makes an ideal base for exploring the D-Day beaches.

These days, Bayeux is a great spot to soak up the gentle Norman atmosphere. The delightful, flowery city centre is crammed with 13th- to 18th-century buildings and a fine Gothic cathedral.

◎ SIGHTS

A 'triple ticket' good for all three of Bayeux' outstanding municipal museums costs €15/13.50 for an adult/child.

Musée d'Art et d'Histoire Baron Gérard   Museum

(MAHB; ☑02 31 92 14 21; www.bayeuxmuseum. com; 37 rue du Bienvenu; adult/child €7/4; ☉9.30am-6.30pm May-Sep, 10am-12.30pm & 2-6pm Oct-Apr, closed Jan–mid-Feb) Opened in 2013, this is one of France's most gorgeously presented provincial museums. The exquisite exhibitions cover everything from Gallo-Roman archaeology to medieval art and paintings from the Renaissance to the 20th century, including a fine work by Gustave Caillebotte. Other highlights include impossibly delicate local lace and Bayeux-made porcelain. Housed in the former bishop's palace.

Cathédrale Notre Dame   Cathedral

(rue du Bienvenu; ☉8.30am-7pm) Most of Bayeux' spectacular Norman Gothic cathedral dates from the 13th century, though the crypt (take the stairs on the north side of the choir), the arches of the nave and the lower parts of the entrance towers are 11th-century Romanesque. The central tower was added in the 15th century; the copper dome dates from the 1860s.

Conservatoire de la Dentelle   Lace Workshop

(Lace Conservatory; ☑02 31 92 73 80; http:// dentelledebayeux.free.fr; 6 rue du Bienvenu; ☉9.30am-12.30pm & 2.30-5pm Mon-Sat) **FREE** Lacemaking, brought to Bayeux by nuns

Cathédrale Notre Dame

in 1678, once employed 5000 people. The industry is long gone, but at the Conservatoire you can watch some of France's most celebrated lacemakers create intricate designs using dozens of bobbins and hundreds of pins; a small shop sells some of their delicate creations. The half-timbered building housing the workshop, decorated with carved wooden figures, dates from the 1400s.

Bayeux War Cemetery   Cemetery

(bd Fabien Ware) The largest of the 18 Commonwealth military cemeteries in Normandy, this peaceful cemetery contains 4848 graves of soldiers from the UK and 10 other countries, including a few from Germany. Across the road is a memorial to 1807 Commonwealth soldiers whose remains were never found; the Latin inscription across the top reads: 'We, once conquered by William, have now liberated the Conqueror's native land'.

Musée Mémorial de la Bataille de Normandie   Museum

(Battle of Normandy Memorial Museum; 02 31 51 46 90; www.bayeuxmuseum.com; bd Fabien Ware; adult/child €7/4; 9.30am-6.30pm May-Sep, 10am-12.30pm & 2-6pm Oct-Apr, closed Jan–mid-Feb) Using well-chosen photos, personal accounts, dioramas and wartime objects, this first-rate museum offers an excellent introduction to the Battle of Normandy. The 25-minute film is screened in both French and English.

EATING

La Reine Mathilde   Patisserie €

(47 rue St-Martin; cakes from €2.50; 9am-7.30pm Tue-Sun) This sumptuously decorated patisserie and *salon de thé* (tearoom), ideal for a sweet breakfast or a relaxing cup of afternoon tea, hasn't changed much since it was built in 1898.

Au Ptit Bistrot   Modern French €€

(02 31 92 30 08; 31 rue Larcher; lunch menu €17-20, dinner menu €27-33, mains €16-19; noon-2pm & 7-9pm Tue-Sat) Near the

Bayeux Tapestry

Two cross-Channel invasions, almost 900 years apart, gave Bayeux a front-row seat at defining moments in Western history. The dramatic story of the Norman invasion of England in 1066 is told – from an unashamedly Norman perspective – in 58 vivid scenes by the world-famous **Bayeux Tapestry** (02 31 51 25 50; www.bayeuxmuseum.com; rue de Nesmond; adult/child incl audioguide €9/4; 9am-6.30pm Mar-Oct, to 7pm May-Aug, 9.30am-12.30pm & 2-6pm Nov-Feb). It was embroidered just a few years after William the Bastard, Duke of Normandy, became William the Conqueror, King of England.

Commissioned by Bishop Odo of Bayeux, William's half-brother, for the opening of Bayeux' cathedral in 1077, the 68.3m-long cartoon strip tells the dramatic, bloody tale with verve and vividness. Fifty-eight action-packed scenes of pageantry and mayhem occupy the centre of the canvas, while religious allegories and illustrations of everyday 11th-century life, some of them naughty, adorn the borders. The final showdown at the Battle of Hastings is depicted in graphic fashion, complete with severed limbs and decapitated heads (along the bottom of scene 52). Halley's Comet, which blazed across the sky in 1066, appears in scene 32.

A 16-minute film gives the conquest historical, political and cultural context, including crucial details on the grooming habits of Norman and Saxon knights.

Edward the Confessor depicted on the tapestry
PHOTOS.COM / GETTY IMAGES ©

Daytrip to Honfleur

Long a favourite with painters such as Monet, Normandy's most charming port town is a popular day-trip destination. The centre can be overrun with visitors, but it's hard not to love the rugged maritime charm of the old harbour, which evokes maritime Normandy of centuries past.

Honfleur is superb for aimless ambling. The harbour, with its bobbing pleasure boats, is Honfleur's focal point. On the west side, **quai Ste-Catherine** is lined with tall, taper-thin houses – many protected from the elements by slate tiles – dating from the 16th to 18th centuries. The **Lieutenance** (12 Place Ste-Catherine), at the mouth of the old harbour, was once the residence of the town's royal governor. Just northeast of the Lieutenance is the **Avant Port**, home to Honfleur's dozen fishing vessels, which sell their catch at the **Marché au Poisson** (Fish Market; Jetée de Transit; ☺8am-noon or later Thu-Sun).

Come lunch, **La Cidrerie** (☑02 31 89 59 85; 26 place Hamelin; mains €8-12; ☺noon-2.30pm & 7-9.30pm Thu-Mon) serves piping-hot *galettes* (savoury buckwheat crêpes) and fizzy Norman ciders served in bowls, while **L'Endroit** (☑02 31 88 08 43; 3 rue Charles et Paul Bréard; weekday lunch menus €25, other menus €30, mains €24-29; ☺noon-1.30pm & 7.30-9pm Thu-Mon) cooks up dishes showcasing the bounty of Normandy's fields and coastline in an eclectic and artfully designed space with open kitchen.

cathedral, this friendly, welcoming eatery whips up creative, beautifully prepared dishes that highlight the Norman bounty without a lick of pretension. Recent hits include chestnut soup, duck breast and bulgur with seasonal fruits and roasted pineapple, and black cod with spinach and spicy guacamole. Reservations essential.

Alchimie   Modern French €€
(lunch menu €12) On a street lined with restaurants, Alchimie has a simple but elegant design that takes nothing from the beautifully presented dishes. Choose from the day's specials listed on a chalkboard menu, which might include hits like *brandade de morue* (codfish baked savoury pie). It's a local favourite, so call ahead.

La Rapière   Italian €€
(☑02 31 21 05 45; www.larapiere.net; 53 rue St-Jean; lunch menus €16-42, dinner menus €30-52; ☺noon-1.30pm Tue & Thu-Sat, 7-9pm Tue-Sat, closed mid-Dec–early Feb) Housed in a late-1400s mansion composed of stone walls and big wooden beams, this atmospheric restaurant specialises in Normandy staples such as terrines, duck and veal with Camembert. The various fixed-price *menus* assure a splendid meal on any budget.

ℹ INFORMATION

Tourist Office (p114) Covers both Bayeux and the surrounding Bessin region, including the D-Day beaches. Has a walking-tour map of town and bus and train schedules, and sells books on the D-Day landings in English. Charges €2 to book hotels and B&Bs.

ℹ GETTING THERE & AWAY

BUS

Bus Verts (☑09 70 83 00 14; www.busverts.fr) Buses 70 and 74 (bus 75 in July and August) link Bayeux' train station and place St-Patrice with many of the villages, memorials and museums along Omaha, Gold and Juno D-Day beaches.

TRAIN

Bayeux' train station is 1km southeast of the cathedral. Direct services:

Caen €7, 20 minutes, at least hourly.

Pontorson (Mont St-Michel) €25, 1¾ hours, three daily.

For Paris' Gare St-Lazare and Rouen, you may have to change at Caen.

GIIMS • SHUTTERSTOCK ©

Quai Ste-Catherine, Honfleur

ℹ️ GETTING AROUND

BICYCLE

Vélos (☑️02 31 92 89 16; www.velosbayeux.com; 5 rue Larcher; per half-/full day from €7.50/10; ⏲️8am-8.30pm) Year-round bike rental from a fruit and veggie store a few paces from the tourist office.

CAR

There's free parking at Parking d'Ornano, at the southern end of rue Larcher.

TAXI

Taxi (☑️02 31 92 92 40; www.bayeux-taxis.com) Can take you around Bayeux or out to the D-Day sites.

Rouen

With its soaring Gothic cathedral, beautifully restored medieval quarter, excellent museums and vibrant cultural life, Rouen is one of Normandy's most engaging destinations.

◉ SIGHTS

The heart of the old city is rue du Gros Horloge, which is two blocks north of the city centre's main east–west thoroughfare, rue Général Leclerc. The main shopping precinct is due north of the cathedral, on pedestrianised rue des Carmes and nearby streets.

Historial Jeanne d'Arc   Museum

(☑️02 35 52 48 00; www.historialjeannedarc.fr; 7 rue St-Romain; adult/child €10/7; ⏲️10am-6pm Tue-Sun) For an introduction to the great 15th-century heroine and the events that earned her fame – and shortly thereafter condemnation – don't miss this excellent new site. It's less of a museum, and more of an immersive, theatre-like experience, where you walk through medieval corridors and watch (and hear via headphones) the dramatic retelling of Joan's visions, her victories, the trial that sealed her fate, and the mythologising that followed in the years after her death.

The site is not coincidentally set inside one part of the archbishop's palace, where

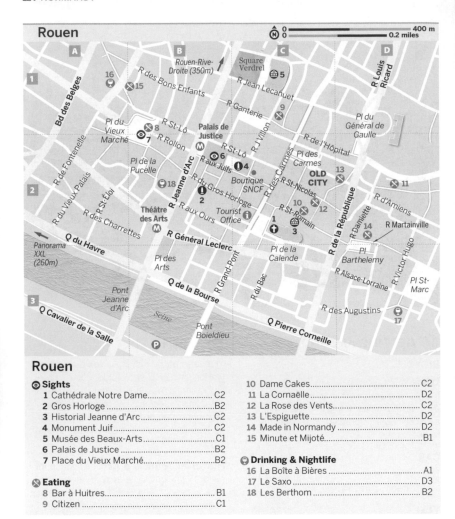

Rouen

Joan was likely tried and condemned in 1431.

Cathédrale Notre Dame   Cathedral
(www.cathedrale-rouen.net; place de la Cathédrale; ⊘2-7pm Mon, 9am-7pm Tue-Sat, 8am-6pm Sun Apr-Oct, shorter hours Nov-Mar) Rouen's stunning Gothic cathedral, built between the late 12th and 16th centuries, was famously the subject of a series of canvases painted by Monet at various times

of the day and year. The 75m-tall **Tour de Beurre** (Butter Tower) was financed by locals in return for being allowed to eat butter during Lent – or so the story goes.

Place du Vieux Marché   Square
The old city's main thoroughfare, rue du Gros Horloge, runs from the cathedral west to place du Vieux Marché. This is where 19-year-old Joan of Arc was executed for heresy in 1431.

Gros Horloge   Clock Tower

(rue du Gros Horloge; adult/child €7/3.50; ⏱10am-1pm & 2-7pm Tue-Sun Apr-Oct, to 6pm Nov-Mar) Spanning rue du Gros Horloge, the Great Clock's Renaissance archway has a gilded, one-handed medieval clock face on each side. High above, a Gothic belfry, reached via spiral stairs, affords spectacular views. The excellent audioguide is a great introduction to Rouen's colourful history and is available in eight languages.

Musée des Beaux-Arts   Art Museum

(☏02 35 71 28 40; www.mbarouen.fr; esplanade Marcel Duchamp; ⏱10am-6pm Wed-Mon) FREE Housed in a grand structure erected in 1870, Rouen's outstanding fine-arts museum features canvases by Rubens, Modigliani, Pissarro, Renoir, Sisley (lots) and, of course, several works by Monet. There's also one jaw-dropping painting by Caravaggio.

Panorama XXL   Gallery

(www.panoramxxl.com; Quai de Boisguilbert; adult/child €10/7; ⏱10am-7pm May-Sep, to 6pm Oct-Apr) In a large, circular column on the waterfront, Panorama XXL lives up to its oversized name, with one massive 360-degree exhibition inside that offers in-depth exploring of one vast landscape, created with photographs, drawings, digital images and recorded audio. Past years have featured Amazonia, Ancient Rome and Rouen in 1431 – often with sunrise and sunset creating different moods. A 15m-high viewing platform in the middle of the room gives a fine vantage point over the scene.

Palais de Justice   Architecture

(place Maréchal Foch & rue aux Juifs) The ornately Gothic Law Courts, little more than a shell at the end of WWII, have been restored to their early-16th-century glory. On rue Jeanne d'Arc, however, you can still see the pock-marked façade, which shows the damages sustained during bombing raids in 1944. Around the corner on pedestrianised rue aux Juifs, you can peer in the spire- and gargoyle-adorned courtyard.

⊗ EATING

Rouen's main dining district, home to dozens of eateries and cafes, is around place du Vieux Marché and adjacent place de la Pucelle. East of the cathedral, there's a row of classy little restaurants along the northern side of rue Martainville, near Église St-Maclou.

Citizen   Cafe €

(4 Rue de l'Écureuil; mains €7-12, Sat brunch €22; ⏱9am-7pm Mon-Fri, from 11am Sat) Citizen is undeniably hip with its chunky wood communal tables, industrial fixtures and groovy tunes playing overhead. More important than the surrounds is the coffee, which is the best in town, and the tasty bites on hand (granola, fresh fruit and fromage blanc for breakfast; smoked salmon salad for lunch), plus beers from Brooklyn Brewery. Outdoor seating on the plaza.

La Cornaëlle   Crêperie €

(☏02 35 08 53 75; 174 rue Eau de Robec; crêpes €8-12; ⏱noon-3pm & 7-10pm Tue-Sat, noon-3pm Sun) Arched ceilings, pale stone walls and some low-playing blues set the scene for an enjoyable night nibbling on delicious savoury *galettes*, while sipping some of the fizzy local cider. Finish off with a decadent dessert crepe (try the *poêlée Normande* with apples, caramel, cream and flambéed *calvados*).

L'Espiguette   Bistro €

(☏02 35 71 66 27; 25 place St-Amand; weekday lunch menu €13, mains €17-24; ⏱noon-10pm Tue-Sat) This charmingly decorated eatery serves excellent bistro classics (think osso buco, fillet of sole, beef tartare), with the day's offerings scribbled on a chalkboard. Grab a seat at one of the outdoor tables on a warm day. It's quite popular with locals, so reserve ahead, even at lunchtime. Speaking of which, the lunch *menu* is a great deal.

La Rose des Vents   Modern French €

(☏02 35 70 29 78; 37 rue St-Nicolas; mains €16; ⏱noon-3pm Tue-Sat) Tucked away inside a retro secondhand shop, this stylish

🍽️ Market-Oyster Lunch

For remarkably fresh seafood, grab a seat at the horseshoe-shaped bar at **Bar à Huîtres** (place du Vieux Marché; mains €10-16, oysters per half-dozen/dozen from €10/17; ⏲10am-2pm Tue-Sat), a casual but polished eatery located inside Rouen's covered market. Specials change daily based on what's fresh, from giant shrimp to fillet of sole, all cooked to perfection. Don't neglect the restaurant's namesake – delicious, locally farmed *huîtres* (oysters), with several different varieties on offer.

Fresh oysters
BIGGEREYE / SHUTTERSTOCK ©

establishment is hugely popular with foodies and hipsters. Patrons rave about the two lunch mains, which change weekly according to what's available in the market. They can usually whip up something for vegetarians as well. Reservations are recommended.

Dame Cakes　　Patisserie €

(☎02 35 07 49 31; www.damecakes.fr; 70 rue St-Romain; lunch menu €16-20, tea & cake menu €9; ⏲10.30am-7pm Mon-Sat; 🖊) Walk through the historic, early-20th-century façade and you'll discover a delightfully civilised selection of pastries, cakes and chocolates. From noon to 3pm you can tuck into delicious quiches, *gratins* and salads in the attached *salon de thé* (tearoom). Lovely.

Minute et Mijoté　　Bistro €€

(☎02 32 08 40 00; http://minutemijote. canalblog.com; 58 rue de Fontenelle; lunch menus €16.50-21, dinner menus €26-31; ⏲noon-2pm & 7.45-10pm Mon-Sat) This smart bistro, with its retro decor, is a longtime favourite dining spot in Rouen. The menu is limited (just two seafood and two meat plates per night on average), but the chef uses quality ingredients, prepared with care, and it's a great value overall.

Made in Normandy　　French €€

(☎02 35 14 07 45; www.lemadeinnormandy. fr; 236 rue Martainville; lunch menu €13-15, dinner menu €19-23; ⏲noon-2pm & 7-9.30pm Thu-Mon) A candle-lit, semiformal restaurant that serves outstanding French and Norman dishes, including succulent beef, Dieppe-style seafood stew and rich crème brûlée.

🍷 DRINKING & NIGHTLIFE

The bars and cafes around place du Vieux Marché and in the old town buzz from noon until the early hours. Rouen is also the centre of Normandy's gay life.

Les Berthom　　Bar

(60 rue de la Vicomte; ⏲5pm-midnight Sun-Wed, to 2am Thu-Sat) Beer lovers should pay a visit to this sleek brewpub near the Vieux Marché. You'll find a changing selection of beers on tap (nine or so at a time, with good Belgian abbey-style ales dominating the list). It's a lively spot for a drink, with bartenders cranking up the beats as the night progresses.

Le Saxo　　Bar

(☎02 35 98 24 92; www.facebook.com/le.saxo. rouen; 11 place St-Marc; ⏲5pm-2am Mon-Sat) Le Saxo swings to jazz, blues, rock, reggae and world music, with free concerts by local bands on Friday and Saturday from 10pm to 1.30am (except in July and August). It hosts jazz jam sessions every other Thursday from 9pm. Serves 13 beers on tap and 120 by the bottle.

La Boîte à Bières　　Bar

(www.laboiteabieres.fr; 35 rue Cauchoise; ⏲5pm-2am Tue-Sat; 🛜) This friendly, often-crowded establishment, with walls plastered with memorabilia, is affectionately known as

BAB. It serves 15 or so beers on tap and another 230 in bottles, including local *bières artisanales* (microbrews).

ℹ INFORMATION

Tourist Office (☑02 32 08 32 40; www.rouen-tourisme.com; 25 place de la Cathédrale; ⊙9am-7pm Mon-Sat, 9.30am-12.30pm & 2-6pm Sun May-Sep, 9.30am-12.30pm & 1.30-6pm Mon-Sat Oct-Apr) Housed in a 1500s Renaissance building facing the cathedral. Can provide English brochures on Normandy and details on guided tours in English (July and August). Rouen's only exchange bureau is at the back.

ℹ GETTING THERE & AROUND

BICYCLE

Cy'clic (☑08 00 08 78 00; http://cyclic.rouen.fr; ⊙5am 1am), Rouen's version of Paris' Vélib', lets you rent a city bike from 20 locations around town. Credit card registration for one/seven days costs €1/5, plus a deposit of €150. Use is free for the first 30 minutes; the 2nd/3rd/4th and subsequent half-hours cost €1/2/4 each.

TRAIN

The train station, **Rouen-Rive-Droite**, is 1.2km north of the cathedral. In the city centre, train tickets are available at the **Boutique SNCF** (cnr rue aux Juifs & rue Eugène Boudin; ⊙12.30-7pm Mon, 10am-7pm Tue-Sat). Direct services:

Caen €28, 1¾ hours, five or six daily.

Paris' Gare St-Lazare €24.10, 1¼ hours, 25 daily Monday to Friday, 13 to 18 Saturday and Sunday.

Trouville & Deauville

The twin seaside towns of Trouville-sur-Mer (population 4800) and Deauville (population 3000), 15km southwest of Honfleur, are hugely popular with Parisians, who flock here year-round on weekends – and all week long from June to September and during Paris' school holidays.

Chic **Deauville** has been a playground of well-heeled Parisians ever since it was founded by Napoléon III's half-brother, the Duke of Morny, in 1861. Expensive, flashy and brash, it's packed with designer boutiques, deluxe hotels and meticulously

Stores in Deauville

KIEV.VICTOR / SHUTTERSTOCK ©

ANTON_IVANOV / SHUTTERSTOCK ©

Trouville

tended public gardens, and hosts two racetracks and the high-profile American Film Festival.

Unpretentious **Trouville** is both a veteran beach resort, graced with impressive mansions from the late 1800s, and a working fishing port. Popular with middle-class French families, the town was frequented by painters and writers during the 19th century (eg Mozin and Flaubert), lured by the 2km-long sandy beach and the laid-back seaside ambience.

◎ SIGHTS

In Deauville, the rich and beautiful strut their stuff along the beachside **Promenade des Planches**, a 643m-long boardwalk that's lined with a row of 1920s cabins named after famous Americans (mainly film stars). After swimming in the nearby 50m **Piscine Olympique** (Olympic swimming pool; ☑02 31 14 02 17; bd de la Mer, Deauville; weekday/weekend from €4/6; ☺10am-2pm & 3.30-7pm Mon-Sat, 10am-4pm Sun, closed 2 weeks in Jan & 3 weeks in Jun), filled with seawater heated to 28°C, they – like

you – can head to the **beach**, hundreds of metres wide at low tide; walk across the street to their eye-popping, neo-something mansion; or head down the block to the spectacularly Italianate **casino**.

Trouville, too, has a waterfront **casino**, wide **beach** and **Promenade des Planches** (boardwalk). At the latter, 583m long and outfitted with Bauhaus-style pavilions from the 1930s, you can swim in a freshwater swimming pool and windsurf; there's also a playground for kids. Trouville's most impressive **19th-century villas** are right nearby.

Musée Villa Montabello   Museum
(☑02 31 88 16 26; 64 rue du Général Leclerc, Trouville; adult/child €3/free, Sun free; ☺2-5.30pm Wed-Mon Apr–mid-Nov, from 11am Sat, Sun & holidays) In a fine mansion built in 1865, this municipal museum recounts Trouville's history and features works by Charles Mozin, Eugène Isabey and Charles Pecrus. Situated 1km northeast of the tourist office, near the beach (and signed off the beach).

The two towns and beach scenes play a starring role in the impressionist works in the small permanent collection. There's also a short film (in French only), vintage travel posters from the 1930s, some early-20th-century clothing and black-and-white photos of beach-goers from days long past. The first floor features temporary exhibitions, with changing shows every three months or so.

✖ EATING

In Trouville, there are lots of restaurants and buzzing brasseries along riverfront bd Fernand Mourcaux; many specialise in fresh fish, mussels and seafood. The area has a fantastic atmosphere on summer evenings. Inland, check out the small restaurants and cafes along and near rue d'Orléans and on pedestrianised rue des Bains.

Deauville has a good selection of eateries scattered around town, with clusters around the tourist office and place Morny.

Les Vapeurs   Brasserie €€
(☑02 31 88 15 24; 160 bd Fernand Moureaux, Trouville; mains €17-32; ☺noon-10pm) Across from the fish market, Les Vapeurs has been going strong since 1927. The huge menu is a showcase for seafood platters, mussels in cream sauce, grilled haddock and classic brasserie fare (like steak tartare). It's served amid old-time ambience, with black-and-white photos, a touch of neon and wicker chairs at the outdoor tables in front.

L'Essentiel   Fusion €€
(☑02 31 87 22 11; 29 rue Mirabeau; lunch menu €20-28, dinner menu €60, mains €23-34; ☺noon-2pm & 7.30-11pm Thu-Mon) One of Deauville's top dining rooms, L'Essentiel serves up an imaginative blend of French ingredients with Asian and Latin American accents. Start off with codfish croquettes with sweet potato aioli before moving on to scallops with broccoli yuzu, or wagyu flank steak with roasted turnips and smoked cashew juice.

ⓘ INFORMATION

Deauville Tourist Office (☑02 31 14 40 00; www.deauville.org; place de la Mairie; ☺10am-

🍽 A Fishy Business

The **Marché aux Poissons** (Fish Market; bd Fernand Moureaux, Trouville; ☺8am-7.30pm) is *the* place in Trouville to head to for fresh oysters with lemon (from €9 to €16 a dozen) and many other maritime delicacies. Even if you don't have access to a kitchen, there's cooked peel-and-eat shrimp, mussels, sea urchins and scallops, which you can enjoy on the tables out front. Located on the waterfront 250m south of the casino.

Poissonnerie Pillet Saiter (www.poissonnerie-pilletsaiter.fr; bd Fernand Moureaux, Trouville; oysters per dozen €10-15; ☺8am-7.30pm), proud of having operated its own fishing boat since 1887, sells platters of seafood (by weight) and oysters (by the six or dozen) that you can eat at little tables.

6pm Mon-Sat, 10am-1pm & 2-5pm Sun) Has a trilingual walking tour brochure with a Deauville map and can help find accommodation. The website has details on cultural events and horse races. Situated 800m west of the train station along rue Désiré le Hoc.

Trouville Tourist Office (☑02 31 14 60 70; www.trouvillesurmer.org; 32 bd Fernand Moureaux; ☺10am-6pm Mon-Sat, 10am-1.30pm Sun Sep-Jun, 9.30am-7pm Mon-Sat, 10am-6pm Sun Jul & Aug) Has a free map of Trouville and sells map-brochures for two self-guided architectural tours (€3.50) and two rural walks (€1) of 7km and 11km. Situated 200m north of pont des Belges.

ⓘ GETTING THERE & AROUND

BICYCLE

Les Trouvillaises (☑02 31 98 54 11; www.lestrouvillaises.fr; place Foch; bicycle per hr/day €5/14; ☺9am-7pm mid-Mar–Oct) Based near Trouville's Casino (next to the footbridge/passenger ferry to Deauville), Les Trouvillaises rents out a variety of two- and four-wheel pedal-powered

The Cider Route

Normandy's signposted, 40km Route du Cidre, about 30km south of Deauville, wends its way through the **Pays d'Auge**, a rural area of orchards, pastures, hedgerows, half-timbered farmhouses and stud farms, through picturesque villages such as Cambremer and Beuvron-en-Auge. Signs reading 'Cru de Cambremer' indicate the way to 17 small-scale, traditional *producteurs* (producers) who are happy to show you their facilities and sell you their homegrown apple cider (about €3.50 a bottle), *calvados* (apple brandy) – affectionately known as *calva* – and *pommeau* (a mixture of apple juice and *calvados*).

Traditional Normandy cider takes about six months to make. Ripe apples are shaken off the trees or gathered from the ground between early October and early December. After being stored for two or three weeks, they are pressed, purified, slow-fermented, bottled and naturally carbonated, just like Champagne.

Normandy's AOC (Appellation d'Origine Contrôlée) cider is made with a blend of apple varieties and is known for being fruity, tangy and slightly bitter. You can enjoy it in crêperies and restaurants throughout Normandy.

Apple cider
DVOEVNORE / SHUTTERSTOCK ©

conveyances, including bicycles, tandems and carts, for both adults and children.

BUS

Deauville and Trouville's joint bus station is next to the Trouville-Deauville train station.

Bus Verts (p122) Bus 20 goes to Caen (€5.15, two hours, seven to 12 daily) and Honfleur (€2.10, 30 minutes, four to seven daily).

TRAIN

The Trouville-Deauville train station is in Deauville right next to pont des Belges (the bridge to Trouville). Getting here usually requires a change at Lisieux (€6.80, 20 minutes, nine to 11 daily), though there are two or three direct trains a day to Paris' Gare St-Lazare (€35, two hours). Destinations that require a change of trains include Caen (€14.50, 1¼ to two hours, six to 11 daily) and Rouen (from €25, 1¼ to two hours, five to eight daily).

Étretat

The dramatic twin cliffs of Étretat, 60km north of Trouville and 90km west of Rouen, made it a favourite of painters like Gustave Courbet and Claude Monet. With the vogue for sea air at the end of the 19th century, fashionable Parisians came and built extravagant villas. Étretat has never gone out of style and still swells with visitors every weekend.

⊙ SIGHTS & ACTIVITIES

The pebbly **beach** is separated from the town centre by a dyke. To the left as you face the sea, you can see the **Falaise d'Aval**, renowned for its free-standing arch – compared by French writer Maupassant to an elephant dipping its trunk in the sea – and the adjacent **Aiguille**, a 70m-high spire of chalk-white rock rising from the waves. Further along the cliff is a second natural arch known as **La Manneporte**. To reach the plateau above, take the steep footpath from the southwestern end of the beachfront.

To the right as you face the sea towers the **Falaise d'Amont**, atop which a memorial marks the spot where two aviators were last seen before attempting to cross the Atlantic in 1927.

The tourist office has a map of trails around town and can also provide details on sail-powered cruises aboard a **two-masted schooner** (March to October).

ℹ️ INFORMATION

Tourist Office (📞02 35 27 05 21; www.etretat. net; place Maurice Guillard; ⏱9.30am-6.30pm mid-Jun–mid-Sep, 10am-noon & 2-6pm Mon-Sat mid-Sep–mid-Jun, Sun during school holidays) Situated inside the town hall.

ℹ️ GETTING THERE & AWAY

Keolis (📞02 35 28 19 88; www.keolis-seine-maritime.com) Scenic bus 24 (seven or more daily) goes to Le Havre's train station (€2, one hour) and to Fécamp (€2, 30 minutes).

Le Havre

A Unesco World Heritage Site since 2005, Le Havre is a love letter to modernism, evoking, more than any other French city, France's postwar energy and optimism. All but obliterated in September 1944 by Allied bombing raids that killed 3000 civilians, the centre was completely rebuilt by the Belgian architect Auguste Perret, whose bright, airy modernist vision remains, miraculously, largely intact. Attractions include a museum full of captivating impressionist paintings, a soaring church with a mesmerising stained-glass tower, and hilltop gardens with views over the city. Le Havre is a regular port of call for cruise ships.

◎ SIGHTS & ACTIVITIES

Musée Malraux Art Museum

(MuMa; 📞02 35 19 62 72; 2 bd Clemenceau; adult/child incl audioguide €5/free; ⏱11am-6pm Mon & Wed-Fri, to 7pm Sat & Sun) Near the waterfront, this luminous modern space houses a fabulous collection of impressionist works – the finest in France outside Paris – by masters such as Monet (who grew up in Le Havre), Pissarro, Renoir and Sisley. You'll also find works by the Fauvist painter Raoul Dufy, born in Le Havre, and paintings by Eugène Boudin, a mentor of Monet and another Le Havre native.

There's a cafe with fine views over the harbour. MuMa is 1km southeast of the tourist office, at the southwestern tip of the city centre.

Église St-Joseph Church

(bd François 1er; ⏱10am-6pm) Perret's masterful, 107m-high Église St-Joseph, visible from all over town, was built using bare concrete from 1951 to 1959. Some 13,000 panels of coloured glass make the soaring, sombre interior particularly striking when it's sunny.

Stained-glass artist Margaret Huré created a cohesive masterpiece in her collaboration with Peret, and her use of shading and colour was thoughtfully conceived, evoking different moods depending on where the sun is in the sky – and the ensuing colours created by the illumination.

Appartement Témoin Architecture

(📞02 35 22 31 22; 181 rue de Paris; adult/child €5/free; ⏱tours 2pm, 3pm, 4pm & 5pm Wed, Sat & Sun, plus 2pm & 3pm Mon, Tue, Thu & Fri Jun-Sep) Furnished in impeccable early-1950s style, this lovingly furnished bourgeois apartment can be visited on a one-hour guided tour that starts at 181 rue de Paris (Maison du Patrimoine), a block north of Le Volcan.

The apartment is a remarkable time capsule of the postwar boom days that Le Havre experienced, complete with clothes, newspapers, furniture and appliances exactly as one would have seen entering a downtown apartment in the decade of the city's reconstruction.

Le Volcan Cultural Centre

(Espace Oscar Niemeyer; 📞02 35 19 10 10; www. levolcan.com; place Charles de Gaulle; ⏱library 10am-7pm) Le Havre's most conspicuous landmark, designed by Brazilian architect Oscar Niemeyer and opened in 1982, is also the city's premier cultural venue. One look and you'll understand how it got its name, which means 'the volcano'. After extensive renovations the complex reopened in 2015, with a new concert hall and an ultramodern *mediathèque* (multimedia library). It's situated at the western end of the Bassin du Commerce, the city centre's former port.

It's worth stopping by the library and cafe while strolling around Le Havre. Check the website for upcoming performances, which tend towards avant-garde and interdisciplinary works.

❌ EATING

You'll find a concentration of restaurants along pedestrian-friendly Rue Victor Hugo, one block north of Le Volcan. There's another cluster of restaurants in Quartier St-François, the area just south of the Bassin du Commerce – check out rue de Bretagne, rue Jean de la Fontaine and rue du Général Faidherbe.

Halles Centrales   Food Market €
(rue Voltaire; ⊙8.30am-7.30pm Mon-Sat, 9am-1pm Sun) Food stalls at Le Havre's main market include a patisserie, a *fromagerie* (cheese shop) and many tempting fruit stands; there's also a small supermarket. Situated a block west of Le Volcan.

La Taverne Paillette   Brasserie €€
(🖉02 35 41 31 50; www.taverne-paillette.com; 22 rue Georges Braque; lunch menu €15, mains €16-26; ⊙noon-midnight daily) Solid brasserie food is the order of the day at this Le Havre institution – think big bowls of mussels, generous salads, gargantuan seafood platters and, in the Alsatian tradition, eight types of *choucroute* (sauerkraut). Situated five blocks north of Église St-Joseph, at the northeast corner of a park called Square St-Roch.

Bistrot des Halles   Bistro €€
(🖉02 35 22 50 52; 7 place des Halles Centrales; lunch menu €14, other menu €25, mains €15-24; ⊙noon-3pm & 7-11pm Mon-Sat, noon-3pm Sun) For a very French dining experience, head to this Lyon-style bistro, decked out with

Interior of Église St-Joseph (p131)

FRANK SHOUT IMAGES/GETTY IMAGES ©

old-time enamel publicity plaques. Specialities include steak, *magret de canard* (duck breast fillet), *cassoulet* and large salads. Situated two blocks west of Le Volcan and across from the covered market (Halles Centrales).

 INFORMATION

Maison du Patrimoine (☎02 35 22 31 22; 181 rue de Paris; ☺1.45-6.30pm year-round, plus 10am-noon Apr-Sep) The tourist office's city centre annexe has an exposition on Perret's postwar reconstruction of the city.

Tourist Office (☎02 32 74 04 04; www.lehavre-tourisme.com; 186 bd Clemenceau; ☺2-6pm Mon, 10am-12.30pm & 2-6pm Tue-Sun) Has a map in English for a two-hour walking tour of Le Havre's architectural highlights and details on cultural events. Situated at the western edge of the city centre, one block south of the La Plage tram terminus.

 GETTING THERE & AWAY

BOAT

Le Havre's car ferry terminal, situated 1km southeast of Le Volcan, is linked with the English port of Portsmouth via **Brittany Ferries** (www.brittany-ferries.co.uk). Ferries depart daily from late March to early November.

BUS

The bus station is next to the train station.

Bus Verts (p122) Heading south, bus 20 (four to six daily) goes to Honfleur (€4.15, 30 minutes) and Deauville and Trouville (€6.25, one hour).

Keolis (p131) For the Côte d'Albâtre, take scenic bus 24 (seven or more daily) to Étretat (€2, one hour).

TRAIN

The train station, **Gare du Havre**, is 1.5km east of Le Volcan, at the eastern end of bd de Strasbourg. The tram stop out front is called 'Gares'.

Fécamp €9.30, one to 1½ hours, eight to 15 daily.

 Norman Cuisine

Normandy may be the largest French region without even a single vineyard, but its culinary riches more than make up for the dearth of local wines – and be sides, any self respecting Norman would rather wash down a meal with a pitcher of tart cider or *calvados* (apple brandy).

Normandy is a land of cream, soft cheeses, apples and an astonishingly rich range of seafood and fish. Classics to look out for include *coquilles St-Jacques* (scallops), available from October to May, and *sole dieppoise* (Dieppe sole). Don't forget your *trou normand* ('Norman hole'), the traditional break between courses of a meal for a glass of *calvados* to cleanse the palate and improve the appetite for the next course!

BENOIST SÉBIRE/GETTY IMAGES ©

Paris' Gare St-Lazare €35, 2¼ hours, 15 daily Monday to Friday, seven to nine Saturday and Sunday.

Rouen €16, one hour, 16 to 20 daily Monday to Saturday, 10 Sunday.

 GETTING AROUND

Two modern tram lines run by LiA (www.transports-lia.fr) link the train station with the city centre and the beach. A single ride costs €1.70; travelling all day is €3.80.

Location de Vélos rents out **bicycles** (two hours/half-day/full day €3/4/7) at two sites, including the train station and a shop on 9 ave René Coty, one block north of the Mairie du Havre.

BRITTANY

Brittany at a Glance...

Brittany is for explorers. Its wild, dramatic coastline, medieval towns and thick forests make an excursion here well worth it. This is a land of prehistoric mysticism, proud tradition and culinary wealth, where fiercely independent locals celebrate Breton culture.

The entire region – Breizh in Breton – has a wonderfully undiscovered feel. Whether you explore world-famous sights like St-Malo and the Carnac megaliths or unexpected Breton gems such as small-town Quiberon or the Morbihan coast, it doesn't take long to realise that there's far more to Brittany than sweet crêpes and homemade cider. Then there's Brittany's much-loved islands, très belle to boot.

Brittany in Two Days

Spend a day cycling between prehistoric **megaliths** (p138) around Carnac; rent wheels at Carnac-Plage, lunch on crêpes in **Carnac town** (p146), and end the day with a refreshing dip in the Breton sea on Carnac's **La Grand Plage** (p146). Dine on seafood in **Quiberon** (p147). Day two, catch a ferry to **Belle Île** (p144) or head to nearby **Vannes** (p148) for scenic old-town mooching and boats to a deserted island in the **Golfe du Morbihan** (p145).

Brittany in Four Days

With four days, you have time to travel further afield. Day three take in the island you didn't do the previous day, and on the last day consider a trip to **St-Malo** (p140) – a two- to three-hour train ride from Vannes (change trains in Rennes) or a scenic two-hour motor across inland Brittany. Explore its old-town streets, walk its ramparts and devour.

Arriving in Brittany

Gare Maritime de St-Malo Ferries to/from the Channel Islands, Portsmouth and Poole.

St-Malo train station Regular trains to/from Paris (€45 to €79, 3½ hours). Change trains in Rennes (€15, one hour) for Vannes (€36, 2½ hours).

Aéroport Dinard Bretagne Ryanair flights from London Stansted, Bradford-Leeds and East Midlands to Dinard, a 20-minute drive from St-Malo and two hours from Carnac.

BreizhGo (www.breizhgo.com) Has a handy website.

Sleeping

From boutique B&Bs to ocean-side campgrounds, Brittany has it all. Advance reservations are essential, especially for St-Malo on the north coast and also Belle Île, which fills up completely in July and August. Small towns Quiberon and Vannes are excellent bases for southern Brittany, with high lodging standards and hotels that stay open year-round. Carnac is equally hotel-loaded, albeit many are seasonal.

PECOLD / SHUTTERSTOCK ©

Carnac Megaliths

Predating Stonehenge by around 100 years, the Carnac (Garnag in Breton) area offers the world's greatest concentration of megalithic sites. There are no fewer than 3000 of these upright stones, erected between 5000 and 3500 BC.

Two perplexing questions arise from Brittany's Neolithic menhirs, dolmens, cromlechs, tumuli and cairns. Just how did the original constructors hew, then haul, these blocks (the heaviest weighs 300 tonnes), millennia before the wheel and the mechanical engine reached Brittany? And why? Theories and hypotheses abound, but common consensus is that they served some kind of sacred purpose – a spiritual impulse like that behind so many monuments built by humankind.

Just north of Carnac, a vast array of monoliths stand in several distinct alignments, all visible from the road, though fenced for controlled admission. The best way to appreciate their sheer size and numbers is to walk or bike between the **Ménec** and **Kerlescan** groups.

Great For...

☑ Don't Miss

Incredible Neolithic artefacts found in the region, on display at Carnac's Musée de Préhistoire (p146).

Alignements de Kermario

Kerlescan ○
Alignements ✪
de Kerlescan

Alignements   ✪***Alignements***
du Ménec   ***de Kermario***
Village du   ✪
Ménec   🏛 ***Maison des Mégalithes***
○

Carnac ○   ✪***Tumulus St-Michel***

ℹ Need to Know

In summer buses shuttle between the main monolith sites, Carnac-Ville and Carnac-Plage.

✗ Take a Break

Wolf down flambéed crêpes and *galettes* (savoury pancakes) at Chez Marie (p146) in Carnac.

★ Top Tip

Rent wheels to cycle between meg-aliths at A Bicyclette (p147) by Carnac-Plage.

Maison des Mégalithes

Near the stones, the **Maison des Méga-lithes** (☎02 97 52 29 81; www.menhirs-carnac.fr; rte des Alignements, D196; tour adult/child €6/free; ⊗9.30am-8pm Jul & Aug, 10am-5pm Sep-Apr, 9am-6pm May & Jun) explores the site's history and offers guided visits. Due to severe erosion, the sites are fenced off to allow the vegetation to regenerate; certain areas are accessible only by guided tour. October to March you can wander freely through parts – the Maison des Mégalithes has maps of what's open.

Alignments

Opposite the Maison des Mégalithes, the largest menhir field – with 1099 stones – is the **Alignements du Ménec**, 1km north of Carnac-Ville. From here, the D196 heads northeast for about 1.5km to the equally

impressive **Alignements de Kermario** (parts of which are open year-round). Climb the stone observation tower midway along the site to see the alignment from above.

The **Tumulus de Kercado** lies just east of Kermario and 500m to the south of the D196. It's the massive burial mound of a Neolithic chieftain dating from 3800 BC. Deposit your fee (€1) in an honour box at the entry gate. About 300m east of the Kercado turnoff along the D196, lies the parking area for the **Géant du Manio**. A 15-minute walk brings you to it, the highest menhir in the complex.

The easternmost of the major groups is the **Alignements de Kerlescan**, a smaller grouping also accessible in winter.

Tumulus St-Michel

Tumulus St-Michel, 400m northeast of the Carnac-Ville tourist office, and accessed off the D781 at the end of rue du Tumulus, is a gigantic burial mound with a church on top. It dates back to at least 5000 BC and offers sweeping views (exterior access only).

Jetty, St-Malo

OLIVER HOFFMANN / SHUTTERSTOCK ©

St-Malo

The enthralling port town of St-Malo on Brittany's north coast has a dramatically changing landscape. With one of the world's greatest tidal ranges, this town is nature's finest theatre – and every tourist's summer heaven.

Photo op paradise, St-Malo is an ancient walled city where brewing storms under blackened skies see waves lash the top of the ramparts ringing its beautiful walled city. Hours later, blue sky merges with the deep cobalt sea as the tide recedes, exposing broad beaches and creating land bridges to granite outcrop islands. Stunning!

Construction of the city fortifications began in the 12th century. The town became a key port during the 17th and 18th centuries as a base for both merchant ships and government-sanctioned privateers (pirates, basically) against the constant threat of the English.

Great For...

☑ Don't Miss

Eye-popping views of the old city from the château's lookout tower.

Intra-Muros

The tangle of streets within the walled city, known as Intra-Muros ('within the walls'), are a highlight of a visit to Brittany. Grand

RIEKEPHOTOS / SHUTTERSTOCK ©

ⓘ Need to Know

Visit the **tourist office** (☑08 25 13 52 00;
www.saint-malo-tourisme.com; esplanade
St-Vincent; ☺9am-7.30pm Mon-Sat, 10am-
6pm Sun Jul & Aug, shorter hours Sep-Jun, 🛜)
for helpful information.

✕ Take a Break

Throw back a Breton beer at **L'Aviso** (12
rue Point du Jour; ☺6pm-2am).

★ Top Tip

A combined ticket (€13/6 per adult/
child) gives you access to St-Malo's
four major monuments; buy it at the
Musée d'Histoire.

merchants' mansions and sea captains'
houses line the narrow lanes, and open
squares are tucked in its heart.

For the finest panoramas, stroll along
the **jetty** that pokes out to sea off the
southwestern tip of Intra-Muros, from
the end of which you'll get the wide-angle
view – or, to zoom in, clamber along the
top of the **ramparts** which surround the
town. Constructed at the end of the 17th
century under military architect Vauban,
and measuring 1.8km, the ramparts can be
accessed at several points, including at all
the main city gates.

The city's centrepiece, **Cathédrale
St-Vincent** (place Jean de Châtillon; ☺9.30am-
6pm), was constructed between the 12th and
18th centuries. During ferocious fighting in
1944 during WWII the cathedral was badly
hit; much of its original structure (including
its spire) was reduced to rubble – as was a

staggering 80% of the city. The cathedral
was rebuilt and reconsecrated in 1971.

For the full lowdown on the life and history of St-Malo, head to the **Musée d'Histoire** (☑02 99 40 71 57; www.ville-saint-malo.fr/
culture/les-musees; Château; adult/child €6/3;
☺10am-12.30pm & 2-6pm Apr-Sep, Tue-Sun
Oct-Mar) inside Château de St-Malo, built by
the dukes of Brittany in the 15th and 16th
centuries.

Île du Grand Bé

At low tide, cross the beach to walk out
via Porte des Bés to Île du Grand Bé, the
rocky islet where the great St-Malo-born
18th-century writer Chateaubriand is buried. About 100m beyond the island is the
privately owned, Vauban-built, 17th-cen-
tury **Fort du Petit Bé**. The owner runs
30-minute guided tours in French; leaflets
are available in English. Once the tide rush-
es in, the causeway remains impassable for
about six hours; check tide times with the
tourist office.

Le Palais (p144), Belle Île

Breton Island Life

Brittany's south coast islands, dotted with black sheep and crossed with craggy coastal paths and windswept cycling tracks, are big draws. Think turquoise waters, abundant wildflowers and little to do but walk, cycle or picnic in perfect peace.

Great For...

ⓘ Need to Know

Belle Île tourist office (☏02 97 31 81 93; www.belle-ile.com; quai Bonnelle, Le Palais; ⊙9am-1pm & 2-7pm Mon-Sat, to 1pm Sun Jul & Aug, shorter hours Sep-Jun; ☏)

★ **Top Tip**

Rent a bicycle on Belle Île in Le Palais; pay about €13 per day.

Belle Île

Belle Île (in full, Belle-Île-en-Mer, 'beautiful island in the sea') lives up to its name: rugged cliffs and rock stacks line the island's west coast while picturesque pastel ports nestle along the eastern side.

Accessed by ferries from Quiberon, the island has a population that swells tenfold in summer. Brittany's largest offshore island (20km by 9km) has two main settlements: the port of **Le Palais** on the east side of the island with a dramatic Vauban citadel, now a **history museum** (☏02 97 31 85 54; www.citadellevauban.com; Le Palais; adult/child €8/5; ☺9am-7pm Jul & Aug, shorter hours Sep-Dec & Feb-Jun); and smaller, even more charming **Sauzon** in the northeast.

The best way to appreciate the island's waterside charms is from the 95km coastal footpath. The fretted western coast has spectacular rock formations and caves, including **Grotte de l'Apothicairerie** where waves roll in from two sides; **Vives Eaux** (☏02 97 31 00 93; www.vives-eaux.fr; chemin de Port Puce, Sauzon; tours adult/child from €34/24, kayak rental per hr €11; ☺May-Oct) organises excellent kayaking expeditions and guided tours.

Just off the western side of the island, the magnificent rock stacks of **Aiguilles de Port Coton** that resemble *aiguilles* (needles) are a must-see for photographers. The name Port Coton comes from the way the sea foams around the rocks, creating foam like cotton wool. These dramatic rock formations were depicted in a series of famous canvases by Claude Monet.

The island's northernmost point juts out at **Pointe des Poulains**. Flanked by craggy

Sauzon

cliffs, this windswept headland is Belle Île's loftiest lookout, and was once the home of renowned actress Sarah Bernhardt. Her former fortress home is open to the public from April to October.

Belle Beaches

Belle Île is blessed with beautiful beaches. The largest is 2km-long **Plage des Grands Sables**, spanning the calm waters of the island's eastern side. Sheltered **Plage d'Herlin**, on the south side, is best for kids.

Don't Miss

Local *agneau de pré salé*, tasty lamb with a distinct savoury taste due to grazing on salty pastures. Pair with a crisp white wine.

CAPTBLACK76 / SHUTTERSTOCK ©

Golfe du Morbihan

Around 40 islands peep out from the shallow waters of the Morbihan Gulf, which forms a breathtakingly beautiful inland sea that's easily accessible from Vannes. Some islands are barely sandy specks of land, while others harbour communities of fishers, farmers and artistic types seduced by the island lifestyle. The bay's largest island is the 6km-long **Île aux Moines**. Nearby **Île d'Arz** is smaller – just 3km long and 1km wide – but it's the most scenic of the lot and features secluded sands and coastal walks. Tempted to stay? Both islands have a slew of B&Bs and eateries.

Lots of companies offer scenic cruises and ferry services to Île aux Moines and Île d'Arz and beyond. In high season check with **Navix** (📞08 25 13 21 00; www.navix.fr; ☺Apr-Sep) and **La Compagnie du Golfe** (📞02 97 01 22 80; www.compagnie-du-golfe.fr; Vannes; cruise adult/child from €16.50/11.50; ☺Apr-Sep). Year-round **Bateaux-Bus du Golfe** (📞02 97 44 44 40; www.ile-arz.fr; adult/child return €10.20/5.60; ☺6.30am-8pm) runs 10 to 14 boats per day between Vannes port or Conleau and Île d'Arz. **Izenah Croisières** (📞02 97 26 31 45; www.izenah-croisieres.com; adult/child return €5/2.70) runs boats from the port at Baden to Île aux Moines year-round.

Take a Break

On Belle Île, enjoy a kettle of mussels at bistro **Le Verre à Pied** (📞02 97 31 29 65; 3 place de la République, Le Palais; mains €13-20, lunch menus €16-19; ☺noon-2pm & 6-10pm Thu-Tue Feb-Dec) in central Le Palais. Finish with a slice of Breton cake for dessert.

Carnac

With enticing beaches and a pretty town centre, Carnac would be a popular tourist town even without its collection of magnificent megalithic sites, but when these are thrown into the mix you end up with a place that is unmissable on any ramble through Brittany.

Carnac, some 32km west of Vannes, comprises the old stone village Carnac-Ville and, 1.5km south, the seaside resort of Carnac-Plage, which is bordered by the 2km-long sandy beach, La Grande Plage.

◎ SIGHTS

Musée de Préhistoire   Museum
(☎02 97 52 22 04; www.museedecarnac.fr; 10 place de la Chapelle, Carnac-Ville; adult/child €6/2.50; ⏱10am-6.30pm Jul & Aug, 10am-12.30pm & 2-6pm Wed-Mon Apr-Jun & Sep, shorter hours Oct-Mar) The Musée de Préhistoire is choc full of the finds from the megalithic sites throughout the region. The museum chronicles life in and around Carnac from the Palaeolithic and Neolithic eras to the Middle Ages, and is a must for seeing beautifully made Neolithic axe heads, pottery, jewellery and other priceless artefacts.

⊗ EATING

Carnac is rife with tourist-focused eateries, but several of the hotels have great restaurants, and there is one gastronomic gem.

Chez Marie   Creperie €
(☎02 97 52 07 93; 3 place de l'Église, Carnac-Ville; mains €6-13, menus €10-15; ⏱noon-2pm & 7-10pm Wed-Sun) Established in 1959, this Carnac institution churns out savoury *galettes* and sweet crêpes in a charmingly traditional stone house opposite the church. Connoisseurs recommend its flambéed specialities, especially the Arzal *galette*, with scallops, apples and cider.

La Côte   Gastronomic €€€
(☎02 97 52 02 80; www.restaurant-la-cote.com; impasse Parc Er Forn, Kermario; lunch menu €26, dinner menus €37-83; ⏱12.15-2pm Wed-Sun, 7.15-9.15pm Tue-Sun) Top recommendation on the Morbihan coast goes to this Carnac

Chez Marie

VICTOR MASCHEK / SHUTTERSTOCK ©

restaurant run by Carnacois *maître-cuisinier* Pierre Michaud, who has won plaudits for his inventive cuisine that combines the very best Breton ingredients. The setting is another drawcard, with an elegant dining room and a soothing terrace overlooking a small fish pond. Find it in a quiet property close to the Alignements de Kermario.

Save room for dessert – homemade ice creams in flavours like lemongrass are delicious.

 INFORMATION

Tourist Office (☏02 97 52 13 52; www.ot-carnac. fr, 74 av des Druides, Carnac-Plage, ☺9.30am-7pm Mon-Sat, 3-7pm Sun Jul-Aug, 9.30am-12.30pm & 2-6pm Mon-Sat, 3-6pm Sun Apr-Jun & Sep, shorter hours rest of year; 🛜) Also has an office at Carnac-Ville, next to the church. Excellent map of nearby Neolithic sites. Has a smartphone app.

❶ GETTING THERE & AROUND

BICYCLE

Hire bikes and cycle buggies from **A Bicyclette** (☏02 97 52 75 08; www.velocarnac.com; 93bis av des Druides, Carnac-Plage; bicycle per day from €10, buggy per hour from €8) **down near the beach.**

BUS

The main bus stops are in Carnac-Ville, outside the police station on rue St-Cornély, and in Carnac-Plage, beside the tourist office. **Tim** (☏08 10 10 10 56; www.morbihan.fr; ticket €2) runs a daily bus (line 1) to Auray, Vannes and Quiberon (€2).

TRAIN

The nearest useful train station is in Auray, 12km to the northeast. SNCF has an office in the Carnac-Plage tourist office where you can buy advance tickets.

Quiberon

Quiberon (Kiberen in Breton) sits at the southern tip of a thin, 14km-long peninsula, called the **Presqu'île de Quiberon**, flanked

Celtic Fest

Celtic communities from Ireland, Scotland, Wales, Cornwall, the Isle of Man and Galicia in northwest Spain congregate with Bretons at the **Festival Interceltique de Lorient** (www.festival-interceltique.com; Lorient) over 10 days in early August. Upwards of 600,000 people descend on the city of Lorient, about 30km northwest of Carnac, so book well ahead if you're planning to stay in town for the festival.

Flag bearers in the parade
FRED TANNEAU / STRINGER ©

on the western side by the rocky, wave-lashed **Côte Sauvage** (Wild Coast). The setting is superb, with a heady mix of lovely beaches and rugged inlets, but the town itself is quite tacky, and finding a parking spot is like looking for a pot of gold at the end of a rainbow. Even so, it's wildly popular in summer and is also the departure point for ferries to Belle Île. For outdoorsy types, there are plenty of water sports available, from diving and snorkelling to sea kayaking and *char à voile* (sand yachting).

◎ SIGHTS & ACTIVITIES

Sillages   Kayaking
(☏06 81 26 75 08; www.kayak-sillages.com; 9 av de Groix, St-Pierre-Quiberon; adult/child from €20/17; ☺daily by reservation) What about a morning paddle far from the crowds along the Côte Sauvage? This reputable outfit based in St-Pierre-Quiberon (look for the 'Base Nautique') runs guided kayaking tours for all levels – beginners are welcome.

 Medieval Vannes

What a beauty! Overlooking the Golfe du Morbihan, Vannes is one of Brittany's most beautiful towns. Spectacular fortifications encircle meandering alleys and cobbled squares, leading down to a sparkling cafe-lined marina. The city preserves much of its medieval atmosphere, has a lively bar and restaurant scene year-round, and is a lovely stop en route to the glittering island-studded Golfe du Morbihan and nearby Neolithic sites.

Vannes' old town is surrounded by massive **ramparts**, in turn lined by a moat, and on the eastern edge flower-filled gardens. Tucked away behind rue des Vierges, stairs lead to the accessible section of the ramparts from which you can see the black-roofed **Vieux Lavoirs** (Old Laundry Houses) along the water. Or walk along rue Francis Decker, on the wall's eastern exterior, to take it all in.

Within the walls, the old city is a jumble of timber-framed houses and wonky merchants' mansions, especially around **place des Lices** and **place Henry IV**. Opposite the cathedral, **La Cohue** ([📞]02 97 01 63 00; www.mairie-vannes.fr; place St-Pierre; adult/child €4.60/free; [🕐]1.30-6pm Jun-Sep, Tue-Sun Oct-May) has variously been a produce market, a law court and the seat of the Breton parliament. Today it's a well-curated fine-arts museum.

Timber-framed houses, Vannes
PERESANZ / SHUTTERSTOCK ©

La Grande Plage   Beach
La Grande Plage is a family-friendly beach; bathing spots towards the peninsula's tip are less crowded.

EATING

Seafood, of course, features on Quiberon menus. **Le Petit Hôtel du Grand Large** ([📞]02 97 58 31 99; www.lepetithoteldugrandlarge. fr; 11 quai St-Ivy, Portivy; d €115-135; [🛜]) has earned a Michelin star for its take.

Le Vivier   Seafood €
([📞]02 97 50 12 60; Côte Sauvage; mains €8-25; [🕐]noon-3pm & 7-8pm Tue-Sun Feb-Nov, plus Mon in Jul & Aug) The food is almost secondary at this convivial eatery dramatically perched on a small cliff on the Côte Sauvage; bookings are essential for the top tables, squeezed onto a sunny terrace hovering above the rocky coastline. The menu is plain and unpretentious – think salads, mussels, smoked fish and shellfish.

From central Quiberon, follow the signs north to 'Côte Sauvage' for about 2km.

Restaurant de La Criée   Seafood €€
([📞]02 97 30 53 09; 11 quai de l'Océan; mains €20-30, menus €19-25; [🕐]12.15-2pm Tue-Sun, 7.15-9pm Tue-Sat) On the harbour front, La Criée has long been a favourite among fish lovers. Nautically themed and run by a talented team, the seafood here is a cut above most of Quiberon's bistros. Dover sole, fillet monkfish, brill cooked with apples, and red mullet in a fennel sauce all feature.

Villa Margot   Modern French €€
([📞]02 97 50 33 89; www.villamargot.fr; 7 rue de Port Maria; mains €23-29, lunch menu €18, other menus €34-45; [🕐]12.15-1.30pm & 7.15-9.30pm Thu-Mon) The interior of this stunning stone restaurant looks like it would be at home in a chic Parisian *quartier,* with original art on the walls, flower-shaped opaque glass light fittings, hot-pink and brown colour schemes, and lobsters clawing in the live tank. That is, until you head out onto the

Restaurants in Quiberon

timber deck, which has direct access to the beach for a post-repast stroll.

ℹ INFORMATION

Tourist Office (☐02 97 50 07 84; www.quiberon. com; 14 rue de Verdun; ☺9am-7pm Mon-Sat, 10am-1pm & 2-5pm Sun Aug, shorter hours rest of year; ☎) Between the train station and La Grande Plage.

ℹ GETTING THERE & AROUND

BICYCLE

Cycles Loisirs (☐02 97 50 31 73; www.cycles loisirs.free.fr; 32 rue Golvan; touring/mountain bikes per day from €9.50/13) 200m north of the tourist office, rents touring/mountain bikes.

Cyclomar (☐02 97 50 26 00; www.cyclomar. fr; 47 place Hoche; touring/mountain bikes per day from €9.50/11, scooters incl helmet per day from €39.50) Around 200m south of the tourist office, rents out bikes at similar prices as well as scooters. It also runs an operation from the train station during July and August.

BOAT

Compagnie Océane (☐02 97 35 02 00, 08 20 05 61 56; www.compagnie-oceane.fr; adult/child return €34.50/18.50) Runs ferries between Quiberon and Belle-Île, and Houat and Hoëdic islands. Park at Sémaphore car park 1.5km north of the harbour front, and take the free shuttle to the port.

BUS

Quiberon is connected by **Tim** (p147) bus line 1 with Carnac (45 minutes), Auray (1¼ hours) and Vannes (1¾ hours). Buses stop at the train station and at place Hoche, near the tourist office and the beach.

CAR

High-summer traffic is hellish – consider leaving your vehicle at the 1100-spot Sémaphore car park (€4.80 for up to four hours, €13.70 for 24 hours, April to September), 1.5km north of the harbour front, and walking or taking the free shuttle bus into town. Parking is much easier in town in winter.

CHAMPAGNE

Champagne at a Glance...

Champagne arouses the senses: eyes feast on vertical processions of tiny, sparkling bubbles; the nose breathes in the heavenly bouquet of fermentation; the ears rejoice at the clink of glasses and the subtle fizz; the palate tingles with every sip. The imagination and intellect are roused as Champagne cellar visits reveal the magical processes that transform the world's most pampered grapes into this Unesco World Heritage–listed region's fabled wines.

Despite the prestige of their vines, the people of Champagne offer a warm, surprisingly easy-going welcome, both in the stylish cities and along the Champagne Routes, which wend their way through villages to family-run cellars and vineyards.

Champagne in Two Days

Begin in the considered capital of Champagne, Épernay. Buy a picnic at the town's covered **food market** (p167) before touring your pick of the world-famous Champagne houses. Head out of town afterwards for a picnic lunch amid vines in Hautvillers, first delightful stop on the picturesque Vallée de la Marne driving route. Day two, head to Reims to visit its **cathedral** (p156) and more Champagne houses.

Champagne in Four Days

With four days, you can linger longer in the countryside. Spend two days slowly meandering along the Côte des Blancs Champagne Route; overnight in an idyllically rural B&B in Avize or Le Mesnil-sur-Oger, and before setting out book a tour in advance at the **Musée de la Vigne et du Vin** (p160).

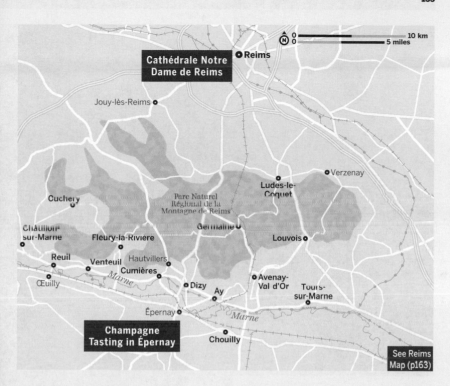

Cathédrale Notre Dame de Reims

Reims

Jouy-lès-Reims

Verzenay

Ludes-le-Coquet

Cuchery

Parc Naturel Régional de la Montagne de Reims

Châtillon-sur-Marne

Fleury-la-Rivière

Germaine

Louvois

Reuil

Venteuil

Hautvillers

Cumières

Marne

Œuilly

Dizy

Ay

Avenay-Val d'Or

Tours-sur-Marne

Épernay

Marne

Champagne Tasting in Épernay

Chouilly

See Reims Map (p163)

Arriving in Champagne

Reims train station Frequent services to/from Paris Gare de l'Est (€19 to €63, 46 minutes to one hour, 12 to 17 daily) and Épernay (€7, 20 to 42 minutes, 16 daily). Car rental agencies next to the station on bd Joffre.

Car The region makes a refreshing and convenient stopover for motorists driving from the Channel ports or Paris southeastward towards Lyon or Provence.

Sleeping

Reims and Épernay are appealing bases for driving tours along the Montagne de Reims, Vallée de la Marne and Côte des Blancs Champagne Routes, with a plentiful supply of characterful hotels and B&Bs. Plan ahead and you can find charming digs in the heart of wine country – local tourist offices and the website www.champagne-ardenne-tourism.co.uk can advise.

PH8.CZ (RICHARD SEMIK) / SHUTTERSTOCK ©

Wine cellar

Champagne Tasting in Épernay

Prosperous Épernay, home to many of the world's most celebrated Champagne houses, is the finest spot on earth for tasting bubbly – in a cinematic labyrinth of ancient subterranean cellars.

Great For...

☑ **Don't Miss**

The stash of 300 Champagne varieties to pick from at C. Comme (p166).

Beneath the streets in 110km of subterranean cellars, more than 200 million bottles of Champagne are being aged. In 1950 one such cellar – owned by the irrepressible Mercier family – hosted a car rally without the loss of a single bottle!

Moët & Chandon

This prestigious **maison de Champagne** (✆03 26 51 20 20; www.moet.com; 20 av de Champagne; adult incl 1/2 glasses €23/28, 10-18yr €10; ⏱tours 9.30-11.30am & 2-4.30pm daily Apr–mid-Nov, Mon-Fri mid-Nov–Mar) offers frequent one-hour tours, offering a peek at part of its 28km labyrinth of *caves* (cellars). At the shop you can pick up a 15L bottle of Brut Impérial for just €1500; a standard bottle costs €31.

Dom Pérignon statue (p166), Moët & Chandon

PHB.CZ (RICHARD SEMIK) / SHUTTERSTOCK ©

ⓘ Need to Know

Reserve cellar tours with *dégustation* (tasting) at Épernay's **tourist office** (☏03 26 53 33 00; www.ot-epernay.fr; 7 av de Champagne; ⊙9am-12.30pm & 1.30-7pm Mon-Sat, 10.30am-1pm & 2-4.30pm Sun, closed Sun mid-Oct–mid-Apr; 🛜).

✕ Take a Break

Coffee and *baba* (a cork-shaped, Champagne-fuelled pastry with vanilla cream) at Pâtisserie Vincent Dallet (p167).

★ Top Tip

Rent bicycles and get cycling maps at the tourist office (p167).

32 06 22; www.georgescartier.com; 9 rue Jean Chandon Moët; adult incl 1/2 glasses €12/16, 2-glass Grand Cru €22, 3-glass vintage €35; ⊙tours 10.30am, noon, 2.30pm & 4pm Tue-Sun) is atmospheric. Look out for the graffiti dating to when they were used as bunkers during WWII.

De Castellane

The 45-minute tours, in French and English, at **De Castellane** (☏03 26 51 19 11; www.castellane.com; 57 rue de Verdun; adult incl 1 glass €14, under 12yr free; ⊙tours 10-11am & 2-5pm, closed Christmas–mid-Mar) take in a museum dedicated to elucidating the *méthode champenoise* and its diverse technologies. The reward for climbing the 237 steps up the 66m-high tower (built 1905) is a fine panoramic view.

Taste Like a Pro

Two-hour workshops at **Villa Bissinger** (☏03 26 55 78 78; www.villabissinger.com; 15 rue Jeanson, Ay; 2hr workshop €25; ⊙2.30pm 1st Sat of month Apr-Nov), home to the International Institute for the Wines of Champagne, are educative and fun. Sessions cover the basics (producers, grape varieties etc) and include tasting of four Champagnes. Find it 3.5km northeast of Épernay in Ay. Reserve.

Mercier

France's most popular brand, **Mercier** (☏03 26 51 22 22; www.champagnemercier.fr; 68-70 av de Champagne; adult incl 1/2/3 glasses €14/19/22 Mon-Fri, €16/21/25 Sat & Sun, 12-17yr €8; ⊙tours 9.30-11.30am & 2-4.30pm, closed mid-Dec–mid-Feb) was founded in 1847 by Eugène Mercier, a trailblazer in the field of eye-catching publicity stunts and the virtual creator of the cellar tour. Everything here is flashy, including the 160,000L barrel that took two decades to build (for the Universal Exposition of 1889), the lift that transports you 30m underground and the laser-guided touring train.

Champagne Georges Cartier

Hewn out of the chalk in the 18th century, the warren of cellars and passageways at **Champagne Georges Cartier** (☏03 26

EVGENY SHMULEV / SHUTTERSTOCK ©

Cathédrale Notre Dame de Reims

There is no finer 360-degree, bird's-eye view of this luxuriant and very flat French region of bubbly vineyards than from the top of Reims' cathedral. Scale its tower and swoon.

Great For...

☑ **Don't Miss**

One-hour tours of the cathedral tower (250-step alert!); book at Palais du Tau.

Imagine the egos and extravagance of a French royal coronation. The focal point of such bejewelled pomposity was Reims' resplendent Gothic cathedral, begun in 1211 on a site occupied by churches since the 5th century. The cathedral was seriously damaged by artillery and fire during WWI, and was repaired during the interwar years, thanks, in part, to significant donations from the American Rockefeller family. It has been inscribed on Unesco's list of World Heritage Sites since 1991.

Façade

Nothing can prepare you for that first sky-ward glimpse of Reims' gargantuan Gothic cathedral, rising golden and imperious above the city. To get the most impressive first view, approach the cathedral from the west, along rue Libergier. Here your gaze will be drawn

Rose window

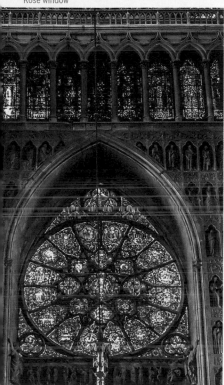

KIEV.VICTOR / SHUTTERSTOCK ©

Cathédrale ❶ Notre Dame

❶ Need to Know

www.cathedrale-reims.culture.fr; place du Cardinal Luçon; tower adult/child €7.50/free, incl Palais du Tau €11/free; ⏰7.30am-7.15pm, tower tours hourly 10am-4pm Tue-Sat, 2-4pm Sun May-Sep, 10am-4pm Sat, 2-4pm Sun mid-Mar-Apr

✕ Take a Break

Enjoy a glass of Champagne at stunning art deco cafe, Café du Palais (p165).

★ Top Tip

Reims' tourist office (p165) rents audioguides (€6) for self-paced cathedral tours.

to the heavily restored architectural features of the façade, lavishly encrusted with sculptures. Among them is the 13th-century **L'Ange au Sourire** (Smiling Angel), presiding beneficently above the central portal, and the worn figure of **Goliath**, held in place with metal straps on the west façade.

Coronations

The single most famous event to take place in the cathedral was the coronation of Charles VII, with Joan of Arc at his side, on 17 July 1429. This is one of 25 coronations that took place here between 1223 and 1825.

Interior Treasures

The interior is a rainbow of stained-glass windows; the finest are the western façade's 12-petalled **great rose window** – under restoration at the time of research – the north

transept's rose window and the vivid **Chagall creations** (1974) in the central axial chapel.

Other interior highlights include a flamboyant Gothic **organ case** (15th and 18th centuries) topped with a figure of Christ, a 15th-century wooden **astronomical clock** and a statue of **Joan of Arc** in full body armour (1901).

Palais du Tau

When in town for their coronations, French princes stayed at Palais du Tau – and threw sumptuous banquets here afterwards. Today another Unesco World Heritage Site, the lavish former archbishop's residence was redesigned in neoclassical style between 1671 and 1710. Its museum displays truly exceptional statuary, liturgical objects and tapestries from the cathedral, some in the impressive, Gothic-style **Salle de Tau** (Great Hall). Treasures worth seeking out include the 9th-century talisman of Charlemagne and Saint Remi's golden, gem-encrusted chalice from the 12th century.

Driving Tours

Vallée de la Marne Champagne Route

A stronghold of pinot meunier vines, this 90km itinerary winds from Épernay to Dormans, heading more or less west along the hillsides north of the River Marne, then circles back to the east along the river's south bank. The GR14 long-distance walking trail and its variants (eg GR141) pass through the area.

Hautvillers

Perched above a sea of emerald vines and ablaze with forsythia and tulips in spring, Hautvillers, 6km north of Épernay, is where Dom Pierre Pérignon (1638–1715) is popularly believed to have created Champagne. He is buried in the **Église Abbatiale**. The village is one of Champagne's prettiest, with ubiquitous medieval-style wrought-iron signs providing pictorial clues to the activities taking place on the other side of the wall.

On the main square, the **tourist office** (✆03 26 57 06 35; www.tourisme-hautvillers. com; place de la République; ⊙9.30am-1pm & 1.30-5.30pm Mon-Sat, 10am-4pm Sun, shorter hours in winter) has maps detailing vineyard walks. For stylish Champagne tasting, hit **Au 36** (www.au36.net; 36 rue Dom Pérignon; ⊙10.30am-6pm Tue-Sun, closed Christmas-early Mar), a slinky wine boutique with a 'wall' of Champagne arranged by aroma and a laid-back tasting room.

Gorge on astonishing **vineyard views** north of the centre along route de Fismes (D386); south along route de Cumières (a road leading to D1); along the GR14 long-distance walking trail; and local vineyard footpaths.

Cuchery

You're assured a warm welcome and a fascinating cellar tour at **Albert Levasseur** (✆03 26 58 11 38; www.champagne-levasseur. fr; 6 rue Sorbier, Cuchery; ⊙9am-noon & 2-5pm Mon-Fri, Sat by appointment), run by a friendly Franco-Irish couple, which turns grapes grown on 4.2 hectares into 35,000 to

Hautvillers and the Marne River

40,000 bottles of Champagne each year. Phone or email ahead if possible – if not drop by and knock. Find the hamlet of Cuchery 18km northwest of Épernay on the D24.

Châtillon-sur-Marne

Sloping picturesquely down a hillside braided with vines, this village's biggest claim to fame is as the home town of Pope Urban II. A map panel on central Place Urbain II details an 11km, four-hour vineyard walk. Its cellars also produce Champagnes worth lingering for. The **tourist office** (☑03 26 58 32 86; www.tourisme-chatillon-marne.fr; 4 rue de l'Église; ⏰10am-1pm & 2.30-6.30pm Tue-Sun, 2.30-6.30pm Mon, shorter hours Oct-Mar) has plenty of info on the village and the surrounding region.

Œuilly

Blink and you'll miss dinky Œuilly, but that would be a shame. This cute grey-stone village, flower-draped in summer, is topped by a 13th-century church and home to the **Écomusée d'Œuilly** (www.ecomusee-oeuilly.fr; cour des Maillets; adult/child €7/4; ⏰tours 10.30am & 2pm Wed-Mon) spotlighting wine-growing life of yore.

Côte des Blancs Champagne Route

This 100km route, planted almost exclusively with white chardonnay grapes (the name means 'hillside of the whites'), begins along Épernay's majestic av du Champagne and then heads south to Sézanne and beyond. The gently rolling landscape is at its most attractive in late summer and autumn.

Cramant

For views of the neatly tended vines and patchwork colours of the Champagne countryside, check out the view from the ridge above this village, whose northern entrance is adorned by a two-storey-high Champagne bottle. Find it 7.5km southeast of Épernay on D10.

Champagne Types

Blanc de Blancs Champagne made using only chardonnay grapes. Fresh and elegant, with very small bubbles and a bouquet reminiscent of 'yellow fruits' such as pear and plum.

Blanc de Noirs A full-bodied, deep-golden Champagne made solely with black grapes (despite the colour). Often rich and refined, with great complexity and a long finish.

Rosé Pink Champagne (mostly served as an aperitif), with a fresh character and summer fruit flavours. Made by adding a small percentage of red pinot noir to white Champagne.

Prestige Cuvée The crème de la crème of Champagne. Usually made with grapes from *grand cru* vineyards and priced and bottled accordingly.

Millésimé Vintage Champagne produced from a single crop during an exceptional year. Most Champagne is nonvintage.

Wine racks
ID1974 / SHUTTERSTOCK ©

Avize

Right in the heart of Blancs des Blancs country and surrounded by rows of immaculately tended vines, Avize is lauded far and wide for its outstanding Champagnes. It's home to the **Champagne High School of Wine Making** (www.avizeviticampus.fr; rue d'Oger) and the renowned **Sanger Cellars** (☑03 26 57 79 79; www.sanger.fr; 33 rue du Rempart du Midi; tour incl 2-/4-/9-flute tasting €10/17.50/30, full-day masterclass €60;

Making Fizz

Champagne is made from the red pinot noir (38%), the black pinot meunier (35%) or the white chardonnay (27%) grape. Each vine is vigorously pruned and trained to produce a small quantity of high-quality grapes. Indeed, to maintain exclusivity (and price), the designated areas where grapes used for Champagne can be grown and the amount of wine produced each year are limited.

Making Champagne according to the traditional method *(méthode champenoise)* is a complex procedure. There are two fermentation processes, the first in casks and the second after the wine has been bottled and had sugar and yeast added. Bottles are then aged in cellars for two to five years, depending on the *cuvée* (vintage).

During the two months in early spring that the bottles are aged in cellars kept at 12°C, the wine turns effervescent. The sediment that forms in the bottle is removed by *remuage,* a painstakingly slow process in which each bottle, stored horizontally, is rotated slightly every day for weeks until the sludge works its way to the cork. Next comes *dégorgement:* the neck of the bottle is frozen, creating a blob of solidified Champagne and sediment, then removed.

FOODPICTURES / SHUTTERSTOCK ©

⊘8am-noon & 2-5pm Mon-Fri) where tours take in both traditional equipment and the latest high-tech production facilities;

they conclude with tasting and a shopping spree in the discounted *cave* (cellar). The entrance is on the D19; if the door is locked, push the intercom button.

Once the abbey church of a Benedictine convent, **Église St-Nicolas** (rue de l'Église, D10) mixes Romanesque, Flamboyant Gothic and Renaissance styles. From here, aptly named rue de la Montagne leads up the hill (towards Grauves), past an oversized Champagne bottle, to **Parc Vix** (D19), which affords panoramic vineyard views; a map sign details a 6.5km, two-hour walk through forest and field.

Oger

The tiny hamlet of Oger is known for its *grand cru* fields, prize-winning flower gardens and the **Musée du Mariage** (www.champagne-henry-devaugency.fr; 1 rue d'Avize, D10; adult/child €8/free; ⊘9.30am-noon & 2-6pm Tue-Sun). Featuring colourful and often gaudy objects associated with 19th-century marriage traditions, highlights include a tableau of newlyweds in their nuptial bed – but they're not alone, for they've been woken up early by family and friends bearing Champagne, chocolate and broad smiles. The collection was assembled by the parents of the owner of Champagne Henry de Vaugency (founded 1732), an eighth-generation Champagne grower. An explanatory sheet in English is available. Admission includes a Champagne tasting.

Le Mesnil-sur-Oger

This comely wine-growing village, 15km south of Épernay, is among the most famous in Champagne, with 100% of its chardonnay vines producing the superlative *grand cru* Champagnes. It's worth the pilgrimage alone for an insight into Champagne making and its history at the **Musée de la Vigne et du Vin** (⊘03 26 57 50 15; www.champagne-launois.fr; 2 av Eugène Guillaume, cnr D10; adult incl 3 flutes €12; ⊘tours 10am Mon-Fri, 10.30am Sat & Sun). This wine museum, assembled by a family that has been making Champagne since 1872, is so outstanding that it's worth planning your day around a two-hour tour. Highlights include a massive 16-tonne oak-beam grape press from 1630. Reservations can be made by phone or through their website; tours are available in French and English.

Montagne de Reims Champagne Route

Linking Reims with Épernay by skirting the Parc Natural Régional de la Montagne de Reims, a regional park covering the forested Reims Mountain plateau, this meandering, 70km route passes through vineyards planted mainly with pinot noir vines.

Verzenay

With vines spreading like a ribbed blanket over the hillsides and top-of-the-beanstalk views from its lighthouse, Verzenay makes an attractive stop on the Montagne de Reims Champagne Route. Its vines are planted mostly with pinot noir grapes – 100% *grand cru*.

For the region's best introduction to the art of growing grapes and the cycles of the seasons, head to its **Phare de Verzenay**

(Verzenay Lighthouse; www.lepharedeverzenay. com; D26; lighthouse adult/child €3/2, museum €8/4, combined ticket €9/5; ⊙10am-5pm Tue-Fri, to 5.30pm Sat & Sun, closed Jan), on a hilltop at the eastern edge of the village. Exactly 101 spiral stairs lead to the top of the lighthouse, constructed as a publicity stunt in 1909, which rewards visitors with unsurpassed 360-degree views of vine, field and forest – and, if you're lucky, a tiny TGV zipping by in the distance.

The Sillery sugar mill, visible on the horizon, turns an astounding 16,000 tonnes of beets (a major regional crop) into 2600 tonnes of sugar each day! After brushing up on the seasonal processes involved in Champagne production in the museum, stop by the tasting room for a glass of fizz (there are 30 varieties to sample).

Parc Natural Régional de la Montagne de Reims

The 500-sq-km Montagne de Reims Regional Park is best known for a botanical curiosity, 800 mutant beech trees known as faux de Verzy (see http://verzy.verzenay.

Vineyard, Épernay (p166)

online.fr for photos). To get a good look at the trees, which have torturously twisted trunks and branches that hang down like an umbrella, take the Balade des Faux forest walk from 'Les Faux' parking lot, 2km up D34 from Verzy (situated on D26).

Across D34, a 500m gravel path leads through the forest to a *point de vue* (panoramic viewpoint) – next to a concrete WWI bunker – atop 288m-high Mont Sinaï.

Reims

Meticulously restored after WWI and again following WWII, Reims is endowed with handsome pedestrian boulevards, Roman remains, art deco cafes and a flourishing fine-dining scene that counts among it four Michelin-starred restaurants. Along with Épernay, it is the most important centre of Champagne production.

◎ SIGHTS

Basilique St-Rémi   Basilica
(place du Chanoine Ladame; ⊘8am-7pm) FREE
This 121m-long former Benedictine abbey church, a Unesco World Heritage Site, mixes Romanesque elements from the mid-11th century (the worn but stunning nave and transept) with early Gothic features from the latter half of the 12th century (the choir, with a large triforium gallery and, way up top, tiny clerestory windows).

Next door, **Musée St-Rémi** (53 rue Simon; adult/child €4/free; ⊘2-6.30pm Mon-Fri, to 7pm Sat & Sun), in a 17th- and 18th-century abbey, features local Gallo-Roman archaeology, tapestries and 16th- to 19th-century military history.

Musée des Beaux-Arts Art Museum
(8 rue Chanzy; adult/child €4/free; ⊘10am-noon & 2-6pm Wed-Mon) Lodged in an 18th-century abbey, this museum's rich collection stars one of four versions of Jacques-Louis David's world-famous *The Death of Marat* (yes, the bloody corpse in the bathtub), 27 works by Camille Corot (only the Louvre has more), 13 portraits by German

Renaissance painters Cranach the Elder and the Younger, lots of Barbizon School landscapes, some art nouveau creations by Émile Gallé, and two works each by Monet, Gauguin and Pissarro.

Joan Of Arc Statue   Statue
(place du Parvis) A strangely expressionless statue of Joan of Arc, raised high on a rearing horse and bearing a sword, graces this square facing the cathedral. The so-called Maid of Orléans stood alongside Charles VII for his coronation at the cathedral on 17 July 1429.

Cryptoportique   Historic Site
(place du Forum; ⊘2-6pm Jun-Sep) FREE One of Reims' Roman standouts, the below-street-level Cryptoportique is thought to have been used for grain storage in the 3rd century AD.

⊕ TOURS

The musty *caves* (cellars) and dusty bottles of the 10 Reims-based Champagne houses (known as *maisons* – literally, 'houses') can be visited on guided tours. The following places both have fancy websites, cellar temperatures of 10°C to 12°C (bring warm clothes!) and frequent English-language tours that end, *naturellement*, with a tasting session.

Taittinger   Champagne House
(📞03 26 85 45 35; www.taittinger.com; 9 place St-Nicaise; tours €17-45; ⊘9.30am-5.30pm, shorter hours & closed weekends Oct-Mar) The headquarters of Taittinger are an excellent place to come for a clear, straightforward presentation on how Champagne is actually made – there's no claptrap about 'the Champagne mystique' here. Parts of the cellars occupy 4th-century Roman stone quarries; other bits were excavated by 13th-century Benedictine monks. No need to reserve. Situated 1.5km southeast of Reims' centre; take the Citadine 1 or 2 bus to the St-Nicaise or Salines stops.

Reims

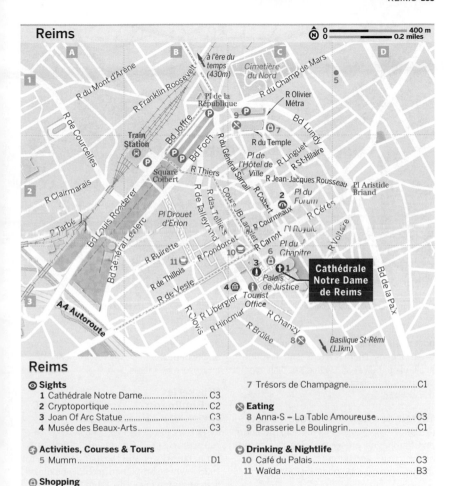

Reims

Mumm   Champagne House

(☎03 26 49 59 70; www.mumm.com; 34 rue du Champ de Mars; tours incl tasting €20-45; ☺tours 9.30am-1pm & 2-6pm, shorter hours & closed Sun Oct-Mar) Mumm (pronounced 'moom'), the only *maison* in central Reims, was founded in 1827 and is now the world's third-largest producer (almost eight million bottles a year). Engaging and edifying guided tours take you through cellars filled with 25 million bottles of fine bubbly and

conclude with a tasting. Wheelchair accessible. Phone ahead if possible.

⋒ SHOPPING

Trésors de Champagne   Wine

(www.boutique-tresors-champagne.com; 2 rue Olivier Métra; ☺2-7pm Tue & Wed, 10.30am-12.30pm & 2-7pm Thu & Fri, 10am-7pm Sat) Strikingly illuminated by Champagne bottles, this swish new wine boutique-cum-bar plays

Café du Palais

host to 28 vintners and more than 170 Champagnes. There is a different selection available to taste each week. Keep an eye out, too, for tasting workshops posted on the website.

Terroir des Rois   Food & Drinks
(8 rue du Préau; ⏱10am-7pm Tue-Sun) Stock up on Champagne, preserves, wine, macarons, *biscuits roses* and other regional treats at this welcoming shop near the cathedral.

🍴 EATING

A tempting array of delis, patisseries and chocolatiers line up along rue de Mars, near Halles du Boulingrin. Place du Forum is a great place to watch the world drift languidly by at bistros, cafes and bars with pavement seating.

à l'ère du temps   Crêperie €
(☎03 26 06 16 88; www.aleredutemps.com; 123 av de Laon; lunch menu €10, mains €7-14; ⏱11.45am-2pm & 6.45-9.30pm Tue-Sat) A short stroll north of place de la République brings you to this sweet and simple crêperie. It does a roaring trade in home-made crêpes, buckwheat *galettes* (savoury pancakes) and gourmet salads.

Brasserie Le Boulingrin   Brasserie €€
(☎03 26 40 96 22; www.boulingrin.fr; 29-31 rue de Mars; menus €20-29; ⏱noon-2.30pm & 7-10.30pm Mon-Sat) A genuine, old-time brasserie – the decor and zinc bar date back to 1925 – whose ambience and cuisine make it an enduring favourite. From September to June, the culinary focus is on *fruits de mer* (seafood) like Breton oysters. There's always a €9.50 lunch special.

Anna-S – La Table Amoureuse   Traditional French €€
(☎03 26 89 12 12; www.annas-latableamoureuse. com; 6 rue Gambetta; 3-course lunch €17.50, dinner menus €29-47; ⏱noon-1.30pm & 7-9pm Tue & Thu-Sat, noon-1.30pm Wed & Sun) So what if the decor is chintzy – there is a reason why this bistro is as busy as a beehive. Friendly service and a menu packed with well-done classics – Arctic char with Champagne jus, fillet of veal in rich, earthy morel sauce –

hit the mark every time. The three-course lunch is a steal at €17.50.

l'Assiette
Champenoise   Gastronomic €€€

(📞03 26 84 64 64; www.assiettechampenoise.com; 40 av Paul-Vaillant-Couturier, Tinqueux; menus €95-255; ⊙noon-2pm & 7.30-10pm Thu-Mon, 7.30-10pm Wed) Heralded far and wide as one of Champagne's finest tables and crowned with the holy grail of three Michelin stars, L'Assiette Champenoise is headed up by chef Arnaud Lallemen. Listed by ingredients, his intricate, creative dishes rely on outstanding produce and play up integral flavours – be it Breton lobster, or milk-fed lamb with preserved vegetables. One for special occasions.

DRINKING & NIGHTLIFE

Though Reims is an upbeat university city, it is still more a place of wine-sipping sophistication than all-night raves. The liveliest bars, cafes and pubs huddle around place Drouet d'Erlon, rue Chanzy and place du Forum. Champagne is, naturally, the tipple of choice.

Café du Palais   Cafe

(www.cafedupalais.fr; 14 place Myron-Herrick; ⊙9am-9.30pm Tue-Sat) Run by the same family since 1930, this art deco cafe is *the* place to sip a glass of Champagne. Lit by a skylight is an extraordinary collection of bric-a-brac ranging from the inspired to the kitsch.

Waïda   Tearoom

(5 place Drouet d'Erlon; ⊙7.30am-7.30pm Tue-Fri, 7.30am-8pm Sat, 8am-2pm & 3.30-7.30pm Sun) A tearoom and confectioner with old-fashioned mirrors, mosaics and marble. This is a good place to pick up a box of Reims' famous *biscuits roses,* traditionally nibbled with Champagne, rainbow-bright macarons and divine *religieuses* (cream-filled puff pastries).

ℹ INFORMATION

The **tourist office** (📞03 26 77 45 00; www.reims-tourisme.com; 6 rue Rockefeller; ⊙10am-6pm Mon-Sat, 10am-12.30pm & 1.30-5pm Sun)

 Visit Troyes

When the bubbles get too much, head south to Troyes, a handsome town graced with one of France's finest ensembles of half-timbered houses and Gothic churches. Often overlooked, it's one of the best places in France to get a sense of what Europe looked like back when Molière was penning his finest plays and the *Three Musketeers* were swashbuckling. Several unique and very worthwhile museums are another lure.

All at once imposing and delicate with its filigree stonework, Troyes' **cathedral** (place St-Pierre; ⊙9am-noon & 1-5pm Mon-Sat, 11.30am-5pm Sun) is a stellar example of Champenois Gothic architecture. The flamboyant west façade dates from the mid-1500s, while the 114m-long interior is illuminated by a spectacular series of 180 stained-glass windows (13th to 17th centuries) that shine like jewels when it's sunny. Also notable is the fantastical baroque organ (1730s) sporting musical *putti* (cherubs), and a tiny treasury (open July and August only) with enamels from the Meuse Valley.

Lunch at **Le Valentino** (📞03 25 73 14 14; http://levalentino.com; 35 rue Paillot de Montabert; menus €28-58; ⊙noon-1.30pm & 7.30-9.30pm Tue-Sat), a rose-hued 17th-century restaurant with cobbled courtyard and top-notch modern French cuisine. Post-lunch, hit Troyes' outlet stores stuffed with brand-name clothing and accessories (a legacy of the city's long-time role as France's knitwear capital).

Nights on the Fizz

It may come as little surprise that the tipple of choice in Épernay is Champagne, and it's as readily available (and almost as reasonably priced) in the bars dotted about town as wine is elsewhere.

Central rue Gambetta is a fine starting point for a night on the fizz. At No 8, the downstairs cellar of wine bar **C. Comme** (www.c-comme.fr; 8 rue Gambetta; light meals €7.50-14.50, 6-glass Champagne tasting €33-39; ☺10am-8.30pm Sun-Wed, to 11pm Thu, to midnight Fri & Sat) stashes away 300 different varieties of Champagne; sample them (from €6 a glass) in the softly lit bar-bistro upstairs. Accompany with a tasting plate of regional cheese, charcuterie and *rillettes* (pork pâté). We love the funky bottle-top tables and relaxed ambience.

A few doors down at No 17, **La Fine Bulle** (The Fine Bubble, 17 rue Gambetta; ☺boutique 10am-midnight, bar 6.30pm-11pm Mon-Thu, 6.30pm-midnight Fri-Sat) (The Fine Bubble) is a smart Champagne bar, boutique and restaurant rolled into one. Each week there are five/six (€15/18) Champagnes available for tasting.

has stacks of information on the Champagne region and Reims (plus free city maps).

GETTING THERE & AROUND

From Reims' train station, 1km northwest of the cathedral, frequent services include:

Paris Gare de l'Est €19 to €63, 46 minutes to one hour, 12 to 17 daily.

Épernay €7, 20 to 42 minutes, 16 daily.

Épernay

Prosperous Épernay, the self-proclaimed capitale du Champagne and home to many of the world's most celebrated Champagne houses, is the best place for touring cellars and sampling bubbly.

SIGHTS

Avenue de Champagne   Street
Épernay's handsome avenue de Champagne fizzes with *maisons de champagne* (Champagne houses). The boulevard is lined with mansions and neoclassical villas, rebuilt after WWI. Peek through wrought-iron gates at Moët's private **Hôtel Chandon**, an early-19th-century pavilion-style residence set in landscaped gardens, which counts Wagner among its famous past guests. The haunted-looking **Château Perrier**, a redbrick mansion built in 1854 in neo–Louis XIII style, is aptly placed at number 13! The roundabout presents photo ops with its giant cork and bottle top.

Dom Pérignon   Statue
Everyone who visits Moët & Chandon invariably stops to strike a pose next to the statue of **Dom Pérignon** (c 1638–1715), after whom the *prestige cuvée* is named. The Benedictine monk played a pivotal role in making Champagne what it is – perfecting the process of using a second, in-the-bottle fermentation to make ho-hum wine sparkle. Apparently, he was so blown away by the result that he rhapsodised about 'tasting the stars'.

EATING

Épernay's main eat street is rue Gambetta and adjacent place de la République. For picnic fixings, head to rue St-Thibault.

Covered Market   Food Market €

(Halle St-Thibault; rue Gallice; ⊘7.30am-12.30pm Wed & Sat) Picnic treats galore.

Pâtisserie
Vincent Dallet   Patisserie €

(www.chocolat-vincentdallet.fr; 26 rue du Général Leclerc; pastries €2.70-4.50; light meals €8-18; ⊘7.30am-7.45pm Tue-Sun) A sweet dream of a chocolaterie, patisserie and tearoom, with delectable pralines, macarons and pastries. A *champenoise* speciality is the 'Baba', vanilla cream topped by a cork-shaped pastry flavoured with Champagne. *Café gourmand*, coffee with a selection of mini desserts, costs €8.90.

La Grillade Gourmande   French €€

(☑03 26 55 44 22; www.lagrilladegourmande. com; 16 rue de Reims; menus €19-59; ⊘noon-2pm & 7.30-10pm Tue-Sat) This chic, red-walled bistro is an inviting spot to try chargrilled meats and dishes rich in texture and flavour, such as crayfish pan-fried in Champagne, and lamb cooked until meltingly tender in rosemary and honey. Diners spill out onto the covered terrace in the warm months.

La Cave à
Champagne   Regional Cuisine €€

(☑03 26 55 50 70; www.la-cave-a-champagne. com; 16 rue Gambetta; menus €20-38; ⊘noon-2pm & 7-10pm Thu-Mon; ⏴) 'The Champagne Cellar' is well regarded by locals for its *champenoise* cuisine (snail and pig's trotter casserole, fillet of beef in pinot noir), served in a warm, traditional, bourgeois atmosphere. You can sample four different Champagnes for €28.

Chez Max   French €€

(☑03 26 55 23 59; www.chez-max.com; 13 av AA Thevenet, Magenta; 3-course lunch menu €15.50, dinner menus €23-41; ⊘noon-1.30pm & 7.30-9.30pm Tue & Thu-Sat, noon-1.30pm Wed & Sun) No fuss, no frills, just good old-fashioned French cooking and a neighbourly vibe is what you'll get at Chez Max. Dishes like confit of duck leg and sea bass with Champagne sauce hit the mark every time.

ⓘ INFORMATION

Tourist Office (☑03 26 53 33 00; www. ot-epernay.fr; 7 av de Champagne; ⊘9am-12.30pm & 1.30-7pm Mon-Sat, 10.30am-1pm & 2-4.30pm Sun, closed Sun mid-Oct–mid-Apr) The super-friendly team here hand out English brochures and maps with walking, cycling and driving tour options. They can make cellar visit reservations. Free wi-fi.

ⓘ GETTING THERE & AROUND

BICYCLE

The tourist office rents out bicycles (city/children's/tandem/electric bicycles €18/11/27/30 per day). Pick up cycling maps and map-cards (€0.50) here.

CAR

Épernay is bang in the heart of Champagne country, making it a perfect base for a driving tour. It's situated on the D951 road 29km south of Reims. Car hire is available locally at **Europcar** (☑03 26 54 90 61; www.europcar.com; 20 rempart Perrier).

TRAIN

The **train station** (place Mendès-France) has direct services to Reims (€7, 24 to 37 minutes, 14 daily) and Paris Gare de l'Est (€24 to €65, 1¼ to 2¾ hours, eight daily).

LYON

Lyon at a Glance...

Commanding a strategic spot at the confluence of the Rhône and the Saône rivers, Lyon has been luring people ever since the Romans named it Lugdunum in 43 BC. Commercial, industrial and banking powerhouse for the past 500 years, grand old Lyon is France's third largest city and the country's gastronomic capital.

Outstanding museums, a dynamic cultural life, Unesco-listed cobbled streets and a thriving university lend the city a distinctly sophisticated air, while adventurous gourmets can indulge in their wildest gastronomic fantasies. Don't leave the city without sampling some traditional Lyonnais specialities in a bouchon *– an old-fashioned bistro with check tablecloths, lace curtains and, invariably, a hand-scrawled menu.*

Lyon in Two Days

Get a city overview with a **guided city tour** (p179), then hit **Vieux Lyon** (p176) for lunch and an afternoon exploring its cobbled streets and secret passages. Hike or ride the funicular up to **Fourvière** (p177) for a fabulous city panorama and dinner with view. Day two, head uphill to **Croix Rousse** (p175): get lost in its rabbit warren of *traboules* (secret passages) visit its **food market** (p183) and discover its **silk-weaving heritage** (p175).

Lyon in Four Days

Spend day three absorbing more of Lyon's rich history at its cache of museums: the **Musée des Beaux-Arts** (p178) followed by lunch on its terrace. In the afternoon catch a **puppet show** (p185) with Guignol, dine in a Lyonnais *bouchon* and enjoy after-dark **drinks** (p184) aboard the Rhône's *péniches* (barges). Day four, sail to the edgy new La Confluence 'hood to visit the cutting-edge **Musée des Confluences** (p179).

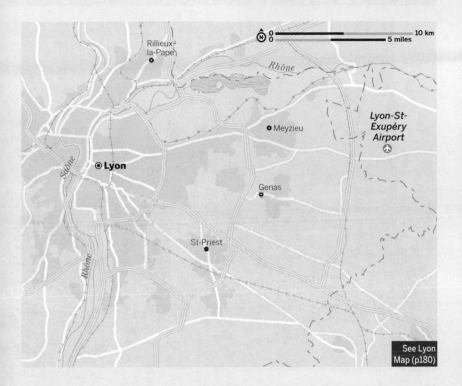

See Lyon
Map (p180)

Arriving in Lyon

Lyon-St-Exupéry Airport (LYS)

Rhônexpress tramway to Part-Dieu train station in under 30 minutes; departures every 15 to 30 minutes from 6am to midnight. Tickets adult/youth €15.90/13.20. By taxi count on paying €50 to €65 for the 30- to 45-minute ride into town.

Part-Dieu & Perrache train stations

Each have their own metro stop, with connections all over the city; single/all-day metro ticket €1.80/5.50.

Sleeping

From B&Bs and apartments to business hotels and boutique ventures, Lyon has a wealth of accommodation to suit every taste and budget. Arriving by car, ask ahead about hotel parking as car parks in Lyon are pricey. Lyon **tourist office** (p186) runs a free reservation service (http://book.lyon-france.com/en/accommodation).

PAUL VANCE / SHUTTERSTOCK ©

Bouchon Dining

A bouchon might be a 'bottle stopper' or 'traffic jam' elsewhere in France, but in Lyon it's a small, friendly bistro that cooks up traditional cuisine using regional produce.

Great For...

☑ Don't Miss

The informal, postdinner history tours run by the gregarious owner at *bouchon* Le Musée (p183).

Bouchons originated in the first half of the 20th century when many large bourgeois families had to let go of their in-house cooks, who then set up their own restaurant businesses. The first of these *mères* (mothers) was Mère Guy, followed by Mère Filloux, Mère Brazier (under whom world-famous Lyonnais chef Paul Bocuse trained) and others.

Many of the best *bouchons* are certified by Les Authentiques Bouchons Lyonnais – look for a metal plaque outside depicting traditional puppet Gnafron with glass of Beaujolais in hand.

What to Drink

Kick-start a memorable gastronomic experience with a *communard*, a blood-red aperitif of Beaujolais wine mixed with *crème de cassis* (blackcurrant liqueur), named after

Sausage dish

❶ Need to Know

Many of the best *bouchons* are shut weekends; advance reservations are recommended.

✖ Take a Break

Mingle with local foodies over a *bouchon* lunch at Le Poêlon d'Or (p183).

★ Top Tip

Get taste buds in gear with a morning stroll around food market Les Halles de Lyon Paul Bocuse (p183)

fish sauce). Die-hard *bouchon* aficionados can't get enough of *andouillette* (a seriously feisty sausage made from pigs' intestines), *gras double* (a type of tripe) and *pieds de mouton/veau/couchon* (sheep/calf/pig trotters).

Cheese & Dessert

For the cheese course, choose between a bowl of *fromage blanc* (a cross between cream cheese and natural yoghurt); *cervelle de canut* ('brains of the silk weaver', *fromage blanc* mixed with chives and garlic), which originated in Croix Rousse and accompanied every meal for 19th-century weavers; or local St Marcellin ripened to gooey perfection.

Desserts are grandma-style: think *tarte aux pommes* (apple tart), or the Lyonnais classic *tarte aux pralines*, a brilliant rose-coloured confection made with crème fraiche and crushed sugar-coated almonds.

Dining Etiquette

Little etiquette is required. Seldom do you get clean cutlery for each course, and mopping your plate with a chunk of bread is fine. In the most popular and traditional spots, you'll often find yourself sitting elbow-to-elbow with your fellow diners at a long row of tightly wedged tables.

the supporters of the Paris Commune killed in 1871. When ordering wine with your meal, ask for a pot – a classically Lyonnais 46cL glass bottle adorned with an elastic band to prevent wine drips – of local Brouilly, Beaujolais, Côtes du Rhône or Mâcon.

Traditional Dishes

Start with *tablier de sapeur* ('fireman's apron'; actually meaning breaded, fried tripe), *salade de cervelas* (salad of boiled pork sausage sometimes studded with pistachios or black truffle specks), or caviar de la Croix Rousse (lentils in creamy sauce). Hearty main dishes include *boudin blanc* (veal sausage), *boudin noir aux pommes* (blood sausage with apples), *quenelles* (feather-light flour, egg and cream dumplings) or *quenelles de brochet* (pike dumplings served in a creamy cray-

Ancient loom at Maison des Canuts

MATZ SJOBERG / ROBERT HARDING ©

Traboules & Canuts

Deep within Vieux Lyon and Croix Rousse, a labyrinth of dark and dingy traboules (secret passages) snakes through apartment blocks, under streets and into courtyards – perfect for off-beat urban exploration.

Great For...

☑ Don't Miss

Four 14th- to 17th-century houses wrapped around a *traboule* and Italianate loggia at **Cour des Loges** (www.courdes loges.com; 2-8 rue du Bœuf, 5e; M Vieux Lyon).

Across the city 315 passages link 230 streets, with a combined length of 50km. Renaissance courtyards, spiral stone staircases, romantic loggias and interesting building façades painted a rainbow of muted hues pepper the route – only sections of which are open to visitors. Many are closed or unmarked, and exploring Lyon's *traboules* is as much about unearthing unmarked doorways as admiring unique architecture.

Traboules v Miraboules

Genuine *traboules* (derived from the Latin *trans ambulare*, meaning 'to pass through') cut from one street to another. Passages that fan out into a courtyard or cul-de-sac aren't *traboules* but *miraboules* (two of the finest examples are at 16 rue Bœuf and 8 rue Juiverie, both in Vieux Lyon).

Cour des Veraces

CORNELIA TOGEA / GETTY IMAGES ©

Vieux Lyon

Some of Vieux Lyon's *traboules* date from Roman times, but most were constructed by *canuts* (silk weavers) in the 19th century to transport silk in inclement weather. Resistance fighters found them handy during WWII.

Vieux Lyon's most celebrated *traboules* include those connecting 27 rue St-Jean with 6 rue des Trois Maries and 54 rue St-Jean with 27 rue du Bœuf (push the intercom button to buzz open the door).

Croix Rousse

Step into Croix Rousse's underworld at 9 place Colbert, crossing **Cour des Voraces** – built by silk weavers in 1840 on the *pentes* (slopes) of Croix Rousse with a monumental open-air, seven-storey staircase – to 14bis montée St Sébastien,

and eventually emerging at 29 rue Imbert Colomes. From further *traboules*, zigzag down the *pentes* to place des Terreaux.

The City's Silk Weavers

Following the introduction of the mechanical Jacquard loom in 1805, Lyonnais *canuts* built tens of thousands of workshops in Croix Rousse, an independent hilltop quarter that only became part of Lyon in 1852. Their workshops sported huge windows to let in light and huge wood-beamed ceilings, more than 4m high, to accommodate the bulky machines. Weavers spent 14 to 20 hours a day hunched over their looms breathing in silk dust. Two-thirds were illiterate and everyone was paid a pittance; strikes in 1830–31 and 1834 resulted in the death of several hundred weavers.

No *traboule* evokes the fate of Lyonnais weavers more than Cour des Voraces, place of refuge for hundreds of weavers during subsequent 19th-century worker revolts. Learn about their labour-intensive life and see manual looms in use at Croix Rousse's fascinating **Maison des Canuts** (☑04 78 28 62 04; www.maisondescanuts.com; 10-12 rue d'Ivry, 4e; adult/child €7/4; ☺10am-6.30pm Mon-Sat, guided tours 11am & 3.30pm Mon-Sat; ⓂCroix Rousse).

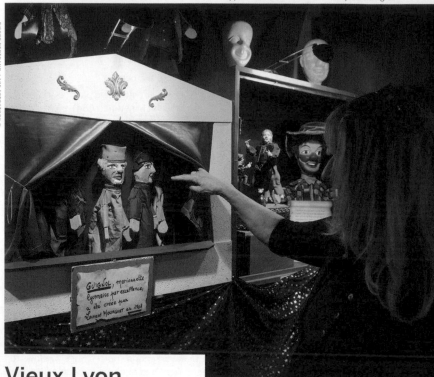

Puppets in Le Petit Musée Fantastique de Guignol

RIEGER BERTRAND / AGE FOTOSTOCK ©

Vieux Lyon

Lyon's old town, with its cobbled lanes and medieval and Renaissance architecture, is a Unesco World Heritage Site. Its atmospheric web of streets divides into three quarters: St-Paul (north), St-Jean (middle) and St-Georges (south).

Great For...

☑ Don't Miss

A traditional puppet show at one of Lyon's most famous puppet theatres, Théâtre Le Guignol de Lyon (p185).

Lovely old buildings line rue du Bœuf, rue St-Jean and rue des Trois Maries. Crane your neck upwards to see gargoyles and other cheeky stone characters carved on window ledges along rue Juiverie, home to Lyon's Jewish community in the Middle Ages.

Cathédrale St-Jean

Lyon's partly Romanesque **cathedral** (place St-Jean, 5e; ⏱8.15am-7.45pm Mon-Fri, to 7pm Sat & Sun; ⓜVieux Lyon) was built between the late 11th and early 16th centuries. The portals of its Flamboyant Gothic façade, completed in 1480 (and recently renovated), are decorated with 280 square stone medallions. Inside, the highlight is the **astronomical clock** in the north transept.

Musées Gadagne

Housed in a 16th-century mansion built for two rich Florentine bankers, this twin-

Basilique Notre Dame de Fourvière

DREAMER COMPANY / SHUTTERSTOCK ©

⊙ Need to Know

Shop (in style): art galleries, antiquarian and secondhand bookshops fill Vieux Lyon's pedestrian streets.

✕ Take a Break

Cool down with a lavender ice cream from Terre Adélice (p182) or a neobistro lunch at Cinq Mains (p182).

★ Top Tip

The tourist office (p186) organises excellent tours through Vieux Lyon with English-speaking guides; book in advance.

2-6.30pm Tue-Sun, 2-6pm Mon, Ⓜ Vieux Lyon) is Guignol, the Lyonnais puppet famous for its slapstick antics and political commentary. Ask staff to set up the English soundtrack on the cute, sensor-activated exhibits.

themed **exhibition space** (☑04 78 42 03 61; www.museegadagne.com; 1 place du Petit Collège, 5e; adult/child museum €6/free, both museums €9/free; ⊙11am-6pm Wed-Sun; Ⓜ Vieux Lyon) incorporates an excellent local history museum, **Musée d'Histoire de Lyon**, chronicling the city's layout as its silk-weaving, cinema and transportation evolved, and an international puppet museum, **Musée des Marionettes du Monde**, paying homage to Lyon's iconic puppet, Guignol. On the 4th floor, a cafe adjoins tranquil, terraced gardens, here since the 14th century.

Le Petit Musée Fantastique de Guignol

The star of this tiny, two-room **museum** (☑04 78 28 62 04; www.le-petit-musee-fantastique-de-guignol.boutiquecardelli.fr; 6 rue St-Jean, 5e; adult/child €5/3; ⊙10.30am-1pm &

What's Nearby

From Vieux Lyon, tree-shaded footpaths and a funicular wind steeply uphill to **Fourvière**, Lyon's so-called 'Hill of Prayer' on the Saône's western bank. Over two millennia ago, the Romans built the city of Lugdunum on these slopes, crowned today by showy 19th-century **Basilique Notre Dame de Fourvière** (www.fourviere.org; place de Fourvière, 5e; rooftop tour adult/child €7/4; ⊙8am-6.45pm, guided tours Apr-Nov; Ⓜ Fourvière) and the landmark **Tour Métallique**, an Eiffel Tower–like structure (minus its bottom two-thirds) built in 1893 and used as a TV transmitter.

◉ SIGHTS

A number of sights lie in the city centre, which occupies a long peninsula between the rivers known as Presqu'île. Rising to the north of the Presqu'île is hillside Croix Rousse, and west across the Saône is medieval Vieux Lyon.

Musée des Beaux-Arts   Museum
(☏04 72 10 17 40; www.mba-lyon.fr; 20 place des Terreaux, 1er; adult/child €8/free; ☺10am-6pm Wed, Thu & Sat-Mon, 10.30am-6pm Fri; ⓂHôtel de Ville) This stunning and eminently manageable museum showcases France's finest collection of sculptures and paintings outside of Paris from antiquity onwards. Highlights include works by Rodin, Rubens, Rembrandt, Monet, Matisse and Picasso. Pick up a free audioguide and be sure to stop for a drink or meal on the delightful stone terrace off its **cafe-restaurant** or take time out in its tranquil **cloister garden**.

> *France's finest collection of sculptures and paintings outside of Paris*

Sculptures in the cloister garden, Musée des Beaux-Arts

Opéra de Lyon   Architecture
(www.opera-lyon.com; 1 place de la Comédie, 1er; ⓂHôtel de Ville) Lyon's neoclassical 1831-built opera house was modernised in 1993 by renowned French architect Jean Nouvel, who added the striking semi-cylindrical glass-domed roof. On its northern side, boarders and bladers buzz around the fountains of **place Louis Pradel**, surveyed by the **Homme de la Liberté** (Man of Freedom) on roller skates, sculpted from scrap metal by Marseille-born César.

Musée des Arts Décoratifs   Museum
(☏04 78 38 42 00; www.mtmad.fr; 34 rue de la Charité, 2e; adult/child €10/7.50; ☺10am-5.30pm Tue-Sun; ⓂAmpère) This well-organised museum displays 18th-century furniture, tapestries, wallpaper, ceramics and silver. Tickets include admission to the adjoining **Musée des Tissus** (☏04 78 38 42 00; www.mtmad.fr; 34 rue de la Charité, 2e; adult/child €10/7.50; ☺10am-5.30pm Tue-Sun; ⓂAmpère), which showcases extraordinary Lyonnais and international silks.

Musée d'Art Contemporain — Art Museum

(☎04 72 69 17 17; www.mac-lyon.com; 81 quai Charles de Gaulle, 6e; adult/child €9/free; ⊙11am-6pm Wed-Fri, 10am-7pm Sat & Sun; ☐C1, C4, C5) Lyon's contemporary art museum mounts edgy temporary exhibitions and a rotating permanent collection of post-1960 art. It sometimes closes for several weeks between exhibitions, so check to make sure there's something on. Buses stop right out front.

Centre d'Histoire de la Résistance et de la Déportation — Museum

(☎04 78 72 23 11; www.chrd.lyon.fr; 14 av Berthelot, 7e; adult/child €4/free; ⊙10am-5.30pm Wed-Sun; MPerrache, Jean Macé) The WWII headquarters of Gestapo commander Klaus Barbie evokes Lyon's role as the 'Capital of the Resistance' through moving multimedia exhibits. Extensively remodelled in 2012, the museum includes sound recordings of deportees and Resistance fighters, plus a varied collection of everyday objects associated with the Resistance (including the parachute Jean Moulin used to re-enter France in 1942).

Musée des Confluences — Museum

(☎04 28 38 11 90; www.museedesconfluences. fr; 86 quai Perrache, 6e; adult/child €9/free; ⊙11am-6.15pm Tue, Wed & Fri, 11am-9.15pm Thu, 10am-6.15pm Sat & Sun; ☐T1) Opened in late 2014, this recent building, designed by the Viennese firm Coop Himmelb(l)au, is the crowning glory of Lyon's newest neighbourhood, the Confluence, at Presqu'île's southern tip. Lying at the confluence of the Rhône and Saône Rivers, this ambitious science-and-humanities museum is housed in a futuristic steel-and-glass transparent crystal. Its distorted structure is one of the city's iconic landmarks.

The museum's permanent exhibitions are arranged thematically into four sections. The 'Origins' exhibition focuses on the origins of the earth and the various theories of evolution; the 'Eternity' exhibition is devoted to death rites; the 'Societies'

Green in the City

If you're museum-ed out, head to lovely **Parc de la Tête d'Or** (www.loisirs-parcde-latetedor.com; bd des Belges, 6e; ⊙6.30am-10.30pm mid-Apr–mid Oct, to 8.30pm rest of year; ☐C1, C5, MMasséna) north of the centre, which provides a green haven for nature lovers and families. Spanning 117 hectares, France's largest urban park was landscaped in the 1860s. It's graced by a lake (rent a rowing boat), botanic gardens with greenhouses, rose gardens, a zoo and a tourist train. Take bus C1 (from Part-Dieu train station) or bus C5 (from Place Bellecour and Hôtel de Ville) to the Parc Tête d'Or-Churchill stop.

A greenhouse in Parc de la Tête d'Or
MAGSPACE / SHUTTERSTOCK ©

exhibition explores how human groups are organised and interact; and the 'Species' exhibition is devoted to natural history.

⊙ TOURS

Lyon City Tour — Bus

(☎04 78 56 32 39; www.lyoncitytour.fr; adult 1-/2-day ticket €19/22, child 1 or 2 days €8; ⊙9.30am-6.30pm Apr-Oct, 9.45am-5.45pm Nov-Mar) Hop-on, hop-off double-decker bus tours. On Thursday and Sunday evenings from mid-June to mid-September, a Lyon by Night tour is also offered at 9.30pm.

Lyon City Boat — Boating

(Navig'inter; ☎04 78 42 96 81; www.lyoncityboat. com; 2 quai des Célestins, 2e; river excursions adult/child €11.50/8; ⊙ Apr-Oct; MBellecour,

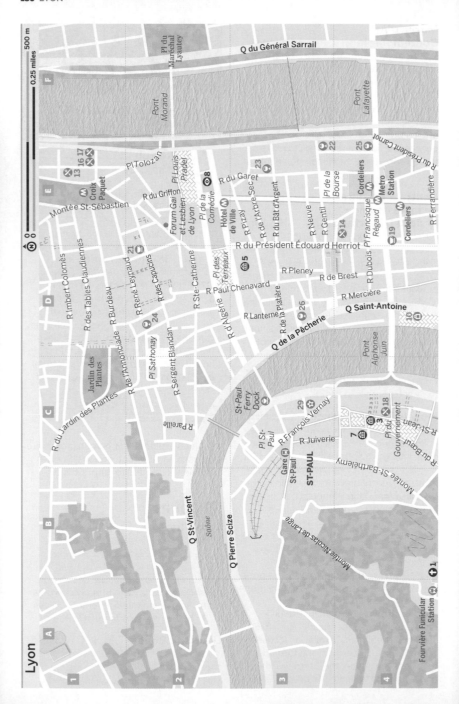

Lyon

500 m
0.25 miles

Q du Général Sarrail

Pont Morand

Pont Lafayette

Pl du Maréchal Lyautey

Pl Tolozan

13 16 17

Croix Paquet

Montée St-Sébastien

R du Griffon

Pl Louis Pradel

Forum Gai et Lesbien de Lyon

Pl de la Comédie

8

R du Garet

23

R de l'Arbre Sec

R du Bât d'Argent

Hôtel de Ville

R Pizay

R du Président Carnot

22

25

Cordeliers

Pl de la Bourse

Metro Station

R du Président Édouard Herriot

R Neuve

R Gentil

Pl Francisque Régaud

14

R Ferrandière

19

Cordeliers

R Imbert Colomès

R des Tables Claudiennes

R Burdeau

R René Leynaud

R des Capucins

21

24

R Ste-Catherine

Pl des Terreaux

5

R Paul Chenavard

R d'Algérie

R Lanterne

R de la Platière

R Pleney

R de Brest

R Mercière

R Dubois

Q Saint-Antoine

10

R du Jardin des Plantes

Jardin des Plantes

R de l'Annonciade

Pl Sathonay

R Sergent Blandan

26

Q de la Pêcherie

Pont Alphonse Juin

R Pareille

St-Paul Ferry Dock

Pl St-Paul

29

R François Vernay

3

18

R St-Jean

7

Pl du Gouvernement

R du Bœuf

Q St-Vincent

Saône

Q Pierre Scize

Gare St-Paul

R Juiverie

ST-PAUL

Montée St-Barthélemy

Montée Nicolas de Lange

1

Fourvière Funicular Station

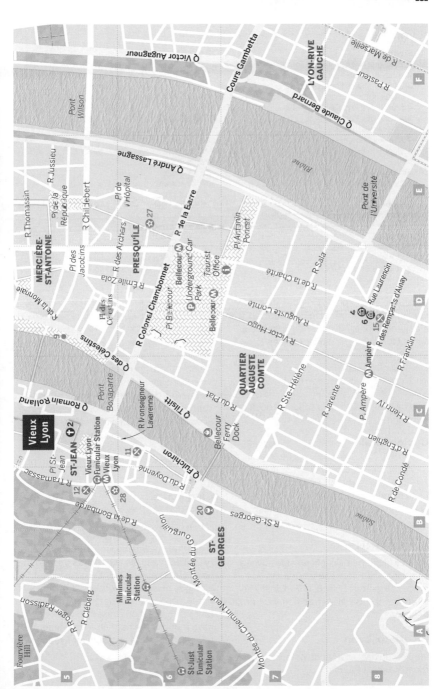

Lyon

Vieux Lyon) From April to October, river excursions depart from Lyon City Boat's dock along the Saône. Advance bookings are essential for lunch and dinner **cruises** (⌨04 78 42 96 81; www.lyoncityboat.com; 23 quai Claude Bernard, 7e; 3hr lunch cruise €50-59, 6hr lunch cruise €55-65, 3hr dinner cruise €59-69; ⏰Tue-Sun by reservation; Ⓜ Ampère, Guillotière, 🚃T1), which leave from a separate dock on the Rhône.

Cyclopolitain   Cycling
(⌨04 78 30 35 90; www.visite-insolite-cyclopolitain.com; tours 2 people €40-130; ⏰noon-7pm Tue-Fri, 10.30am-7pm Sat) Tiny and/or tired feet can rest aboard a cycle-taxi tour. Choose from nine different itineraries.

 ## EATING

A flurry of big-name chefs presides over a sparkling restaurant line-up that embraces all genres: French, fusion, fast and international, as well as traditional Lyonnais *bouchons*.

⊗ Vieux Lyon

Vieux Lyon has a surfeit of restaurants, most aimed at tourists.

Terre Adélice   Ice Cream €
(⌨04 78 03 51 84; www.terre-adelice.eu; 1 place de la Baleine, 5e; 1/2/3 scoops €2.60/4.70/6.50; ⏰10am-midnight Apr-Oct, noon-7pm Nov-Mar; Ⓜ Vieux Lyon) It's hard to resist the 150 flavours, both divine and daring, at this ice-cream shop on Vieux Lyon's main pedestrian thoroughfare. Play it safe with Valrhona dark chocolate, organic pistachio or vanilla from Madagascar; experiment gently with cardamom, Grand Marnier or lavender; or take a walk on the wild side with a scoop of wasabi, yoghurt and pepper or tomato-basil.

Cinq Mains   Neobistro €€
(⌨04 37 57 30 52; www.facebook.com/cinq mains; 12 rue Monseigneur Lavarenne, 5e; lunch menus €12-19, dinner menus €28-35; ⏰noon-2pm & 8-10pm) When young Lyonnais Grégory Cuilleron and his two friends opened this neobistro in early 2016, it was an instant hit. They're working wonders at this cool loft-like space with a mezzanine, serving up tantalising creations based on what they have found at the market. A new generation of chefs and a new spin for Lyonnais cuisine.

Daniel et Denise Bouchon €€

(☎04 78 42 24 62; www.danieletdenise-stjean.fr; 36 rue Tramassac, 5e; mains €15-25, lunch menu €21, dinner menus €30-40; ⊗noon-2pm & 7.30-9.30pm Tue-Sat) One of Vieux Lyon's most dependable and traditional eateries, this classic spot is run by award-winning chef Joseph Viola, who was elected president of Lyon's *bouchon* association in 2014. Come here for elaborate variations on traditional Lyonnais themes.

Presqu'île

Le Poêlon d'Or Bouchon €€

(☎04 78 37 65 60; www.lepoelondor-restaurant. fr; 29 rue des Remparts d'Ainay, 2e; lunch menus €17-20, dinner menus €27-32; ⊗noon-2pm & 7.30-10pm Mon-Fri; ⒨Ampère-Victor Hugo) This upmarket *bouchon*, around the corner from the Musée des Tissus, is well known among local foodies who recommend its superb *andouillette* and pike dumplings. Save room for the delicious chocolate mousse or the vanilla crème brûlée. Well worth the detour.

Le Musée Bouchon €€

(☎04 78 37 71 54; 2 rue des Forces, 2e; lunch mains €14, lunch menus €19-26, dinner menus €23-32; ⊗noon-1.30pm & 7.30-9.30pm Tue-Sat; ⒨Cordeliers) Housed in the stables of Lyon's former Hôtel de Ville, this delightful *bouchon* serves a splendid array of meat-heavy Lyonnais classics, including a divine *poulet au vinaigre* (chicken cooked in vinegar). The daily changing *menu* features 10 appetisers and 10 main dishes, plus five scrumptious desserts, all served on cute china plates at long family-style tables.

La Mère Brazier Gastronomic €€€

(☎04 78 23 17 20; www.lamerebrazier.fr; 12 rue Royale; lunch menus €57-70, dinner menus €100-155; ⊗noon-1.15pm & 7.45-9.15pm Mon-Fri Sep-Jul; ⒨Croix Paquet) Chef Mathieu Vianney has reinvented the legendary early-20th-century restaurant that earned Mère Eugénie Brazier Lyon's first trio of Michelin stars in 1933 (a copy of the original guidebook takes pride of place). Vianney is doing admirable justice to Brazier's

Lyon Food Markets

Food shopping in Lyon is an unmissable part of the city's experience. And with so many urban spaces and parks there are plenty of picnic spots too.

Lyon's famed indoor food market **Les Halles de Lyon Paul Bocuse** (☎04 78 62 39 33; www.hallespaulbocuse.lyon.fr; 102 cours Lafayette, 3e; ⊗7am 10.30pm Tue-Sat, to 4.30pm Sun; ⒨Part-Dieu) has over 60 stalls selling their renowned wares. Pick up a round of impossibly runny St Marcellin from legendary cheesemonger Mère Richard, and a knobbly Jésus de Lyon (dry-cured sausage) from pork butcher Collette Sibilia. Or enjoy a sit-down lunch of local produce at the stalls, lip-smacking *coquillages* (shellfish) included.

Lyon has two main outdoor food markets: **Croix Rousse** (bd de la Croix Rousse, 1er; ⊗6am-1pm Tue-Sun; ⒨Croix Rousse) and **Presqu'île** (quai St-Antoine, 1er; ⊗6am-1pm Tue-Sun; ⒨Bellecour, Cordeliers). Each has over 100 vendors.

Stall, Les Halles de Lyon Paul Bocuse
TRAVELSTOCK44.DE / AGE FOTOSTOCK ©

legacy, claiming two Michelin stars himself for his assured cuisine accompanied by an impressive wine list.

☒ Croix Rousse

L'Ourson qui Boit Fusion €€

(☎04 78 27 23 37; 23 rue Royale, 1er; lunch/dinner menu €18/32; ⊗noon-1.30pm & 7.30-9.30pm Mon, Tue & Thu-Sat; ⒨Croix Paquet) On the fringes of Croix Rousse, Japanese chef

LGBT
Lyon

Declared France's most gay-friendly city in 2014 by the magazine *Têtu*, Lyon has scads of venues.

Guys' favourite places to party include **United Café** (www.united-cafe.com; impasse de la Pêcherie, 1er; ⏾midnight-5am; ⓂHôtel de Ville), **Le XS Bar** (19 rue Claudia, 2e; ⏾5pm-3am; ⓂCordeliers) and the city's oldest gay bar, **La Ruche** (22 rue Gentil, 2e; ⏾5pm-3am; ⓂCordeliers). Lesbian venues include **Le L Bar** (19 rue du Garet, 1er; ⏾6pm-4am; ⓂHôtel de Ville) and **Le Marais** (www.lemarais-lyon.fr; 3 rue Terme, 1er; ⏾9pm-3am Thu, 11pm-5am Fri & Sat; ⓂHôtel de Ville, Croix Paquet). For up-to-the-minute listings, visit the websites Gay in Lyon (www.gayinlyon.com) and Hétéroclite (www.heteroclite.org), or check with the **Forum Gai et Lesbien de Lyon** (☑04 78 39 97 72; www.fgllyon.org; 17 rue Romarin, 1er; ⓂCroix Paquet), which organises social events.

Lyon's **Lesbian & Gay Pride** (www.fierte.net) march and festivities hit the streets each year in June. In March, the city hosts a popular week-long LGBT film festival, **Écrans Mixtes** (www.festival-em.org).

Gay Pride celebration in Lyon
PIERRE JEAN DURIEU / GETTY IMAGES ©

Akira Nishigaki puts his own splendid spin on French cuisine, with plenty of locally sourced fresh vegetables and light, clean flavours. The ever-changing *menu* of two daily appetisers and two main dishes is complemented by good wines, attentive service and scrumptious desserts. Well worth reserving ahead.

In early 2016, Akira Nishigaki opened **L'Ourson qui Boit – Pâtisserie** (☑04 78 72 90 54; 2 rue Roger Violi, 1er; pastries €3.50; ⏾10.30am-7pm Mon, Tue & Thu-Sat) next door.

L'Instant   Cafe €
(☑04 78 29 85 08; www.linstant-patisserie.fr; 3 place Marcel Bertone, 4e; breakfast €6.50, lunch mains €6.50-13, weekend brunch €20; ⏾8am-7pm Mon-Sat, to 1pm Sun; 🛜; ⓂCroix Rousse) The best spot in Croix Rousse to start the day, this hybrid cafe-pastry shop overlooking lovely place Marcel Bertone packs a punch. The continental breakfast (and brunch on weekends) is the highlight, while the pastries and pies will leave your taste buds reeling. The wonderfully mellow setting and relaxed urban vibe add to the appeal. Ample outdoor seating on warm days.

🍸 DRINKING & NIGHTLIFE
Along quai Victor Augagneur on the Rhône's left bank, a string of *péniches* (barges with onboard bars) serve drinks from mid-afternoon onwards, many of them rocking until the wee hours with DJs and/or live bands. To study your options, stroll the quayside between Pont Lafayette and Pont de la Guillotière.

Grand Café des Négociants   Cafe
(www.lesnegociants.com; 1 place Francisque Régaud, 2e; ⏾7am-4am; ⓂCordeliers) The tree-shaded terrace and Second Empire decor of chandeliers and mirror-lined walls are the big draws at this centrally located cafe-brasserie, a Lyonnais institution since 1864. Food is served from noon to midnight.

La Boite à Café –
Café Mokxa   Cafe
(www.cafemokxa.com; 3 rue Abbé Rozier, 1er; ⏾8am-7pm Mon-Fri, 9am-7pm Sat, 11am-7pm Sun; 🛜; ⓂCroix Paquet, Hôtel de Ville) A favourite haunt of Lyonnais caffeine fiends and students, this laid-back place on the Croix

Opéra de Lyon

Rousse slopes roasts its own beans and serves Sunday brunch. In summer, tables spill onto charming, circular place du Forez. It also serves superb pastries.

Johnny Walsh's — Pub
(56 rue St-Georges, 5e; ⊙9pm-3am Tue-Sun; 🛜; MVieux Lyon) Local connoisseurs claim this is the best pub in Lyon. It has live music four nights a week. At the south end of Vieux Lyon.

⭐ ENTERTAINMENT

Catching a performance in Lyon is a treat, with a wide array of venues hosting opera, ballet and theatre as well as concert venues.

The leading what's-on guide with both print and online editions is *Le Petit Bulletin* (www.petit-bulletin.fr/lyon). Other helpful websites with entertainment listings include www.monweekendalyon.com, www. lyonclubbing.com and www.lyon.2night.fr (all in French).

Tickets are sold at **Fnac Billetterie** (www. fnacspectacles.com; 85 rue de la République, 2e; ⊙10am-7.30pm Mon-Sat; MBellecour).

Opéra de Lyon — Opera
(www.opera-lyon.com; place de la Comédie, 1er; MHôtel de Ville) Lyon's premier venue for opera, ballet and classical music.

Le Sucre — Live Music
(www.le-sucre.eu; 50 quai Rambaud, 2e; ⊙6pm-midnight Wed & Thu, 7pm-5am Fri & Sat) Down in the Confluence neighbourhood, Lyon's most innovative club hosts DJs, live shows and eclectic arts events on its super-cool roof terrace atop a 1930s sugar factory, La Sucrière.

Théâtre Le Guignol de Lyon — Puppet Theatre
(📞04 78 28 92 57; www.guignol-lyon.com; 2 rue Louis Carrand, 5e; adult/child €10/7.50; MVieux Lyon) One of Lyon's most famous puppet theatres, Théâtre Le Guignol de Lyon has a collection of about 300 puppets. It was renovated in 2016.

Musée des Confluences (p179)

Le Transbordeur Live Music

(www.transbordeur.fr; 3 bd de Stalingrad, Villeurbanne; ⊘Wed-Sat; 🚌Cité Internationale/ Transbordeur) In an old industrial building near the Parc de la Tête d'Or's northeastern corner, Lyon's prime concert venue draws international acts on the European concert-tour circuit.

Hangar du Premier Film Cinema

(www.institut-lumiere.org; 25 rue du Premier Film, 8e; Ⓜ Monplaisir-Lumière) This former factory and birthplace of cinema now screens films of all genres and eras in their original languages. From approximately June to September, the big screen moves outside.

ℹ️ INFORMATION

Lyon City Card (www.en.lyon-france.com/Lyon-City-Card; 1/2/3 days adult €22/32/42, child €13.50/18.50/23.50) This excellent-value card offers free admission to every Lyon museum, the roof of Basilique Notre Dame de Fourvière, guided city tours, Guignol puppet shows and river excursions (April to October), along with numerous other discounts.

The card also includes unlimited citywide transport on buses, trams, the funicular and metro. Full-price cards are available at the tourist office and some hotels, or save 10% by booking online and presenting your confirmation number at the tourist office.

Tourist Office (☑ 04 72 77 69 69; www. lyon-france.com; place Bellecour, 2e; ⊘9am-6pm; Ⓜ Bellecour) In the centre of Presqu'île, Lyon's exceptionally helpful, multilingual and well-staffed main tourist office offers a variety of city walking tours and sells the Lyon City Card. There's a smaller branch just outside the Vieux Lyon metro station.

ℹ️ GETTING THERE & AWAY

AIR

Lyon-St-Exupéry Airport (www.lyonaeroports. com) Located 25km east of the city, with 40 airlines (including many budget carriers) serving over 100 direct destinations across Europe and beyond.

TRAIN

Lyon has two main-line train stations: **Gare de la Part-Dieu** (place Charles Béraudier, 3e; MPart-Dieu), 1.5km east of the Rhône, and **Gare de Perrache** (cours de Verdun Rambaud, 2e; MPerrache). There's also a TGV station at Lyon-St-Exupéry Airport.

Destinations by direct TGV include the following:

Marseille €53, 1¾ hours, every 30 to 60 minutes.

Paris Charles de Gaulle Airport €97, two hours, at least 11 daily.

Paris Gare de Lyon €75, two hours, every 30 to 60 minutes.

ℹ️ GETTING AROUND

BICYCLE

Pick up a red-and-silver bike at one of 200-odd bike stations throughout the city and drop it off at another with Lyon's **Vélo'v** (www.velov.grand-lyon.com; 1st 30min free, next 30min €1, each subsequent 30min period €2) bike rental scheme. Start by paying a one-time flat fee for a *carte courte durée* (short-duration card, €1.50 for 24 hours, €5 for seven days). Once equipped with the card, you're entitled to unlimited rentals. Pay all fees with a chip-enabled credit card using machines installed at bike stations.

BOAT

Le Vaporetto (08 20 20 69 20; www.confluence.fr/W/do/centre/navette) operates *navettes* (passenger ferry boats) to Lyon's new Confluence neighbourhood. Boats (€2) depart hourly between 10am and 9pm from riverbank docks on the Saône near place St-Paul and place Bellecour, returning from the Confluence dock between 10.30am and 9.30pm. Travel time is 30 minutes from the **St-Paul dock** (quai de Bondy, 5e; MHôtel de Ville, Vieux Lyon) and 20 minutes

❄️ Winter Date: Festival of Lights

Fête des Lumières (Festival of Lights; www.fetedeslumieres.lyon.fr; ☉Dec) is Lyon's premier festival. Over four days around the Feast of the Immaculate Conception (8 December), magnificent sound and light shows are projected onto key buildings, while locals illuminate windowsills with candles. It's so colourful that it's worth timing your trip around it. Note that every hotel is fully booked.

EDDY GALEOTTI / SHUTTERSTOCK ©

from the **Bellecour dock** (quai Tilsitt, 2e; MBellecour, Vieux Lyon).

PUBLIC TRANSPORT

Buses, trams, a four-line metro and two funiculars linking Vieux Lyon to Fourvière and St-Just are operated by **TCL** (www.tcl.fr). Public transport runs from around 5am to midnight.

Tickets cost €1.80 (€16.20 for a *carnet* of 10) and are available from bus and tram drivers as well as machines at metro entrances. Tickets allowing two consecutive hours of travel after 9am or unlimited travel after 7pm cost €3, and an all-day ticket costs €5.50. Bring coins as machines don't accept notes (or some international credit cards). Time-stamp tickets on all forms of public transport or risk a fine.

PROVENCE

Provence at a Glance...

Travelling in this sun-blessed part of southern France translates as touring scenic back roads strewn with stunning landscapes: fields of lavender, ancient olive groves and snow-tipped mountains. It's home to Europe's deepest canyon, oldest road and highest mountain pass.

Food is a central part of French life, but in Provence it's an all-consuming passion. Dominated by the hallowed ingredients of Mediterranean cooking – olive oil, wine, tomatoes and garlic – the region's cuisine is a highlight, be it savouring a simple bowl of soupe au pistou or shopping for delicate courgette flowers and sweet Cavaillon melons at the market.

Provence in Two Days

Spend day one in **Avignon** (p202), exploring the old town and the **Palais des Papes** (p202). On day two, depending on your interests, make a day trip to either **Les Baux de Provence** (p194) for hilltop-village meandering – stop en route at Cavaillon's morning **market** (p199) – or to the **Pont du Gard** (p200) for Roman history and memorable canoeing action on the **River Gard** (p201).

Provence in Four Days

Day three, motor an hour southeast to **Aix-en-Provence** (p198) for market shopping and lunch. Either spend the afternoon here too or drive another hour north into the Lubéron to hop between hilltop villages – don't miss a red-rock hike in **Roussillon** (p194) and sunset in **Gordes** (p194). Devote the fourth day to exploring **Moustiers Ste-Marie** (p208).

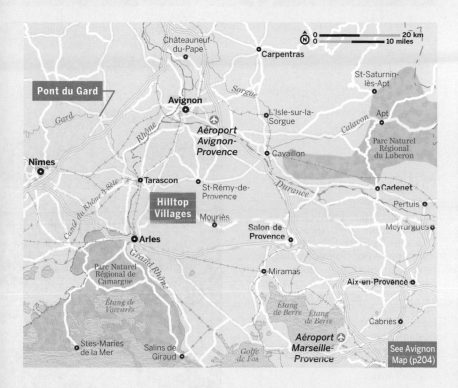

Arriving in Provence

Aéroport Marseille-Provence Buses to Aix-en-Provence every 20 minutes. Direct trains to Avignon Centre (€17.70, 50 minutes to 1½ hours, hourly) and Nîmes (€18.70, one hour, several daily).

Aéroport Avignon-Provence Bus 30 (www.tcra.fr; €1.30, 25 minutes, Monday to Saturday) to the post office and LER bus 22 (www.info-ler.fr; €1.50) to Avignon bus station and TGV station. Taxis about €35.

Sleeping

Provence has a huge, varied range of accommodation, from urban hotel to countryside *chambre d'hôte*. Prices go through the roof in summer. Avignon is an excellent base for the Vaucluse and Pont du Gard (a 30-minute drive); Apt and its rural surrounds are perfect for touring the Lubéron's hilltop villages; magical Moustiers Ste-Marie is a key stop for Gorge du Verdon explorers.

Gordes (p194)

Hilltop Villages

Impossibly perched on a rocky peak, gloriously lost in back country, fortified or château-topped: Provence's impressive portfolio of villages perchés calls for go-slow touring – on foot, by bicycle or car. Most villages are medieval, built from golden stone and riddled with cobbled lanes, flower-filled alleys and fountain-pierced squares. Combine with a long lazy lunch for a perfect day.

Great For...

Need to Know

Apt tourist office (☏04 90 74 03 18; www.luberon-apt.fr; 20 av Philippe de Girard; ☺9.30am-1pm & 2.30-7pm Mon-Sat, 9.30am-12.30pm Sun Jul & Aug, 9.30am-12.30pm & 2-6pm Mon-Sat Sep-Jun)

★ **Top Tip**

Visit early in the morning or just before sunset for the best light and fewer crowds.

Les Baux-de-Provence

Clinging precariously to an ancient limestone *baou* (Provençal for 'rocky spur'), this fortified hilltop village is among France's most visited. Narrow cobbled streets wend up to the splendid ruined castle of **Château des Baux** (☎04 90 54 55 56; www.chateau-baux-provence.com; adult/child €10/8 Apr-Sep, €8/6 Oct-Mar; ☉9am-8pm Jul & Aug, to 7pm Apr-Jun & Sep, shorter hours Oct-Mar), whose dramatic maze-like ruins date to the 10th century. The clifftop castle was largely destroyed in 1633, during the reign of Louis XIII, and is a thrilling place to explore – climb crumbling towers for incredible views, descend into disused dungeons and flex your knightly prowess with giant medieval weapons dotting the open-air site. Medieval-themed entertainment abounds in summer.

Gordes

Like a giant wedding cake rising over the rivers Sorgue and Calavon, the tiered village of Gordes juts spectacularly out of the white-rock face of the Vaucluse plateau. Come sunset, the village glows gold.

From the central square, meander downhill along rue Baptistin Picca to **Boulangerie de Mamie Jane** (☎04 90 72 09 34; rue Baptistin Picca; lunch menus from €6.50; ☉6.30am-1pm & 2-6pm Thu-Tue), a pocket-sized family-run bakery with outstanding bread, pastries, cakes and biscuits, including lavender-perfumed *navettes* and delicious peanut-and-almond brittle known as *écureuil* (from the French for squirrel).

Roussillon

Dazzling Roussillon was once the centre of local ochre mining and is still unmistakably

Lacoste

marked by its vivid crimson colour. Artist workshops lace its streets and the **Sentier des Ocres** (Ochre Trail; adult/child €2.50/free; ⊘9.30am-5.30pm; 🖮) plunges intrigued visitors into a mini-desert landscape of chestnut groves, pines and sunset-coloured ochre formations – it's like stepping into a Georgia O'Keeffe painting. Information panels along the two circular trails (30 or 50 minutes) highlight flora to spot. Wear walking shoes and avoid white clothing!

Ménerbes

Hilltop Ménerbes gained fame as the home of expat British author Peter Mayles, whose book *A Year in Provence* recounts his tales of renovating a farmhouse just outside the village in the late 1980s. Opposite the village's 12th-century church, the **Maison de la Truffe et du Vin** (House of Truffle & Wine;

DUCHY / SHUTTERSTOCK ©

📞04 90 72 38 37; www.vin-truffe-luberon.com; place de l'Horloge; ⊘10am-noon & 2.30-6pm Apr-Oct, Thu-Sat Nov-Mar) represents 60 local *domaines* (wine-growing estates). April to October, there is free wine tasting and wine sales at bargain-basement prices. Winter brings truffle workshops.

Lacoste

Lacoste has nothing to do with the designer brand – although it does have couturier connections. In 2001 designer Pierre Cardin purchased the 9th-century **Château de Lacoste** (📞04 90 75 93 12, www. chateau-la-coste.com), where the Marquis de Sade (1740–1814) retreated in 1771, when his writings became too scandalous for Paris. The château was looted by revolutionaries in 1789, and the 45-room palace remained an eerie ruin until Cardin arrived. He created a 1000-seat theatre and opera stage adjacent, only open during July's month-long **Festival de Lacoste** (www. festivaldelacoste.com). Daytime visits are possible only by reservation.

Bonnieux

Settled during the Roman era, Bonnieux in Le Petit Lubéron is another bewitching hilltop town that still preserves its medieval character. It's intertwined with alleyways, cul-de-sacs and hidden staircases: from place de la Liberté, 86 steps lead to the 12th-century church. The **Musée de la Boulangerie** (📞04 90 75 88 34; 12 rue de la République; adult/student/child €3.50/1.50/free; ⊘10am-12:30pm & 2.30-6pm Wed-Mon Apr-Oct), in an old 17th-century bakery building, explores the history of bread-making. Time your visit for the lively Friday market, which takes over most of the old town's streets.

★ Don't Miss

Rows of summertime lavender in bloom at **Abbaye Notre-Dame de Sénanque** (www.abbayedesenanque.com), a supremely peaceful and graceful Cistercian abbey 4km northwest of Gordes.

Aix-en-Provence food market (p198)

Provençal Markets

Stalls groaning with fruit and veg, trays of cheese and saucisson (dry cured sausage) to sample, stallholders loudly plying their wares – markets are an essential element of Provençal life. Practically every village has at least one weekly morning market, packed with locals shopping and gossiping, and dozens of stalls selling everything from locally farmed produce to spices, soaps and handmade crafts.

Great For...

❶ Need to Know

Aix-en-Provence tourist office (☎04 42 16 11 61; www.aixenprovencetourism.com; 300 av Giuseppe Verdi; ◷8.30am-7pm Mon-Sat, 10am-1pm & 2-6pm Sun, to 8pm Mon-Sat Jun-Sep; 🛜)

★ **Top Tip**

Take your own woven straw basket to blend in with the local crowd.

Aix-en-Provence

A pocket of left-bank Parisian chic deep in Provence, Aix (pronounced like the letter X) is all class: its leafy boulevards and public squares are lined with 17th- and 18th-century mansions, punctuated by gurgling moss-covered fountains. Haughty stone lions guard its grandest avenue, cafe-laced **cours Mirabeau**, where fashionable Aixois pose on polished pavement terraces sipping espresso.

At the city's **food market** (place Richelme; ☉7am-noon), trestle tables groan under the weight of marinated olives, goat's cheese, garlic, lavender, honey, peaches, melons, cherries and a bounty of other sun-kissed fruit, veg and seasonal foods. Plane trees shade the atmospheric T-shaped square where Aixois catch up over *un café* on cafe terraces after shopping.

Flower markets fill place des Prêcheurs (Sunday morning) and place de l'Hôtel de Ville (Tuesday, Thursday and Saturday mornings); and a **flea market** (place de Verdun; ☉Tue, Thu & Sat mornings) promises quirky vintage finds three mornings a week.

Breads baked by artisanal *boulanger* Benoît Fradette delight at **Farinoman Fou** (www.farinomanfou.fr; 3 rue Mignet; breads €1-3; ☉7am-7pm Tue-Sat), a phenomenal bakery with a constant queue outside.

Carpentras

For all-round atmosphere Carpentras' Friday-morning market is unbeatable. Streets spill over with more than 350 stalls laden with bread, honey, cheese, olives, fruit and a rainbow of *berlingots*, Carpentras' striped, pillow-shaped hard-boiled sweets. During winter a pungent **truffle**

Salami and sausages for sale at Aix-en-Provence's food market

market murmurs with hushed-tone transactions. The truffle season is kicked off by Carpentras' biggest fair, held during the **Fête de St-Siffrein** on 27 November, when more than 1000 stalls spread across town.

Markets aside, this slightly rundown agricultural town has but a handful of historic sights. A Greek trading centre and later a Gallo-Roman city, it became papal territory in 1229, and was also shaped by a strong Jewish presence; Jews who had been expelled from French crown territory took refuge here.

Apt

Apt's huge Saturday-morning *marché Provençal* attracts hordes of locals and tourists alike. The principal town in the Luberon, Apt is edged on three sides by sharply rising plateaux surrounding a river that runs through town. At the market, look out for Apt's local speciality: *fruits confits* (candied fruits, sometimes also known as glacé or crystallised fruit), made with real fruit, in which the water is removed and replaced with a sugar syrup to preserve them.

Cavaillon

Cavaillon is synonymous with sweet cantaloupe melons – best shopped for at the small town's early-morning Monday market, May to September, or during July's four-day **Fête du Melon**.

L'Isle-sur-la-Sorgue

A moat of flowing water encircles the ancient and prosperous town of L'Isle-sur-la-Sorgue. This 'Venice of Provence' is home to several antiques villages, housing 300 dealers between them. Sunday is the big market day, with antique vendors participating as well, while Thursday offers a smaller market through the village streets.

L'Isle dates to the 12th century, when fishers built huts on stilts above what was then a marsh. By the 18th century, canals lined with 70 giant wheels powered silk factories and paper mills. The exceptional historic centre is contained within canals dotted by creaking waterwheels – the one by the tiny park at ave des Quatre Otages is particularly photogenic. The ancient fishers' quarter, a tangle of narrow passageways, dead-ends in L'Isle's eastern corner and retains a town-within-a-town feeling.

A **tourist-office** (☏04 90 38 04 78; www.oti-delasorgue.fr; place de la Liberté; ☉9am-12.30pm & 2.30-6pm Mon-Sat, 9.30am-1pm Sun) brochure details the attractions, and there's an app you can download.

ADRIAN HANCU / GETTY IMAGES ©

Take a Break

Lunch in Carpentras at fashionable brasserie **Chez Serge** (☏04 90 63 21 24; www.chez-serge.com; 90 rue Cottier; lunch/dinner menus from €17/27; ☉noon-2pm & 7.30-10pm Jun-Sep, noon-1.30pm & 7.30-9.30pm Oct-May; 🛜🛝) – truffles in season!

SIGURCAMP / SHUTTERSTOCK ©

Pont du Gard

Southern France has some fine Roman sites, but nothing can top the Unesco World Heritage–listed Pont du Gard, a breathtaking three-tiered aqueduct 25km west of Avignon.

The extraordinary three-tiered Pont du Gard was once part of a 50km-long system of channels built around 19 BC to transport water from Uzès to Nîmes. The scale is huge: the bridge is 48.8m high, 275m long and graced with 35 precision-built arches; it was sturdy enough to carry up to 20,000 cu metres of water per day.

Musée de la Romanité

Each block was carved by hand and transported from nearby quarries – no mean feat, considering the largest blocks weighed over 5 tonnes. The height of the bridge descends by 2.5cm across its length, providing just enough gradient to keep the water flowing – an amazing demonstration of the precision of Roman engineering. The Musée de la Romanité

Great For...

☑ **Don't Miss**

With kids: fun, hands-on learning in the Ludo play area.

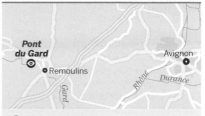

ⓘ Need to Know

☐04 66 37 50 99; www.pontdugard.fr; car
& up to 5 passengers €18, after 8pm €10, by
bicycle or on foot €7, after 8pm €3.50; ⊘site
24hr year-round, visitor centre & museum
9am-8pm Jul & Aug, shorter hours Sep–mid-
Jan & mid-Feb–Jun

✖ Take a Break

Dine at outstanding restaurant **Le
Tracteur** (www.lucietestud.com/
lctracteur/) in nearby Argilliers.

★ Top Tip

Evening is a good time to visit: admission is cheaper and the bridge is
illuminated.

provides background on the bridge's
construction.

Mémoires de Garrigue

You can walk across the tiers for panoramic
views over the Gard River, but the best perspective on the bridge is from downstream,
along the 1.4km Mémoires de Garrigue
walking trail.

Canoeing on the Gard

Paddling beneath the Pont du Gard is
unforgettable. The best time to do it is early
spring between April and June, as winter
floods and summer droughts can sometimes make the river impassable.

The Gard flows from the Cévennes
mountains all the way to the aqueduct,
passing through the dramatic **Gorges du
Gardon** en route.

Hire companies are in Collias, 8km from
the bridge, a journey of about two hours by
kayak. Depending on the season and height
of the river, canoe further by being dropped
upstream at Pont St-Nicholas (19km, four
to five hours) or Russan (32km, six to seven
hours); the latter includes a memorable
paddle through the Gorges du Gardon.

There's a minimum age of six. Life jack-
ets are always provided, but you must be a
competent swimmer.

Avignon

Attention, quiz fans: name the city where the pope lived during the 14th century. Answered Rome? Bzzz: sorry, wrong answer. For 70-odd years, the Provençal town of Avignon served as the centre of the Roman Catholic world, and though its stint as the seat of papal power only lasted a few decades, it's been left with an impressive legacy of ecclesiastical architecture, most notably the soaring, World Heritage–listed fortress-cum-palace known as the Palais des Papes.

Avignon is now best known for its annual arts festival, the largest in France, which draws thousands of visitors for several weeks in July. The rest of the year it's a lovely city to explore, with boutique-lined streets, leafy squares and some excellent restaurants – as well as an impressive medieval wall that entirely encircles the old city.

> *testament to the medieval might of the Roman Catholic church*

Palais des Papes

⊚ SIGHTS

Palais des Papes   Palace

(Papal Palace; www.palais-des-papes.com; place du Palais; adult/child €11/9, with Pont St-Bénezet €13.50/10.50; ⊗9am-8pm Jul, to 8.30pm Aug, shorter hours Sep-Jun) The largest Gothic palace ever built, the Palais des Papes was built by Pope Clement V, who abandoned Rome in 1309 as a result of violent disorder following his election. It served as the seat of papal power for seven decades, and its immense scale provides ample testament to the medieval might of the Roman Catholic Church. Ringed by 3m-thick walls, its cavernous halls, chapels and antechambers are largely bare today, but an audioguide (€2) provides a useful backstory.

Musée du Petit Palais   Museum

(⌨04 90 86 44 58; www.petit-palais.org; place du Palais; adult/child €6/free; ⊗10am-1pm & 2-6pm Wed-Mon) The archbishops' palace during the 14th and 15th centuries now houses outstanding collections of primitive, pre-Rennaissance, 13th- to 16th-century Italian religious paintings by artists includ-

THANH DROMARD / 500PX ©

ing Botticelli, Carpaccio and Giovanni di Paolo – the most famous is Botticelli's *La Vierge et l'Enfant* (1470).

Pont St-Bénezet   Bridge
(bd du Rhône; adult/child 24hr ticket €5/4, with Palais des Papes €13.50/10.50; ⊙9am-8pm Jul, to 8.30pm Aug, shorter hours Sep-Jun) Legend says Pastor Bénezet had three saintly visions urging him to build a bridge across the Rhône. Completed in 1185, the 900m-long bridge with 20 arches linked Avignon with Villeneuve-lès-Avignon. It was rebuilt several times before all but four of its spans were washed away in the 1600s.

If you don't want to pay to visit the bridge, admire it for free from Rocher des Doms park, Pont Édouard Daladier or on Île de la Barthelasse's chemin des Berges.

Musée Angladon   Art Museum
(☑04 90 82 29 03; www.angladon.com; 5 rue Laboureur; adult/child €8/6.50; ⊙1-6pm Tue-Sun Apr-Sep, 1-6pm Tue-Sat Oct-Mar) Tiny Musée Angladon harbours an impressive collection of impressionist treasures, including works by Cézanne, Sisley, Manet and Degas – but the star piece is Van Gogh's *Railway Wagons*, the only painting by the artist on display in Provence. Impress your friends by pointing out that the 'earth' isn't actually paint, but bare canvas.

Collection Lambert   Art Museum
(☑04 90 16 56 20; www.collectionlambert.com; 5 rue Violette; adult/child €10/8; ⊙11am-6pm Tue-Sun Sep-Jun, to 7pm daily Jul & Aug) Reopened in summer 2015 after significant renovation and expansion, Avignon's contemporary-arts museum focuses on works from the 1960s to the present. Work spans from minimalist and conceptual to video and photography – in stark contrast to the classic 18th-century mansion housing it.

🟢 ACTIVITIES
Le Carré du Palais   Wine Tasting
(☑04 90 27 24 00; www.carredupalaisavignon.com; 1 place du Palais) The historic Hôtel Cal-

Lessons at the Market

Avignon's covered food market, **Les Halles** (www.avignon-leshalles.com; place Pie; ⊙6am-1.30pm Tue-Fri, to 2pm Sat & Sun), has over 40 food stalls showcasing seasonal Provençal ingredients. Even better, free cooking demonstrations are held at 11am on Saturdays. Outside on place Pie, admire Patrick Blanc's marvellous vegetal wall.

Fresh shrimp at Les Halles
STEVE ESTVANIK / SHUTTERSTOCK ©

vet de la Palun building in central Avignon has been renovated into a wine centre promoting and serving Côtes du Rhône and Vallée du Rhône appellations. Stop in to get a taste of the local vintages.

Avignon Wine Tour   Tours
(☑06 28 05 33 84; www.avignon-wine-tour.com; per person €80-100) Visit the region's vineyards with a knowledgeable guide, leaving you free to enjoy the wine.

❌ EATING
Place de l'Horloge is crammed with touristy restaurants that don't offer the best cuisine or value in town. Delve instead into the pedestrian old city where ample pretty squares tempt: place des Châtaignes and place de la Principe are two particularly beautiful restaurant-clad squares.

Restaurants open seven days during the summer festival season, when reservations become essential.

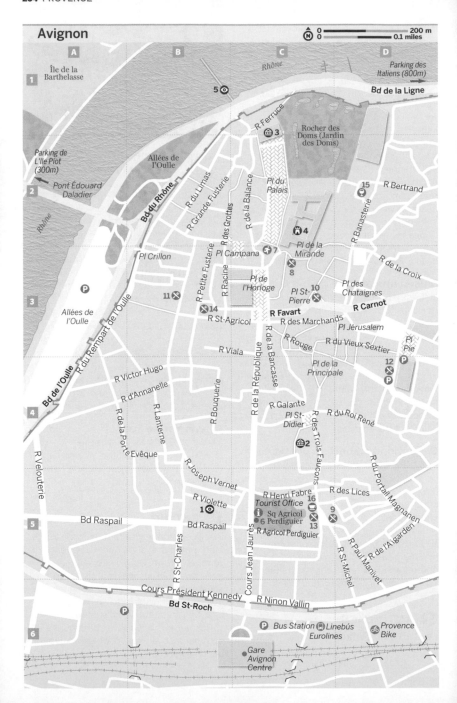

Avignon

Maison Violette   Boulangerie €

(☑06 59 44 62 94; place des Corps Saints; ☺7am-7.30pm Mon-Sat) We simply defy you to walk into this bakery and not instantly be tempted by the stacks of baguettes, *ficelles* and *pains de campagnes* loaded up on the counter, not to mention the orderly ranks of éclairs, *millefeuilles*, fruit tarts and cookies lined up irresistibly behind the glass. Go on, a little bit of what you fancy does you good, non?

Ginette et Marcel   Cafe €

(☑04 90 85 58 70; 27 place des Corps Saints; tartines €4.30-6.90; ☺11am-11pm Wed-Mon; ⊞) Set on one of Avignon's most happening plane-tree-shaded squares, this vintage cafe styled like a 1950s grocery is a charming spot to hang out and people-watch over a *tartine* (open-face sandwich), tart, salad or other light dish – equally tasty for lunch or an early-evening *apéro*. Kids adore Ginette's cherry- and violet-flavoured cordials and Marcel's glass jars of old-fashioned sweets.

Restaurant L'Essentiel   French €€

(☑04 90 85 87 12; www.restaurantlessentiel. com; 2 rue Petite Fusterie; menus €32-46; ☺noon-2pm & 7-9.45pm Tue-Sat) Snug in an elegant, caramel-stone *hôtel particulier* (private mansion) the Essential is one of the finest places to eat in town – inside or in the wonderful courtyard garden. Begin with courgette flowers poached in a crayfish and truffle sauce, then continue with rabbit stuffed with candied aubergine, perhaps.

L'Épicerie   Bistro €€

(☑04 90 82 74 22; www.restaurantlepicerie.fr; 10 place St-Pierre; lunch/dinner menus from €16/23; ☺noon-2.30pm & 8-10pm) Traditional and unashamedly so, this cosy bistro is a fine spot for hearty French dishes, from homemade foie gras to a mixed platter of Provençal produce (€19). All the bistro boxes receive a big tick: checked tablecloths, vintage signs, friendly waiters, great local wines by the glass.

Christian Etienne   Provençal €€€

(☑04 90 86 16 50; www.christian-etienne.fr; 10 rue de Mons; lunch/dinner menus from €35/75; ☺noon-2pm & 7.30-10pm Tue-Sat) One of Avignon's top tables, this much-vaunted restaurant occupies a 12th-century palace with a leafy outdoor terrace, adjacent to Palais des Papes. Interiors feel slightly dated, but the refined Provençal cuisine remains exceptional, and the restaurant has earned a Michelin star.

Les 5 Sens   Gastronomic €€€

(☑04 90 85 26 51; www.restaurantles5sens.com; 18 rue Joseph Vernet; menus lunch €16-22, dinner €40-59; ☺noon-1.30pm & 7.45-11.30pm Tue-Sat) Chef Thierry Baucher, one of France's *meilleurs ouvriers* (top chefs), reveals his southwestern origins in specialities such as *cassoulet* and foie gras but skews contemporary-Mediterranean in gastronomic dishes such as butternut-squash ravioli with *escargots*. Surroundings are sleek; service is impeccable.

🍷 DRINKING & NIGHTLIFE

Chic yet laid-back Avignon is awash with gorgeous, tree-shaded pedestrian squares buzzing with cafe life. Favourite options, loaded with pavement terraces and drinking opportunities, include place Crillon, place Pie, place de l'Horloge and Place des Corps Saints.

Students tend to favour the many bars dotted along the aptly named rue de la Verrerie (Glassware St).

La Manutention   Bar

(4 rue des Escaliers Ste-Anne; ⊘noon-midnight) No address better reflects Avignon's artsy soul than this bistro-bar at cultural centre La Manutention. Its leafy terrace basks in the shade of Palais des Papes' stone walls and, inside, giant conservatory-style windows open onto the funky decor of pocket-size bar Utopia. There's a cinema too.

Milk Shop   Cafe

(🗩09 82 54 16 82; www.milkshop.fr; 26 place des Corps Saints; ⊘7.45am-7pm Mon-Fri, 9.30am-7pm Sat; 🛜) Keen to mingle with Avignon students? Make a beeline for this *salon*

au lait ('milk bar') where super-thick ice-cream shakes (€4.50) are slurped through extra-wide straws. Bagels (€5 to €7), cupcakes and other American snacks create a deliberate US vibe, while comfy armchairs and wi-fi encourage hanging out.

ℹ️ INFORMATION

Tourist Office (🗩04 32 74 32 74; www.avignon-tourisme.com; 41 cours Jean Jaurès; ⊘9am-6pm Mon-Sat, 10am-5pm Sun Apr-Oct, shorter hours Nov-Mar) Offers guided walking tours and information on other tours and activities, including boat trips on the Rhône and wine-tasting trips to nearby vineyards. Smartphone apps too.

Tourist Office Annex (Gare Avignon TGV; ⊘Jun-Aug) During summer, Avignon has an information booth at the TGV station.

ℹ️ GETTING THERE & AWAY

AIR

Aéroport Avignon-Provence (AVN; 🗩04 90 81 51 51; www.avignon.aeroport.fr; Caumont)

From left: Les Baux-de-Provence (p194); Moustiers Ste-Marie (p208); Pont St-Bénezet (p203) and Palais des Papes (p202), Avignon

In Caumont, 8km southeast of Avignon. Direct flights to London, Birmingham and Southampton in the UK.

BUS

The **bus station** (bd St-Roch; ⊙information window 8am-7pm Mon-Fri, to 1pm Sat) is next to the central train station. Tickets are sold on board. For schedules, see www.lepilote.com, www.info-ler.fr and www.vaucluse.fr. Long-haul companies **Linebús** (☑04 90 85 30 48; www.linebus.com) and **Eurolines** (☑04 90 85 27 60; www.eurolines.com) have offices at the far end of bus platforms and serve places like Barcelona.

Aix-en-Provence €17.40, LER Line 23, 1¼ hours, six daily Monday to Saturday, two on Sunday.

Carpentras €2, Transvaucluse Line 5.1, 45 minutes, two or three hourly Monday to Saturday, every two hours Sunday.

TRAIN

Avignon has two train stations: **Gare Avignon Centre** (42 bd St-Roch), on the southern edge of the walled town, and **Gare Avignon TGV**, 4km southwest in Courtine. Local shuttle trains link the two every 20 minutes (€1.60, five minutes,

6am to 11pm). Note that there is no luggage storage at the train station.

Destinations served by TGV include Paris Gare du Lyon (€35 to €80, 3½ hours), Marseille (€17.50, 35 minutes) and Nice (€31 to €40, 3¼ hours). **Eurostar** (www.eurostar.com) services operate one to five times weekly between Avignon TGV and London (from €59.50, 5¾ hours) en route to/from Marseille.

Marseille €17.50, 1¼ to two hours.

Marseille airport (Vitrolles station) €14.50, one to 1½ hours.

ⓘ GETTING AROUND

BICYCLE

Vélopop (☑08 10 45 64 56; www.velopop.fr) Shared-bicycle service, with 17 stations around town. The first half-hour is free; each additional half hour is €1. Membership per day/week is €1/5.

Provence Bike (☑04 90 27 92 61; www.provence-bike.com; 7 av St-Ruf; bicycles per day/week from €12/65, scooters €25/150; ⊙9am-6.30pm Mon-Sat, plus 10am-1pm Sun Jul)

Avignon Pass

An excellent-value discount card, **Avignon Passion** yields cheaper admission to big-hitter museums and monuments in Avignon and Villeneuve-lès-Avignon. The first site visited is full price, but each subsequent site is discounted. The pass is free, valid 15 days, covers a couple of tours too, and is available at the **tourist office** (p206) and at museums.

Rents city bikes, mountain bikes, scooters and motorcycles.

CAR & MOTORCYCLE

Find car-hire agencies at both train stations (reserve ahead, especially in July). Narrow, one-way streets and impossible parking make driving within the ramparts difficult: park outside the walls. The city has 900 free spaces at **Parking de L'Ile Piot**, and 1150 at **Parking des Italiens**, both under surveillance and served by the free **TCRA shuttle bus** (Transports en Commun de la Région d'Avignon; ☑04 32 74 18 32; www.tcra.fr). On directional signs at intersections, 'P' in yellow means pay lots; 'P' in green, free lots. Pay **Parking Gare Centre** (☑04 90 80 74 40; bd St-Roch; ☺24hr) is next to the central train station.

Moustiers Ste-Marie

Dubbed 'Étoile de Provence' (Star of Provence), jewel-box Moustiers Ste-Marie crowns towering limestone cliffs, which mark the beginning of the Alps and the end of Haute-Provence's rolling plains. A 227m-long chain, bearing a shining gold star, is stretched high above the village – a tradition, legend has it, begun by the Knight of Blacas, who was grateful to have returned safely from the Crusades. Twice a century, the weathered chain snaps, and the star gets replaced, as happened in 1996. In summer, it's clear that Moustiers' charms are no secret.

◎ SIGHTS

Chapelle Notre Dame de Beauvoir
Church

(guided tours adult/child €3/free) Lording over the village, beneath Moustiers' star, this 14th-century church clings to a cliff ledge like an eagle's nest. A steep trail climbs beside a waterfall to the chapel, passing 14 stations of the cross en route. On 8 September, Mass at 5am celebrates the nativity of the Virgin Mary, followed by flutes, drums and breakfast on the square.

Musée de la Faïence
Museum

(☑04 92 74 61 64; rue Seigneur de la Clue; adult/student/under 16yr €3/2/free; ☺10am-12.30pm Jul & Aug, to 5pm or 6pm rest of year, closed Tue year-round) Moustiers' decorative *faïence* (glazed earthenware) once graced the dining tables of Europe's most aristocratic houses. Today each of Moustiers' 15 ateliers has its own style, from representational to abstract. Antique masterpieces are housed in this little museum, adjacent to the town hall.

✪ ACTIVITIES

Des Guides pour l'Aventure
Outdoors

(☑06 85 94 46 61; www.guidesaventure.com) Offers activities including canyoning (from €45 per half-day), rock climbing (€40 for three hours), rafting (€45 for 2½ hours) and 'floating' (€50 for three hours) – which is like rafting, except you have a buoyancy aid instead of a boat.

✪ EATING

La Grignotière
Provençal €

(☑04 92 74 69 12; rte de Ste-Anne; mains €6-15; ☺11.30am-10pm May-Sep, to 6pm Feb–mid-May) Hidden behind the soft pink façade of Moustier's Musée de la Faïence is this utterly gorgeous, blissfully peaceful garden restaurant. Tables sit between olive trees and the colourful, eye-catching decor – including the handmade glassware – is the handiwork of talented, dynamic owner

Moustiers Ste-Marie

Sandrine. Cuisine is 'picnic chic', meaning lots of creative salads, tapenades, quiches and so on.

La Treille Muscate   Provençal €€

(☎04 92 74 64 31; www.restaurant-latreille muscate.fr; place de l'Église; lunch/dinner menus from €24/32; ⊗noon-2pm Fri-Wed, 7.30-10.30pm Fri-Tue) The top place to eat in the village proper: classic Provençal cooking served with panache, either in the stone-walled dining room or on the terrace with valley views. Expect tasty dishes like oven-roasted lamb served with seasonal veg, and rainbow trout with *sauce vierge*. Reservations recommended.

La Ferme Ste-Cécile   Gastronomic €€

(☎04 92 74 64 18; D952; menus €29-38; ⊗noon-2pm Tue-Sun, 7.30-10pm Tue-Sat) Just outside Moustiers, this wonderful *ferme auberge* (country inn) immerses you in the full Provençal dining experience, from the sunsplashed terrace and locally picked wines right through to the chef's meticulous

Mediterranean cuisine. It's about 1.2km from Moustiers; look out for the signs as you drive towards Castellane.

La Bastide de Moustiers   Gastronomic €€€

(☎04 92 70 47 47; www.bastide-moustiers.com; chemin de Quinson; lunch menus €40-50, dinner menus €64-82; ⊗noon-2pm & 7.30-9.30pm May-Sep, closed Tue & Wed Oct-Apr; 🌲) Legendary chef Alain Ducasse has created his own Provençal bolthole here, and it's an utter treat from start to finish, from the playful *amuses bouches* to the rich, sauce-heavy mains and indulgent desserts. The views from the terrace are dreamy too. Dress smartly and reserve ahead in high season. It's 500m down a country lane, signposted off the D952 to Ste-Croix de Verdon.

ⓘ GETTING THERE & AROUND

A car makes exploring the gorges much more fun, though if you're very fit, cycling is an option too. Bus services run to Castellane and Moustiers, but there's scant transport inside the gorges.

NICE

In This Chapter

Nice at a Glance...

With its mix of real-city grit, old-world opulence, year-round sunshine and stunning seaside location, Nice is the unofficial capital of the French Riviera (known as the Côte d'Azur in French), and a must-see for every visitor. A magnet for sunseekers since the 19th century, this bewitching coastal city has so much going for it, it's almost embarrassing – fabulous markets, an enticing old town, glorious architecture and a wealth of super restaurants. It's far from perfect – the traffic's horrendous and the beach is made entirely of pebbles – but if you really want to soak up the Riviera vibe, there's really no better place to do it.

Nice in Two Days

Explore **Vieux Nice** (p214); lunch local at **Chez René Socca** (p225) and end on a natural high in **Parc du Château** (p215). Spend the afternoon on **Promenade des Anglais** (p220), then dine at **Le Bistrot d'Antoine** (p225). Day two, discover Matisse and Chagall in **Cimiez** (p221), and spend the afternoon learning about belle époque Nice at the **Musée Masséna** (p220). Enjoy an aperitif at **Les Distilleries Idéales** (p215) and dinner at **Olive et Artichaut** (p226).

Nice in Four Days

Shop for picnic supplies at cours Saleya food market, then head out of town and be wowed by huge sea views along the hair-raising **Grande Corniche** (p218); visit La Turbie's **Trophée des Alpes** (p218) and picnic. Drop down to the **Moyenne Corniche** (p218), ending in **Èze** (p218) for extraordinary Riviera views. Last day, follow the **Corniche Inférieure** (p219) along the coast to **Monaco** (p228); lunch in **Villefranche-sur-Mer** (p219).

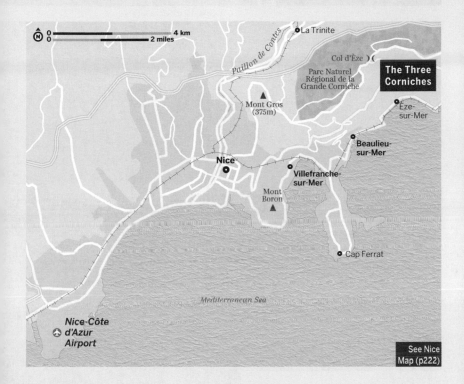

Arriving in Nice

Nice-Côte d'Azur Airport Buses 98 and 99 to Promenade des Anglais and Nice train station respectively (€6, 35 minutes, every 20 minutes). Taxi to downtown Nice €23 to €31.

Nice train station In the centre of Nice, a 15-minute walk to Promenade des Anglais or 15 minutes to the waterfront by bus 12.

Sleeping

Accommodation is excellent and caters to all budgets, unlike many cities on the Côte d'Azur. Hotels charge substantially more during the Monaco Grand Prix and get booked up quickly in July and August; book well in advance in summer. For accommodation info online see **Nice Tourisme** (http://en.nicetourisme. com).

Place Massena, Vieux Nice

ANDREA KAMAL / GETTY IMAGES ©

Vieux Nice

Getting lost among the narrow, winding alleyways of Nice's old town is a highlight. The layout has barely changed since the 1700s, and restaurants, boutiques and bars pack out its atmospheric streets.

Great For...

☑ Don't Miss

A slice of *socca* (chickpea-flour pancake) on the raucous pavement terrace at Chez René Socca (p225).

Cours Saleya

This joyous, thriving market square – permanently thronged in summer – is the life and soul of Vieux Nice. Every morning, Tuesday to Sunday, from 6am until lunchtime, a massive **food market** (cours Saleya; ☉6am-1.30pm Tue-Sun) fills much of the square, stalls laden with fruit and vegetables, olives marinated a dozen different ways, every herb and spice known under the Provençal sun – no market is a finer reflection of local Niçois life. An adjoining **flower market** (cours Saleya; ☉6am-5.30pm Tue-Sat, to 1.30pm Sun) is worth a meander just for its vibrant colours and fragrances; Monday ushers in a **flea market** (cours Saleya; ☉8am-5pm Mon).

Cathédrale Ste-Réparate

WENDY CONNETT / ROBERT HARDING ©

ℹ Need to Know

Themed walking tours in English at the Centre du Patrimoine (p223).

✕ Take a Break

Queue for a lavender and violet or tomato ice cream from master ice-cream maker Fenocchio (p224).

★ Top Tip

Duck and dive your way through the old town to Nice's fish market, place St-François.

Baroque Gems

Baroque aficionados will adore architectural gems **Cathédrale Ste-Réparate** (place Rossetti), honouring the city's patron saint; and exuberant **Chapelle de la Miséricorde** (cours Saleya), a chapel from 1740 renowned for its exceptionally rich architecture. Tricky to spot because of the narrow lane it sits on, **Palais Lascaris** (📞 04 93 62 72 40; 15 rue Droite; guided visit €6; ⏰10am-6pm Wed-Mon) **FREE**, is a 17th-century mansion housing a frescoed orgy of Flemish tapestries, faïence and gloomy religious paintings. On the ground floor is an 18th-century pharmacy.

Bird's-Eye Panorama

For the best views over Vieux Nice's red-tiled rooftops, climb the winding staircases up to **Parc du Château** (⏰8.30am-8pm Apr-Sep, to 6pm Oct-Mar) **FREE**, a wooded outcrop on the eastern edge of the old town. It's been occupied since ancient times; archaeological digs have revealed Celtic and Roman remains, and the site was later occupied by a medieval castle that was razed by Louis XIV in 1706 – only the 16th-century Tour Bellanda remains. There are various entrances, including one beside the tower – or cheat and ride the free lift.

People Watching over Drinks

Lounging on an old-town cafe terrace, watching the world go by over a glass of pastis or post beach cocktail, is a national pastime in Nice. **Les Distilleries Idéales** (📞04 93 62 10 66; www.lesdistilleriesideales. fr; 24 rue de la Préfecture; ⏰9am-12.30am) is best for beer on tap and local wine in the old town, and choices abound on cafe-lined cours Saleya.

Or nip around to La Shounga (p227), and all-day cocktail bar with ice-cream sundaes and other desserts. Snag a seat outside gazing out at the Med and know you've hit Nice's jet-setter jackpot.

Villefranche-sur-Mer (p219)

The Three Corniches

This trio of corniches (coastal roads) hugs the cliffs between Nice and Monaco, each higher than the last, with dazzling views of the Med. For the grandest views, it's the Grande Corniche you want, but the Moyenne Corniche runs a close scenic second. The lowest of all, the Corniche Inférieure, allows access to a string of snazzy coastal resorts.

Great For...

ⓘ Need to Know

Take bus 116 from Nice to La Turbie along the Grande Corniche; bus 82 along the Moyenne Corniche to Èze; trains and bus 100 along Corniche Inférieure.

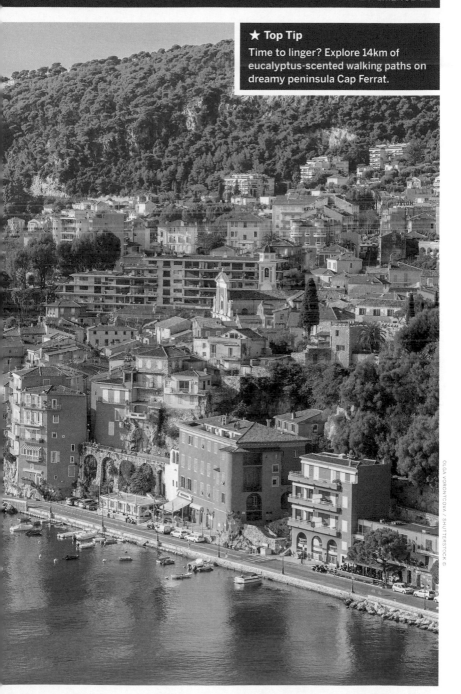

★ **Top Tip**
Time to linger? Explore 14km of
eucalyptus-scented walking paths on
dreamy peninsula Cap Ferrat.

Grande Corniche

Views from the spectacular cliff-hanging Grande Corniche are mesmerising. Alfred Hitchcock was sufficiently impressed by Napoléon's Grande Corniche to use it as a backdrop for his film *To Catch a Thief* (1956), starring Cary Grant and Grace Kelly. Ironically, Kelly died in 1982 after crashing her car on this very same road.

Sitting 675m above the sea and just below Èze, **Fort de la Revère** is the perfect place to revel in 360-degree views. The fort was built in 1870 to protect Nice (it served as an Allied prisoner camp during WWII). There are picnic tables under the trees for an al fresco lunch and dozens of walking trails in the surrounding **Parc Naturel Départemental de la Grande Corniche**, a protected area that stretches along the D2564 from Col d'Èze to La Turbie.

There are no villages of note along the Grande Corniche until you reach hilltop **La Turbie**, known for its monumental Roman triumphal monument called Trophée des Alpes, visible from all directions. This amazing monument was built by Emperor Augustus in 6 BC to celebrate his victory over the Celto-Ligurian Alpine tribes that had fought Roman sovereignty (the names of the 45 tribes are carved on the western side of the monument). The tower teeters on the highest point of the old Roman road, with dramatic views of Monaco.

Moyenne Corniche

Cut through rock in the 1920s, the Moyenne Corniche takes drivers from Nice past the Col de Villefranche (149m) to **Èze**, a rocky little village perched on an impossible

View of the Mediterranean Sea from Èze

peak. A jewel in the Riviera crown, Èze is a medieval village stitched from a rabbit warren of small stone houses, winding lanes and second-to-none coastal views.

Gorge on the best panorama from **Jardin Exotique d'Èze** (📞04 93 41 10 30; adult/child €6/2.50; ⏱9am-7.30pm Jul-Sep, to 6.30pm Apr-Jun, to 5.30pm rest of year), a cactus garden at the top of the village, next to old castle ruins. Take time to sit here or in the garden's Zen area to contemplate the stunning view: few places on earth offer such a wild panorama.

Corniche Inférieure

Skimming the villa-lined waterfront between Nice and Monaco, the lowest coastal road – the Corniche Inférieure – was built in the 1860s. It passes through a string of snazzy coastal resorts and is perfect for a dip in the sea.

Villefranche-sur-Mer is a gorgeous seaside village heaped above a picture-postcard harbour, with an imposing citadel. Its 14th-century old town, with evocatively named streets broken by twisting staircases and glimpses of the sea, is a delight to amble. Villefranche was a favourite of Jean Cocteau (1889–1963), who sought solace here in 1924 after the death of his companion Raymond Radiguet and went on to decorate the interior of 14th-century **Chapelle St-Pierre** (admission €3; ⏱10am-noon & 3-7pm Wed-Mon Apr-Sep, 10am-noon & 2-6pm Oct-Mar) with a mirage of mystical frescoes.

In chic **St-Jean-Cap Ferrat** follow the crowds to **Villa Ephrussi de Rothschild** (📞04 93 01 33 09; www.villa-ephrussi.com/en; adult/child €13/10; ⏱10am-7pm Jul & Aug, 10am-6pm Feb-Jun, Sep & Oct, 2-6pm Mon-Fri, 10am-6pm Sat & Sun Nov-Jan), an over-the-top belle époque confection commissioned by Baroness Béatrice Ephrussi de Rothschild in 1912. The villa is filled with Fragonard paintings, Louis XVI furniture and Sèvres porcelain, and its nine exquisite themed gardens are stunning – sea views are supreme and fountains 'dance' to classical music every 20 minutes.

★ Don't Miss

In the old town of Villefranche-sur-Mer, don't miss eerie, arcaded rue Obscure, a historical monument a block in from the water.

WEI HAO HO / GETTY IMAGES ©

✗ Take a Break

Swoon-worthy sea views over a chic aperitif and/or a Michelin-starred meal at boutique restaurant-hotel **Château Eza** (www.chateaueza.com) in Èze.

⊙ SIGHTS

Promenade
des Anglais   Architecture

The most famous stretch of seafront in Nice – if not France – is this vast paved promenade, which gets its name from the English expat patrons who paid for it in 1822. It runs for the whole 4km sweep of the Baie des Anges with a dedicated lane for cyclists and skaters; if you fancy joining them, you can rent skates, scooters and bikes from Roller Station.

Musée Masséna   Museum

(☑04 93 91 19 10; 65 rue de France; adult/child €6/free; ◷10am-6pm Wed-Mon) Originally built as a holiday home for Prince Victor d'Essling (the grandson of one of Napoléon's favourite generals, Maréchal Masséna), this lavish belle époque building is another of the city's iconic architectural landmarks. Built between 1898 and 1901 in grand neoclassical style with an Italianate twist, it's now a fascinating museum dedicated to the history of the Riviera – taking in everything from holidaying monarchs to expat Americans, the boom of tourism and the enduring importance of carnival.

Musée d'Art Moderne
et d'Art Contemporain Art Museum

(MAMAC; ☑04 97 13 42 01; www.mamac-nice.org; place Yves Klein; ◷10am-6pm Tue-Sun) **FREE** European and American avant-garde works from the 1950s to the present are the focus of this museum. Highlights include many works by Christo and Nice's New Realists: Niki de Saint Phalle, César, Arman and Yves Klein. The building's rooftop also works as an exhibition space (with knockout panoramas of Nice to boot).

✪ ACTIVITIES

Roller Station   Skating

(☑04 93 62 99 05; www.roller-station.fr; 49 quai des États-Unis; skates, boards & scooters per hr/day €5/10, bicycles €5/15; ◷9am-8pm Jul & Aug, 10am-7pm Sep-Jun) For a fantastic family

> *The most famous stretch of seafront in Nice*

Promenade des Anglais

BELLENA / SHUTTERSTOCK ©

outing, rent inline skates, skateboards, scooters and bicycles at this rental outlet to whizz along Nice's silky-smooth Promenade des Anglais. You'll need some ID as a deposit. Count an extra €1/2 per hour/day for protective gear (helmet and pads).

Mobilboard Nice   Segway

(☑04 93 80 21 27; www.mobilboard.com/nice-promenade; 2 rue Halévy; 30min initiation €17, 1/2hr tour €30/50) For an effortless cruise along Promenade des Anglais, hop aboard an electric Segway. Rental includes a 15-minute lesson on how to ride the two-wheeled, battery-powered 'vehicle', protective helmet and audioguide.

🟢 Beaches

Officially there are 25 named beaches strung out along the Baie des Anges, some of which are free, while others are reserved solely for paying clientele. All are pebbly, so sensitive behinds might opt for one of the private beaches (€15 to €22 per day) which come with sun-loungers and comfy mattresses.

Free cold-water showers, lifeguards and first-aid posts are available most of the way along the bay, including on the public beaches; there are also a few public toilets for which you have to pay a small charge. Most beaches also offer activities, from beach volleyball to jet skis and pedalos.

Nudity is perfectly acceptable on Nice's beaches, and locals certainly aren't shy about letting it all hang out – but of course, there's no obligation to bare all (or anything).

Plage Publique
des Ponchettes   Beach

Right opposite Vieux Nice, this is generally the busiest beach of all, with oiled bodies either baking in the sun or punching a ball on the beach-volleyball court.

🟢 TOURS

Trans Côte d'Azur   Boating

(www.trans-cote-azur.com; quai Lunel; ☺Apr-Oct) Trans Côte d'Azur runs one-hour boat

 Modern Art in Cimiez

North of Nice centre is the wealthy residential neighbourhood of Cimiez, home to some outstanding museums and belle époque architecture.

Musée Matisse (☑04 93 81 08 08; www.musee-matisse-nice.org; 164 av des Arènes de Cimiez; ☺10am-6pm Wed-Mon) This museum houses a fascinating assortment of works by Matisse, including oil paintings, drawings, sculptures, tapestries and Matisse's famous paper cut-outs. The permanent collection is displayed in a red-ochre 17th-century Genoese villa in an olive grove. Temporary exhibitions are in the futuristic basement building. Matisse is buried in the **Monastère Notre Dame de Cimiez** (place du Monastère; ☺8.30am-12.30pm & 2.30-6.30pm) cemetery, across the park from the museum.

Musée National Marc Chagall (☑04 93 53 87 20; www.musee-chagall.fr; 4 av Dr Ménard; adult/child €9/7; ☺10am-6pm Wed-Mon May-Oct, to 5pm Nov-Apr) The strange, dreamlike and often unsettling work of the Belarusian painter Marc Chagall (1887–1985) is displayed at this small museum, which owns the largest public collection of the painter's work. The main hall displays 12 huge interpretations (1954–67) of stories from Genesis and Exodus. From the city centre, allow about 20 minutes to walk to the museum (signposted from av de l'Olivetto).

Musée Matisse

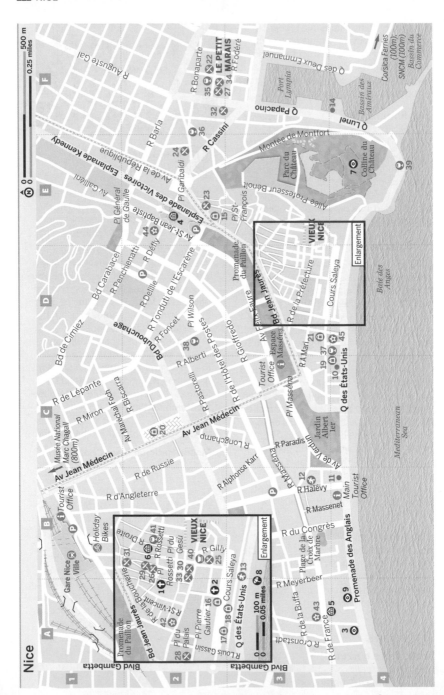

Nice

Nice

cruises along the Baie des Anges and Rade de Villefranche (adult/child €18/12.50) April to October. Mid-June to mid-September it sails to Île Ste-Marguerite (€40/30, one hour), St-Tropez (€65/50, 2½ hours), Monaco (€38/29.50, 45 minutes) and Cannes (€40/30, one hour).

Centre du Patrimoine   Walking
(75 quai des Etats-Unis; adult/child €5/free; ⊙8.30am-1pm & 2-5pm Mon-Thu, to 3.45pm Fri) The Centre du Patrimoine runs two-hour thematic walking tours. English-language tours must be booked two days in advance. The tourist office has a full listing.

L'OpenTour   Bus
(www.nice.opentour.com; opposite 109 quai des Etats-Unis; 1-/2-day pass adult €22/25, child €8) With headphone commentary in several languages, the open-topped bus tours (1½ hours) give you a good overview of Nice. Hop on or off at any one of 14 stops.

ⓐ SHOPPING

Shops abound in Nice, ranging from the touristy boutiques of Vieux Nice to the designer temples to fashion around rue de France and the enormous **Nice Étoile** (www.nicetoile.com; av Jean Médecin) shopping mall. For vintage (fashion and objects) and contemporary art, meander the hip Petit Marais north of Port Lympia. For gourmet gifts to take home, head for the market, where you'll find olive oil, wine, biscuits, candied fruits and much more.

Cave de la Tour   Wine
(☑04 93 80 03 31; www.cavedelatour.com; 3 rue de la Tour; ⊙7am-8pm Tue-Sat, 7am-12.30pm Sun) Since 1947 locals have been trusting this atmospheric *cave* (wine seller) to find the best wines from across the Alpes Maritimes and Var. It's a ramshackle kind of place, with upturned wine barrels and blackboard signs, and a loyal clientele,

 Le Petit Marais

Parisians might scoff at the idea, but Le Petit Marais in Nice is nicknamed after the trendy Marais district in Paris for good reason. The Niçois *quartier* – the area of town wedged between place Garibaldi and Port Lympia – buzzes with happening eating, drinking and boutique shopping addresses, firmly off the tourist radar but in the address book of every trendy local. Stroll the lengths of rue Bonaparte, rue Bavestro, rue Lascaris and surrounding streets to catch the city's latest hot new opening.

Our favourites: for bistro food and weekend drinks with local trendies, **L'Uzine** (📞04 93 56 42 39; 18 rue François Guisol; mains €14-20; ⊗11am-11pm Tue-Sat); for lunchtime salads, coffee, cakes and Sunday brunch, **Déli Bo** (📞04 93 56 33 04; 5 rue Bonaparte; mains €12-20; ⊗7am-8pm); for fine wine, many organic, wine bar and bistro **Vinivore** (📞04 93 14 68 09; www.vinivore.fr; 10 rue Lascaris; dinner menu €32-25, mains €18-25; ⊗noon-2pm & 7.30-10.30pm Tue-Fri, 7.30-10.30pm Sat); and for cocktails on slouchy sofas in an old lighting factory, **Comptoir Central Électrique** (📞04 93 14 09 62; www.comptoircentralelectrique.fr; 10 rue Bonaparte; ⊗8.30am-12.30am Mon-Sat).

Croissants, coffee and orange juice
MATT MUNRO/LONELY PLANET ©

including market traders and fishmongers getting their early-morning wine fix. Lots of wines are available by the glass.

Moulin à Huile d'Olive Alziari Food

(📞04 93 62 94 03; www.alziari.com.fr; 14 rue St-François de Paule; ⊗8.30am-12.30pm & 2.15-7pm Mon-Sat) Superb (but very expensive) hand-pressed olive oil, fresh from the mill on the outskirts of Nice. It comes in several flavours of differing fruitiness. The shop also sells delicious tapenades, jams, honeys and other goodies. From Monday to Friday, you can visit the mill to see the process in action: catch bus no 3 to the Terminus stop.

Pâtisserie Henri Auer Confiserie Food

(📞04 93 85 77 98; www.maison-auer.com; 7 rue St-François de Paule; ⊗9am-6pm Tue-Sat) With its gilded counters and mirrors, this looks more like a 19th-century boutique than a sweet shop, but this is where discerning Niçois have been buying their *fruits confits* (crystallised fruit) since 1820.

✖ EATING

Booking is advisable at most restaurants, particularly during the busy summer season. To lunch with locals, grab a pew in the midday sun on one of the many place Garibaldi cafe terraces. There are lots of restaurants on cours Saleya, but quality can be variable, so choose carefully.

Fenocchio Ice Cream €

(📞04 93 80 72 52; www.fenocchio.fr; 2 place Rossetti; 1/2 scoops €2.50/4; ⊗9am-midnight Feb-Oct) There's no shortage of ice-cream sellers in Vieux Nice, but *maître glacier* (master ice-cream maker) Fenocchio has been king of the scoops since 1966. The array of flavours is mind-boggling – olive, tomato, fig, beer, lavender and violet are just a few to try. Dither too long over the 70-plus flavours and you'll never make it to the front of the queue. For a Niçois twist, ask for *tourte de blette* (a sweet chard tart with raisins, pine nuts and parmesan). The queues at the main branch are long on hot summer days, but they're generally shorter at the **second branch** (📞04 93 62

88 80; www.fenocchio.fr; 6 rue de la Poissonerie; ⊙9am-midnight Wed-Mon) around the corner.

La Rossettisserie — French €
(☏04 93 76 18 80; www.larossettisserie.com; 8 rue Mascoïnat; mains €13.50-14.50; ⊙noon-2pm & 7.30-10pm Mon-Sat) Roast meat is the order of the day here: make your choice from beef, chicken, veal or lamb, and pair it with a choice of mashed or sautéed potatoes and ratatouille or salad. Simple and sumptuous, and the vaulted cellar is a delight.

Chez Pipo — Niçois €
(☏04 93 55 88 82; 13 rue Bavastro; socca €2.70; ⊙11.30am-2.30pm & 5.30-11pm Tue-Sun) Everyone says the best socca (chickpea-flour pancakes) can be found in the old town, but don't believe them – this place near Port Lympia has been in the biz since 1923, and for our money, knocks socca-shaped spots off anywhere else in Nice.

Chez René Socca — Niçois €
(☏04 93 92 05 73; 2 rue Miralhéti; small plates €3-6; ⊙9am-9pm Tue-Sun, to 10.30pm Jul & Aug, closed Nov; ☏) Don't expect service with a smile at this chaotic, no-frills corner restaurant – but do expect a slice of socca or a plate of petits farcis (stuffed vegetables), just like grande-mère used to make. Wines are available by the glass at the bar across the street.

La Merenda — Niçois €
(www.lamerenda.net; 4 rue Raoul Bosio; mains €14-16; ⊙noon-2pm & 7-10pm Mon-Fri) Simple, solid Niçois cuisine – stockfish, calf tripe à la Niçoise with panisse (chunky, pan-fried sticks of chickpea-flour batter) and the like – by former Michelin starred chef Dominique Le Stanc draws the crowds to this pocket-sized bistro where diners rub shoulders, literally. The tiny open kitchen stands proud at the back of the room, and the equally small menu is chalked on the board. No phone, no credit cards.

Le Bistrot d'Antoine — Modern French €€
(☏04 93 85 29 57; 27 rue de la Préfecture; menus €25-43, mains €15-25; ⊙noon-2pm & 7-10pm Tue-Sat) A quintessential French bistro, right down to the checked tablecloths,

Nice Étoile (p223)

DE AGOSTINI PICTURE LIBRARY / AGE FOTOSTOCK ©

Musée Masséna (p220)

> ❝ *fascinating museum dedicated to the history of the Riviera* ❞

street-side tables and impeccable service – not to mention the handwritten blackboard, loaded with classic dishes like rabbit pâté, pot-cooked pork, blood sausage and duck breast. If you've never eaten classic French food, this is definitely the place to start; and if you have, you're in for a treat.

Olive et Artichaut   Provençal €€

(☏04 89 14 97 51; www.oliveartichaut.com; 6 rue Ste-Réparate; 3-course menu €32, mains €16-22; ☉noon-2pm & 7.30-10pm Wed-Sun) There's barely enough room to swing a pan in this tiny street bistro, especially when it's full of diners (as it often is), but it doesn't seem to faze young Niçois chef Thomas Hubert and his friendly team. He sources as much produce as possible from close-to-home suppliers (Sisteron lamb, Niçois olives, locally caught fish) and likes to give the old classics his own individual spin. Wise diners reserve.

Jan   Modern French €€€

(☏04 97 19 32 23; www.restaurantjan.com; 12 rue Lascaris; 2-/3-course lunch menu €30/35, dinner menu €75; ☉ noon-2pm Fri & Sat, 6.30-10pm Tue-Sat) For the full-blown fine-dining experience, Jan Hendrik's restaurant is the top table in town. Born in South Africa, Jan laces his dishes with Antipodean and New World flavours and they crackle with artistic and culinary flair. There's nothing à la carte – Jan decides his *menus* on the day. It's high-end (dress smart) and sought after; reservations essential.

🍷 DRINKING & NIGHTLIFE

Cafe terraces on cours Saleya are lovely for an early-evening aperitif. Vieux Nice's bounty of pubs attracts a noisy, boisterous crowd; most bars have a happy hour from 6pm to 8pm.

El Merkado   Bar

(www.el-merkado.com; 12 rue St-François de Paule; ☉11am-1.30am) Footsteps from cours Saleya, this hip tapas bar (strapline: 'In Sangria We Trust') struts its vintage stuff on the ground floor of a quintessential Niçois town house. Lounging on its pavement terrace or a sofa with an after-beach cocktail is the thing to do here.

La Part des Anges — Wine Bar

(☑04 93 62 69 80; www.la-part-des-anges-nice. fr; 17 rue Gubernatis; ⏱10am-8.30pm Mon-Sat) The focus at this classy wine-shop-bar is organic wines – a few are sold by the glass, but the best selection is available by the bottle, served with homemade tapenades and charcuterie platters. The name means the 'Angel's Share', referring to the alcohol which evaporates as wines age. There are only a few tables, so arrive early or reserve ahead.

La Shounga — Cocktail Bar

(☑04 92 27 75 93; http://shounga.bar; 12 place Guynemer; ⏱8.30am-12.30am; ☎) Decadent, all-day desserts, ice-cream sundaes and cocktails (€8.50) are the reason to hit the sea-facing terrace of this vibrant mojito bar.

BaR'Oc — Wine Bar

(☑06 43 64 68 05; 10 rue Bavastro; ⏱7pm-12.30am) Fine wine and even finer tapas – from parma ham to oven-baked *figatelli* (a type of salami from Corsica) – plus tasting platters of cheese and cold cuts.

Snug & Cellar — Pub

(☑04 93 80 43 22; www.snugandcellar.com; 22 rue Droite; ⏱noon-12.30am) A more chilled retreat than many of the pubs in the old town, especially if you can bag one of the prime tables in the cosy cellar. Quizzes, bands and one-off events keep the interest going. Happy hour is from 8pm to 10pm.

✪ ENTERTAINMENT

Opéra de Nice — Opera

(www.opera-nice.org; 4-6 rue St-François de Paule) The vintage 1885 grande dame hosts operas, ballets and orchestral concerts.

Chez Wayne's — Live Music

(www.waynes.fr; 15 rue de la Préfecture; ⏱10am-2am) One of a strip of raucous drinking holes on the edge of the old town, Wayne's

🍽 Niçois Specialities

Nice's eponymous salad (crunchy lettuce, anchovies, olives, green beans and tomatoes in its purest form) has travelled far beyond its original shores. But there is much more to Niçois cuisine than *salade niçoise*. Here are five local specialities to try:

Stockfish Dried cod soaked in running water for a few days and then simmered with onions, tomatoes, garlic, olives and potatoes.

Socca A pancake made of chickpea flour and olive oil cooked on a griddle with sneezing quantities of black pepper.

Daube A rich beef stew of wine, onions, carrots, tomatoes and herbs; the sauce is often served with gnocchi or ravioli.

Petits farcis Stuffed vegetables (generally onions, courgette, courgette flowers, tomatoes and aubergines).

Pissaladière A pizza-like base topped with onions, garlic, olives and anchovies.

Daube
TRAVELLIGHT / SHUTTERSTOCK ©

Place is a proper pub, through and through: plenty of beers on tap, a nightly roster of bands and big-screen sports action. Scruffy as it comes, but great fun if that's what you're in the mood for.

Le Volume — Live Music

(www.source001.com; 6 rue Defly; ⏱11am-9pm Mon, to 12.30am Tue-Thu, to 1am Fri & Sat, 8.30pm-12.30am Sun; ☎) This dynamic cafe, cultural centre and live-music venue is the place to tune into the current and emerging

Daytrip to Monaco

Squeezed into just 200 hectares (2.8 sq km), this glitzy, glam confetti principality – the world's second-smallest country – is truly beguiling. Day trip it from Nice, an easy 25-minute train journey (€3.30) along the coast.

Ogling at Carlo's legendary marble-and-gold **casino** (☑98 06 21 21; www.montecarlocasinos.com; place du Casino; 9am-noon €10, from 2pm Salons Ordinaires/ Salons Privées €10/20; ☉visits 9am-noon, gaming 2pm-2am or 4am or when last game ends) is a Monaco essential. The building, open to visitors every morning, is Europe's most lavish example of belle époque architecture. To gamble or watch the poker-faced play, visit after 2pm (strictly over-18s).

Monaco's other must-see is the **Musée Océanographique de Monaco** (☑93 15 36 00; www.oceano.mc; av St-Martin; adult €11-16, child €7-12; ☉9.30am-8pm Jul & Aug, 10am-7pm Apr-Jun & Sep, to 6pm Oct-Mar), stuck dramatically to the edge of a cliff since 1910. Its centrepiece is its aquarium with a 6m-deep lagoon where sharks and marine predators are separated from colourful tropical fish by a coral reef. Enjoy sweeping views of Monaco and the Med from the rooftop cafe terrace.

For motor sports fans, Monaco **tourist office** (www.visitmonaco.com; 2a bd des Moulins; ☉9am-7pm Mon-Sat, 11am-1pm Sun) has maps of the iconic, 3.2km F1 circuit that tears around town in late May.

Monte Carlo Casino
ANDRII LUTSYK / SHUTTERSTOCK ©

music scene. Live music and jam sessions most nights from 9pm.

Cinéma Rialto Cinema
(http://lerialto.cine.allocine.fr; 4 rue de Rivoli) Undubbed films, with French subtitles.

ℹ INFORMATION

Nice's main **tourist office** (Promenade des Anglais; ☑08 92 70 74 07; www.nicetourisme. com) has recently reopened after renovations. There are also two smaller branches on **Promenade du Paillon** (☑08 92 707 407; ☉9am-6pm Mon-Sat) and outside the **train station** (Gare de Nice; ☑08 92 70 74 07; av Thiers; ☉9am-7pm daily Jun-Sep, 9am-6pm Mon-Sat & 10-5pm Sun Oct-May).

ℹ GETTING THERE & AWAY

AIR

Nice-Côte d'Azur Airport (☑08 20 42 33 33; www.nice.aeroport.fr; ☎) is France's second-largest airport and has international flights to Europe, North Africa and the US, with regular and low-cost airlines. The airport has two terminals, linked by a free shuttle bus.

BOAT

Nice is the main port for ferries to Corsica. **SNCM** (www.sncm.fr; quai du Commerce) and **Corsica Ferries** (www.corsicaferries.com; quai du Commerce) are the two main companies.

TRAIN

Nice has excellent train connections to pretty much everywhere on the coast, and many towns further afield too.

Monaco €4.60, 35 minutes, hourly.

Marseille €35 to €38, 2½ hours, hourly.

Paris €66 to €140, 5¾ hours, hourly.

ℹ GETTING AROUND

BUS

Buses and trams in Nice are run by **Lignes d'Azur** (www.lignesdazur.com). Tickets cost just

Les Distilleries Idéales (p215)

€1.50 (or €10 for a 10-journey pass) and include one connection, including intercity buses within the Alpes-Maritimes *département*.

Buses are particularly handy to get to Cimiez and the port. Night buses run from around 9pm until 2am.

BICYCLE

Vélo Bleu (☑04 93 72 06 06; www.velobleu.org) is Nice's shared-bicycle service. It's great value and very convenient for getting round town, with 100-plus stations around the city – pick up your bike at one, return it at another.

One-day/week subscriptions cost €1/5, plus usage: free for the first 30 minutes, €1 the next 30, then €2 per hour thereafter. Some stations are equipped with terminals to register directly with a credit card; otherwise you'll need a mobile phone (beware of roaming charges).

The handy Vélo Bleu app allows you to find your nearest station, gives real-time information about the number of bikes available at each and calculates itineraries.

CAR & MOTORCYCLE

Traffic, a confusing one-way system, and pricey parking mean driving in Nice is a bad idea – it's better to explore the city first, then head back out to the airport and rent your car there instead.

Holiday Bikes (☑04 93 160 162; http://loca-bike.fr; 23 rue de Belgique; ⊙9.30am-12.30pm & 2.30-6.30pm Mon-Sat, 10am-noon & 5-6.30pm Sun) rents 50cc scooters/125cc motorcycles for €30/55.

TRAM

Nice's sleek tram is great for getting across town, particularly from the train station to Vieux Nice and the old bus station. Trams run from 4.30am to 1.30am.

A second line running east–west from the airport to the port is currently under construction. It's officially scheduled for completion in 2017, but there's still a lot of work to do, and construction is causing considerable upheaval on several streets and around the edge of Port Lympia.

ST-TROPEZ

St-Tropez at a Glance...

Pouting sexpot Brigitte Bardot came to St-Tropez in the 1950s to star in Et Dieu Créa la Femme *(And God Created Woman; 1956) and overnight transformed the peaceful fishing village into a sizzling jet-set favourite. Tropeziens have thrived on their sexy image ever since.*

Manicured vineyards and narrow lanes dotted with châteaux, solitary stone bastides *(country houses) and private villas unfurl along the Presqu'île de St-Tropez. A coastal path and fine-sand beaches − easily the loveliest on the French Riviera − ring this luxuriant peninsula. Inland, the flower-dressed hilltop villages of Gassin and Ramatuelle charm visitors.*

St-Tropez in Two Days

Explore St-Tropez, not missing its jam-packed **market** (p240) on **place des Lices** (p240), the **Musée de l'Annonciade** (p234) and the old fishing quarter of **La Ponche** (p240). Stroll along the coastal path and come dusk, hobnob over an aperitif at the bewitching **Vieux Port** (p234). Make day two a beach day; reserve a table at **La Plage des Jumeaux** (p242) or one of Pampelonne's celebrity beach clubs.

St-Tropez in Four Days

Third day, head inland to the flowery hilltop village of **Ramatuelle** (p241). Continue to medieval **Gassin** (p241) for a 360-degree view of the St-Tropez peninsula and bay. Dine and dance the evening away back in St-Tropez. Last day, take a boat trip with **Les Bateaux Verts** (p239) to Port Grimaud or Porquerolles.

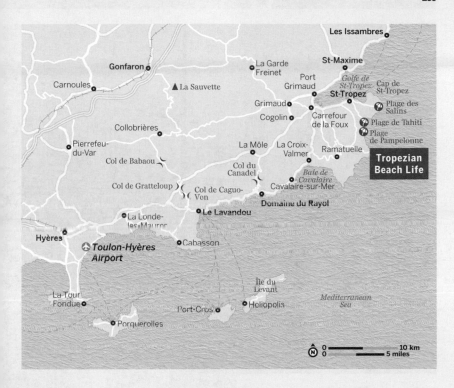

Les Issambres

Gonfaron
La Garde Freinet
St-Maxime
Port Grimaud
Golfe de St-Tropez
Cap de St-Tropez
Carnoules
▲ La Sauvette
St-Tropez
Grimaud
Plage des Salins
Collobrières
Cogolin
Carrefour de la Foux
Plage de Tahiti
Plage de Pampelonne
Pierrefeu-du-Var
La Môle
La Croix-Valmer
Ramatuelle
Tropezian Beach Life
Col de Babaou
Col du Canadel
Col de Gratteloup
Col de Caguo-Von
Baie de Cavalaire
Cavalaire-sur-Mer
Domaine du Rayol
La Londe-les-Maures
Le Lavandou
Hyères
Cabasson
⊙ Toulon-Hyères Airport
Île du Levant
Mediterranean Sea
La Tour Fondue
Port-Cros
Heliopolis
Porquerolles

Ⓝ 0 ──── 10 km
0 ──── 5 miles

Arriving in St-Tropez

Aéroport Toulon-Hyères Bus shuttles between the airport and St-Tropez (€15, 1½ hours); some require a transfer.

St-Raphäel train station Les Bateaux de St-Raphaël boats run April to mid-October (€15, one hour; www.bateauxdestraphael.com) from the dock, 200m from the station; and VarLib buses (www.varlib.fr, €3, 1¼ hours to three hours depending on traffic) to St-Tropez.

Sleeping

St-Tropez is home to celebrity-studded hangs, with prices to match – this is no shoestring destination, though campgrounds do sit southeast along Plage de Pampelonne. Most hotels close occasionally in winter; the tourist office lists what's open and also has a list of B&Bs. If you're driving, double-check the parking arrangements.

Vieux Port

It is not without good reason that the Old Port quays – hub of local life – are chockablock with 60,000 seasonal inhabitants, tourists, artist easels, tourist stalls and yachties a day in summer.

Great For...

☑ **Don't Miss**

Old fishing quarter, La Ponche (p240), northeast of Vieux Port.

Three medieval towers guard the port: Portalet, Jarlier and Suffren, the oldest building in St-Tropez, dating from the 15th century.

Musée de l'Annonciade

In a gracefully converted 16th-century chapel, this small but famous museum showcases an impressive collection of modern art infused with that legendary Côte d'Azur light. Pointillist Paul Signac bought a house in St-Tropez in 1892 and introduced other artists to the area. The museum's collection includes his *St-Tropez, Le Quai* (1899) and *St-Tropez, Coucher de Soleil au Bois de Pins* (1896).

The Fauvist collection includes works by Derain and Matisse, who spent the summer of 1904 here. Cubists George Braque and Picasso are also represented.

Bravadeurs at Les Bravades

ℹ Need to Know

St-Tropez tourist office (☏08 92 68 48 28; www.sainttropeztourisme.com; quai Jean Jaurès; ⊙9.30am-1.30pm & 3-7.30pm Jul & Aug, 9.30am-12.30pm & 2-7pm Apr-Jun, Sep & Oct, to 6pm Mon-Sat Nov-Mar)

✕ Take a Break

Grab a signature steak tartare at popular pub **Le Gorille** (☏04 94 97 03 93; 1 quai Suffren; 7am-7pm).

★ Top Tip

Duck beneath the archway by the tourist office to uncover St-Tropez' fish market on place aux Herbes.

Bailli de Suffren

At the Vieux Port, a statue of the Bailli de Suffren, cast from a 19th-century cannon, peers out to sea. The bailiff (1729–88) was a sailor who fought with a Tropezien crew against Britain and Prussia during the Seven Years' War.

Festive Fun

An ear-splitting army of 140 musket-firing *bravadeurs* parade around the Vieux Port carrying a bust of patron saint, St-Torpes, during **Les Bravades** (Provençal for 'bravery'), the town's traditional festival held 16 to 18 May since 1558. Torpes was a Roman officer, beheaded in AD 68 as punishment for becoming a Christian. The emperor Nero packed the decapitated body into a small boat, along with a dog and a rooster, who were to devour his remains. Miraculously, the body came ashore in St-Tropez without a nibble being taken from it, and the village adopted the headless Torpes as its saint.

Cafe Life

Cafes, restaurants, bistros and bars frame the Vieux Port quays. Sartre wrote parts of *Les Chemins de la Liberté* (Roads to Freedom) at **Sénéquier** (☏04 94 97 20 20; www.senequier.com; quai Jean Jaurès; ⊙8am-1am), a portside cafe – in business since 1887 – which is hugely popular with boaties, bikers and tourists. Look for the terrace crammed with pillar-box-red tables and director's chairs. Count €8 for a mere coffee.

The terrace of friendly **Café de Paris** (www.cafedeparis.fr; 15 quai Suffren; ⊙8am-2am) is *the* place to sport your new strappy sandals at afternoon aperitifs. Or don your glad rags and order a cocktail at **Bar du Port** (www.barduport.com; quai Suffren; ⊙7am-3am), a young and happening bar for beautiful people, with chichi decor in shades of white and silver.

Tropezien Beach Life

Few beaches are as sizzling or storied as St-Tropez's. Don your hottest beach wear, grab your shades and get set to hobnob on some of Europe's finest golden sands.

Great For...

☑ Don't Miss

The Sentier du Littoral (p241) that snakes from beach to beach.

Plage de Pampelonne

France's most chic beach, celebrity-studded Plage de Pampelonne is a divine 9km stretch of golden sand with exclusive beach restaurants and clubs. Find public access (and parking for €5.50) near Moorea Plage. The northern edge of the beach begins 4km southeast of St-Tropez with Plage de Tahiti.

Taste and buy excellent, crisp rosé from the verdant St-Tropez Peninsula at **Mas de Pampelonne**, a winery a few hundred metres inland from Pampelonne beach.

Sémaphore de Camarat

Pampelonne stretches for 9km from Cap du Pinet to **Cap Camarat**, a rocky cape dominated by France's second-tallest lighthouse (110m), operational since 1861, electrified in 1946 and automated from

Plage de la Briande

Golfe de St-Tropez

Mediterranean Sea

St-Tropez

Plage des Salins

Plage de Pampelonne

La Croix- Valmer

ⓘ Need to Know

Ramatuelle tourist office (☑04 98 12 64 00; www.ramatuelle-tourisme.com; place de l'Ormeau; ⊙9am-1.30pm & 2-7pm Mon-Fri, 9 30am-1 30pm & 3.30 6.30pm Sat & Sun Jul & Aug, shorter hours rest of year)

✕ Take a Break

Seafood at Pampelonne's top lunch ad dress, La Plage des Jumeaux (p242).

★ Top Tip

Beach clubs generally open May to September; table and sun-lounger (€15 to €20) reservations are essential.

197/. Scale it for giddy views of St-Tropez and its peninsula. Guided tours run June to September; book at Ramatuelle tourist office.

Plage des Salins

Just east of St-Tropez, **Plage des Salins** (rte des Salins) is a long, wide sandy beach at the southern foot of Cap des Salins. At the beach's northern end, on a rock jutting out to sea, is the tomb of Émile Olivier (1825–1913), who served as first minister to Napoléon III until his exile in 1870. It looks out towards **La Tête de Chien** (Dog's Head), named after the legendary dog who declined to eat St Torpes' remains.

Beach Clubs

St-Tropez' seaside scene is defined by its club-restaurants on the sand.

Club 55 (☑04 94 55 55 55; www.leclub55.fr; 43 bd Patch, Plage de Pampelonne; ⊙10am-late Apr-Sep) The longest-running beach club dates to the 1950s and was originally the crew canteen during the filming of *And God Created Woman*. Now it caters to celebs who do not want to be seen.

Nikki Beach (☑04 94 79 82 04; www.nikkibeach. com/sttropez; rte de l'Épi, Plage de Pampe-lonne; ⊙10am-midnight Apr-Sep) Favoured by dance-on-the-bar celebs keen to be seen on Pampelonne.

Aqua Club (☑04 94 79 84 35; www.aqua-club-plage.fr; rte de l'Épi, Plage de Pampelonne; mains €22-29; ⊙Feb-Oct) A friendly mixed gay and straight crowd, the most diverse by far on Pampelonne, settles in here for relaxed drinks or steaks.

Moorea Plage (☑04 94 97 18 17; www. mooreaplage.fr; rte des Plages, Plage de Tahiti; mains €23-52; ⊙Mar-Sep) Relatively laid-back club-restaurant on Tahiti beach, ideal for conver-sation, backgammon and top steak.

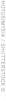

Boat Tours

In the height of summer when horrendous, four-hour traffic bottlenecks jam up the one road into town, boat is by far the coolest, quickest and most serene means of navigating St-Tropez.

April to September, St-Tropez operators offer various boat trips from the port, including celebrity villa-spotting sailings around Baie des Cannebiers. Our tip: make a day of it and hit Port Grimaud for chic strolling and lunch or Porquerolles for walking, cycling and beach-lounging on an idyllic island.

Port Grimaud

It is a 20- to 30-minute sail (single/return €7/12.30) to the so-called 'Venice of Provence', built on the edge of the Golfe de St-Tropez on what was a mosquito-filled swamp in the 1960s. Inside the high wall that barricades the modern pleasure port from the busy N98, cottages painted every colour of the rainbow stand gracefully alongside yacht-laced waterways comprising 12km of quays, 7km of canals and

Great For...

☑ **Don't Miss**

A canal-side seafood platter at **La Table du Mareyeur** (www.mareyeur.com) in Port Grimaud.

Port Grimaud

the 114 bird species. Pottering along the island's rough unpaved trails on foot or by bicycle, breaking with a picnic lunch on the beach and a dip in crystal-clear turquoise water, is heavenly.

Porquerolles' northern coast is laced with beautiful sandy beaches: the island's largest and loveliest beach, **Plage de Notre Dame**, is about 3.5km east of the port (follow the track uphill behind the tourist office); sandy **Plage de la Courtade** is a mere 800m walk from the port. West of the village, **Plage d'Argent**, a good 2km along a potholed track past vineyards, is popular with families because of its seasonal beach cafe-restaurant, lifeguards and toilets.

Bike-hire outfits line the port and central square, **place d'Armes**. At the port, the **tourist office** (📞04 94 58 33 76; www. porquerolles.com; ⊙9am-6.15pm Mon-Sat, to 1pm Sun Jul & Aug, shorter hours rest of year) sells maps showing four cycling itineraries, 6.5km to 13.8km long.

mooring space for thousands of luxury yachts. Thursday and Sunday mornings a market fills place du Marché, from where a bridge leads to Port Grimaud's modernist church – don't miss its beautiful stained-glass windows by Hungarian artist Victor Vasarely. Red rooftops fan out from atop the church bell tower.

Île de Porquerolles

Count on 2½ hours (return €43) to sail to Porquerolles, a beautiful island that is wholly unspoilt: two-thirds of its sandy white beaches, pine woods, maquis and eucalypts are protected by the **Parc National de Port-Cros**, and a wide variety of indigenous and tropical flora thrive, including Requien's larkspur, which grows nowhere else in the world. April and May are the best months to spot some of

◉ SIGHTS

La Ponche
Historic Site

Shrug off the hustle of the port in St-Tropez's historic fishing quarter, La Ponche, northeast of the Vieux Port. From the southern end of quai Frédéric Mistral, place Garrezio sprawls east from 10th-century **Tour Suffren** to place de l'Hôtel de Ville. From here, rue Guichard leads southeast to sweet-chiming **Église de St-Tropez** (place de l'Ormeau), a St-Trop landmark built in 1785 in Italian baroque style. Inside is a bust of St Torpes, honoured during Les Bravades in May.

Follow rue du Portail Neuf south to **Chapelle de la Miséricorde** (rue de la Miséricorde), built in 1645 with a pretty bell tower and colourful tiled dome.

Citadelle de St-Tropez
Museum

(☏04 94 54 84 14; admission €3; ☉10am-6.30pm Apr-Sep, to 5.30pm Oct-Mar) Built in 1602 to defend the coast against Spain, the citadel dominates the hillside overlooking St-Tropez to the east. The views are fantastic. Its dungeons are home to the excellent **Musée de l'Histoire Maritime**, an all-interactive museum inaugurated in July 2013 retracing the history of humans at sea, from fishing, trading and exploration to travel and the navy.

Place des Lices
Square

St-Tropez' legendary and very charming central square is studded with plane trees, cafes and *pétanque* players. Simply sitting on a cafe terrace watching the world go by or jostling with the crowds at its extravaganza of a twice-weekly **market** (place des Lices; ☉8am-1pm Tue & Sat), jam-packed with everything from fruit and veg to sandals and antique mirrors, is an integral part of the St-Tropez experience.

Artists and intellectuals have met for decades in St-Tropez's famous Café des Arts, now simply called Le Café – and not to be confused with the newer, green-canopied Café des Arts on the corner of the square. Aspiring *pétanque* players can borrow a set of boules from the bar.

> *solitary stone bastides and private villas unfurl along the Presqu'île de St-Tropez*

Stone buildings in St-Tropez

INU / SHUTTERSTOCK / GETTY IMAGES ©

✚ ACTIVITIES

Sentier du Littoral   Walking

A spectacular coastal path wends past rocky outcrops and hidden bays 35km south from St-Tropez, around the peninsula to the beach at Cavalaire-sur-Mer. In St-Tropez the yellow-flagged path starts at **La Ponche**, immediately east of Tour du Portalet, and curves around Port des Pêcheurs, past St-Tropez' citadel. It then leads past the walled **Cimitière Marin** (Marine Cemetery), **Plage des Graniers** and beyond.

The tourist office has maps with distances and walking times (eg to Plage des Salins: 8.5km, 2½ hours).

🔒 SHOPPING

St-Tropez is loaded with couture boutiques, gourmet food shops and art galleries.

Atelier Rondini   Shoes

(🖉04 94 97 19 55; www.rondini.fr; 16 rue Georges Clémenceau; ⏰9.30am-6.30pm Tue-Sat, 10.30am-1.30pm & 3.30-6.30pm Sun) French novelist Colette brought a pair of sandals from Greece to Atelier Rondini (open since 1927) to be replicated. It's still making the iconic sandals for about €135.

K Jacques   Shoes

(🖉04 94 97 41 50; www.kjacques.com; 39bis rue Allard; ⏰10am-1pm & 3-7pm Mon-Sat, 10.30am-1pm & 3.30-7pm Sun) Handcrafting sandals (€145 to €220) since 1933 for such clients as Picasso and Brigitte Bardot. There's another **branch** (16 rue Seillon; ⏰10am-1pm & 3-7pm Mon-Sat, 10.30am-1pm & 3.30-7pm Sun) nearby.

Benoît Gourmet & Co   Food & Drinks

(🖉04 94 97 73 78; 6 rue des Charrons; ⏰10am-noon & 2-5pm Mon-Sat) Everything gourmet (caviar, Champagne and foie gras included).

🍴 EATING

Le Café   Cafe €€

(🖉04 94 97 44 69; www.lecafe.fr; place des Lices; lunch/dinner menus €18/32; ⏰8am-11pm)

Ramatuelle & Gassin

Nine kilometres inland, into the lush St-Tropez peninsula, is the labyrinthine walled village of **Ramatuelle**. Its name originates from 'Rahmatu'llah', meaning 'Divine Gift' – a legacy of the 10th-century Saracen occupation. Jazz and theatre fill the tourist-packed streets during August's **Festival de Ramatuelle** (www.festivalderamatuelle.com) and **Jazz Fest** (www.jazzfestivalramatuelle.com), and its tree-studded central square and old world lanes make for an enchanting stroll.

Follow route des Moulins de Paillas up over the hilltop for 2.5km towards Gassin. Grand views and historic windmills unfold, but nothing beats the magnificent 360-degree panorama of the peninsula and St-Tropez bay from **Gassin** village itself. Teetering atop a rocky promontory, the medieval village with 16th-century church is gold.

Whetting whistles since 1789, this historic cafe is where artists and painters preferred to hang out back in the days when St-Trop was still a sleepy port. Happily, it's clung on to its no-nonsense roots – you'll find solid dishes like pot-roasted chicken, mussels and grilled fish on the menu, as well as a lovely interior bar with globe lights and wooden fixtures that still give it a cosy *fin-de-siècle* vibe. They'll lend you a set of boules if you want to take on some *pétanque* players on the square.

Don't confuse it with the other, more modern cafe (with green awnings) just along the square.

Bistro Canaille   Fusion €€

(🖉04 94 97 75 85; 28 rue des Remparts; plates €8-24; ⏰7-11pm Fri & Sat Mar-May & Oct-Dec, 7-11pm Tue-Sun Jun-Sep) Probably the pick of the places to eat in town – creative, cosy and great value while still hitting the gourmet heights. It's got the soul of a

🍽 La Tarte Tropézienne

Don't leave town without sampling *tarte Tropézienne,* an orange blossom–flavoured double sponge cake filled with thick cream, created by Polish baker A Mickla in 1955. Cafe-bakery **La Tarte Tropézienne** (📞04 94 97 04 69; www.latartetropezienne.fr; place des Lices; mains €13-15, cakes €3-5; ⏲6.30am-7.30pm & noon-3pm) is the creator of the eponymous sugar-crusted cake. There are other smaller branches around town.

Tarte Tropézienne
EQROY / SHUTTERSTOCK ©

bistro, but specialises in fusion-style tapas dishes inspired by the owners' travels. More filling mains are chalked on the board. It's on the street leading up to the château.

Le Sporting   Brasserie €€

(place des Lices; lunch menu €13, mains €16-30; ⏲8am-1am) The locals' hang-out of choice at any time of day: a knockabout bistro-bar where everyone knows everyone and the patio overlooking place des Lices is packed with evening pastis-drinkers. Expect simple brasserie grub – entrecôte, hamburgers, salads.

Le G'   Bistro €€

(📞07 86 31 11 22; 67 rue du Portail Neuf; lunch/dinner menus €16/35; ⏲noon-midnight Tue-Sun) Run by full-of-life owners Alain and Nuno, this pint-sized restaurant is a great tip. There are only a few tables and it's popular, so expect to queue – but the wonders worked up in the little open-plan kitch-

en make it worth the wait. Fresh market ingredients drive the menu, which changes regularly.

La Plage des Jumeaux   Seafood €€€

(📞04 94 58 21 80; www.plagedesjumeaux.com; rte de l'Épi, Plage de Pampelonne; mains €25-40; ⏲noon-3pm; 📱🚼) The top pick of St-Tropez' beach restaurants, Jumeaux serves beautiful seafood (including fabulous whole fish, ideal to share) and sun-busting salads on its dreamy white-and-turquoise-striped beach. Families are well catered for, with playground equipment, beach toys and a kids' menu.

Auberge des Maures   Provençal €€€

(📞04 94 97 01 50; www.aubergedesmaures.fr; 4 rue du Docteur Boutin; mains €35-45; ⏲7.30-10pm Apr-Oct) The town's oldest restaurant remains the locals' choice for always-good, copious portions of earthy Provençal cooking, like *daube* (braised beef stew) or tapenade-stuffed lamb shoulder. Book a table (essential) on the leafy courtyard.

La Vague d'Or   Gastronomic €€€

(📞04 94 55 91 00; www.residencepinede.com; Résidence de la Pinède, Plage de la Bouillabaisse; menus from €205; ⏲7.30-10pm mid-Apr–mid-Oct) Wonder-chef Arnaud Donckele has established a gastronomic temple with three Michelin stars at the Résidence de la Pinède: expect Mediterranean ingredients and flavours, with a one-of-a-kind twist.

🍷 DRINKING & NIGHTLIFE

Dress to kill. And bring more money than you think you'll need. Many places close in winter, but in summer it's party central seven days a week.

To tap into the local gay scene, hit **Chez les Garçons** (📞04 94 49 42 67; 11/13 rue du Cépoun; menus €32; ⏲9-11pm May-Sep, Thu-Sun Mar, Apr & Oct) or **L'Esquinade** (2 rue du Four; ⏲midnight-7am daily Jun-Sep, Thu-Sat only Oct-May).

St-Topez nightclub

White 1921   Bar

(www.white1921.com; place des Lices; ⊘8pm-late mid-May–Sep) One of the newest entries on the St-Tropez scene, White 1921 is owned by Louis Vuitton. It's a chic al fresco Champagne lounge in a renovated all-white town house on place des Lices. Can't make it home? Stay over in one of the swank rooms (from €345).

Les Caves du Roy   Club

(www.lescavesduroy.com; Hôtel Byblos, av Paul Signac; ⊘7pm-5am Jul & Aug, Fri & Sat Apr-Oct) This star-studded bar at the infamous Hôtel Byblos remains the perennial champion of nightclubs in St-Tropez, if not the whole Riviera. Dress to impress if you hope to get in and mingle with starlets and racing-car drivers.

VIP Room   Club

(📋04 94 97 14 70; www.viproom.fr; av du 11 Novembre 1918; ⊘Apr-Aug) New York loft–style club at the Nouveau Port; around for aeons and still lures in the occasional VIP.

ⓘ INFORMATION

Tourist Office (p235) Runs occasional walking tours April to October, and also has a kiosk in Parking du Port in July and August. Rather stingily, you have to pay for a town map (€2).

ⓘ GETTING THERE & AROUND

BICYCLE

Rolling Bikes (📋04 94 97 09 39; www.rolling-bikes.com; 14 av du Général Leclerc; per day bikes/scooters/motorcycles from €17/46/120, plus deposit; ⊘10am-6pm Mon-Sat, to 5pm Sun) Do as the locals do and opt for two wheels.

CAR

During high season, those in the know avoid horrendous four-hour traffic bottlenecks on the one road into St-Tropez (or €40 parking, which is hard to find) by parking in Port Grimaud or Ste-Maxime and taking a **Les Bateaux Verts** (p239) shuttle boat.

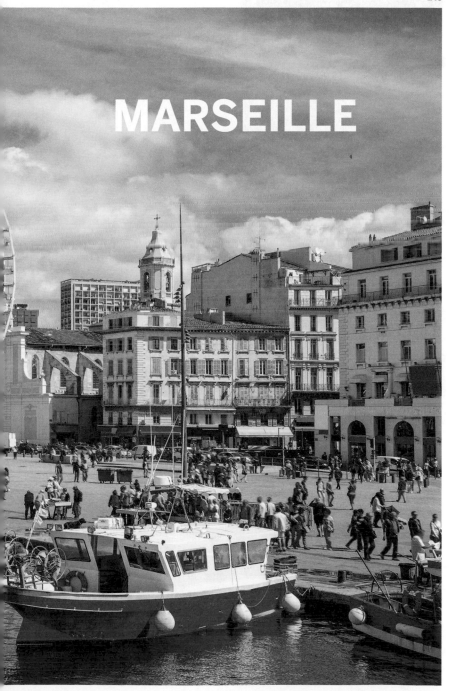

MARSEILLE

In This Chapter

Marseille at a Glance...

Radiating from the boat-lined Vieux Port, Marseille's irresistible magnetism draws you into its vibrant, polyglot heart. France's second-biggest city has a rich history that harks back more than 1500 years. In recent years, this rebel of a city has undergone a major facelift, its stint as European City of Culture in 2013 injecting it with world-class museums, myriad galleries and top-notch performing arts. It also retains earthy, bustling markets and districts spiced with Middle Eastern flavour.

Allow yourself at least 48 hours to take in Marseille's compelling sights, its azure coast and the dramatic Les Calanques – the spectacular coastline that snakes southeast.

Marseille in Two Days

Start at the **Vieux Port** (p254) with breakfast at **La Caravelle** (p263) and a waterside stroll to **MuCEM** (p248) and **Villa Méditerranée** (p249). Lunch at **Le Café des Épices** (p260), then hike up to the **Basilique Notre Dame de la Garde** (p254). Day two, take in magnificent turquoise waters at **Les Calanques** (p252), or catch a boat to revel in Monte Cristo intrigues at **Château d'If** (p263). **Bouillabaisse by the sea** (p260) beckons for dinner.

Marseille in Four Days

Explore **Le Panier** (p250) day three, not missing the **Centre de la Vieille Charité** (p250). Gorge on more art and architecture at the **Musée des Beaux Arts** (p255). Come dusk enjoy an aperitif on artsy cours Julien before dinner at **La Cantinetta** (p261). Fourth day, sail to the **Îles du Frioul** (p263) to frolic and picnic in a natural paradise of birdlife and pebble beach; soak up Marseille's **ebullient nightlife** (p262) after dark.

Arriving in Marseille

Aéroport Marseille-Provence (p264) buses link the airport and Gare St-Charles (adult/child €8.20/4.10) every 15 to 20 minutes. The airport's train station has direct services to several French cities; a free shuttle bus runs to/from the airport terminal.

Gare St-Charles Metro line 1 every six minutes to Vieux Port (two stops), or a 1km walk via La Canebière.

Sleeping

There are modest hotels close to the train station, but the good local-transit system means that it's easy to reach the more charming hotels – many with a big blue sea view – scattered around the Vieux Port and along the coast. Few hotels have their own parking facilities, but most central ones offer discounted rates at one of the city's car parks.

POSZTOS / SHUTTERSTOCK ©

MuCEM

The icon of modern Marseille, this stunning museum explores the history, culture and civilisation of the Mediterranean region through anthropological exhibits, art exhibitions and film. Its striking architecture is breathtakingly contemporary.

One of a clutch of swanky new museums to open in celebration of the city's brief stint as European City of Culture in 2013, the Musée des Civilisations de l'Europe et de la Méditerranée is as much about experiencing stunning city and sea views from unusual viewpoints as delving into the Mediterranean's rich heritage.

J4

The collection sits in a bold, contemporary building, J4, designed by Algerian-born, Marseille-educated architect Rudi Ricciotti. The main focus of the museum is a semipermanent exhibition ranging across the history, genealogy and culture of the Mediterranean, taking in everything from archaeological artefacts to oil paintings. It's supplemented by temporary exhibitions that vary widely in theme: recent highlights were investigations of Jean Genet and Pi-

Great For...

☑ **Don't Miss**

The walkway hidden between the glass wall and outer lace shell of the J4 building.

Fort St-Jean

COLIN MATTHIEU / AGE FOTOSTOCK ©

casso, and an interesting history of French involvement in Algeria.

Fort St-Jean

A vertigo-inducing footbridge links J4 with the 13th-century Fort St-Jean. It was founded by the Knights Hospitaller of St John of Jerusalem and is one of two forts guarding Marseille's ancient harbour. The fort grounds and its gardens are free to explore – allow ample time to lap up the stupendous views of the Vieux Port and Mediterranean Sea. The history of the fort itself is explained in the **Salle du Corps de Garde** (guardhouse room).

Villa Méditerranée

Next to J4, the eye-catching white structure of **Villa Méditerranée** (www.villa-mediterranee. org; bd du Littoral, esplanade du J4; ⊙noon-6pm

Tue-Fri, 10am-6pm Sat & Sun; 🚻) **FREE** is no ordinary 'villa'. Designed by architect Stefano Boeri in 2013, the sleek white edifice sports a spectacular cantilever overhanging an ornamental pool. Inside, a viewing gallery with glass-panelled floor (look down if you dare!) and two or three temporary multimedia exhibitions evoke aspects of the Mediterranean. But it's the building itself that's the undisputed highlight here.

Musée Régards de Provence

Across the busy road from Villa Méditerranée, this curious **museum** (☎04 96 17 40 40; www. museeregardsdeprovence.com; ave Vaudoyer; adult/child €4/free, plus temporary exhibition €8.50/free; ⊙10am-6pm Tue-Sun) is housed in the city's former sanitary station, operational from 1948 until 1971. It's essentially an art museum exploring different depictions of Provence, but it also explores many other aspects of Marseille's past. Its rooftop cafe is a prime spot for bird's-eye city-and-sea views.

Centre de la Vieille Charité

DRABANTH / GETTY IMAGES ©

Le Panier

Around 600 BC, Greek mariners founded the Mediterranean trading post of Massilia, settling on the steep streets of Le Panier – Marseille's oldest quarter today with a rabbit warren of apricot alleyways and distinct shabby-chic charm.

Great For...

☑ Don't Miss

Place de Lenche and rue des Pistoles, two pretty squares ideal for soaking up local boho charm.

Lapping up local life is a big draw of this artsy neighbourhood where narrow, sun-bleached streets give way to artist workshops and bijou squares. Main street Grande Rue follows the ancient road of the Greeks to place de Lenche, location of the original Greek *agora* (marketplace) – hence Le Panier's name, which means 'the basket'.

A Charitable Affair

In the heart of Le Panier is the gorgeous architectural complex of the **Centre de la Vieille Charité** (www.vieille-charite-marseille. com; 2 rue de la Charité; ⊘10am-6pm Tue-Sun; Ⓜ Joliette) **FREE**. It was built in 1749 as a charity shelter for the town's poor by local architect and sculptor Pierre Puget (1620–94), born just a couple of streets away. With its neoclassical central chapel and vast arcaded courtyard, it's a reminder of a

Marseillais soap

MIKHAIL BERKUT / SHUTTERSTOCK ©

Le Panier ⊙

❶ Need to Know

Ask at the tourist office (p264) about guided walks and rambles in Le Panier.

✕ Take a Break

Chill with locals over a glass of pastis and bistro fare at Bar des 13 Coins (p260).

★ Top Tip

Savour multicultural Le Panier with spicy Moroccan tajines, pastillas and curries at Place Lorette (p262).

Savonnerie (⌨ 09 50 63 80 35; www.lagrande savonnerie.com; 36 Grande Rue; soaps from €2.50; ⊘10am-7pm Mon-Sat; ⓂVieux Port), an artisan soapmaker on Le Panier's fringe with a mini-factory just outside town. Shop here for the genuine Marseillais article, made with olive oil and no added perfume, and shaped into cubes.

72% Pétanque (⌨ 04 91 91 14 57; www. philippechailloux.com; 10 rue du Petit Puits; ⊘10.30am-6.30pm; ⓂVieux Port or Joliette) is known for its unusual perfumes like chocolate, verbena and aniseed.

Game for Boules

Pick up your very own travelling set of handmade boules (complete with matching carry bag), plus plenty of other souvenirs relating to France's iconic game at **Maison de la Boule** (⌨ 04 91 43 27 20; www.museede laboule.com; Montée de St Menet; ⊘10am-noon & 2-7pm Wed-Sun; ⓂVieux Port). A little museum illustrates the history of the sport, including the curious figure of Fanny: tradition dictates if you lose a game 13-nil, you must kiss her bare bum cheeks.

more elegant age – ponder this remarkable space from the delightful courtyard cafe.

Entry is free, or pay to visit the **Musée d'Archéologie Méditerranéenne** (⌨ 04 91 14 58 59; http://musee-archeologie-mediterraneenne. marseille.fr; 2 rue de la Charité; adult/child €5/free; ⊘10am-6pm Tue-Sun; ⓂJoliette), an archaeological museum exploring Mediterranean history. Look for a famous decorated Minoan vase and a Mesopotamian enamel panel.

A second museum, the **Musée d'Arts Africains, Océaniens et Améridiens** (⌨ 04 91 14 58 38; http://maaoa.marseille.fr; 2 rue de la Charité; adult/child €5/free; ⊘10am-6pm Tue-Sun; ⓂJoliette), delves into American, African and Pacific culture.

Marseillais Soap

Soap-making has been a Marseille tradition since the 18th century. Enter **La Grande**

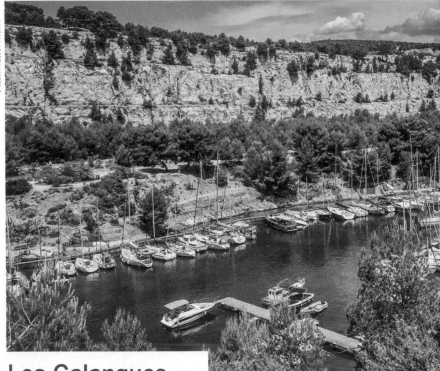

Les Calanques

Marseille abuts the spectacularly wild Parc National des Calanques, a 20km stretch of high, rocky promontories, rising from brilliant-turquoise Mediterranean waters. Sheer cliffs interrupt small idyllic beaches, some accessible only by kayak.

The Marseillais cherish Les Calanques, and come here to soak up the sun or take a long hike. The promontories have been protected since 1975 and shelter an extraordinary wealth of flora and fauna: 900 plant species, Bonelli's eagle, and Europe's largest lizard (the 60cm eyed lizard) and longest snake (the 2m Montpellier snake).

October to June, the best way to see the calanques – including the 500 sq km of the rugged inland **Massif des Calanques** – is to hike the many trails scented with aromatc maquis (scrub). Of the many calanques along the coastline, the most easily accessible are Calanque de Sormiou and Calanque de Morgiou; remote inlets like Calanque d'En Vau and Calanque de Port-Miou take dedication and time to reach – on foot or by kayak (p258).

Great For...

☑ Don't Miss

The stunning rock and sea views (and seafood) at Calanque de Morgiou's Nautic Bar (p253); reserve.

Calanque de Port-Miou

ⓘ Need to Know

In July and August trails close due to fire danger: arrive only by boat tour (p258) from Marseille.

✕ Take a Break

Dine al fresco at **Le Château** (☑04 91 25 08 69; http://lechateausormiou.fr; mains €19-25; ⊘noon-2.30pm & 7.30-9.30pm Apr-Sep) or **Le Lunch** (☑04 91 25 05 37; www.restaurant-lunch.com; mains €25-38; ⊘noon-2.30pm & 8-10pm late Mar–mid-Oct), both in Calanque de Sormiou.

★ Top Tip

Marseille's tourist office (p264) leads guided walks and has information about trail and road closures.

€18-27; ⊘noon-2.30pm & 7.30-9.30pm May-Oct, closed Sun evening & Mon Apr), is dreamy. No credit cards.

Morgiou beach is a one-hour walk from the car park. The hair-raisingly steep, narrow road (3.5km) is open to motorists weekdays only mid-April to May and closed entirely June to September (motorists with a Nautic Bar reservation are always allowed through).

Calanque de Sormiou

The largest calanque hit headlines in 1991 when diver Henri Cosquer from Cassis swam through a 150m-long passage 36m underwater into a cave to find its interior adorned with wall paintings dating from around 20,000 BC. Now named Grotte Cosquer, the cave is a protected historical monument and closed to the public. Many more are believed to exist. Take bus 23 from Marseille's Rond-Point du Prado metro to the La Cayolle stop, from where it is a 3km walk.

Calanque de Morgiou

Windswept Cap Morgiou separates Sormiou from Morgiou, with a pretty little port bobbing with fishing boats, and sheer rock faces from which climbers dangle. An evening spent at its sole (seasonal) restaurant, **Nautic Bar** (☑04 91 40 06 37; mains

En-Vau

East of Calanque de Morgiou, the stone-sculptured coast brings you to a remote calanque: **Calanque d'En-Vau** has a pebbly beach and emerald waters encased by cliffs. Its entrance is guarded by the **Doigt de Dieu** (God's Finger), a giant rock pinnacle. A steep three-hour marked trail leads from the car park (closed July to mid-September) on the Col de la Gardiole to En-Vau. The slippery and sheer descents into En-Vau are for the truly hardcore only.

◎ SIGHTS

Greater Marseille is divided into 16 *arrondissements* (districts), which are indicated in addresses (eg 1er for the first *arrondissement* and so on). The city's main thoroughfare, La Canebière (from the Provençal word *canebe*, meaning 'hemp', after the city's traditional rope industry), stretches eastwards from the Vieux Port towards the train station, a 10-minute walk or two metro stops from the water. North is Le Panier, Marseille's oldest quarter; south is the bohemian concourse of cours Julien; and southwest is the start of the coastal road.

Vieux Port   Historic Site

(Ⓜ Vieux Port) Ships have docked for more than 26 centuries at the city's birthplace, the colourful old port. The main commercial docks were transferred to the Joliette area north of here in the 1840s, but the old port remains a thriving harbour for fishing boats, pleasure yachts and tourists.

The port's southern quay is dotted with bars, brasseries and cafes, and there are more to be found around place Thiars

and cours Honoré d'Estienne d'Orves, where the action continues until late. For supremely lazy sightseers, there's also a **cross-port ferry** (⊘10am-1.15pm & 2-7pm; Ⓜ Vieux Port).

Perched at the edge of the peninsula, the Jardin du Pharo (p264) is a perfect picnic and sunset spot.

Basilique Notre Dame
de la Garde   Church

(Montée de la Bonne Mère; www.notredamedelagarde.com; rue Fort du Sanctuaire; ⊘7am-8pm Apr-Sep, to 7pm Oct-Mar; 🚌60) This opulent 19th-century Romano-Byzantine basilica occupies Marseille's highest point, La Garde (162m). Built between 1853 and 1864, it is ornamented with coloured marble, murals depicting the safe passage of sailing vessels and superb mosaics. The hilltop gives 360-degree panoramas of the city. The church's bell tower is crowned by a 9.7m-tall gilded statue of the Virgin Mary on a 12m-high pedestal. It's a 1km walk from the Vieux Port, or take bus 60 or the tourist train.

Basilique Notre Dame de la Garde interior

MARIA GOLOVIANKO / SHUTTERSTOCK ©

Musée d'Histoire de Marseille

Museum

(📞04 91 55 36 00; http://musee-histoire.
marseille.fr; 2 rue Henri-Barbusse; adult/child
€5/free; 🕙10am-6pm Tue-Sun; Ⓜ️Vieux Port) In
a completely renovated, 15,000-sq-metre
modern space within the Centre Bourse
shopping centre, this museum offers
fascinating insight into Marseille's long
history. Highlights include the remains of
a 3rd-century AD merchant vessel, discovered in the Vieux Port in 1974. To preserve
the soaked and decaying wood, it was
freeze-dried where it now sits behind glass.

Musée des Beaux Arts

Art Museum, Palace

(📞04 91 14 59 30; http://musee-des-beaux-
arts.marseille.fr; 7 rue Édouard Stephan; adult/
child €5/free; 🕙10am-6pm Tue-Sun; ♿; Ⓜ️Cinq
Avenues-Longchamp, 🚋Longchamp) Spectacularly set in the colonnaded Palais de
Longchamp, Marseille's oldest museum
is a treasure trove of Italian and Provençal
painting and sculpture from the 17th to
21st centuries. The palace's shaded park
is one of the centre's few green spaces,
and is popular with local families. The
spectacular fountains were constructed in
the 1860s, in part to disguise a water tower
at the terminus of an aqueduct from the
River Durance.

Musée Cantini

Art Museum

(📞04 91 54 77 75; http://musee-cantini.
marseille.fr; 19 rue Grignan; adult/child €5/
free; 🕙10am-6pm Tue-Sun; Ⓜ️Estrangin-Pré-
fecture) Though it's often overshadowed by
Marseille's multimillion-euro flagship museums, this excellent art museum conceals
some surprising – and impressive – finds
behind its wrought-iron gates. The core
collection contains some fantastic examples of 17th- and 18th-century Provençal
art, including André Derain's *Pinède,
Cassis* (1907) and Raoul Dufy's *Paysage de
l'Estaque* (1908). A second section is dedicated to depictions of Marseille, with works
by Max Ernst, Joan Miró, André Masson
and others.

📖🍴 A Spot of History

Around 600 BC, Greek mariners
founded Massilia, a trading post, at
what is now Marseille's Vieux Port. In
the 1st century BC, the city lost out by
backing Pompey the Great rather than
Julius Caesar: Caesar's forces captured
Massilia in 49 BC and directed Roman
trade elsewhere.

Marseille became part of France in
the 1480s, but its citizens embraced
the Revolution, sending 500 volunteers
to defend Paris in 1792. Heading north,
they sang a rousing march, ever after
dubbed 'La Marseillaise' – now the national anthem. Trade with North Africa
escalated after France occupied Algeria
in 1830 and the Suez Canal opened in
1869. After the World Wars, a steady
flow of migration from North Africa
began and with it the rapid expansion of
Marseille's periphery.

Vieux Port

La Cité Radieuse

Architecture

(The Radiant City; L'Unité d'Habitation; 📞04
91 16 78 00; www.marseille-citeradieuse.org;
280 bd Michelet; 🕙9am-6pm; 🚌83 or 21, stop
Le Corbusier) **FREE** Visionary international-
style architect Le Corbusier redefined
urban living in 1952 with the completion
of his vertical 337-apartment 'garden city',
popularly known as La Cité Radieuse. Today
it is mostly private apartments, plus a hotel,
Hôtel Le Corbusier, the high-end restaurant
Le Ventre de l'Architecte and a rooftop
terrace. Architecture buffs can book guided
tours (adult/child €10/5) that include

Marseille

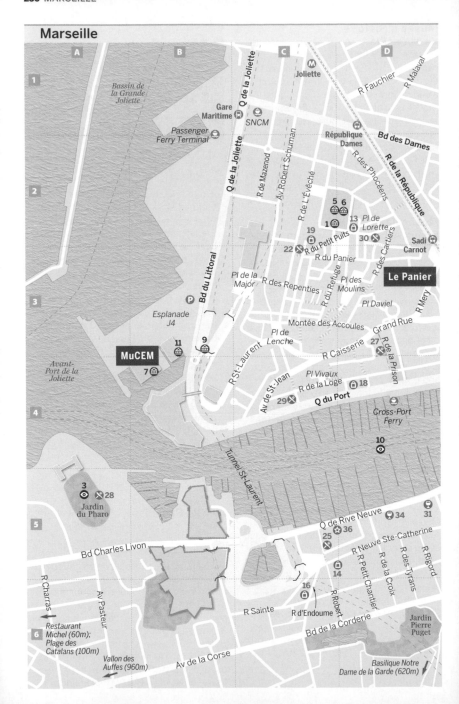

A1 **Bassin de la Grande Joliette**

B1

C1 M **Joliette**

D1 R Fauchier · R Malaval

Gare Maritime
SNCM

Q de la Joliette

Passenger Ferry Terminal

République Dames
Bd des Dames

Q de la Joliette
R de Mazenod
Av Robert Schuman
R des Phocéens
R de la République

R de L'Évêché

5 6
1
13 Pl de Lorette
19
30 🅧
22 🅧 R du Petit Puits
Sadi Carnot

R du Panier
R des Cartiers

Pl de la Major
R des Repenties
Le Panier

Bd du Littoral

P

Pl des Moulins

Pl Daviel
R Mery

Esplanade J4

R du Refuge

Montée des Accoules
Grand Rue

Pl de Lenche
27 🅧 R de la Prison

11
9
MuCEM
7

R St-Laurent
R Caisserie

Pl Vivaux
R de la Loge
18

Avant-Port de la Joliette

Av de St-Jean
29 🅧 **Q du Port**

Cross-Port Ferry

10

Tunnel St-Laurent

3 ◉
🅧 28
Jardin du Pharo

Q de Rive Neuve 34
31
25 🅧 36
Bd Charles Livon

R Neuve Ste-Catherine

14

R Charras

Av Pasteur

16

R Sainte
R d'Endoume
R Robert
R Petit Chantier
R de la Croix
R des Tyrans
R Rigord

Jardin Pierre Puget

Restaurant Michel (60m); Plage des Catalans (100m)

Vallon des Auffes (960m)

Av de la Corse
Bd de la Corderie

Basilique Notre Dame de la Garde (620m)

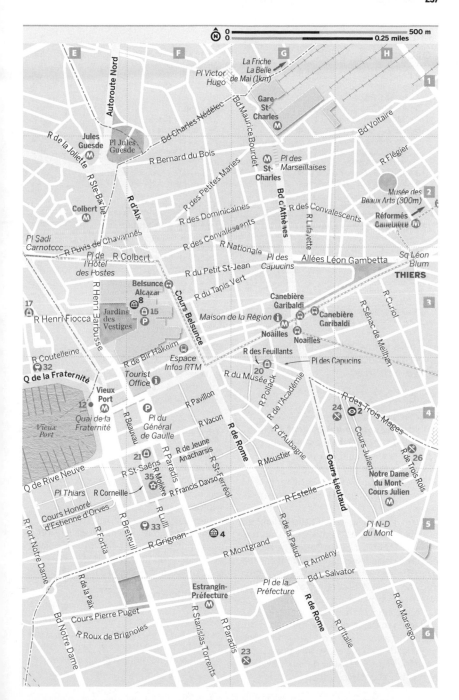

Marseille

a model apartment; contact the tourist office. It's about 5km south of the centre along ave du Prado.

⊚ Beaches

Mesmerising views of another Marseille unfold along **corniche Président John F Kennedy**, the coastal road that cruises south to small, beach volleyball–busy **Plage des Catalans** (3 rue des Catalans; ⊗8.30am-6.30pm; ⊒83) and fishing cove Vallon des Auffes (p260), crammed with boats.

Further south, the vast **Prado beaches** are marked by Jules Cantini's 1903 marble replica of Michelangelo's *David*. The beaches, all gold sand, were created from backfill from the excavations for Marseille's metro. They have a world-renowned **skate park**. Nearby lies expansive Parc Borély.

Promenade Georges Pompidou continues south to **Cap Croisette**, from where the beautiful calanques can be reached on foot.

To head down the coast, take bus 83 from the Vieux Port. At av du Prado switch to bus 19 to continue further.

Raskas Kayak   Kayaking
(⌨04 91 73 27 16; www.raskas-kayak.com; Marseille; half-/full day €35/65) Organises half- and full-day sea-kayaking excursions around Les Calanques.

⊕ TOURS

Croisières Marseille Calanques   Boating
(⌨04 91 33 36 79; www.croisieres-marseille-calanques.com; Vieux Port; MVieux Port) Runs two-hour return trips from the Vieux Port taking in six calanques (adult/child €23/18); three-hour return trips to Cassis passing 12 calanques (€29/22); and 1½-hour trips around the Baie de Marseille (€10), including Château d'If (add €5.50).

Marseille Provence Greeters   Walking
(www.marseilleprovencegreeters.com) A great idea: free walking tours led by locals, covering street art, history, food, shops, football culture and lots more. Sign up in advance

online and check whether your guide speaks English.

Guided Tour   Walking

(www.resamarseille.com; tours €10; ⊗May-Aug; MVieux Port) Run by the tourist office, taking in everything from the city's history to Le Corbusier's architectural experiments at the Cité Radieuse. There's an English-language tour of Le Panier every Saturday at 2pm.

L'Open Tour   Bus

(☑04 91 91 05 82; www.marseille.opentour.com; adult/child €19/8) Travel between key sights and museums aboard a hop-on, hop-off open-top bus. Buy tickets at the tourist office or on board.

🔒 SHOPPING

For chic shopping and large chains, stroll west of the Vieux Port to the 6th *arrondissement*, especially pedestrianised rue St-Ferréol. Major chains fill the **Centre Bourse shopping centre** (www.centre-bourse.com; 17 cours Belsunce; ⊗10am-7.30pm Mon-Sat) and line rue de la République.

Atelier du Santon   Arts & Crafts

(☑04 91 13 61 36; 47 rue Neuve Ste-Catherine; ⊗10am-12.30pm & 2-6.30pm Tue-Sat; MVieux Port) Musée du Santon with its boutique and neighbouring Atelier du Santon are home to tiny handcrafted kiln-fired figures, or *santons* (from *santoùn* in Provençal, meaning 'little saint'). The custom of creating a nativity scene with figurines dates from the Avignon papacy of John XII (1319–34).

La Maison du Pastis   Drinks

(☑04 91 90 86 77; www.lamaisondupastis. com; 108 quai du Port; ⊗10am-5pm Mon-Sat; MVieux Port) A bit touristy, perhaps, but if you're keen to sample a few different kinds of Provence's favourite aperitif – the aniseed-flavoured firewater known as pastis – then this place is an ideal place to do it. It also offers the chance to try absinthe, the

Cours Julien

For a mainline into the city's multicultural make-up, head for **cours Julien** (MNotre Dame du Mont-Cours Julien), an elongated concrete square shaded by palm trees. It's surrounded by hip bars and cafes, and the graffiti-covered streets running north are home to a wealth of bookshops, galleries, tattoo shops and ethnic restaurants. Markets are held on the square on several days of the week: flowers on Wednesday and Saturday, antique books alternate Saturdays, and stamps or antique books on Sunday.

Street art on cours Julien
WENDY CONNETT / ROBERT HARDING ©

notorious spirit known as *la fée verte* (the green fairy) for its supposedly hallucinogenic properties.

Four des Navettes   Food

(☑04 91 33 32 12; www.fourdesnavettes.com; 136 rue Sainte; ⊗7am-8pm Mon-Sat, 9am-1pm & 3-7.30pm Sun; MVieux Port) Opened in 1781, this is the oldest bakery in Marseille (and has apparently only had three owners since then). It is the address to pick up Marseille's signature biscuits, the orange-perfumed *navettes de Marseille* (€17 for a box of 12).

Virginie Monroe   Jewellery

(☑04 91 33 78 70; www.virginiemonroe.com; 1 rue Pythéas; ⊗11am-1.30pm & 2.30-7pm Mon, 10.30am-1.30pm & 2.30-7pm Tue-Fri, 10am-7pm Sat; MVieux Port) Marseille's favourite designer creates delicate necklaces and

Signature Dish: Bouillabaisse

Originally cooked by fishermen from the scraps of their catch, bouillabaisse is Marseille's signature dish. True bouillabaisse includes at least four kinds of fish, and sometimes shellfish. Don't trust tourist traps that promise cheap bouillabaisse; the real deal costs €50 to €65 per person. It's served in two parts: the *soupe de poisson* (broth), rich with tomato, saffron and fennel; and the cooked fish, deboned table side and presented on a platter. On the side are croutons, *rouille* (a bread-thickened garlic-chilli mayonnaise) and grated cheese, usually gruyère. Spread *rouille* on the crouton, top with cheese, and float it in the soup.

Le Rhul (☎04 91 52 01 77; www.hotel-restaurant-le-rhul.com/le-restaurant; 269 corniche Président John F Kennedy; bouillabaisse €53; ◷noon-2pm & 5-9pm; 🚍83) This 1940s seaside hotel with Mediterranean views is a reliably consistent spot for authentic bouillabaisse.

Restaurant Michel (Chez Michel; ☎04 91 52 30 63; www.restaurant-michel-13.fr; 6 rue des Catalans; bouillabaisse €65; ◷6-9.30pm; 🚍83) This deceptively shabby-looking restaurant opposite Plage des Catalans has been the culinary pride and joy of the Michel family since 1946.

Vallon des Auffes (🚍83) Nestled around this picture-postcard fishing village are traditional *cabanons* (seaside cabins), built by fishermen to store tackle and cook traditional Sunday bouillabaisse. Restaurants here serve tip-top bouillabaisse. A narrow staircase (behind the bus stop) links corniche Président John F Kennedy with the harbour.

EATING

Vieux Port and the surrounding pedestrian streets teem with cafe terraces, but choose carefully. For world cuisine, try cours Julien and nearby rue des Trois Mages. For pizza, roast chickens, and Middle Eastern food under €10, nose around the streets surrounding **Marché des Capucins** (place des Capucins; ◷8am-7pm Mon-Sat; Ⓜ Noailles, 🚇Canebière Garibaldi).

Les Buffets du Vieux Port
French €

(☎04 13 20 11 32; www.clubhousevieuxport.com; 158 quai du Port; adult/child menu €23/13; ◷noon-2.30pm & 7.30-10.30pm; 🖼; Ⓜ Vieux Port) What a great idea – a high-class, on-trend self-service canteen, with a vast array of starters, mains, salads and desserts laid out like a banquet for diners to help themselves to. Premium cold cuts, fresh seafood, bouillabaisse, mussels, fish soup – it's all here and more. Portside tables go fast, but there's plenty of room inside.

Bar des 13 Coins
Brasserie €

(☎04 91 91 56 49; 45 rue Sainte-Françoise; mains €12-18; ◷9am-11pm; Ⓜ Vieux Port) Night and day this corner bar is a classic Le Panier hang-out – whether you're old, young, hip or in need of a hip replacement. It's on a quiet backstreet with tables on the square, and serves bistro standards such as steak, mussels, burgers and salads – but it's the chilled vibe you come for, best tasted over an evening pastis.

Le Café des Épices
Modern French €€

(☎04 91 91 22 69; www.cafedesepices.com; 4 rue du Lacydon; lunch/dinner menus from €25/45; ◷noon-3pm & 6-11pm Tue-Fri, noon-3pm Sat; 🖼; Ⓜ Vieux Port) One of Marseille's best chefs, Arnaud de Grammont, infuses his cooking with a panoply of flavours: squid-ink spaghetti with sesame and perfectly cooked scallops, or coriander- and citrus-spiced potatoes topped with the catch of the day. Presentation is impeccable, the decor playful, and the colourful outdoor terrace

bracelets strung with tiny beads. Her ethnic-chic jewellery is wholly affordable to boot.

between giant potted olive trees nothing short of superb.

L'Arome   Modern French €€

(☎04 91 42 88 80; rue de Trois Rois; mains €16-25; ⊙7.30-10pm; ⓂNotre Dame du Mont) The current hot tip in the trendy area around cours Julien is this tiny bistro, on a graffiti-clad street flanked by ethnic restaurants. The no-frills decor, relaxed service and focused menu of French market classics have made this diner deservedly popular. Chef-owner Romain has worked in plenty of fancy restaurants, but aims for sophisticated simplicity here. Reservations essential.

Café Populaire   Bistro €€

(☎04 91 02 53 96; www.cafepopulaire.com; 110 rue Paradis; tapas €6-16, mains €17-22; ⊙noon-2.30pm & 8-11pm Tue-Sat; ⓂEstrangin-Préfecture) Vintage furniture, old books on the shelves and a fine collection of glass soda bottles lend a retro air to this trendy, 1950s-styled *jazz comptoir* (counter) – a restaurant despite its name. The crowd is chic and smiling chefs in the open kitchen mesmerise with daily specials like king

prawns *à la plancha* (grilled) or beetroot and coriander salad.

La Cantinetta   Italian €€

(☎04 91 48 10 48; 24 cours Julien; mains €12-19; ⊙noon-2pm & 7.30-10.30pm Mon-Sat; ⓂNotre Dame du Mont-Cours Julien) Top-class Italian trattoria on the buzzy setting of cours Julien. All the pasta here is homemade, and ingredients are sourced from top Italian suppliers. Ask for a table in the lovely little garden, paved with terracotta tiles and shaded by palms. The *bresaola* (air-dried beef) and parma ham platter are superb.

La Passarelle   Provençal €€

(☎04 91 33 03 27; www.restaurantlapassarelle. fr; 52 rue Plan Fourmiguier; mains €16-22; ⊙noon-2.30pm & 8-10.30pm May-Oct, shorter hours rest of year; ⓂVieux Port) This admirably unpretentious bistro grows most of its organic veggies in its own *potager* (kitchen garden), from tomatoes to courgettes,

> *True bouillabaisse includes at least four kinds of fish, and sometimes shellfish*

Bouillabaisse

Coastal Marseille

salad leaves and aubergines. It's a cosy, friendly place for sampling delicious Mediterranean flavours, with mix-and-match tables and chairs arranged on a decked terrace beneath a spreading sail. Charming and simple.

Place Lorette
Moroccan €€

(☑09 81 35 66 75; place Lorette; mains €13-15; ☺11am-6pm Thu-Sat, to 4pm Sun; Ⓜ Colbert) Tucked away on a quiet square in the middle of polyglot Le Panier, this Moroccan restaurant serves up a fantastic lunch with a spicy Moroccan kick – lamb and chicken tagines, semolina bread, crunchy pastillas, fiery curries, washed down with fresh orange juice and mint tea. The Sunday brunch is a sharing feast.

Le Môlé Passédat
Modern French €€€

(www.passedat.fr; 1 esplanade du J4, MuCEM; La Table lunch/dinner menus from €52/73, La Cuisine 2-/3-course menus €22/35; ☺12.15-2.30pm & 7.30-10.30pm Mon & Wed-Sat, lunch only Sun; Ⓜ Vieux Port, Joliette) Few kitchens are so stunningly located as this one. On the top floor of Marseille's flagship museum, MuCEM, Michelin-starred chef Gérald Passédat cooks up exquisite French fare alongside views of the Mediterranean and Marseillais coastline. **La Table** is the gastronomic restaurant; **La Cuisine** (open noon to 4pm), with self-service dining around shared tables (no sea view), is the cheaper choice. Reserve both online.

🍷 DRINKING & NIGHTLIFE

Near the Vieux Port, head to place Thiars and cours Honoré d'Estienne d'Orves for cafes that bask in the sun by day and buzz into the night. Cours Julien is a fine place on a sunny day to watch people come and go at the many characterful shops, cafes and restaurants in one of Marseille's most interesting neighbourhoods.

La Part des Anges
Wine Bar

(☑04 91 33 55 70; www.lapartdesanges.com; 33 rue Sainte; ☺9am-2am Mon-Sat, 9am-1pm & 6pm-2am Sun; Ⓜ Vieux Port) No address buzzes with Marseille's hip, buoyant crowd more than this fabulous all-rounder wine bar, named after the alcohol that evaporates through a barrel during wine or whisky fermentation: the angels' share. Take your pick of dozens of wines by the glass.

La Caravelle   Bar
(www.lacaravelle-marseille.com; 34 quai du Port; ⊙7am-2am; Ⓜ Vieux Port) Look up or miss this standout upstairs hideaway, styled with rich wood and leather, a zinc bar and yellowing murals. If it's sunny, snag a coveted spot on the port-side terrace. On Friday there's live jazz from 9pm.

Bar de la Marine   Bar
(☑04 91 54 95 42; 15 quai de Rive Neuve; ⊙7am-1am; Ⓜ Vieux Port) Though it is often erroneously thought that Marcel Pagnol filmed the card-party scenes in *Marius* at this Marseille institution, it did figure in the film *Love, Actually*. Come for a drink, not the food, and a lounge on this simple bar's waterside pavement along the Vieux Port. Don't leave without peeking at the original vintage interior.

Trolleybus   Club
(☑04 91 54 30 45; www.letrolley.com; 24 quai de Rive Neuve; ⊙midnight-6am Thu-Sat; Ⓜ Vieux Port) Shake it to techno, funk and indie in between games of *pétanque* at this mythical Marseillais club with four *salles* (rooms) beneath 17th-century stone vaults at the Vieux Port.

✪ ENTERTAINMENT

Cultural events are covered in *L'Hebdo* (€1.20), available around town, or www.marseillebynight.com and www.journalventilo.fr. Tickets for some events are sold at the tourist office (p264).

La Friche La Belle de Mai   Cultural Centre
(☑04 95 04 95 04; www.lafriche.org; 41 rue Jobin; ⊙information & ticket kiosk 11am-6pm Mon, to 7pm Tue-Sun; 🚌49, stop Jobin) This former sugar-refining plant and subsequent tobacco factory is now a vibrant arts centre with a theatre, artists' workshops, cinema,

 Island Life

Located 3.5km west of the Vieux Port, the island fortress-prison of **Château d'If** (www.if.monuments-nationaux.fr; adult/child €5.50/free; ⊙10am-6pm Apr-Oct, to 5pm rest of year) was immortalised in Alexandre Dumas' classic 1844 novel *The Count of Monte Cristo*. Many political prisoners were incarcerated here, including the Revolutionary hero Mirabeau and the Communards of 1871. Other than the island itself there's not a great deal to see, but it's worth the trip just for the views of the Vieux Port. Frioul If Express boats (€10.50 return, 20 minutes, around nine daily) run from the quay.

A few hundred metres west of Île d'If are the **Îles du Frioul**, embracing the barren, dyke-linked, white-limestone islands of Ratonneau and Pomègues. Seabirds and rare plants thrive on these tiny islands, which are each about 2.5km long, totalling 200 hectares. Ratonneau has three beaches. Frioul If Express boats to Château d'If also serve the Îles du Frioul (one/two islands €10.50/15.60 return, 35 minutes, around 20 daily).

Château d'If
LEONID ANDRONOV / SHUTTERSTOCK ©

multimedia displays, skateboard ramps, electro and world-music parties etc. Check its program online.

The quickest way by public transport is to catch the metro to Gare St-Charles and walk along rue Guibal, or take line M2 to Cinq Avenues Longchamp, cross Parc Longchamp and then take Rue Bénédit.

 The Perfect Sunset

Only Marseillais and those in the know are privy to **Le Chalet du Pharo** (☑04 91 52 80 11; www.le-chalet-du-pharo.com; Jardin du Pharo, 58 bd Charles Livon; mains €18-30; ⊗noon-3pm daily, 7.30-9.30pm Mon-Sat; MVieux Port), a little chalet with a very big view, secreted in the **Jardin du Pharo** (MVieux Port). Its hillside terrace, shaded by pines and parasols, stares across the water at Fort St-Jean, MuCEM and the Villa Méditerranée beyond. Grilled fish and meat dominate the menu. Online reservations are essential. No credit cards.

Le Chalet du Pharo
GARDEL BERTRAND / AGE FOTOSTOCK ©

Opéra Municipal de Marseille
Opera

(☑04 91 55 11 10; http://opera.marseille.fr; 2 rue Molière; MVieux Port) Hosts large-scale performances by internationally renowned artists. The season runs September to June.

Théâtre National d e Marseille
Theatre

(La Criée, ☑04 91 54 70 54; www.theatre-lacriee. com; 30 quai de Rive Neuve; MVieux Port) Dance and drama, sometimes in English.

Nouveau Stade Vélodrome
Stadium

(www.lenouveaustadevelodrome.com; 3 bd Michelet; MRond-Point du Prado) Marseille's cherished football team plays at Stade Vélodrome, which also hosts concerts. Occasional guided tours are available via

the tourist office. It's 4km or so south of the Vieux Port, along av du Prado.

INFORMATION

Marseille City Pass (www.resamarseille.com; 24/48/72hr €24/31/39) Covers admission to city museums, public transport, a guided city tour, Château d'If boat trip and more, plus other discounts. It's not necessary for children under 12, as many attractions are greatly reduced or free. Buy it online or at the tourist office.

Tourist Office (☑04 91 13 89 00; www.mar-seille-tourisme.com; 11 La Canebière; ⊗9am-7pm Mon-Sat, 10am-5pm Sun; MVieux Port) Marseille's useful tourist office has plenty of information on everything, including guided city tours on foot or by bus, electric tourist train or boat, as well as to Les Calanques. Has free wi-fi too.

Maison de la Région (www.regionpaca.fr; 61 La Canebière; ⊗11am-6pm Mon-Sat; MNoailles) Info on the surrounding Provence and Côte d'Azur region.

GETTING THERE & AWAY

AIR

Aéroport Marseille-Provence (Aéroport Marseille-Marignane; MRS; ☑04 42 14 14 14; www.marseille.aeroport.fr) is located 25km northwest of Marseille in Marignane. There are regular year-round flights to nearly all major French cities, plus major conurbations in the UK, Germany, Belgium, Italy and Spain.

BOAT

The **passenger ferry terminal** (www.marseille-port.fr; MJoliette) is located 250m south of place de la Joliette.

SNCM (☑08 91 70 18 01; www.sncm.fr; 61 bd des Dames; MJoliette) has regular ferries from Nice and Marseille to Corsica and Sardinia, plus long-distance routes to Algeria and Tunisia.

TRAIN

Eurostar (www.eurostar.com) has one-to-five times weekly services between Marseille and London (from €99, 6½ hours) via Avignon and

Nouveau Stade Vélodrome

Lyon. As always, the earlier you book, the cheaper the potential fare.

Regular and TGV trains serve **Gare St-Charles** (⊗ticket office 5.15am-10pm; Ⓜ Gare St-Charles SNCF), which is a junction for both metro lines. The **left-luggage office** (⊗8.15am-9pm) is next to platform A. Sample fares:

Nice €28, 2½ hours.

Paris Gare de Lyon From €75, three hours on TGV.

① GETTING AROUND

BICYCLE

With the **Le Vélo** (www.levelo-mpm.fr) bike-share scheme, pick up/drop off a bike from 100-plus stations across the city and the coastal road to the beaches. Users must subscribe online first (€1/5 a week/year), after which the first 30 minutes is free, then €1 per hour. Stations only take credit cards with chips.

CAR

Trust us, you'll regret bringing a car into Marseille – car parks and on-street parking are very expensive, and the traffic can be horrendous. Central car parks include **Parking Bourse** (rue Reine Elisabeth; ⊗24hr; Ⓜ Vieux Port) and **Parking de Gaulle** (22 place du Général de Gaulle; ⊗24hr; Ⓜ Vieux Port) off La Canebière. Expect to pay at least €2 per hour, €30 per 24 hours.

PUBLIC TRANSPORT

Marseille has two metro lines (Métro 1 and Métro 2), two tram lines (yellow and green) and an extensive bus network. Bus, metro or tram tickets (per hour/day €1.60/5.20) are available from machines in the metro, at tram stops and on buses. Most buses start in front of the **Espace Infos RTM** (⊘04 91 91 92 10; www.rtm.fr; 6 rue des Fabres; ⊗8.30am-6pm Mon-Fri, 8.30am-noon & 1-4.30pm Sat; Ⓜ Vieux Port), where you can obtain information and tickets.

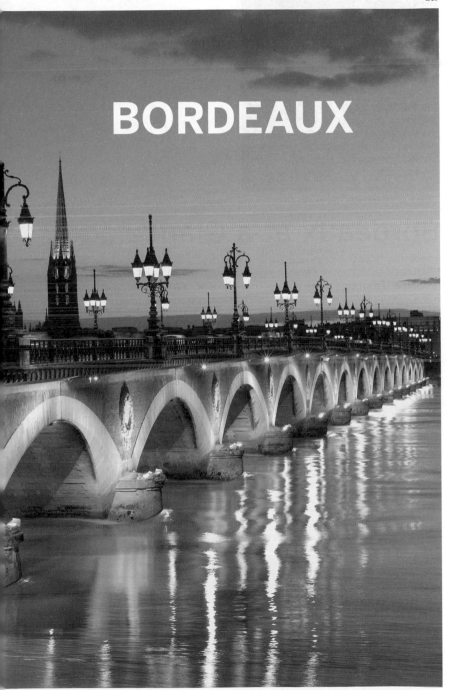

BORDEAUX

Bordeaux at a Glance...

Bordeaux is among France's most exciting, vibrant and dynamic cities. Visionary city mayor Alain Juppé has pedestrianised boulevards, restored neoclassical architecture, created a high-tech public transport system and reclaimed Bordeaux's former industrial wet docks at Bassin à Flots. Half the city (18 sq km) is Unesco-listed, making it the largest urban World Heritage Site.

Bolstered by its high-spirited university-student population and 5.5 million visitors annually, La Belle Bordeaux scarcely sleeps: think barista-run coffee shops, super-food food trucks, an exceptional dining scene and more fine wine than you could ever possibly drink. Santé!

Bordeaux in Two Days

Begin with coffee at **Black List** (p281) then explore the **cathedral** (p276) and its belfry. Visit the **Musée d'Aquitaine** (p276) then walk south to **Marché des Capucins** (p279) for an early oyster lunch. Devote the afternoon to **La Cité du Vin** (p270). Day two, consider one of the tourist office's exceptional themed tours and a tasting workshop at the **École du Vin de Bordeaux** (p273).

Bordeaux in Four Days

Head out of the city day three to either **St-Émilion** (p282) or the **Médoc** (p277); reserve your lunch table well in advance. Day four, consider a day trip to the **Dune du Pilat** (p274); pack your beach gear and cycling legs.

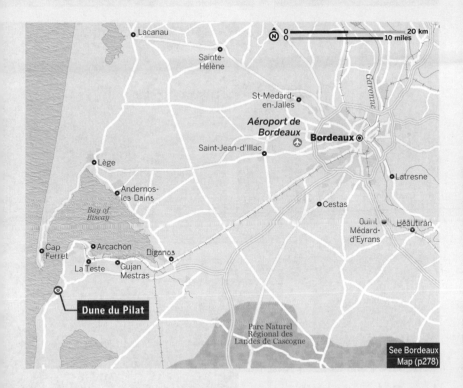

Dune du Pilat

Parc Naturel
Régional des
Landes de Cascogne

See Bordeaux
Map (p278)

Arriving in Bordeaux

Aéroport de Bordeaux Hourly shuttle bus (www.navetteaeroport-bordeaux.com; €7.20, 30 minutes) to the train station, place Gambetta and Esplanade des Quinconces. Otherwise, urban bus line 1 every 10 minutes to the train station; journey time is 40 minutes (longer at rush hour) and a ticket costs €1.50. Taxi to the city centre: around €50.

Sleeping

Accommodation options are plentiful across all categories, with several delightful options sitting splendidly in the town centre around the cathedral. Another charming area is the atmospheric wine-merchant district of Chartrons, midway between the cathedral and the rejuvenated wet-dock area, Bassin à Flots. For chic B&B accommodation between vines, head out of town into Bordeaux's lush wine regions.

Wine cellar

La Cité du Vin

The complex world of wine is explored in depth in Bordeaux's ground-breaking La Cité du Vin, a stunning piece of contemporary architecture resembling a swirling wine decanter of sorts on the banks of the River Garonne.

Great For...

☑ Don't Miss

One-hour architecture tours (€6) of the building inside and out, departing at 3pm daily.

Iconic Architecture

The swirl of white wine in a glass? A gnarled and knotted vine? Precisely what the shimmering gold creation of Paris-based architects Anouk Legendre and Nicolas Desmazières (built at a cost of €81 million) is meant to be is unclear. One thing is certain: the curvaceous riverside building that glitters gold in the sun is enticing, seductive and a brilliant photo op thanks to the thousands of silk-screen-printed glass and aluminium panels tiling its façade.

Voyage of Discovery

La Cité du Vin has no permanent exhibition: with the aid of a digital companion, visitors follow a tour through 20 different themed zones covering everything from vine culti-vation and grape varieties to ancient wine trade and celebrated wine personalities.

PHILIP BIRD LRPS CPAGB / SHUTTERSTOCK ©

La Cité ◉
du Vin

Central
Bordeaux

❶ Need to Know

☎05 56 81 38 47; www.laciteduvin.com; 1 Esplanade de Pontac; adult/child €20/free; ⊙9.30am-7.30pm Apr-Oct, Tue-Sun Nov-Mar

✗ Take a Break

Reserve a table at **Le 7 Restaurant** (www. le7restaurant.com), on the 7th floor.

★ Top Tip

Arrive by boat, a 20-minute voyage (€1.50) from Esplanade des Quinconces, downtown Bordeaux.

Le Belvédère

Tours end with a complimentary glass of wine in Le Belvédère, a panoramic tasting space on the 8th floor with a huge 30m-long oak bar, monumental chandelier made out of hundreds of recycled wine bottles, and a magnificent 360-degree panorama of Bordeaux city laid out at your feet. Interject sensational river and city views with a *dégustation* (tasting) of 20 different Bordeaux wines; kids taste grape juices.

Vineyard Siestas

In hot, south-of-France style, visitors can indulge in an afternoon vineyard siesta in July and August. Film screenings focusing on vineyards and winemakers in Bordeaux and the world, nonalcoholic tasting workshops for families, and creative cork workshops and wine-label decoding sessions for kids are other appealing experiential activities.

Musée du Vin et du Négoce

Too high-tech? From futuristic La Cité du Vin stroll back in time, along the river south, to the ancient wine-trading district of **Chartrons**. Here, hidden in one of the city's oldest buildings – an Irish merchant's house dating to 1720 – this small wine and trade museum offers a more traditional insight into the historic origins of Bordeaux's wine trade and the importance of the *négociant* (merchant trader) in the 19th century. Its vaulted cellars, 33m long, display dozens of artefacts, including handcrafted stave oak barrels and every size of wine bottle from an Avion to a Melchior.

Digital-Smart Tasting

It's been dubbed the 'Guggenheim of wine' for good reason: the multi-sensory workshops whereby visitors can pair virtual food with real wines in a fully immersive space (think smells, sounds, 360-degree imagery) are sensational.

Bordeaux Wine Trail

Thirsty? The 1000-sq-km wine-growing area around the city of Bordeaux is, along with Burgundy, France's most important producer of top-quality wines. Wine aficionados, be prepared to enter viticulture heaven.

Great For...

☑ Don't Miss

A glass of wine on the stunning rooftop terrace of luxurious 18th-century **Le Grand Hôtel** (📞05 57 30 44 44; www.ghbordeaux.com; 2-5 place de la Comédie).

The Bordeaux region is divided into 57 appellations (production areas) that are grouped into seven *familles* (families), and subdivided into a hierarchy of designations (eg *premier grand cru classé,* the most prestigious) that vary from appellation to appellation. Most Bordeaux wines have earned the right to include the abbreviation AOC (Appellation d'Origine Contrôlée) on their labels, indicating that the contents have been grown, fermented and aged according to strict regulations that govern such viticultural matters as the number of vines permitted per hectare and acceptable pruning methods.

Bordeaux has over 5000 châteaux (also called *domaines* or *clos*), referring not to palatial residences but to the estates where grapes are raised, picked, fermented and then matured as wine. Some accept walk-in

JUSTIN FOULKES / LONELY PLANET ©

Wine). It hosts introductory two-hour workshops on the last Saturday of each month and daily July to September (€39), and more complex two- to three-day courses (€350 to €600) from May to October. Food lovers will appreciate the two-day 'Practical Level' course, which includes food pairings and a cooking session.

Cooking Courses

There are a couple of courses open to tourists and, this being Bordeaux, most involve food and wine.

Le Saint James   Cooking

(☑05 57 97 06 00; www.saintjames-bouliac. com; 3 place Camille Hostein, Bouliac) Memorable cooking courses are organised at **Côté Cours**, the prestigious but highly accessible cooking school of chic lifestyle hotel Le Saint James, a stunning piece of architecture by Jean Nouvel, between vines in the village of Bouliac, 10km southeast of Bordeaux. Themed classes last three to 3½ hours and cost €75 to €155 per person. Afterwards indulge in a drink at **Café de l'Esperance**, Bouliac's uber-cool village cafe also run by Le Saint James.

---

visitors; most require a reservation. Many close during the *vendange* (grape harvest) in October.

Tours & Tastings

Whet your palate with the tourist office's **city tour**, a two-hour session (€14) starting at 10am daily, which includes wine tasting. Or go for the **Urban Wine Tour** (€49) that introduces wine lovers to châteaux and *bars à vin* (wine bars) in the city, or a 1½-hour **river cruise** with oysters and wine tasting (€15).

École du Vin de Bordeaux   Wine

(Bordeaux Wine School; ☑05 56 00 22 85; www. bordeaux.com; 3 cours du 30 juillet) Serious students of the grape can enrol at this highly regarded wine school inside the Maison du Vin de Bordeaux (Bordeaux House of

Dune du Pilat

This colossal sand dune is Europe's largest. Scampering up and along its near-hallucinatory golden sands is a once-in-a-lifetime experience, making the easy 70km day trip from Bordeaux an absolute essential.

Great For...

☑ Don't Miss

The pine-scented cycle path linking Dune du Pilat with Arcachon, 8km south.

Sometimes referred to as the Dune de Pyla because of its location 4km from the bijou seaside town of Pyla-sur-Mer, this gargantuan sand dune stretches from the mouth of the Bassin d'Arcachon southwards for 2.7km. Already Europe's largest, the dune is growing eastwards 1.5m a year – it has swallowed trees, a road junction and even a hotel, so local lore claims.

The view from the top – approximately 115m above sea level – is magnificent. To the west you see the sandy shoals at the mouth of the Bassin d'Arcachon, including Cap Ferret and the **Banc d'Arguin** bird reserve where up to 6000 couples of sandwich terns nest each spring. Dense dark-green forests of maritime pines, oaks, ferns and strawberry trees (whose wood is traditionally used to build oyster-farmer

Bay of Biscay

Bordeaux

⊙ **Dune du Pilat**

❶ Need to Know

Parking costs €4/6 per four hours/day in July and August (€1/2 September to June).

✕ Take a Break

Picnic on the sand or see and be seen over lunch at chic La Co(o)rniche.

★ Top Tip

Take care swimming: powerful currents swirl out to sea from deceptively tranquil little bays.

shacks) stretch from the base of the dune eastwards almost as far as the eye can see.

Dune Panorama

Snack bars and touristy restaurants abound next to the Dune du Pilat car park – although on warm, sunny days with no wind, you might prefer to picnic on the sand. Before leaving Bordeaux, stock up with traditional Bordelais supplies at gourmet food store, Le Comptoir Bordelaise (p279).

For an unforgettable meal with golden dune view, there is only one address: **La Co(o)rniche** (☏05 56 22 72 11; www.lacoorniche-pyla.com; 46 av Louis Gaume, Pyla-sur-Mer; 2-/3-course lunch menu €53/58, seafood platters €40-85) is a glamorous 1930s hunting lodge, reinvented by French designer

Philippe Starck. Perfectly placed for a meal or tapas-fuelled drink after a sandy walk on the dune, this sensational seaside address is beach chic at its best. Snag a table by the infinity pool to feast on the chef's modern French cuisine. Or, should you prefer a cheaper or lighter meal (€12 to €20), stop for a cocktail and seafood tapas in the bar. If you fall madly in love with the place and find yourself unable to leave, doubles in the designer five-star hotel start at €255.

Sunset Walks

The helpful **Espace Accueil** (☏05 56 22 12 85; www.ladunedupilat.com; Dune du Pilat, Pyla-sur-Mer; ⊙9.30am-6pm Jul & Aug, to 5.30pm rest of year) has information on the dune and runs fascinating guided walks on the sand, including at sunset. Be warned that it can be desperately windy atop the dune: swirling, whip-lashing sand can be particularly unpleasant for younger children.

⊙ SIGHTS

Mirroir d'Eau   Fountain

(Water Mirror; place de la Bourse; ⏰10am-10pm summer) `FREE` A fountain of sorts, the Mirroir d'Eau is the world's largest reflecting pool. Covering an area of 3450 sq metres of black granite on the quayside opposite the imposing Palais de la Bourse, the 'water mirror' provides hours of entertainment on warm sunny days when the reflections in its thin slick of water – drained and refilled every half-hour – are stunning. Every 23 minutes a dense fog-like vapour is ejected for three minutes to add to the fun (and photo opportunities).

Cathédrale St-André   Cathedral

(www.cathedrale-bordeaux.fr; place Jean Moulin; ⏰2-6pm Mon, 10am-noon & 2-6pm Tue-Sun) Lording over the city, and a Unesco World Heritage Site prior to the city's classification, the cathedral's oldest section dates from 1096; most of what you see today was built in the 13th and 14th centuries. Enjoy exceptional masonry carvings in the north portal.

Even more imposing than the cathedral itself is the gargoyled, 50m-high Gothic belfry, **Tour Pey-Berland** (place Jean Moulin; adult/child €5.50/free; ⏰10am-1.15pm & 2-6pm Jun-Sep, 10am-12.30pm & 2-5.30pm Oct-May), erected between 1440 and 1466.

Musée d'Aquitaine   Museum

(📞05 56 01 51 00; www.musee-aquitaine-bordeaux.fr; 20 cours Pasteur; adult/child €4/2; ⏰11am-6pm Tue-Sun) Gallo-Roman statues and relics dating back 25,000 years are among the highlights at this bright and spacious, well-curated history and art museum. Grab a bilingual floor plan at the entrance and borrow an English-language catalogue to better appreciate the exhibits that span prehistory through to 18th-century Atlantic trade and slavery, world cultures and the emergence of Bordeaux as a world port in the 19th century.

Musée des Beaux-Arts   Art Museum

(📞05 56 96 51 60; www.musba-bordeaux.fr; 20 cours d'Albret; adult/child €4/2; ⏰11am-6pm mid-Jul–mid-Aug, closed Tue rest of year) The evolution of Occidental art from the Renais-

Mirroir d'Eau and Palais de la Bourse

sance to the mid-20th century is on view at Bordeaux's Museum of Fine Arts, which occupies two wings of the 1770s-built Hôtel de Ville, either side of elegant city park Jardin de la Mairie. The museum was established in 1801; highlights include 17th-century Flemish, Dutch and Italian paintings. Temporary exhibitions are regularly hosted at its nearby annexe, **Galerie des Beaux-Arts** (place du Colonel Raynal; adult/child €6.50/3.50; ☺11am-6pm mid-Jul–mid-Aug, closed Tue rest of year).

Jardin Public   Garden
(cours de Verdun) Landscaping is artistic as well as informative at the Jardin Public. Established in 1755 and laid out in the English style a century later, the grounds incorporate duck ponds, the meticulously catalogued **Jardin Botanique** dating from 1629, and the city's **Musée d'Histoire Naturelle** (Natural History Museum; 5 place Bardineau) closed for renovation work and slated to open again in late 2017.

 TOURS

The tourist office (p282) runs a packed program of city tours in English, including gourmet and wine tours, river cruises in the warmer months and child-friendly tours. All tours take a limited number of participants; reserve ahead on the tourist office website or in situ.

🔒 SHOPPING

Europe's longest pedestrian shopping street, rue Ste Catherine, stretches north from place de la Victoire to place de la Comédie, with 19th-century shopping arcade **Galerie Bordelaise** (rue de la Porte Dijeaux & rue Ste-Catherine) nearby. Trendy independent boutiques are concentrated on hip rue St-James in the St-Pierre quarter and rue Notre-Dame in Chartrons.

Les Dock des Épices   Food
(http://dockdesepices.com; 20 rue St-James; ☺10am-7pm Tue-Sat) For red Sauternes- or Syrah-flavoured rock salt, *fleur de sel* from

 ### The Médoc

Northwest of Bordeaux, along the western shore of the Gironde Estuary, lie some of Bordeaux's most celebrated vineyards.

On the riverbanks of the muddy Gironde, **Pauillac** (population 1300) is at the heart of the wine country, surrounded by the distinguished Haut-Médoc, Margaux and St-Julien appellations. Extraordinary châteaux pepper these parts, from world-famous **Château Ducru-Braucaillou** on its southeast fringe to **Château Margaux**, with striking cellars designed by Lord Norman Foster. The Pauillac wine appellation encompasses 18 *crus classés*, including the world-renowned Mouton Rothschild, Latour and Lafite Rothschild.

Pauillac tourist office houses the **Maison du Tourisme et du Vin** (☎05 56 59 03 08; www.pauillac-medoc.com; La Verrerie, Pauillac; ☺9.30am-7pm Mon-Sat, 10am-1pm & 2-6pm Sun), with information on visiting châteaux, colour-coded maps of production areas and driving itineraries along **Les Routes des Vins de Bordeaux**.

In the gold-stone hamlet of Bages, near Pauillac, lunch on the picture-postcard village square at 1930s-styled **Café Lavinal** (www.jmcazes.com/en/cafe-lavinal; Passage du Desquet, Bages; menus €28 & €38, mains €12-25; ☺8am-2pm & 7.30-9pm; ❄🛜). With twin Michelin-starred chef Jean-Luc Rocha from neighbouring Château Cordeillan-Bages overseeing the menu and 120 wines on the *carte de vin,* a brilliant bistro dining experience is guaranteed. The menu features French classics (veal kidneys, *magret de canard,* fish stew), burgers, salads and charcuterie platters.

Île de Ré and Bordeaux tea, look no further than this incredible spice shop and upmarket *épicerie* (grocery).

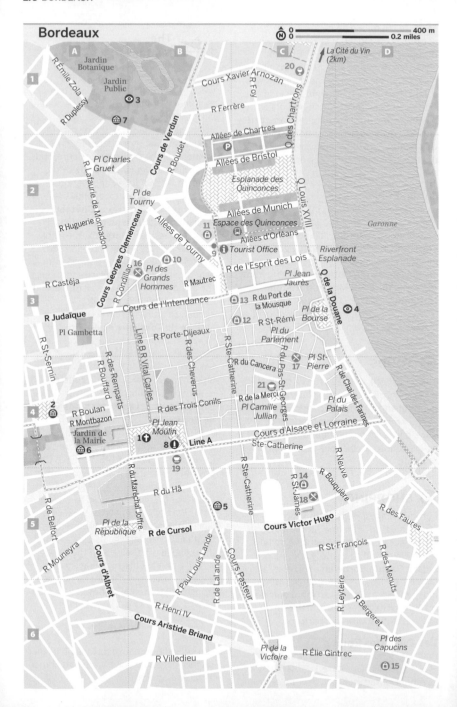

Bordeaux

N

0   400 m
0   0.2 miles

La Cité du Vin
(2km)

Jardin
Botanique

R Émile Zola

R Duplessy

Cours Xavier Arnozan

R Foy

R Ferrère

Jardin
Public ⊙ 3

Allées de Chartres

7

Q des Chartrons

P

Allées de Bristol

Cours de Verdun

R Boudet

Pl Charles
Gruet

R Lafaurie de Monbadon

Pl de
Tourny

Esplanade des
Quinconces

R Huguerie

Allées de Tourny

Allées de Munich

Espace des Quinconces

11

Q Louis XVIII

Garonne

Allées d'Orléans

9 ℹ Tourist Office

R de l'Esprit des Lois

Riverfront
Esplanade

R Castéja

Cours Georges Clemenceau

R Condillac

16 ⊗

10

Pl des
Grands
Hommes

R Mautrec

Cours de l'Intendance

13

R du Port de
la Mousque

Pl Jean
Jaurès

Q de la Douane

R Judaïque

R St-Sernin

Pl Gambetta

R des Remparts

R Bouffard

Line B R Vital Carles

12

R Porte-Dijeaux

R des Cheverus

R Ste-Catherine

R du Cancera

R St-Rémi

Pl du
Parlement

Pl de la
Bourse

⊙ 4

17 ⊗

Pl St-
Pierre

R du Pas-St-Georges

R des Trois Conils

21

R de la Merci

Pl Camille
Jullian

R du Palais

R de Chai des Farines

Pl du
Palais

R Boulan

R Montbazon

Jardin de
la Mairie

6

Pl Jean
Moulin

1 ℹ

8 ℹ

Line A

Cours d'Alsace et Lorraine

Ste-Catherine

R Neuve

R St-James

14

18 ⊗

R Bouquière

R de Belfort

R du Maréchal Joffre

19

R du Hâ

R Ste-Catherine

5

Cours Victor Hugo

R des Faures

Pl de la
République

R de Cursol

Pl de la
République

Cours d'Albret

R Mouneyra

R Paul Louis Lande

R de Lalande

Cours Pasteur

R St-François

R Leyteire

R des Menuts

R Bergeret

R Henri IV

Cours Aristide Briand

R Villedieu

Pl de la
Victoire

R Élie Gintrec

Pl des
Capucins

15

A   B   C   D

1   2   3   4   5   6

Bordeaux

Le Comptoir Bordelaise
Food & Drinks

(www.lecomptoirbordelais.com; 1 rue Piliers de Tutelle; ◷9am 7.30pm) Rev up your taste buds in this gourmet boutique selling local and regional food and drink specialities. Be tempted by local cheese, *canalés* (sand-castle-shaped cakes from Bordeaux), *bouchons de Bordeaux* (cork-shaped pastries filled with almonds), *raisins au Sauternes* (chocolate-enrobed raisins soaked in Sauternes wine), salted caramels, chocolate sardines, olive oils, sauces and condiments, artisan beers – the list is endless. Then, of course, there is wine...

Beillevaire
Food

(☑09 54 86 80 03; www.fromagerie-beillevaire.com; 8 rue Michel Montaigne; ◷8.30am-7.30pm Tue-Sat) This artisan *fromagerie* and *crémerie* (dairy shop) is a sheer delight for local foodies who shop here for boutique cheeses and creamy yellow butter hand-moulded in fat curvaceous patties near Nantes. Don't miss the *demi-sel croquant* butter, studded with crunchy crystals of rock salt. If you want to take some cheese home with you, ask for it to be vacuum-packed.

Bordeaux Magnum
Wine

(☑05 56 48 00 06; 3 rue Gobineau; ◷9am-8pm Mon-Sat, 10am-6pm Sun) Speciality wine shop with rack upon rack of Bordeaux's gift to the world.

⊗ EATING

Magasin Général
International €

(☑05 56 77 88 35; www.magasingeneral.camp; 87 quai des Queyries; 2-/3-course menu €14/18, mains €9-19; ◷8.30am-6pm Wed-Fri, 8.30am-midnight Sat, 10am-midnight Sun, kitchen noon-2.15pm & 7-10pm; 🛜) Follow the hip crowd across the river to this huge industrial hangar on the right bank, France's biggest and best organic restaurant with gargantuan terrace complete with vintage sofa seating, ping-pong table and table football. Everything here, from the vegan burgers and super-food salads to smoothies, pizzas, wine and French bistro fare, is *bio* (organic) and sourced locally. Sunday brunch (€24) is a bottomless feast.

Marché des Capucins
Market

(http://marchedescapucins.com; place des Capucins; ◷6am-1pm Tue-Sun) A classic Bordeaux experience is a Saturday morning spent slurping oysters and white wine from a seafood stand in the city's legendary covered food market. Stalls overflowing with fruit, veg, cheese, meats, fish and all sorts fill the space to bursting. Walk south down cours Pasteur to place de la Victoire, then turn left onto rue Élie Gintrec.

Potato Head
Modern French €€

(http://potatoheadbordeaux.com/; 27 rue Buhan; mains lunch €13, dinner €18-25, 5-course tasting menu €41; ⊙11am-3pm Sun) With its eclectic mix of seating (bar stool, bistro and armchair), moss-clad vegetal wall and industrial-style lighting, this trendy bistro is a fabulous space to dine in. Throw in a creative kitchen known for surprise combos (foie gras, beetroot, ginger and chocolate, anyone?) and the finest summer garden in the city and, well, you need to reserve well in advance.

Sunday brunch (€24) in the garden is a languid and sensational affair.

Le Petit Commerce   Seafood €€

(05 56 79 76 58; 22 rue Parlement St-Pierre; 2-course lunch menu €14, mains €15-25; ⊙noon-midnight) This iconic bistro, with dining rooms both sides of a narrow pedestrian street and former Michelin-starred chef Stéphane Carrade in the kitchen, is the star turn of the trendy St-Pierre quarter. It's best known for its excellent seafood menu that embraces everything from Arcachon sole and oysters to eels, lobsters and *chipirons* (baby squid) fresh from St Jean de Luz.

End your meal, as locals do, with a bowl of *riz au lait à l'orange* (orange-perfumed rice pudding).

La Tupina   Regional Cuisine €€€

(✆05 56 91 56 37; www.latupina.com; 6 rue Porte de la Monnaie; lunch menu €18, dinner menus €39 & €74; ⊙noon-2pm & 7-11pm Tue-Sun) Filled with the aroma of soup simmering inside a *tupina* ('kettle' in Basque) over an open fire, this bistro is feted for its seasonal southwestern French fare: think foie gras and egg *cassoullette* (mini casserole), milk-fed lamb, tripe and goose wings. Hopefully nothing will change following the 2016 retirement of the gregarious Jean-Pierre Xiradakis, life and soul of La Tupina since 1968.

Le Chapon Fin   Gastronomic €€€

(✆05 56 79 10 10; www.chapon-fin.com; 5 rue Montesquieu; lunch menus €28 & €39, dinner menus €69-99) A meal at Bordeaux's most historic dining address, open since 1825, is worth it, if only to gawp in astonishment at the extravagant rococo interior: think mountains of fake rock, lush greenery and exuberant furnishings – and relive the gran-

From left: Jardin Public (p277); Cathédrale St-André (276); Musée des Beaux-Arts (p276)

deur of belle époque Bordeaux. Caviar, foie gras and seasonal asparagus followed by roast pigeon or saddle of lamb feature on the very classical, gastronomic menu.

🔵 DRINKING & NIGHTLIFE

Bar à Vin Wine Bar

(📋05 56 00 43 47; http://baravin.bordeaux.com; 3 cours du 30 Juillet; ⊙11am-10pm Mon-Sat) This ultrastylish but very accessible wine bar, inside the hallowed halls of the Maison du Vin de Bordeaux, is the designer hot spot to tipple with Bordelais who really know their wine. Lounge between walls of stacked bottles, on armchairs or at the bar, and allow gracious sommeliers to guide you through the choice of 30 odd different Bordeaux wines by the glass (€3 to €8).

Symbiose Cocktail Bar

(Old-fashioned Stories; 📋05 56 23 67 15; www.facebook.com/symbiosebordeaux/; 4 quai des Chartrons; ⊙noon-2.30pm Mon, noon-2.30pm & 6.30pm-2am Tue-Fri, 6.30pm-2am Sat) There is something eminently inviting about this clandestine address with soft green façade across from the river on the fringe of the Chartrons district. This is the secret speakeasy that introduced good cocktails with gastronomic food pairings to Bordeaux. The chef uses locally sourced, artisan products, and cocktails rekindle old-fashioned recipes packed with homemade syrups and 'forgotten', exotic or unusual ingredients.

Utopia Cafe, Bar

(www.cinemas-utopia.org; 3 place Camille Jullian; ⊙10am-1am summer, to 10.30pm winter) At home in an old church, this much-venerated art space is a local institution. Art-house cinema, mellow cafe, hot lunch spot and bar rolled into one, it is one of the top addresses in the city to mingle over a drink, *tartine* (open sandwich, €7) or good-value meal (mains €13 to €15) with local Bordelais at any time of day. Its atmospheric pavement terrace on a car-free square catches the morning sun.

Black List Cafe

(📋06 89 91 82 65; www.facebook.com/blacklistcafe; 27 place Pey Berland; ⊙8am-6pm Mon-Fri, 9.30am-6pm Sat) For serious coffee lovers, nothing beats the beans that arrive at this

Daytrip to St-Émilion

The medieval village of St-Émilion, 40km east of Bordeaux, perches above vineyards renowned for producing full-bodied, deeply coloured red wines. Named after Émilion, a miracle-working Benedictine monk who lived in a cave here between AD 750 and 767, it soon became a stop on pilgrimage routes, and the village and its vineyards are now Unesco-listed.

For foodies, there is one address: **La Terrasse Rouge** (☑05 57 24 47 05; www.laterrasserouge.com; 1 Château La Dominique; lunch menu €28; ◷noon-2.30pm & 7-11pm Jun-Sep, noon-2.30pm & 7-11pm Fri & Sat, noon-2.30pm Sun-Thu Oct-May) is a spectacular vineyard restaurant, borne out of Jean Nouvel's designer revamp of Château La Dominique's wine cellars. Oysters are fresh from Cap Ferret, caviar comes from Neuvic in the neighbouring Dordogne and the iPad mini wine list is naturally extraordinary. Watch for the monthly cooking classes held here, built around lunch and *dégustation* (tasting) of two St-Émilion wines. Advance reservations essential.

Hiking and cycling circuits loop through the greater World Heritage jurisdiction; St-Émilion **tourist office** (☑05 57 55 28 28; www.saint-emilion-tourisme.com; place des Créneaux; ◷9.30am-7.30pm Jul & Aug, shorter hours rest of year) has maps and rents bicycles; reserve in advance online.

Vineyard near St-Émilion
JUSTIN FOULKES / LONELY PLANET ©

coffee shop freshly roasted from Paris' Belleville Brûlerie. In a tiny but stylishly retro, ceramic-tiled interior, barista Laurent Pierre serves espresso and filtered *grand cru* coffee to a discerning Bordelais crowd. Granola breakfasts, veggie-packed salads and creative sandwiches (lunch menus €8.50 to €11.50), and fresh organic juices complement the fantastic coffee.

I.Boat   Club
(☑05 56 10 48 35; www.iboat.eu; quai Armand Lalande, Bassins à Flot 1; ◷7pm-6am) Hip-hop, rock, indie pop, psyche blues rock, punk and hardcore are among the varied sounds that blast out of this fun nightclub and concert venue, afloat a decommissioned ferry moored in the increasingly trendy, industrial Bassins à Flot district in the north of the city. Live music starts at 7pm, with DJ sets kicking in on the club dance floor from 11.30pm.

ⓘ INFORMATION

Consider investing in a **Bordeaux City Pass** (www.bordeauxcitypass.com). A one-/two-/three-day card costs €26/33/40 and covers admission to many museums and monuments, unlimited public transport and various other discounts. The tourist office sells it.

Tourist Office (☑05 56 00 66 00; www.bordeaux-tourisme.com; 12 cours du 30 Juillet; ◷9am-7.30pm Mon-Sat, 9.30am-6.30pm Sun Jul & Aug, shorter hours Sep-Jun) Runs an excellent range of city and regional tours; reserve in advance online or in situ. It also rents pocket modems to hook you up with wi-fi.

ⓘ GETTING THERE & AWAY

AIR

Aéroport de Bordeaux (www.bordeaux.aeroport.fr) is in Mérignac, 10km southwest of the city centre, with domestic and increasing numbers of international flights to many Western European and North African destinations.

Bar à Vin (p281)

TRAIN

Bordeaux is one of France's major rail-transit points. The station, **Gare St-Jean** (cours de la Marne), is about 3km from the city centre at the southern terminus of cours de la Marne.

Paris Gare Montparnasse €79, 3¼ hours, at least 16 daily.

ⓘ GETTING AROUND

BICYCLE

Public bike sharing scheme VCub (www.vcub. fr) has 1700 bicycles available for use at 166 stations all over the city. Pay €1.50 to access a bike for 24 hours, plus €2 per hour after the first 30 minutes (free) is up; you'll need to initially register online or with your credit card at a VCub station.

BUS & TRAM

Urban buses and trams are run by TBC. Get time-table information and tickets from its **Espace des Quinconces** (☏05 57 57 88 88; www.infotbc. com; Esplanade des Quinconces; ⊙7am-7.30pm Mon-Fri, 9am-6pm Sat) information office on Esplanade des Quinconces, the main bus and tram hub. Tram line C links the latter with the train station via the riverside; tram B cruises north along the river to La Cité du Vin. Single tickets cost €1.50.

FRENCH ALPS

French Alps at a Glance...

It took something as monumental as the collision of Africa and Europe to produce the Alps. Inconceivable forces buckled the land, driving it high into the sky and creating a place of enchantment and danger: colossal peaks, crevasse-fissured glaciers, tumbling crystal-clear rivers, sapphire lakes and snow-covered mountain passes.

Flanked to the east by the Swiss and Italian Alps, Savoie (Savoy) rises from the southern shores of Lake Geneva, Europe's largest alpine lake, and culminates at the roof of Europe, mighty 4810m Mont Blanc. At higher elevations you'll find legendary ski resorts such as Chamonix and, lower down to the west, the elegant lakeside town of Annecy.

The French Alps in Two Days

Acclimatise day one with some gentle skiing (winter) or hiking (summer) in Chamonix. Join the après-ski crowd on rue des Moulins for an apéro or head to **Office** (p298) in Argentière. Dine on cheesy Savoyard specialities at **Crèmerie du Glacier** (p298). Day two, assuming the sky is blue, hit the heady heights of the **Aiguille du Midi** (p288) and beyond into Italy with a cable-car ride of a lifetime.

The French Alps in Four Days

Devote a second day to exploring Chamonix' exceptional ski slopes or hiking trails – **Lac Blanc** (p297) is a summertime essential. Day four, move onto **Lac d'Annecy** (p292) where lunch or afternoon tea at **Auberge du Père Bise** (p293) in the beautiful lakeside village of Talloires beckons. End the day exploring **Annecy old town** (p300).

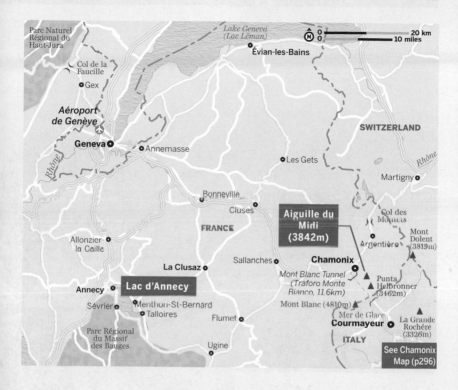

Arriving in the French Alps

Aéroport de Genève Buses from airport and train station to Chamonix (€25, 1½ to two hours, up to eight daily). Grenoble, Chambéry and Lyon are other major points of entry by air.

Chamonix & Annecy train stations Both are just footsteps from the town centre.

Tunnel du Mont Blanc (www.atmb. com) An 11.6km road link between Chamonix and Courmayeur in Italy's Val d'Aosta.

Sleeping

Savoie is well geared up for visitors, with everything from humble mountain *refuges* (huts), open only in summer, to grand hotel-spas going strong since the belle époque. Demand skyrockets in Chamonix during the ski season (December to April), while July and August are busiest in and around Annecy. In the mountains, many places close for a while in spring and autumn.

Aiguille du Midi

A great broken tooth of rock rearing amongst the Alpine fastness of the Mont Blanc massif, the Aiguille du Midi (3842m) is one of Chamonix' most distinctive – and dramatic – geographical features.

Great For...

☑ **Don't Miss**

Scaring yourself senseless with Step into the Void.

Téléphérique de l'Aiguille du Midi

If you can handle the altitude, the 360-degree views of the French, Swiss and Italian Alps from the summit are (quite literally) breath-taking. Year-round, you can float in a cable car from downtown Chamonix, over forests and beyond the tree line, to the Aiguille du Midi on the vertiginous **Téléphérique de l'Aiguille du Midi** (www.compagniedumontblanc. co.uk; place de l'Aiguille du Midi; adult/child return to Aiguille du Midi €58.50/49.70, to Plan de l'Aiguille summer €31/26.40, winter €17/14.50; ⊗1st ascent btwn 7.10am & 8.30am, last btwn 3.30pm & 5pm) – a series of two cable cars and a gondola.

In summer (especially mid-July to mid-August) there are massive lines (we're talking two-hour waits) so you may need to obtain a boarding card (marked with the number of your departing and returning cable cars) along with your ticket. Essential

ⓘ Need to Know

Advance reservations are essential. Check weather and buy tickets online at www.compagniedumontblanc.co.uk.

✕ Take a Break

Over traditional Savoyard *tartiflette* (potatoes, cheese and bacon baked in a casserole) at 3842m at **Restaurant Le 3842** (www.aiguilledumidi-restaurant. com/3842); reserve.

★ Top Tip

Dress warmly: temperatures at the top range from -10°C (summer) to -25°C (winter).

items to include in your daypack: sunglasses, sun hat, sunscreen, warm clothes, sturdy shoes, snacks and water.

Step into the Void

Halfway up, **Plan de l'Aiguille** (2317m) is a terrific place to start hikes or to paraglide. Count on paying around €220 per adult to fly in tandem with other colourful paragliders in the sky wheeling down from heady heights.

Up top at a breathtaking 3842m, you can gorge on the mountain panorama in literally every direction – including 1000m straight down – thanks to the glass-floored **Step into the Void**, a transparent viewing platform.

Télécabine Panoramique Mont Blanc

From the Aiguille du Midi, between late May and September, you can continue for a

further 50 minutes of mind-blowing Alpine scenery – think glaciers and spurs, seracs and shimmering ice fields – in the smaller bubbles of the **Télécabine Panoramique Mont Blanc** (☑04 50 53 22 75; Aiguille du Midi; adult/child return from Chamonix €80/68; ☺last departure from Aiguille du Midi 2.30pm) to Pointe Helbronner (3466m) on the France–Italy border.

Skyway Monte Bianco

Three years in the making, the spectacular, international cable car **Skyway Monte Bianco** (www.montebianco.com; Pointe Helbronner; one way adult/child €36/25.20; ☺8.30am-4.30pm, earlier starts in summer) continues 4km from Pointe Helbronner to Courmayeur in the Val d'Aosta, on the Italian side of Mont Blanc (Monte Bianco in Italian). The cars rotate a full 360 degrees, affording peerless views of Mont Blanc, the Matterhorn and Gran Paradiso.

Skiers at the starting point of La Vallée Blanche

Winter Skiing

Thrilling descents, glorious off-piste terrain and unbeatable Mont Blanc views – skiing in Chamonix is so fantastic that skiers don't even mind the less-than-convenient transport links to access the slopes.

With the sheer white heights of the Mont Blanc massif as its sensational backdrop, the Chamonix Valley shows the Alps at their most dramatic. First 'discovered' as a tourist destination by Brits William Windham and Richard Pococke in 1741, it has become a wintertime playground of epic proportions, more than satisfying the most demanding skiers as well as the après-ski revellers who pack themselves into its boot-stompin' bars.

Ski Areas

Of Chamonix' nine main areas, **Le Tour**, **Les Planards**, **Les Chosalets** and **La Vormaine** are best for beginners. For speed and challenge, it has to be **Brévent-Flégère**, above Chamonix, and **Les Grands Montets**, accessible from the attractive village of Argentière, 9km north of the town. Boarders

---

Great For...

☑ **Don't Miss**

A world-famous *croûte aux fromages* at Crèmerie du Glacier (p298).

Skiers on Mont Blanc

STEPHENMESSE / GETTY IMAGES ©

Maison de la Montagne; ☺8.30am-noon & 2.30-7.30pm, closed Sun & Mon late Apr-mid-Jun & mid-Sep-mid-Dec) which is nearly 200 years old, offers wintertime tours around the Mont Blanc range into Switzerland and Italy and romantic night tours through the forest with dinner. It also runs the Mont Blanc Ski & Guide Compagnie, which does ski guiding, ice climbing and mountaineering.

Other recommended companies offering extreme skiing expeditions, glacier trekking and other guided adventures: **Chamonix Experience** (☑09 77 48 58 69; www.chamex.com; 49 place Edmond Desailloud; ☺8.30-11am & 3-7pm 1 Dec–5 May & 1 Jun–30 Sep)

Association Internationale des Guides du Mont Blanc (☑04 50 53 27 05; www.guides-du-montblanc.com; 9 passage de la Varlope)

Lift Passes

Chamonix Le Pass (one/three/six days €49/136/246) Gets you up to most Chamonix ski domains.

Mont Blanc Multipass (one/three/six days €61/86/124) In summer, this pass affords access to all operating lifts.

Mont Blanc Unlimited Pass (one/three/six days €60/176/293) A worthwhile investment for serious skiers, this pass grants access to 400km of runs, including all lifts in the Chamonix Valley, Courmayeur in Italy and Verbier in Switzerland, plus the Aiguille du Midi cable car and the Montenvers-Mer de Glace train.

seeking big air zip across to the kickers and rails at **Les Grands Montets snow park** and the natural halfpipe in **Le Tour**.

La Vallée Blanche

This jaw-dropping 2800m descent is the off-piste ride of a lifetime. Beginning at the Aiguille du Midi, zipping over the crevasse-riddled Mer de Glace glacier and returning to Chamonix through the forest, it can only be tackled with a *guide de haute montagne* (specially trained mountain guide). Skiers should be red-piste level and in reasonable physical shape.

Guided Adventure

Chamonix' most prestigious guides association, the **Compagnie des Guides de Chamonix** (☑04 50 53 00 88; www.chamonix-guides.com; 190 place de l'Église,

Lac d'Annecy

The purity of its turquoise water and natural beauty make Lake Annecy a hardcore seductress who demands outdoor action, be it lounging on cafe terraces, mountain-gazing on the lakefront, swimming, walking or cycling.

Great For...

☑ Don't Miss

A romantic lake cruise with **Compagnie des Bateaux** (☎04 50 51 08 40; www.annecy-croisieres.com; 2 place aux Bois; 1hr lake cruises adult/child €14.2/9.60; ☻late Mar–mid-Dec).

Cycling & Blading

Biking and blading are big, with 46km of cycling track encircling the lake.

Family bike shop **Roul' ma Poule** (☎04 76 39 77 20; www.roulemapoule.com; 4 rue des Marquisats; ☻9.30am-7pm) rents roller-blades (€15/20 per half/full day), bicycles (€15/20), tandems (€34/44) and kids' trailers (€15/20), and is a great source of day-trip recommendations.

Water Sports

The most relaxed way to see the lake is from the water. March to October, pedal and motor boats can be hired for €15/50 per hour/day along the Annecy waterfront. **Société des Régates à Voile d'Annecy** (☎04 50 45 48 39; www.srva.info; 31 rue des Marquisats, Base Nautique; ☻10am-12.30pm & 1.30-7pm Mon-Sat, 10am-7pm Sun) rents sailing boats (from

€44 for two hours on a single-person Laser dinghy) and windsurfers (€28).

Beaches

When the sun's out, the beaches fringing the lake beckon. Some are patrolled in summer, and can become very crowded. On the lakefront in Annecy, **Plage Impérial** (☑️04 50 19 19 73; www.plage-imperial.com; 30 ave d'Albigny; per day €15; ⊙10am-7pm Jun-Aug, Sat & Sun May & Sep) is a manicured private beach with bags of family-friendly attractions next to Annecy's elegant, pre-WWI casino. **Plage des Marquisats** (58 rue des Marquisats; ⊙lifeguard present Jul-Aug) **FREE** is a pebbly beach, very popular with sunbathers and lake-frolickers alike, 1km southeast of town. Kid-clad families tend to frequent the gentle, shallow beach of **Plage d'Albigny à Annecy-le-Vieux** (av du Petit Port) **FREE**, 1km northeast of Annecy.

Lakeside Legends

Lac d'Annecy is the stunning setting for two of the most-celebrated restaurants in the French Alps. The eponymous **Yoann Conte** (☑️04 50 09 97 49; www.yoann-conte.com; 13 Vieille rte des Pensières, Veyrier-du-Lac; lunch menus €85-126, dinner menus €189-220; ⊙noon-1.30pm & 7-8.30pm Wed-Sun, plus 7-8.30pm Tue in summer) has taken over from his mentor, Marc Veyrat, while at **Auberge du Père Bise** (☑️04 50 60 72 01; www.perebise.com; 303 rte du Port, Talloires; menus €85; ⊙12.30-2pm & 7.30-9pm Thu-Mon late Sep–mid-Dec & mid-Feb–May, Wed Jun-Sep), Sophie Bise draws on her heritage as a third-generation chef and Annecy local to craft food that expresses its provenance.

Beautiful Villages

On warm summer days the villages of **Sévrier**, 5km south on Lac d'Annecy's western shore, and **Menthon-St-Bernard**, 8.5km southeast on the lake's eastern shore, make good day trips from Annecy.

Don't miss 1000-year-old **Château de Menthon-St-Bernard** (☑️07 81 74 39 72; www.chateau-de-menthon.com; Menthon-St-Bernard; guided tours adult/child €8.50/4; ⊙noon-6pm Jul & Aug, 2-6pm Fri-Sun May, Jun & Sep) – one of the inspirations for Walt Disney's Sleeping Beauty castle (so they say) – where St Bernard was born in 1008.

South of Menthon, **Talloires** is the most exclusive lakeside spot.

Chamonix

⊙ SIGHTS

Mer de Glace Viewpoint
France's largest glacier, the 200m-deep 'Sea of Ice' flows 7km down the northern side of Mont Blanc, moving up to 1cm an hour (about 90m a year). The **Train du Montenvers** (☏04 50 53 22 75; www.compagniedumontblanc.fr; 35 place de la Mer de Glace; adult/child return €31/26.40; ⊘10am-4.30pm), a picturesque, 5km-long cog railway opened in 1909, links Gare du Montenvers with Montenvers (1913m), from where a cable car takes you down to the glacier and the **Grotte de Glace** (⊘closed last half of May & late Sep–mid-Oct). Your ticket also gets you into the Glaciorium, which looks at the birth, life and future of glaciers.

On foot, the Mer de Glace can be reached from **Plan de l'Aiguille** on the **Grand Balcon Nord trail**. The two-hour uphill trail from Chamonix starts near the summer luge track. Traversing the crevassed glacier requires proper equipment and an experienced guide.

Le Brévent Viewpoint
The highest peak on the western side of the Chamonix Valley, Le Brévent (2525m) has tremendous views of the Mont Blanc massif, myriad hiking trails through a nature reserve, ledges to paraglide from and some vertiginous black runs. Reach it by linking the **Télécabine de Planpraz** (☏04 50 53 22 75; www.compagniedumontblanc.co.uk; 29 rue Henriette d'Angeville; adult/child return €30.50/25.90; ⊘from 8.50am Dec-Apr, Jun-Sep & late Oct-Nov), 400m west of the tourist office, with the **Téléphérique du Brévent** (www.compagniedumontblanc.co.uk; 29 rue Henriette d'Angeville; adult/child one way €23/19.60, return €31/26.40; ⊘mid-Dec–mid-Apr & mid-Jun–mid-Sep). Plenty of family-friendly trails begin at **Planpraz** (2000m), and the Liaison cable car connects to the adjacent ski fields of La Flégère.

Musée Alpin Museum
(☏04 50 53 25 93; 89 av Michel Croz; adult/child €5.90/free; ⊘2-6pm Wed-Mon Sep-Jun, 10am-noon & 2-7pm Wed-Mon Jul & Aug) Perhaps better titled the Musée Chamonix-Mont Blanc, this engaging little collection richly

View of Mer de Glace from the Grand Balcon Nord trail

illustrates the area's long history of Alpine adventure, including the cliffhanging feats of crystal-hunter Jacques Balmat and the first ascent of Mont Blanc by a woman (Marie Paradis, a local maidservant, in 1808). Ask at the ticket counter for printed information in English.

Musée des Cristaux   Museum

(☑04 50 55 53 93; www.mineralogie-chamonix. org; 615 allée Recteur Payot; adult/child €5.90/ free; ⊙2-6pm Sep-Jun, 10am-6pm Jul & Aug) Has a truly dazzling collection of crystals, rocks and minerals, many from around Mont Blanc. **L'Espace Alpinisme** focuses on the art and science of mountaineering with creative interactive displays and spectacular photos and videos of seemingly impossible ascents. Situated behind the church.

❸ ACTIVITIES

When enough snow melts (usually sometime in June), hikers can take their pick of 350km of spectacular high-altitude trails, many easy to get to by cable car (running mid-June to September). In June and July there's enough light to walk until at least 9pm.

Balcon (literally 'balcony') trails, both *grand* and *petit*, run along both sides of the valley, the former up at around 2000m, the latter a bit above the valley's villages.

CYCLING

Lower-altitude trails such as the Petit Balcon Sud from Argentière to Servoz are perfect for biking. Most outdoor-activity specialists arrange guided mountain-biking expeditions.

MOUNTAINEERING & HIGH-ALPINE TOURS

Local guide companies offer exhilarating climbs for those with the necessary skill, experience and stamina. Options include five-day **rock-climbing courses** (€630 to €920) and the incomparable **Mont Blanc**

 Kidding Around Chamonix

There's plenty to amuse *les petits* (the little ones) around Chamonix. In the warm season, kids will love getting close to free-roaming chamois, ibex and whistling marmots at the **Parc de Merlet** (www.parcdemerlet.com; 2495 chemin de Merlet, Les Houches; adult/child €7/4; ⊙10am-6pm Tue-Sun May, Jun & Sep, 9.30am-7.30pm Jul & Aug, by appointment 4 Jan–31 Mar), 13km by road (5km on foot) southwest of central Chamonix in Coupeau. Or treat them to a fun-packed day on the trampolines and funfair rides at the **Parc de Loisirs de Chamonix** (☑04 50 53 08 97; www.chamonixparc. com; 351 chemin du Pied du Grépon; 1-day ski passes €21.90, 1/10 luge rides €5.50/45; ⊙11.30am-6pm high season, reduced hours other times), near the chairlift in Les Planards, 500m east of Gare du Montenvers.

Cham' Aventure (☑04 50 53 55 70; www.cham-aventure.com; 190 place de l'Église, Maison de la Montagne) also has a wide variety of outdoor programs for children.

Back in Chamonix, the indoor **ice-skating rink** (☑04 50 53 12 36; 165 rte de la Patinoire; adult/child €6.20/4.60, skate hire €4.10; ⊙2-6pm Thu-Tue year-round, Wed during peak periods) provides amusement when the weather packs up, as do sports activities at the adjacent **Centre Sportif Richard Bozon** (☑04 50 53 23 70; 214 av de la Plage; ⊙noon-7.30pm Mon-Fri, 2-7.30pm Sat & Sun), with indoor and (in summer) outdoor swimming pools.

ascent (from €920). For hikers, a big draw is the classic six- to 10-day **Tour du Mont Blanc** (€795 to €1395), taking in majestic glaciers and peaks in France, Italy and Switzerland. Prices usually include half-board in *refuges* (mountain huts), picnics, lift tickets and luggage transport.

Chamonix

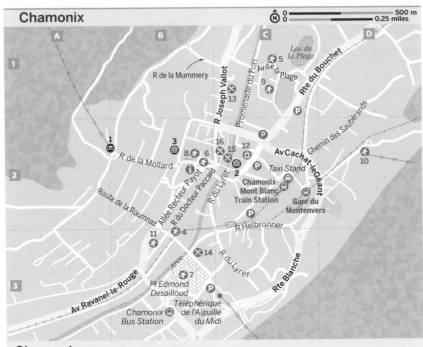

Chamonix

🔒 SHOPPING

Cooperative Fruitière
Val d'Arly   Food
(☎04 50 93 15 89; www.coopflumet.com; 93
rue Whymper; ⏰9am-7.30pm) A shopfront
for a venerable collective of more than 70
artisanal producers, this *fruitière* is the best
place in Chamonix to stock up on Reblochon, *raclette* (a kind of cheese), Tomme

de Savoie, Morteau sausage and all those
other Savoyard delicacies.

✗ EATING

From post-piste burgers to Michelin-starred
gastronomy, Chamonix has something for
everyone. Restaurants and British-style
pubs serving food cluster most densely ·

around rue des Moulins, but all neighbourhoods are pretty well served, in season.

Most restaurants open seven days a week in season but have reduced (or no) hours out of season.

Hibou Deli
Deli €

(☑04 50 96 65 13; www.hibou-chamonix.com; 416 rue Joseph Vallot; mains €8-10; ⊙11am-9pm mid-Dec–early May & mid-Jun–early Oct; ☑) This tiny shopfront kitchen, owned by a British chef, pumps out fantastic Asian and North African–inspired dishes to takeaway. The lamb *mechoui* is rubbed with spices and cooked over 24 hours to an almost buttery consistency, the Bangkok chicken is fragrant with lime leaves and coconut, and there are always plenty of veggie options and an interesting *plat de jour* (dish of the day).

Les Vieilles Luges
French €€

(☑06 84 42 37 00; www.lesvieillesluges.com; Les Houches; menus €20-35; ⊙lunch winter, lunch & dinner by reservation summer, min 25 people) This impossibly atmospheric 250-year-old farmhouse can only be reached by skis or by a scenic 20-minute hike from the Maison Neuve chairlift. Hunker under low wood beams to savour dishes such as *grand-mère*'s bœuf bourguignon and creamy *farçon* (potato bake prepared with prunes, bacon and cream), washed down with *vin chaud* (mulled wine) warmed over a wood fire. Magic.

Le Cap Horn
Modern French €€

(☑04 50 21 80 80; www.caphorn-chamonix.com; 78 rue des Moulins; lunch menus €20, dinner menus €32-39; ⊙noon-3pm & 7-10.30pm) Housed in a gorgeous, two-storey chalet decorated with model sailing boats – joint homage to the Alps and Cape Horn – this highly praised restaurant, opened in 2012, serves French and Asian-inflected dishes such as pan-seared duck breast with honey and soy sauce, fisherman's stew and, for dessert, *souffle au Grand Marnier*. Reserve for dinner Friday and Saturday in winter and summer.

Munchie
Fusion €€

(☑04 50 53 45 41; www.munchie.eu; 87 rue des Moulins; mains €22-24; ⊙7pm-2am winter & sum-

Hiking to Lac Blanc

Two gentle hours from **Télésiège de l'Index** (www.compagniedumontblanc.co.uk; adult/child one way from Les Praz €23/19.60; ⊙Dec-Apr & Jun-Sep) leads along the western valley to stunning Lac Blanc (2352m). There's also the steeper trail from the **Téléphérique de la Flégère** (☑04 50 53 22 75; www.compagniedumont blanc.co.uk; 35 rte des Tines; adult/child from Les Praz €13/11.70; ⊙8.45am-4pm Dec-Apr & Jun-Sep) or the even-more challenging 1050 vertical-metre hike from Argentière (3½ hours one way). Reserve a place at the **Refuge du Lac Blanc** (☑04 50 53 49 14; refugedulacblanc@gmail.com; dm incl half-board €55; ⊙mid-Jun–Sep), a wooden chalet famed for its top-of-Europe Mont Blanc views.

mer) Franco-Asian-Scandinavian fusion may not be a tried and true recipe for success, but this casual, Swedish-skippered restaurant has been making diners happy since 1997. Dishes such as Sichuan-spiced lamb tataki, Japanese coconut rice with egg yolk confit and Thai 'pesto', and cod with ash and leek are so popular that reservations are recommended during the ski season.

Le Chaudron
French €€

(☑04 50 53 40 34; www.le-chaudron-chamonix. com; 79 rue des Moulins; menus €27-34; ⊙7-9.30pm or later mid-Dec–Apr & mid-Jun–Sep) Making stylish yet cosy use of a 100-year-old mule stable (the faux cowhide recalling its rustic origins), the Cauldron is guaranteed to give you a warm inner glow on a cold winter's day. Go-to dishes include terrine of Beaufort cheese and beef cheek, slow-cooked in red wine and served with creamy risotto.

Le Bistrot
Modern French €€€

(☑04 50 53 57 64; www.lebistrotchamonix. com; 151 av de l'Aiguille du Midi; lunch menus €20, dinner menus €55-85; ⊙noon-1.30pm & 7-9pm) Sleek and hushed, this is a real

🍽 Lunch in the Forest

A wooden forest chalet is the fairy-tale setting for Chef Claudy's world-famous *croûte aux fromages* (bread drenched in a secret white-wine sauce, topped with cheese and baked) and other cheesy Savoyard delights (including nine kinds of fondue) at **Crèmerie du Glacier** (📞04 50 54 07 52; www.lacremerieduglacier.fr; 766 chemin de la Glacière; lunch menus €13, fondue €15-20; ⏱lunch & dinner mid-Dec–mid-May & late Jun–mid-Sep, closed Wed in winter). Reserve by phone and follow the signpost from the roundabout near the bridge at the southern entrance to Argentière.

To get here, you have several options. In winter, ski down on Piste de la Pierre à Ric (red) or cross-country ski over on Piste de la Moraine. In summer, hike over from the Petit Balcon Nord trail, 15 minutes away.

In winter or summer, walk or drive east for about 1km from the base of Téléphérique Lognan-Les Grands Montets; take one-lane chemin de la Glacière in summer and equally narrow chemin de la Rosière in winter.

Fondue
SILKENPHOTOGRAPHY / GETTY IMAGES ©

gastronome's paradise. Chef Daniele Raimondi, a protégé of Alain Ducasse, experiments with textures and seasonal flavours in creations such as duck breast with polenta, turnip and sour cherry sauce; pan-fried scallops with pumpkin, truffle and hazelnuts; and chocolate and coriander profiteroles with vanilla ice cream.

🍷 DRINKING & NIGHTLIFE

Whether you're looking for a glammed-up cocktail bar, a spit-and-sawdust pub or something in between, Chamonix nightlife rocks. For a bar crawl, head (along with the locals) to central rue des Moulins, where wall-to-wall watering holes keep buzzing until about 1am.

Office   Bar
(📞04 50 54 15 46; 274 rue Chalet Stratton, Argentière; ⏱3pm-1am Mon-Fri & noon-1am Sat & Sun summer & winter; 🛜) This mellow pub cranks things up in the après-ski (or, in summer, après-mountain bike) hours, with DJs a couple of nights a week and live music on Friday (from 10.30pm). Rib-sticking food (burgers €13, ribs €14) provides ballast for the journey.

ℹ INFORMATION

Tourist Office (📞04 50 53 00 24; www.chamonix.com; 85 place du Triangle de l'Amitié; ⏱8.30am-7pm winter & summer, 9am-12.30pm & 2-6pm in low season; 🛜) Information on accommodation, activities, the weather and cultural events.

ℹ GETTING THERE & AWAY

BUS

Services to/from Chamonix' **bus station** (📞04 50 53 01 15; 234 av Courmayeur, Chamonix Sud; ⏱8am-noon & 1.15-6.30pm in winter, shorter hours rest of year):

Geneva, Switzerland (airport and bus station) One way/return €25/50, 1½ to two hours, eight daily in winter; six at other times. Operated by **Starshipper** (📞04 56 12 40 59; www.starshipper.com).

Courmayeur, Italy One way/return €15/21, 45 minutes, four daily. Run by **Savda** (📞+39 01 65 36 70 11; www.savda.it), with onward connections to Aosta and Milan.

See the websites or drop by the bus station for timetables and reservations (highly recommended).

Lac Blanc (p297)

TRAIN

The scenic, narrow-gauge **Mont Blanc Express** glides from St-Gervais-Le-Fayet to the Swiss town of Martigny, taking in Les Houches, Chamonix, Argentière and Vallorcine en route.

From St-Gervais-Le-Fayet, there are somewhat infrequent trains to cities around France, often with a change in Bellegarde or Annecy. Destinations:

Annecy €15.70, 1½ hours, 12 daily.

Lyon €36.60, 3½ to 5 hours, 10 daily.

Paris €98.50 to €128, 4¾ to seven hours, 11 daily.

❶ GETTING AROUND

BICYCLE

You can hire cross-country, mountain and downhill bikes from **Zero G** (☑04 50 53 01 01; www. zerogchamonix.com; 90 ave Ravanel-le-Rouge; ⊙9am-12.30pm & 3.30-7pm), which also rents out snowboard gear.

BUS

Public buses run by **Chamonix Bus** (www. chamonix-bus.com) serve all the towns, villages, ski lifts and attractions in the Chamonix Valley, from Argentière (Col des Montets in summer) in the northeast, to Servoz and Les Houches in the southwest.

The buses all travel circuits that include the **bus station** (p298) in Chamonix Sud throughout the year, and have added destinations and are more frequent in winter (mid-December to mid-April) and summer (late June to early September).

CAR

Parking in Chamonix involves either paying for a spot in a city-centre **parking garage** (per 1½/12/24 hours €2/8.50/10.50) or heading to one of the seven **free lots** on Chamonix' outskirts, five of them towards Argentière.

TAXI

For a taxi, call ☑06 11 86 93 43, or try the **taxi rank** in front of the train station.

Palais de l'Isle

Annecy

Reclining gracefully by the shores of its mountain-fringed lake, cut by limpid canals, studded with geranium-bedecked houses and dominated by its turreted château, Annecy is one of the ornaments of Savoy. Wandering its medieval Old Town – a photogenic jumble of narrow pedestrians-only streets, crystal-clear canals (hence Annecy being dubbed 'Venice of the Alps') and colonnaded passageways – is one of Alpine life's great simple pleasures.

⊙ SIGHTS

Château d'Annecy   Castle

(www.musees.agglo-annecy.fr; rampe du Château; adult/child €5.20/2.60; ⊘10am-noon & 2-5pm Wed-Mon Oct-May, 10.30am-6pm daily Jun-Sep) Rising dramatically above the old town, this 13th- to 16th-century castle was once home to the Counts of Geneva. The exhibits inside are diverse, ranging from medieval sculpture and Savoyard furniture to Alpine landscape painting and contemporary art, with a section on the natural history of Lac d'Annecy. Some signage is multilingual.

Palais de l'Isle   Museum

(☑04 56 49 40 37; www.musees.agglo-annecy.fr; 3 passage de l'Île; adult/child €3.80/2; ⊘10am-noon & 2-5pm Wed-Mon Oct-May, 10am-5pm Wed-Mon Jun-Sep) Sitting on a triangular islet surrounded by the Canal du Thiou, the 12th-century Palais de l'Isle has been a lordly residence, a courthouse, a mint and a prison over the centuries. The central landmark of Annecy's gorgeous Vieille Ville (Old Town), it now houses permanent exhibits on local architecture and history, and temporary displays of art.

⊗ EATING

Food Market   Market €

(cnr rues Ste-Claire & de la République; ⊘7am-1pm Sun, Tue & Fri) Growing organically through the picturesque arteries of the Vieille Ville, this sprawling market has all the Savoyard delicacies, fresh fruit and vegetables and cheap souvenirs you could possibly need.

Le Denti — French €€

([☎]04 50 64 21 17; 25bis av de Loverchy; lunch menus €22, dinner menus €32-42; [◷]noon-1.15pm Thu-Mon, 7.30-9.15pm Mon & Thu-Sat) A few blocks off the beaten track but worth seeking out, this unassuming restaurant serves traditional French cuisine – their speciality is fish – prepared so the taste of the super-fresh ingredients shines through. The menu changes twice a month according to the seasonal produce available in the markets.

La Ciboulette — Gastronomic €€€

([☎]04 50 45 74 57; www.laciboulette-annecy.com; Cour du Pré Carré, 10 rue Vaugelas; menus €38-75; [◷]noon-1pm & 7.30-8.45pm Tue-Sat) Crisp white linen sets the scene at this elegant restaurant, where chef Georges Paccard prepares innovative delights such as veal sweetbreads with bitter gentian juice, and grilled turbot with pigs' trotter croquette and tarragon sauce.

L'Esquisse — Gastronomic €€€

([☎]04 50 44 80 59; www.esquisse-annecy.fr; 21 rue Royale; lunch menus €25, dinner menus €39-65; [◷]12.15-1.15pm & 7.30-9pm Mon, Tue & Thu-Sat) A talented husband-and-wife team runs the show at this intimate seven-table restaurant. Their passion shines through in the service, wine list and carefully composed menus dotted with delights such as pumpkin consommé with Beaufort cheese and roast scallops with brown butter. Reserve ahead.

🍷 DRINKING & NIGHTLIFE

The winding streets of the Vieille Ville contain plenty of charismatic little wine bars, plus a few pubs which cater to the younger and noisier.

Beer O'Clock — Bar

([☎]04 50 65 83 78; 18 rue du Faubourg Ste-Claire; 250mL beer €3-5.25; [◷]5pm-midnight Tue-Fri, to 1am Sat, to 11pm Sun; [📶]) This laid-back,

Festive Fun

Annecy celebrates the flamboyant **Venetian Carnival** in February (two weeks after its namesake in Venice, Italy); the **Fête du Lac**, with a spectacular 70 minutes of fireworks over the lake, on the first Saturday in August; and **Le Retour des Alpages**, when the cows come home from summer pasturage in the Alps, wreathed in flowers and bells, on the second Saturday in October. Street performers wow evening crowds at **Les Noctibules**, over four nights in July.

high-tech establishment serves beer like petrol stations sell gasoline: you only pay for what you pump. After buying credit on a computerised magnetic card, you can drink as much or as little of the 12 brews on offer as you like – a fantastic way to compare and savour lots of microbrews side-by-side.

ℹ️ INFORMATION

Tourist Office ([☎]04 50 45 00 33; www.lac-annecy.com; 1 rue Jean Jaurès, courtyard of Centre Bonlieu; [◷]9am-12.30pm & 1.45-6pm Mon-Sat year-round, plus Sun mid-May–mid-Sep, 9am-12.30pm Sun Apr & early Oct & Dec) Has free maps and brochures, and details on cultural activities all around the lake.

ℹ️ GETTING THERE & AWAY

Direct services from Annecy **train station** (place de la Gare):

Lyon Part-Dieu €26 to €50, two hours, eight to 13 daily.

Paris Gare de Lyon €80 to €101, 3¾ hours, four to seven daily.

St-Gervais-le-Fayet For Chamonix; €15.30, 1½ hours, up to five daily.

Vallon des Auffes (p260), Marseille

In Focus

Arc de Triomphe (p57), Paris

France Today

France has not escaped economic crisis, terrorism and the unexpected rise of the far-right in Europe. But this ancient country of Gallic pride and tradition has weathered greater storms and it's far from sunk. Wine tourism is on the up, politicians have redrawn the local-government map and, across the board, French people are turning to grass-roots culture and gastronomy for strength and inspiration.

The Fruits of the Land

French wine growers are riding high. In 2015 fabled vineyards in the ancient wine-growing region of Champagne were inscribed on the Unesco World Heritage list as extraordinary world treasures – think exceptional scenery, unique know-how shared between generations and a remarkable cultural heritage. And with the French more passionate than ever about their *terroir* (land) and the fruits it bears, it is with a celebratory pop of corks that *viticulteurs* (wine growers) in Champagne prepare to plant new vines in 40 new Champagne-producing villages in 2017.

Developments in the urban wine world are equally exciting – and a gentle reminder of just how intrinsic wine culture is to contemporary life in France. In the city of Bordeaux, the fabulously flamboyant and sassy, €81 million La Cité du Vin opened in 2016. Its mission: to explore

belief systems
(% of population)

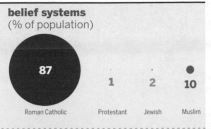

87	**1**	**2**	**10**
Roman Catholic	Protestant	Jewish	Muslim

if France were 100 people

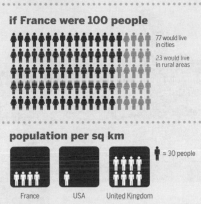

77 would live in cities

23 would live in rural areas

population per sq km

≈ 30 people

France   USA   United Kingdom

the global world of wine. In the vine-laced countryside around Bordeaux meanwhile, architects are designing state-of-the-art wine cellars, cooking schools and urban-chic dining spaces for ancient châteaux whose daily existence has, for centuries, been charted by the seasons and languid rhythm of nature. Wine tourism in France is the new gold.

A Shift to the Right

As the country gears up for presidential elections in May 2017, all eyes are on the increasingly powerful Front National (FN), known for its fervent anti-immigrant stance. In the 2014 municipal elections, the far-right party led by Marine Le Pen won 7% of votes, trumping the ruling left-centre Socialists in several towns. In European elections a month later the FN won a quarter of votes, ahead of the main opposition party UMP (21%) and governing left-wing Socialists (14%). The ultimate humiliation came during parliamentary elections a few months later: the FN won its first ever two seats in the French Senate and the Socialists lost majority control of the Upper Chamber.

Terrible Times

On 7 January 2015 the Paris offices of newspaper *Charlie Hebdo* were attacked in response to satirical images it had published of the prophet Muhammad. Eleven staff and one police officer were killed and a further 22 people injured. #JeSuisCharlie ('I am Charlie') became a worldwide slogan of support. Worse followed. On 13 November 2015 terrorist attacks occurred in Paris and St-Denis. During a football match watched by 80,000 spectators, three explosions were heard outside the stadium. Soon after, gunmen fired on customers drinking on pavement terraces outside several cafes and restaurants in Paris' 10e and 11e *arrondissements*. At 9.40pm three gunmen stormed concert hall Le Bataclan and fired into the audience. In all that evening 130 people lost their lives and 368 were injured. Months later, during festive Bastille Day celebrations in Nice on 14 July 2016, a lorry ploughed at high speed through crowds on Promenade des Anglais. The driver subsequently got out and started shooting into the crowd before being shot himself by police. Death toll: +80.

Tossed but Not Sunk

Fluctuat nec mergitur (tossed but not sunk) has been the motto of the French capital since 1853 when Baron Haussmann etched it for eternity onto the city coat of arms. And since the fatal terrorist attacks on Paris in November 2015, it has become the rallying cry of French people countrywide who stand in complete solidarity with Parisians; who tenaciously cling more than ever to their grass-roots culture that sees the French shop for food at the weekly market and chit-chat in all weathers over coffee or an *apéro* on cafe pavement terraces. Little wonder that a love for local, seasonal and organic is taking off at such a terrific pace.

Carnac megaliths (p138)

History

With everything from ancient artworks to Gothic cathedrals and regal châteaux, France is a living history textbook. Even the tiniest villages are littered with reminders of the nation's often turbulent past. Encompassing everything from courtly intrigue to intellectual enlightenment, artistic endeavour and bloody revolution, French history is far from dull.

c 7000 BC

Neolithic people turn their hands to monumental menhirs and dolmen during the New Stone Age, creating a fine collection in Brittany.

1500–500 BC

Celtic Gauls move into the region and establish trading links with the Greeks, whose colonies included Massilia on the Mediterranean coast.

c AD 455–70

France remains under Roman rule until the 5th century, when the Franks and the Alemanii invade the country from the east.

WWII tank, Utah Beach (p118)

JCARILLET / GETTY IMAGES ©

Prehistory

The first people to settle in France in significant numbers were small tribes of hunter-gatherers, who arrived around 35,000 to 50,000 years ago. These nomadic tribes lived seasonally from the land while pursuing game such as mammoth, aurochs, bison and deer. They used natural caves as temporary shelters, leaving behind sophisticated artworks.

The next great wave of settlers arrived after the end of the last ice age, from around 7500 BC to 2500 BC. These Neolithic people were responsible for the construction of France's megalithic monuments, including dolmens, burial tombs, stone circles and Brittany's massive stone alignments in Carnac. During this era, warmer weather allowed the development of farming and animal domestication, and humans increasingly established themselves in settled communities, often protected by defensive forts.

987
With the crowning of Hugh Capet, a dynasty that will rule one of Europe's most powerful countries for the next eight centuries is born.

1066
William the Conqueror occupies England, making Normandy and Plantagenet-ruled England formidable rivals of France.

1152
Eleanor of Aquitaine weds Henry of Anjou, sparking a French–English rivalry that will last three centuries.

MuCEM

★ **Best History Museums**

MuCEM (p248), Marseille

Musée d'Art et d'Histoire Baron Gérard (p120), Bayeux

Mémorial – Un Musée pour la Paix (p119), Caen

Centre d'Histoire de la Résistance et de la Déportation (p179), Lyon

Gauls & Romans

Communities were further developed from around 1500 BC to 500 BC by the Gauls, a Celtic people who migrated westwards from present-day Germany and Eastern Europe. But the Gauls' reign was short lived; over the next few centuries their territories were gradually conquered or subjugated by the Romans. After decades of sporadic warfare, the Gauls were finally defeated in 52 BC when Caesar's legions crushed a revolt led by the Celtic chief Vercingetorix.

France flourished under Roman rule. The Romans constructed roads, temples, forts and grand aqueducts like Provence's Pont du Gard to transport water from one town to another. They also planted the country's first vineyards, notably around Burgundy and Bordeaux.

The Rise of the Kings

Following the collapse of the Roman Empire, control of France passed to the Frankish dynasties, who ruled from the 5th to the 10th century, and effectively founded France's first royal dynasty. Charlemagne (AD 742–814) was crowned Holy Roman Emperor in 800, around the same time that Scandinavian Vikings (also called Norsemen, thus Normans) began to raid France's western and northern coasts. Having plundered and pillaged to their hearts' content, the Normans eventually formed the independent duchy of Normandy in the early 11th century. In 1066, the Normans launched a successful invasion of England, making William the Conqueror both Duke of Normandy and King of England. The tale of the invasion is graphically recounted in the embroidered cloth known as the Bayeux Tapestry.

During this time, Normandy was one of several independent duchies or provinces (including Brittany, Aquitaine, Burgundy, Anjou and Savoy) within the wider French kingdom. While each province superficially paid allegiance to the French crown, they were effectively self-governing and ruled by their own courts.

Intrigue and infighting were widespread. Matters came to a head in 1152 when Eleanor, Queen of Aquitaine, wed Henry, Duke of Anjou (who was also Duke of Normandy and, as

1337	1530s	1789
Incessant struggles between the Capetians and King Edward III over the French throne degenerate into the Hundred Years' War.	The Reformation sweeps through France, pitting Catholics against Protestants and leading to the Wars of Religion (1562–98).	The French Revolution begins when a mob arms itself with weapons from the Hôtel des Invalides and storms the prison at Bastille.

William the Conqueror's great-grandson, heir to the English crown).

Henry's ascension to the English throne in 1154 brought a third of France under England's control, with battles that collectively became known as the Hundred Years' War (1337–1453).

Following heavy defeats for the French at Crécy and Agincourt, John Plantagenet was made regent of France on behalf of Henry VI in 1422, and less than a decade later he was crowned king of France. The tide of the war seemed to have taken a decisive turn, but luckily for the French, a 17-year-old warrior by the name of Jeanne d'Arc (Joan of Arc) rallied the French forces and inspired the French king Charles VII to a series of victories, culminating in the recapture of Paris in 1437.

Joan was subsequently betrayed to the English, accused of heresy and witchcraft, and burnt at the stake in Rouen in 1431.

Renaissance to Revolution

During the reign of François I (r 1515–47), the Renaissance arrived from Italy, and prompted a great flowering of culture, art and architecture across France. Lavish royal châteaux were built along the Loire Valley, showcasing the might and majesty of the French monarchy.

The pomp and profligacy of the ruling elite didn't go down well with everyone, however. Following a series of social and economic crises that rocked the country during the 18th century, and incensed by the corruption and bourgeois extravagance of the aristocracy, a Parisian mob took to the streets in 1789, storming the prison at Bastille and kickstarting the French Revolution.

Inspired by the lofty ideals of *liberté, fraternité, égalité* (freedom, brotherhood, equality), the Revolutionaries initially found favour with the French people. France was declared a constitutional monarchy, but order broke down when the hard-line Jacobins seized power. The monarchy was abolished and the nation was declared a republic on 21 September 1792. Three months later Louis XVI was publicly guillotined on Paris' place de la Concorde. His ill-fated queen, Marie-Antoinette, suffered the same fate a few months later.

Off with His Head!

Prior to the Revolution, public executions in France depended on rank: the nobility were generally beheaded with a sword or axe (with predictably messy consequences), while commoners were usually hanged (particularly nasty prisoners were also drawn and quartered).

In the 1790s a group of French physicians, scientists and engineers set about designing a clinical new execution machine involving a razor-sharp weighted blade, guaranteed to behead people with a minimum of fuss or mess. Named after one of its inventors, the anatomy professor Ignace Guillotin, the machine was first used on 25 April 1792.

During the Reign of Terror, at least 17,000 met their death beneath the machine's plunging blade. By the time the last was given the chop in 1977 (behind closed doors – the last public execution was in 1939), the contraption could slice off a head in 2/100 of a second.

1851	**1905**	**1918**
Louis Napoléon leads a coup d'état and proclaims himself Emperor Napoléon III of the Second Empire (1852–70).	The emotions aroused by the Dreyfus Affair lead to the promulgation of *läcité* (secularism), the legal separation of church and state.	The armistice ending WWI sees the return of Alsace and Lorraine, but the war brings about the loss of a million French soldiers.

Chaos ensued. Violent retribution broke out across France. During the Reign of Terror (September 1793 to July 1794), churches were closed, religious monuments were desecrated, riots were suppressed and thousands of aristocrats were imprisoned or beheaded. The high ideals of the Revolution had turned to vicious bloodshed, and the nation was rapidly descending into anarchy. France desperately needed someone to re-establish order, give it new direction and rebuild its shattered sense of self. Enter a dashing (if diminutive) young Corsican general called Napoléon Bonaparte.

The Napoléonic Era

Napoléon's military prowess turned him into a powerful political force. In 1804 he was crowned emperor at Paris' Notre Dame Cathedral, and he subsequently led the French armies to conquer much of Europe. His ill-fated campaign to invade Russia ended in disaster, however; in 1812, his armies were stopped outside Moscow and decimated by the brutal Russian winter. Two years later, Allied armies entered Paris and exiled Napoléon to Elba.

But in 1815 Napoléon escaped, re-entering Paris on 20 May. His glorious 'Hundred Days' ended with defeat by the English at the Battle of Waterloo. He was exiled again, this time to St Helena in the South Atlantic, where he died in 1821. His body was later reburied under Hôtel des Invalides in Paris.

New Republics

France was dogged by a string of ineffectual rulers until Napoléon's nephew, Louis Napoléon Bonaparte, came to power. He was initially elected president, but declared himself Emperor (Napoléon III) in 1851.

While the so-called Second Empire ran roughshod over many of the ideals set down during the Revolution, it proved to be a prosperous time. France enjoyed significant economic growth and Paris was transformed by urban planner Baron Haussmann, who created the famous 12 boulevards radiating from the Arc de Triomphe.

But like his uncle, Napoléon III's ambition was his undoing. A series of costly conflicts, including the Crimean War (1854–56), culminated in humiliating defeat by the Prussian forces in 1870. France was once again declared a republic – for the third time in less than a century.

The Belle Époque

The Third Republic got off to a shaky start: another war with the Prussians resulted in a huge war bill and the surrender of Alsace and Lorraine. But the period also ushered in a new era of culture and creativity that left an enduring mark on France's national character.

The belle époque ('beautiful age') was an era of unprecedented innovation. Architects built a host of exciting new buildings and transformed many French cities. Engineers laid

1939	1944	1968
Nazi Germany occupies France and divides it into a zone under direct German occupation, and a puppet state led by General Pétain.	Normandy and Brittany are the first to be liberated following the D-Day landings in June, followed by Paris on 25 August.	Large-scale anti-authoritarian student protests, aimed at de Gaulle's style of government by decree, escalate into a countrywide protest.

the tracks of France's first railways and tunnelled out Paris' metro system. Designers experimented with new styles and materials, while young artists invented a host of new 'isms' (including impressionism, which took its title from one of Claude Monet's seminal early paintings, *Impression, Soleil Levant*).

The era culminated in a lavish World Fair in Paris in 1889, an event that summed up the excitement and dynamism of the age, and inspired the construction of one of France's most iconic landmarks – the Eiffel Tower.

The Great War

The *joie de vivre* of the belle époque wasn't to last. Within months of the outbreak of WWI in 1914, the fields of northern France had been transformed into a sea of trenches and shell craters; by the time the armistice had been signed in November 1918, some 1.3 million French soldiers had been killed and almost one million crippled.

Desperate to forget the ravages of the war, Paris sparkled as the centre of the avant-garde in the 1920s and '30s. The liberal atmosphere (not to mention the cheap booze and saucy nightlife) attracted a stream of foreign artists and writers to the city, and helped establish Paris' enduring reputation for creativity and experimentation.

A Date with the Revolution

Along with standardising France's system of weights and measures with the metric system, the Revolutionary government adopted a 'more rational' calendar from which all 'superstitious' associations (ie saints' days and mythology) were removed. Year 1 began on 22 September 1792, the day the First Republic was proclaimed.

The names of the 12 months – Vendémaire, Brumaire, Frimaire, Nivôse, Pluviôse, Ventôse, Germinal, Floréal, Prairial, Messidor, Thermidor and Fructidor – were chosen according to the seasons. Each month was divided into three 10-day 'weeks' called *décades*. The five remaining days of the year were used to celebrate Virtue, Genius, Labour, Opinion and Rewards. These festivals were initially called *sans-culottides*.

The Revolutionary calendar was ditched and the old system restored in 1806 by Napoléon Bonaparte.

WWII

The interwar party was short-lived. Two days after Germany invaded Poland in 1939, France joined Britain in declaring war on Germany. Within a year, Hitler's blitzkrieg had swept across Europe, and France was forced into humiliating capitulation in June the same year. Following the seaborne retreat of the British Expeditionary Force at Dunkirk, France – like much of Europe – found itself under Nazi occupation.

The Germans divided France into two zones: the west and north (including Paris), which was under direct German rule; and a puppet state in the south based around the spa town

1994
The 50km-long Channel Tunnel linking France with Britain opens after seven years of hard graft by 10,000 workers.

1995
Jacques Chirac becomes president, winning popular acclaim for his direct words and actions.

2002
The French franc, first minted in 1360, is thrown onto the scrap heap of history as the country adopts the euro as its official currency.

Bayeux Tapestry

of Vichy. The anti-Semitic Vichy regime proved very helpful to the Nazis in rounding up Jews and other undesirables for deportation to the death camps.

After four years of occupation, on 6 June 1944 Allied forces returned to French soil during the D-Day landings. Over 100,000 Allied troops stormed the Normandy coastline and, after several months of fighting, liberated Paris on 25 August. But the cost of the war had been devastating for France: many cities had been razed to the ground and millions of French people had lost their lives.

Poverty to Prosperity

Broken and battered from the war, France was forced to turn to the USA for loans as part of the Marshall Plan to rebuild Europe. Slowly, under the government of French war hero Charles de Gaulle, the economy began to recover and France began to rebuild its shattered infrastructure. The debilitating Algerian War of Independence (1954–62) and the subsequent loss of French colonies seriously weakened de Gaulle's government, however, and following widespread student protests in 1968 and a general strike by 10 million workers, de Gaulle was forced to resign from office in 1969. He died the following year.

Subsequent French presidents Georges Pompidou (in power 1969–74) and Giscard d'Estaing (1974–81) were instrumental in the increasing political and economic integration of Europe, a process that had begun with the formation of the EEC (European Economic Community) in 1957, and continued under François Mitterrand with the enlarged EU (European Union) in 1991. During Mitterrand's time in office, France abolished the death penalty, legalised homosexuality, gave workers five weeks' annual holiday and guaranteed the right to retire at 60.

In 1995 Mitterrand was succeeded by the maverick Jacques Chirac, who was re-elected in 2002. Chirac's attempts at reform led to widespread strikes and social unrest, while his opposition to the Iraq war alienated the US administration (and famously led to the rebranding of French fries as Freedom fries).

2004
France bans the wearing of crucifixes, the Islamic headscarf and other overtly religious symbols in state schools.

2007
Pro-American pragmatist Nicolas Sarkozy beats Socialist candidate Ségolène Royal to become French president.

2011
French parliament bans burkas in public. Muslim women wearing the burka can be fined and required to attend 'citizenship classes'.

Recent Politics

Following Chirac's retirement, the media-savvy Nicolas Sarkozy was elected president in 2007, bringing a more personality-driven, American-style approach to French politics. Despite initial popularity, Sarkozy's time in office was ultimately marred by France's fallout from the 2008 financial crisis, as well as controversy about his personal affairs – particularly his marriage to Italian supermodel and singer Carla Bruni.

Presidential elections in 2012 ushered in France's first Socialist president since 1995, François Hollande (b 1954). His firmly left-wing policies (including increases in corporation tax, the minimum wage and income tax for high-earners) initially proved popular, but Hollande has had a rocky ride since coming to power.

The French Resistance

Despite the myth of *'la France résistante'* (the French Resistance), the underground movement never actually included more than 5% of the population. The other 95% either collaborated or did nothing. Resistance members engaged in railway sabotage, collected intelligence for the Allies, helped Allied airmen who had been shot down and published anti-German leaflets, among other activities. Though the impact of their actions was relatively slight, the Resistance served as an enormous boost to French morale – not to mention the inspiration for numerous literary and cinematic endeavours.

Scandal broke in 2013 after finance minister Jerome Cahuzac admitted to having a safe-haven bank account in Switzerland and was forced to resign. Two months later France officially entered recession – again. France's AA+ credit rating was downgraded still further to AA and unemployment dipped to 11.1% – the highest in 15 years. Rising anger at Hollande's failure to get the country's economy back on track saw his popularity plunge fast and furiously, and his Socialist party was practically wiped out in the 2014 municipal elections as the vast majority of the country swung decisively to the right. Paris, with the election of Spanish-born Socialist Anne Hidalgo as Paris' first female mayor, was one of the few cities to remain on the political left.

France's economy remains stubbornly in the doldrums, while Hollande's own personal affairs have come under uncomfortable scrutiny – in 2014 his alleged affair with actress Julie Gayet hit the tabloids, and led to the end of his relationship with France's First Lady, Valérie Trierweiler. With his popularity at an all-time low, it remains to be seen whether Hollande can turn things around.

2012

France loses its top AAA credit rating. Presidential elections usher in François Hollande, France's first Socialist president in 17 years.

2013

Same-sex marriage is legalised in France. By the end of the year, 7000 gay couples have tied the knot.

2014

Municipal elections usher in Paris' first female mayor Anne Hidalgo.

ZONESIX / SHUTTERSTOCK ©

Architecture

From prehistoric megaliths in Brittany to Vauban's star-shaped citadels built to defend France's 17th-century frontiers, French architecture has always been of grand-projet proportions. Paris' skyline shimmers with Roman arenas, Gothic cathedrals, postmodernist cubes and futuristic skyscrapers, while provincial France cooks up the whole gamut of mainstream architectural styles.

Roman to Gothic

The Romans left behind a colossal architectural legacy in Provence and on the French Riviera. Thousands of men took three to five years to haul the 21,000 cu metres of local stone needed to build the Pont du Gard.

Several centuries later, architects adopted elements from Gallo-Roman buildings to create *roman* (Romanesque) masterpieces such as the exquisitely haunting Basilique St-Rémi in Reims, Caen's twinset of famous Romanesque abbeys and Provence's lavender-framed Abbaye de Sénanque. In Normandy the nave and south transept of the abbey-church on Mont St-Michel are beautiful examples of Norman Romanesque.

Northern France's extraordinary wealth in the 12th century lured the finest architects, engineers and artisans, who created impressive Gothic structures with ribbed vaults carved with great precision, pointed arches, slender verticals and stained-glass windows – Rouen cathedral is a lovely example. Avignon's pontifical palace is Gothic architecture on a gargantuan scale.

Renaisssance

The Renaissance, which began in Italy in the early 15th century, set out to realise a 'rebirth' of classical Greek and Roman culture. It impacted France at the end of that century when Charles VIII began a series of invasions of Italy, returning with new ideas.

To trace the shift from late Gothic to Renaissance, travel along the Loire Valley. During the very early Renaissance period, châteaux were used for the first time as pleasure palaces rather than defensive fortresses. Many edifices built during the 15th century to early 16th century in the Loire Valley – including Château d'Azay-le-Rideau and Château de Villandry – were built as summer or hunting residences for royal financiers, chamberlains and courtiers. Red-patterned brickwork – such as that on the Louis XII wing of Château Royal de Blois – adorned the façade of most châteaux dating from Louis XII's reign (1498–1515).

Art Nouveau

Art nouveau (1850–1910) combined iron, brick, glass and ceramics in ways never before seen. See for yourself in Paris with Hector Guimard's noodle-like metro entrances or the fine art nouveau interiors in the Musée d'Orsay.

Neoclassicism

Neoclassicism peaked under Napoléon III, who used it extensively for monumental architecture intended to embody the grandeur of imperial France and its capital: the Arc de Triomphe, the Arc du Carrousel at the Louvre, the Assemblée Nationale building and the Palais Garnier.

It was during this period that urban planner Baron Haussmann, between 1850 and 1870 as Prefect of the Seine, completely redrew Paris' street plan, radically demolishing the city's maze of narrow, cramped medieval streets and replacing it with wide boulevards, sweeping parks and attractive *passages couverts* (covered passages).

The true showcase of this era is Casino de Monte Carlo in Monaco, created by French architect Charles Garnier (1825–98) in 1878.

Contemporary

For centuries French political leaders sought to immortalise themselves through the erection of huge public edifices (aka *grands projets*) in Paris. Georges Pompidou commissioned the once reviled, now much-loved Centre Pompidou (1977) in which the architects – in order to keep the exhibition halls as uncluttered as possible – put the building's insides out. Under François Mitterrand, IM Pei's glass pyramid at the hitherto sacrosanct and untouchable Louvre appeared.

France's arguably most talented architect, Jean Nouvel is the creative talent behind Paris' Institut du Monde Arabe (1987), one of the most beautiful and successful of France's contemporary buildings. He also designed the Philharmonie de Paris, an experimental concert hall for the city's symphonic orchestra, and is the architect behind the current €600 million renovation of Gare d'Austerlitz (with one-third of the budget going on restoring the amazing glass roof).

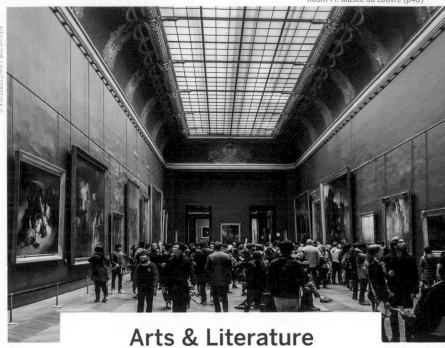

KIEVVICTOR / SHUTTERSTOCK ©

Arts & Literature

Painting, literature, music: France's vast artistic heritage is the essence of French art de vivre. French painting continues to break new ground with provocative street art, while French writers Voltaire, Victor Hugo, Marcel Proust and Simone de Beauvoir fill the literary world's hall of fame. Music is embedded in the French soul, with world-class sounds coming out of Paris.

Painting France

Classical to Romantic

According to Voltaire, French painting proper began with Baroque painter Nicolas Poussin (1594–1665), known for his classical mythological and biblical scenes bathed in golden light. Wind forward a couple of centuries and modern still life popped up with Jean-Baptiste Chardin (1699–1779). A century later, neoclassical artist Jacques Louis David (1748–1825) wooed the public with vast history paintings; some are in the Louvre.

While Romantics such as Eugène Delacroix (1798–1863) revamped the subject picture, the Barbizon School effected a parallel transformation of landscape painting. Jean-François Millet (1814–75), son of a Normandy farmer, took many of his subjects from peasant life, and reproductions of his *L'Angélus* (The Angelus; 1857) – the best-known painting in France after the *Mona Lisa* – are strung above mantelpieces all over rural France. The original hangs in Paris' Musée d'Orsay.

The Impressionists

It was in a flower-filled garden in a Normandy village that Claude Monet (1840–1926) expounded impressionism, a term of derision taken from the title of his experimental painting *Impression: Soleil Levant* (Impression: Sunrise; 1874).

An arthritis-crippled Renoir painted out his last impressionist days in a villa on the French Riviera, a part of France that inspired dozens of artists. In St-Tropez pointillism took off with Georges Seurat (1859–91), the first to apply paint in small dots or uniform brush strokes of unmixed colour. His pupil Paul Signac (1863–1935) is best known for pointillist works.

Street Art

Street art is big, thanks in part to the pioneering work of **Blek Le Rat** (http://bleklerat.free.fr) in the 1980s. The Parisian artist, born as Xavier Prou, began by spraying tiny rats in hidden corners of the streets of Paris, went on to develop stencil graffiti as a recognised form, and notably inspired British street artist Banksy.

In 2013 the world's largest collective street-art exhibition, **La Tour Paris 13** (www.tourparis13.fr), opened in a derelict apartment block in Paris' 13e arrondissement. Its 36 apartments on 13 floors showcased works by 100 international artists. The blockbuster exhibition ran for one month, after which the tower was shut and demolished. Itself an artwork, the three-day demolition was filmed and streamed live on the internet – where the street artworks remain.

Matisse, Picasso & Klein

Twentieth-century French painting is characterised by a bewildering diversity of styles, including cubism, and Fauvism, named after the slur of a critic who compared the exhibitors at the 1906 autumn Salon in Paris with *fauves* (wild animals) because of their radical use of intensely bright colours. Spanish cubist Pablo Picasso (1881–1973) and Fauvist Henri Matisse (1869–1954) both chose southern France to set up studios.

With the close of WWII, Paris' role as artistic world capital ended. The focus shifted back to southern France in the 1960s with new realists such as Arman (1928–2005) and Yves Klein (1928–62), both from Nice. In 1960 Klein famously produced *Anthropométrie de l'Époque Bleue,* a series of imprints made by naked women (covered from head to toe in blue paint) rolling around on a white canvas, in front of an orchestra of violins and an audience in evening dress.

1990s Urban Minutiae

Artists in the 1990s turned to the minutiae of everyday urban life to express social and political angst. Conceptual artist Daniel Buren (b 1938) reduced his painting to a signature series of vertical 8.7cm-wide stripes that is applied to any surface imaginable – white marble columns in the courtyard of Paris' Palais Royal included. The painter (who in 1967, as part of the radical group BMPT, signed a manifesto declaring he was not a painter) was the *enfant terrible* of French art in the 1980s.

Current Art Trends

Paris-born conceptual artist Sophie Calle (b 1953) brazenly exposes her private life in public with eye-catching installations such as *Prenez Soin de Vous* (Take Care of Yourself;

Musée National Picasso

★ **Best Art Museums**

Musée du Louvre (p40), Paris

Musée d'Orsay (p62), Paris

Musée National Picasso (p60), Paris

Musée de l'Annonciade (p236), St-Tropez

Musée Matisse (p221), Nice

THOMAS CRAIG / GETTY IMAGES ©

2007), a compelling and addictive work of art in book form exposing the reactions of 107 women to an email Calle received from her French lover, dumping her.

Her *Rachel, Monique* (2010) evoked the death and lingering memory of her mother in the form of a photographic exhibition first shown in Paris, later as a live reading performance at the Festival d'Avignon, and subsequently in a chapel in New York. In 2015 *Suite Vénitienne* was published, a beautiful hardback rendition, on gilt-edged Japanese paper, of her first art book in 1988 in which she followed Henri B around Venice for two weeks, anonymously photographing the enigmatic stranger.

Literary Drama

Courtly Love to Symbolism

Troubadours' lyric poems of courtly love dominated medieval French literature, while the *roman* (literally 'romance', now meaning 'novel') drew on old Celtic tales. With the *Roman de la Rose*, a 22,000-line poem by Guillaume de Lorris and Jean de Meung, allegorical figures like Pleasure, Shame and Fear appeared.

French Renaissance literature was extensive and varied. La Pléiade was a group of lyrical poets active in the 1550s and 1560s. The exuberant narrative of Loire Valley–born François Rabelais (1494–1553) blends coarse humour with encyclopedic erudition in a vast panorama of every kind of person, occupation and jargon in 16th-century France. Michel de Montaigne (1533–92) covered cannibals, war horses, drunkenness, the resemblance of children to their fathers and other themes.

Le grand siècle (golden age) ushered in classical lofty odes to tragedy: François de Malherbe (1555–1628) brought a new rigour to rhythm in poetry; and Marie de La Fayette (1634–93) penned the first French novel, *La Princesse de Clèves* (1678).

French Romanticism

The philosophical Voltaire (1694–1778) dominated the 18th century. A century on, Besançon gave birth to French Romantic Victor Hugo (1802–85).

In 1857 literary landmarks *Madame Bovary* by Gustave Flaubert (1821–80) and Charles Baudelaire's (1821–67) poems *Les Fleurs du Mal* (The Flowers of Evil) were published. Émile Zola (1840–1902) saw novel-writing as a science in his powerful series, Les Rougon-Macquart.

Evoking mental states was the dream of symbolists Paul Verlaine (1844–96) and Stéphane Mallarmé (1842–98). Verlaine shared a tempestuous homosexual relationship with poet Arthur Rimbaud (1854–91): enter French literature's first modern poems.

Modern Literature

The world's longest novel – a seven-volume 9,609,000-character giant by Marcel Proust (1871–1922) – dominated the early 20th century. *À la Recherche du Temps Perdu* (Remembrance of Things Past) explores in evocative detail the true meaning of past experience recovered from the unconscious by involuntary memory.

Surrealism proved a vital force until WWII. André Breton (1896–1966) captured the spirit of surrealism – a fascination with dreams, divination and all manifestations of the imaginary – in his autobiographical narratives.

Bestsellers

Marc Levy is France's bestselling writer. The film rights of his first novel were snapped up for the Steven Spielberg box-office hit, *Just Like Heaven* (2005), and his novels have been translated into 42 languages. *Une Autre Idée de Bonheur* (Another Idea of Happiness; 2013) was published a year later in English, as will his latest – *L'Horizon à l'Envers* (2016) – in due course no doubt.

In Paris the bohemian Colette (1873–1954) captivated and shocked with her titillating novels detailing the amorous exploits of heroines such as schoolgirl Claudine. In New York meanwhile, what would become one of the bestselling French works of all time was published in 1943: *Le Petit Prince* (The Little Prince), by Lyon-born writer and pilot, Antoine de Saint-Exupéry (1900–44). He captured the hearts of millions with his magical yet philosophical tale for children about an aviator's adventures with a little blonde-haired Prince from Asteroid B-612.

After WWII, existentialism developed around the lively debates of Jean-Paul Sartre (1905–80), Simone de Beauvoir (1908–86) and Albert Camus (1913–60) in Paris' Left Bank cafes.

The nouveau roman of the 1950s saw experimental young writers seek new ways of organising narratives. *Histoire d'O* (Story of O), an erotic sadomasochistic novel written by Dominique Aury under a pseudonym in 1954, sold more copies outside France than any other contemporary French novel.

Radical young writer Françoise Sagan (1935–2004) shot to fame overnight at the age of 18 with her first novel, *Bonjour Tristesse* (Hello Sadness, 1954). The subsequent fast-paced, hedonistic lifestyle pursued by the party-loving, bourgeois-born writer ensured she remained in the spotlight until her death in 2004.

The New Generation

No French writer better delves into the mind, mood and politics of France's notable ethnic population than Faïza Guène (b 1985), who writes in a notable 'urban slang' style.

Born and bred on a ghetto housing estate outside Paris, she stunned critics with her debut novel, *Kiffe Kiffe Demain* (2004), sold in 27 countries and published in English as *Just Like Tomorrow* (2006).

Faïza Guène's father moved from a village in western Algeria to northern France in 1952, aged 17, to work in the mines. Only in the 1980s could he return to Algeria. There he met his wife, whom he brought back to France, to Les Courtillières housing estate in Seine-St-Denis, where 6000-odd immigrants live in five-storey, high-rise blocks stretching for 1.5km. Such is the setting for Guène's first book and her second semi-autobiographical novel, *Du Rêve pour les Oeufs* (2006), published in English as *Dreams from the Endz* (2008). Her most recent work, *Un Homme ça ne Pleure Pas* (Real Men Don't Cry, 2014), shifts to Nice in southern France.

A Contemporary Proust

French laureate Patrick Modiano (b 1945) is a French writer whose novels are often set in Paris during the Nazi occupation of WWII. Often compared to Proust, he won the Nobel Prize in Literature in 2014, confirming France's ranking as the country with the most literary Nobel Prize winners – 15 to date. *Missing Person* (2005) is one of a handful of Modiano's many French bestsellers translated into English.

Musical Encounters

Classical

French Baroque music heavily influenced European musical output in the 17th and 18th centuries. French musical luminaries – Charles Gounod (1818–93), César Franck (1822–90) and *Carmen* creator Georges Bizet (1838–75) among them – were a dime a dozen in the 19th century. Modern orchestration was founded by French Romantic Hector Berlioz (1803–69). He demanded gargantuan forces: his ideal orchestra included 240 stringed instruments, 30 grand pianos and 30 harps.

Claude Debussy (1862–1918) revolutionised classical music with *Prélude à l'Après-Midi d'un Faune* (Prelude to the Afternoon of a Fawn), creating a light, almost Asian musical impressionism.

Jazz & French Chansons

Jazz hit 1920s Paris in the banana-clad form of Josephine Baker, an African-American cabaret dancer. Post-WWII ushered in a much-appreciated bunch of musicians, mostly black Americans who opted to remain in Paris' bohemian Montmartre rather than return to the brutal racism and segregation of the US: Sidney Bechet called Paris home from 1949, jazz drummer Kenny 'Klook' Clarke followed in 1956, pianist Bud Powell in 1959 and saxophonist Dexter Gordon in the early 1960s.

The *chanson française,* a French folk-song tradition dating from the troubadours of the Middle Ages, was eclipsed by the music halls and burlesque of the early 20th century, but was revived in the 1930s by Édith Piaf and Charles Trenet. In the 1950s, Paris' Left Bank cabarets nurtured *chansonniers* (cabaret singers) such as Léo Ferré, Georges Brassens, Claude Nougaro, Jacques Brel and the very charming, very sexy, very French Serge Gainsbourg.

Rap

France is known for its rap, an original 1990s sound spearheaded by Senegal-born, Paris-reared rapper MC Solaar and Suprême NTM (NTM being an acronym for a French expression far too offensive to print). Most big-name rappers are French 20-somethings of Arabic or African origin whose prime preoccupations are the frustrations and fury of fed-up immigrants in the French *banlieues* (suburbs). France's best-known rap band is Marseille's home-grown IAM (www.iam.tm.fr).

No artist has sealed France's reputation in world music more than Paris-born, Franco-Congolese rapper, slam poet and three-time Victoire de la Musique–award winner, Abd al Malik (www.abdalmalik.fr). His albums, including his latest, *Scarifications* (2015), are all classics.

Rock & Pop

One could be forgiven for thinking that French pop is becoming dynastic. The distinctive M (for Mathieu) is the son of singer Louis Chédid; Arthur H is the progeny of pop-rock musician Jacques Higelin; and Thomas Dutronc is the offspring of 1960s idols Jacques and Françoise Hardy. Serge Gainsbourg's daughter with Jane Birkin, Charlotte Gainsbourg (b 1971) made her musical debut in 1984 with the single 'Lemon Incest' and – several albums later – released a cover version of the song 'Hey Joe' as soundtrack to the film *Nymphomaniac* (2013) in which she also starred as the leading lady. For her latest album she collaborated with Guy Man from Daft Punk and French electronic music producer SebastiAn.

Indie rock band Phoenix, from Versailles, headlines festivals in the US and UK. The band was born in the late 1990s in a garage in the Paris suburbs.

Always worth a listen is the group Louise Attaque (http://loulseattaque.com) who, after a 10-year break, released its new album, *L'Anomalie,* with huge success in early 2016. Nosfell (www.nosfell.com), one of France's most creative and intense musicians, sings in his own invented language called *le klokobelz*. In 2015 Nosfell wrote the music for *Contact,* a musical comedy by French dancer and choreographer Philippe Decouflé.

Christophe Maé mixes acoustic pop with soul, with stunning success. His jazzy third album, *Je Veux du Bonheur* (2013), was heavy influenced by the time the Provence-born singer spent travelling in New Orleans. Travels abroad likewise provide the inspiration for the spring 2016 album, *Palermo Hollywood,* by talented singer and songwriter Benjamin Biolay (b 1973).

Marseille-born Marina Kaye (b 1998) won *France's Got Talent* TV show at the age of 13, as well as huge acclaim with her debut single 'Homeless', and released her first album *Fearless* in 2015. Celebrity singer Nolwenn Leroy (b 1982) performs in Breton, English and Irish as well as French; while Paris' very own Indila (b 1984) woos France with her edgy pop and *rai* (a style derived from Algerian folk music).

Zaz

Jazz fans adore the gypsy jazz style of young French pop singer Zaz – an experimental voice from the Loire Valley, often compared to Édith Piaf – who stormed to the top of the charts with her debut album *Zaz* (2010). Her subsequent third album, *Paris* (2014), is a musical ode to the French capital with 13 songs evoking Paris' irresistible charm and romance. Her first live album, *Sur la Route* (2015), only confirmed that Zaz is one of France's hottest contemporary female voices.

Electronica & Dance

David Guetta, Laurent Garnier, Martin Solveig and Bon Sinclair – originally nicknamed 'Chris the French Kiss' – are top Parisian electronica music producers and DJs who travel the international circuit. In the late 1990s David Guetta, with his wife Cathy, directed Paris' mythical nightclub Les Bains Douches, today a trendy club-hotel in Le Marais.

Algerian Rai to Zouglou

With styles from Algerian *rai* to other North African music (artists include Cheb Khaled, Natacha Atlas, Jamel, Cheb Mami) and Senegalese *mbalax* (Youssou N'Dour), West Indian zouk (Kassav', Zouk Machine) and Cuban salsa, France's world beat is strong. Manu Chao (www.manuchao.net), the Paris-born son of Spanish parents, uses world elements to stunning effect.

Magic System from Côte d'Ivoire popularised *zouglou* (a kind of West African rap and dance music) with its album *Premier Gaou,* and Congolese Koffi Olomide still packs the halls. Also try to catch blind singing couple, Amadou and Mariam; Rokia Traoré from Mali; and Franco-Algerian DJ-turned-singer Rachid Taha (www.rachidtaha.fr) whose music mixes Arab and Western musical styles with lyrics in English, Berber and French.

French Cuisine

French cuisine waltzes taste buds through a dizzying array of dishes sourced from aromatic street markets, seaside oyster farms, sun-baked olive groves and ancient vineyards. The freshness of ingredients, natural flavours, regional variety and range of cooking methods are phenomenal. The very word 'cuisine' was borrowed from the French – no other language could handle all the nuances.

Cheese

No French food product is a purer reflection of *terroir* (land) than cheese, an iconic staple that – with the exception of most coastal areas – is made all over the country, tiny villages laying claim to ancient variations made just the way *grand-père* (grandfather) did it. France boasts more than 500 varieties, made with *lait cru* (raw milk), pasteurised milk or *petit-lait* ('little-milk', the whey left over after the fats and solids have been curdled with rennet).

Chèvre, made from goat's milk, is creamy, sweet and faintly salty when fresh, but hardens and gets saltier as it matures. Among the best is Ste-Maure de Touraine, a mild creamy cheese from the Loire Valley; Cabécou de Rocamadour from Midi-Pyrénées, often served warm with salad or marinated in oil and rosemary; and Lyon's St-Marcellin, a soft white cheese that should be served impossibly runny.

Roquefort, a ewe's-milk veined cheese from Languedoc, is the king of blue cheeses and vies with Burgundy's pongy Époisses for the strongest taste award. Soft, white, orange-skinned Époisses, created in the 16th century by monks at Abbaye de Cîteaux, takes a month to make, using washes of saltwater, rainwater and Marc de Bourgogne – a local pomace brandy and the source of the cheese's final fierce bite.

Equal parts of Comté, Beaufort and Gruyère – a trio of hard, fruity, cow's milk cheeses from the French Alps – are grated and melted in a garlic-smeared pot with a dash of nutmeg, white wine and *kirsch* (cherry liqueur) to create fondue Savoyarde. Hearty and filling, this pot of melting glory originated from the simple peasant need of using up cheese scraps. It is now the chic dish to eat on the ski slopes.

Bread

In northern France wheat fields shade vast swathes of agricultural land a gorgeous golden copper, and nothing is more French than *pain* (bread). Starved peasants demanded bread on the eve of the French Revolution when the ill-fated Queen Marie-Antoinette is purported to have said 'let them eat cake'.

Le Gavage

Fattened duck and goose liver have been enjoyed since time immemorial, but it wasn't until the 18th century that it was introduced on a large scale.

Traditionally, back in the 11th century, local farmers in the Dordogne would slaughter the farm goose then pluck out its liver and soak it in warm milk to ensure a succulent swollen liver, ripe for feasting on with a chilled glass of sweet Monbazillac white. Today, in order to fatten the livers, ducks and geese are controversially force-fed twice a day for two or three weeks with unnatural amounts of boiled corn. During *le gavage* (force-feeding), a tube is threaded down the throat into the bird's stomach, enabling 450g or so of boiled corn to be pneumatically pumped into the bird in just a few seconds.

Force feeding is illegal in 12 countries in the EU, Norway, Switzerland, Israel and the USA; and foie gras imports are forbidden in many countries. Within France itself, there is a growing movement to end *le gavage*.

And bread today – no longer a matter of life or death but a cultural icon – accompanies every meal. It's rarely served with butter, but when it is, the butter is always *doux* (unsalted).

Every town and almost every village has its own *boulangerie* (bakery) which sells bread in all manner of shapes, sizes and variety. Artisan *boulangeries* bake their bread in a wood-fired, brick bread oven pioneered by Loire Valley châteaux in the 16th century.

Plain old *pain* is a 400g, traditional-shaped loaf, soft inside and crusty out. The iconic classic is *une baguette*, a long, thin crusty loaf weighing 250g. Anything fatter and it becomes *une flûte*, thinner *une ficelle*. While French baguettes are impossibly good, they systematically turn unpleasantly dry within four hours, unbelievably rock-hard within 12.

Charcuterie & Foie Gras

Charcuterie, the backbone of every French picnic and a bistro standard, is traditionally made from pork, though other meats are used in making *saucisse* (small fresh sausage, boiled or grilled before eating), *saucisson* (salami), *saucisson sec* (air-dried salami), *boudin noir* (blood sausage or pudding made with pig's blood, onions and spices) and other cured and salted meats. Pâtés, terrines and *rillettes* are also considered charcuterie. The difference between a pâté and a terrine is academic: a pâté is removed from its container and sliced before it is served, while a terrine is sliced from the container itself. *Rillettes*, spread cold over bread or toast, is potted meat or even fish that has been shredded with two forks, seasoned and mixed with fat.

★ Top Tables

Restaurant David Toutain (p71), Paris
La Côte (p146), Carnac
l'Assiette Champenoise (p165), Reims
Jan (p226), Nice
La Terrasse Rouge (p282), St-Émilion

The key component of *pâté de foie gras* is foie gras, which is the liver of fattened ducks and geese. It was first prepared *en croûte* (in a pastry crust) around 1780 by one Jean-Pierre Clause, chef to the military governor of Alsace, who was impressed enough to send a batch to the king of Versailles. Today, it is a traditional component of celebratory or festive meals – particularly Christmas and New Year's Eve – in family homes countrywide, and is consumed year-round in regions in southwest France where it is primarily made.

Sweet Treats

Patisserie is a general French term for pastries and includes *tartes* (tarts), *flans* (custard pies), *gâteaux* (cakes) and *biscuits* (cookies) as well as traditional croissants, *pains au chocolat* and other typical pastries. *Sablés* are shortbread biscuits, *tuiles* are delicate wing-like almond cookies, madeleines are small scallop-shaped cakes often flavoured with a hint of vanilla or lemon, and *tarte tatin* is an upside-down caramelised apple pie that's been around since the late 19th century. Louis XIV (1643–1715), known for his sweet tooth, is credited with introducing the custom of eating dessert – once reserved for feast days and other celebrations – at the end of a meal.

Breton Crêpes & Seafood

Brittany is a paradise for seafood lovers (think lobster, scallops, sea bass, turbot, mussels and oysters from Cancale) as well as kids, thanks to the humble crêpe and *galette,* an ancient culinary tradition that has long-ruled Breton cuisine. Pair a sweet wheat-flour pancake or savoury buckwheat *galette* with *une bolée* (a stubby terracotta goblet) of apple-rich Breton cider, and taste buds enter gourmet heaven. Royal Guillevic and ciders produced by the Domaine de Kervéguen are excellent quality, artisanal ciders to try. If cider is not your cup of tea, order a local beer like Coreff or nonalcoholic *lait ribot* (fermented milk). *Chouchen* (hydromel), a fermented honey liqueur, is a typical Breton aperitif.

Cheese is not big, but *la beurre de Bretagne* (Breton butter) is. Traditionally sea-salted and creamy, a knob of it naturally goes into crêpes, *galettes* and the most outrageously buttery cake you're likely to ever taste in your life – *kouign amann* (Breton butter cake). Bretons, unlike the rest of the French, even butter their bread. Butter handmade by Jean-Yves Bordier ends up on tables of top restaurants around the world.

Seaweed is another Breton culinary curiosity, and 80% of French shallots are grown here.

Normandy Cream & Cider

Cream, apples and cider are the essentials of Norman cuisine, which sees mussels simmered in cream and a splash of cider to make *moules à la crème normande* and tripe thrown in the slow pot with cider and vegetables to make *tripes à la mode de Caen.* Creamy Camembert is the local cow's milk cheese, and on the coast *coquilles St-Jacques* (scallops) and *huîtres* (oysters) rule the seafood roost. Apples are the essence of the region's main tipples: tangy cider and the potent *calvados* (apple brandy), exquisite straight or splashed on apple sorbet.

À la Provençal

Cuisine in sun-baked Provence is laden with tomatoes, melons, cherries, peaches, olives, Mediterranean fish and Alpine cheese. Farmers gather at the weekly market to sell their fruit and vegetables, woven garlic plaits, dried herbs displayed in stubby coarse sacks, and olives stuffed with a multitude of edible sins. *À la Provençal* still means anything with a generous dose of garlic-seasoned tomatoes, while a simple *filet mignon* sprinkled with olive oil and rosemary fresh from the garden makes the same magnificent Sunday lunch it did generations ago.

Yet there are exciting culinary contrasts in this region, which see fishermen return with the catch of the day in seafaring Marseille; grazing bulls and paddy fields in the Camargue; black truffles in the Vaucluse; cheese made from cow's milk in Alpine pastures; and an Italianate accent to cooking in seaside Nice.

Bouillabaisse, Marseille's mighty meal of fish stew, is Provence's most famous contribution to French cuisine. The chowder must contain at least three kinds of fresh saltwater fish, cooked for about 10 minutes in a broth containing onions, tomatoes, saffron and various herbs, and eaten as a main course with toasted bread and *rouille* (a spicy red mayonnaise of olive oil, garlic and chilli peppers).

The fish stew *bourride* is similar to bouillabaisse but has fewer ingredients, a less prescriptive recipe, and often a slightly creamier sauce. It's customarily served with *aïoli* (garlic mayonnaise).

When in Provence, do as the Provençaux do: drink pastis. An aniseed-flavoured, 45% alcoholic drink, it was invented in Marseille by industrialist Paul Ricard in 1932. Amber-coloured in the bottle, it turns milky white when mixed with water. An essential lunch or dinner companion is a chilled glass of the region's irresistibly pink, AOC Côtes de Provence rosé wine.

Piggy Parts in Lyon

All too often Lyon is dubbed France's gastronomic capital. And while it doesn't compete with France's capital when it comes to variety of international cuisine, it certainly holds its own when it comes to titillating taste buds with the unusual and inventive. Take the age-old repertoire of feisty, often pork-driven dishes served in the city's legendary *bouchons* (small bistros): breaded fried tripe, big fat *andouillettes* (pig-intestine sausage), silk-weaver's

The Zany Macaron

No sweet treat evokes the essence of French patisserie quite like the elegant, sophisticated and zany macaron, a legacy of Catherine de Médicis who came to France in 1533 with an entourage of Florentine chefs and pastry cooks adept in the subtleties of Italian Renaissance cooking and armed with delicacies such as aspic, truffles, *quenelles* (dumplings), artichokes – and macarons.

Round and polished smooth like a giant Smartie, the macaron (nothing to do with coconut) is a pair of crisp-shelled, chewy-inside discs – egg whites whisked stiff with sugar and ground almonds – sandwiched together with a smooth filling. Belying their eggshell fragility, macarons are created in a rainbow of lurid colours and flavours that's wild and inexhaustible: rose petal, cherry blossom, caramel with coconut and mango, mandarin orange and olive oil...

Croissants

brains (a herbed cheese spread, not brains at all) – there is no way you can ever say Lyonnais cuisine is run of the mill. A lighter, less meaty speciality is *quenelle de brochet,* a poached dumpling made of freshwater fish (usually pike) and served with sauce Nantua (a cream and freshwater-crayfish sauce).

Equally fine is the Lyonnais wine list where very fine Côtes de Rhône reds vie for attention with local Brouilly and highly esteemed Mâcon reds from nearby Burgundy. In *bouchons,* local Beaujolais is mixed with a dash of blackcurrant liqueur to make a blood-red *communard* aperitif.

The Cheesy French Alps

Savoyard food is justifiably famous, and features in the preponderance of French restaurants in the region. Like all regional French cuisines, it's a product of the *terroir*, and all that grows within it. This means plenty of dairy, cured meats and pasta such as *crozets* and *ravioles*.

Every restaurant in the Alps with a Savoyard menu offers *raclette*, *tartiflette* or fondue, but to save on costs and maximise the cheese you can opt for DIY: many *fruitières* (cheese-mongers) will lend you the required apparatus, provided you buy their ingredients.

Fondue Savoyarde

Made with three types of cheeses in equal proportions (Gruyère, Beaufort and Comté) and dry white wine (about 0.4L of wine for 1kg of cheese). Melt the mix in a cast-iron dish on a hob, then keep it warm with a small burner on the table. Dunk chunks of bread in the cheesy goo.

Our tip: rub garlic on the bread or add some to the dish – you'll have cheesy breath anyway, so what the hell.

Tartiflette

Easy-peasy. Slice a whole Reblochon cheese lengthwise into two rounds. In an ovenproof dish, mix together slices of parboiled potatoes, crème fraiche, onions and lardons (diced bacon). Whack the cheese halves on top, bake for about 40 minutes at 180°C, and ta-da!

Our tip: more crème fraiche and more lardons (a sprinkle of nutmeg is also good).

Raclette

Named after the Swiss cheese, *raclette* is a combination of melting cheese, boiled pota-toes, charcuterie and baby gherkins. The home *raclette* kit is an oval hotplate with a grill underneath and dishes to melt slices of cheese.

Our tip: avoid a sticky mess by greasing and preheating your grill, and go easy on the ingredients (less is more).

Picnic Perfect

Baguette French simplicity at its best: buy a baguette from the *boulangerie*, stuff it with a chunk of Camembert, pâté and *cornichons* (miniature gherkins), or a few slices of *rosette de Lyon* or other salami, and, *voilà*, picnic perfection! If you're sweet-toothed, do it the French-kid way – wedge a slab of milk chocolate inside.

Macarons No sweeter way to end a gourmet picnic, most famously from Ladurée (p64) in Paris.

Kouign amann The world's most buttery, syrupy cake, aka Breton butter cake.

Fruit Big juicy black cherries from Apt; peaches, apricots and tomatoes from the Rhône Valley, Provence and the Riviera.

Provençal olives or peppers Marinated and stuffed with a multitude of edible sins from market stands.

Champagne from Reims and *biscuits roses*.

Country produce Pâté, walnuts and foie gras from the Dordogne.

Niçois Specialities

Niçois specialities include *socca* (a savoury, griddle-fried pancake made from chickpea flour and olive oil, sprinkled with a liberal dose of black pepper), *petits farcis* (stuffed vegetables), *pissaladière* (onion tart topped with black olives and anchovies) and the many vegetable *beignets* (fritters). Try them at **Chez René Socca** (p225) or Lou Pilha Leva.

Dining Lexicon

Auberge Country inn serving traditional fare, often attached to a small hotel.

Ferme auberge Working farm that cooks up meals from local farm products; usually only dinner and frequently only by reservation.

Bistro (also spelled *bistrot*) Anything from a pub or bar with snacks and light meals to a small, fully fledged restaurant.

Neobistro Trendy in Paris and large cities where this contemporary take on the traditional bistro embraces everything from checked-tablecloth tradition to contemporary minimalism.

Brasserie Much like a cafe except it serves full meals, drinks and coffee from morning until 11pm or later. Typical fare includes *choucroute* (sauerkraut) and *moules frites* (mussels and fries).

Restaurant Born in Paris in the 18th century, restaurants today serve lunch and dinner five or six days a week.

Buffet (or *buvette*) Kiosk, usually at train stations and airports, selling drinks, filled baguettes and snacks.

Cafe Basic light snacks as well as drinks.

Crêperie (also *galetterie*) Casual address specialising in sweet crêpes and savoury *galettes* (buckwheat crêpes).

Salon de thé Trendy tearoom often serving light lunches (quiche, salads, cakes, tarts, pies and pastries) as well as green, black and herbal teas.

Table d'hôte (literally 'host's table') Some of the most charming B&Bs serve *table d'hôte* too, a delicious homemade meal of set courses with little or no choice.

Outdoor Activities

France takes outdoor activities and elevates them to a fine art. In the birthplace of the Tour de France, the cycling is world-class; in Mont Blanc's backyard, the skiing is second to none. And everywhere – from Brittany's coastal wilds to the sun-blazed vines and lavender meadows of Provence – the hiking is, ah, just magnifique.

Skiing & Snowboarding

Just whisper the words 'French Alps' to a skier and watch their eyes light up. The ski season goes with the snow, generally running from early or mid-December to around mid-April: the higher you go, the more snow-sure the resort and the longer the season. Crowds and room rates skyrocket during school holidays (Christmas, February half-term, Easter), so avoid these times if you can.

Météo France (www.meteofrance.com) Weather and daily avalanche forecast during the ski season.

École du Ski Français (ESF; www.esf.net) The largest ski school in the world, with first-class tuition. Search by region.

France Montagnes (www.france-montagnes.com) Official website of French ski resorts, with guides, maps, snow reports and more.

Hiking & Walking

Hikers have a high time of it in the Alps, with mile after never-ending mile of well-marked trails. Lifts and cable cars take the sweat out of hiking here in summer. Chamonix (p294) is the trailhead for the epic 10-day, three-country Tour de Mont Blanc, but gentler paths, such as the **Grand Balcon Sud**, also command Mont Blanc close-ups.

Club Alpin Français (French Alpine Club; www.ffcam.fr) has guides for alpine sports and manages 127 *refuges* (mountain huts).

Cycling & Mountain Biking

France is fabulous freewheeling country, with routes leading along its lushly wooded valleys and mighty rivers begging to be explored in slow motion. Among the best options is chateau-studded Loire Valley – **Loire à Vélo** (www.loireavelo.fr) maintains 800km of signposted routes. Provence's 236km **Autour du Luberon** *véloroute* (bike path) links one gold stone village to another. Or partner wine tasting with a pedal through Bordeaux vines. Bike hire is widely available and costs from €10 per day for a classic bike to €35 for a top-of-the-range mountain bike or ebike. Tourist offices have details.

Véloroutes et Voies Vertes (www.af3v.org) has the inside scoop on 250 signposted *véloroutes* and *voies vertes* (greenways), plus an interactive map to pinpoint them.

Kayaking & Canoeing

Top options include the looking-glass Lake Annecy in the French Alps, the River Gard and Provence's highly scenic Gorges du Verdon. Sea kayakers adore the ragged, cove-indented Parc National des Calanques near Marseille; pay around €10 to €15 for kayak or canoe rental per day, and €25/50 for a half-/full-day excursion.

Rock Climbing & Via Ferrata

For intrepid souls, the holy grail of rock climbing is France's highest of the high: 4810m Mont Blanc. Chamonix guide companies organise ascents of this monster mountain, as well as five-day rock-climbing courses in the surrounding Alps. If you are less experienced but fancy flirting with climbing, *via ferrate* (fixed-rope routes) lace the Alps. Guide companies charge around €50 for half-day escapades.

Paragliding

Many a peak, perfect thermals, and glacier-frosted mountains and forests to observe while drifting down to ground level attract paragliders to Alpine resorts such as Chamonix. Lake Annecy is a favourite. Tandem flights with a qualified instructor cost anything between €65 and €220.

Monaco (p228)

MEDIOIMAGES / PHOTODISC / GETTY IMAGES ©

Survival Guide

Directory A–Z

Accommodation

Be it a fairy-tale château, a boutique hideaway or floating pod on a lake, France has accommodation to suit every taste and pocket. If you're visiting in high season (especially August), reserve ahead – the best addresses on the coast fill up months in advance.

Reservations

Midrange, top-end and many budget hotels require a credit card number to secure an advance reservation made by phone; some hostels do not take bookings. Many tourist offices can advise on availability and reserve for you, often for a fee of €5 and usually only if you stop by in person. In the Alps, ski-resort tourist offices run a central reservation service for booking accommodation.

Seasons

o In ski resorts, high season is Christmas, New Year and the February–March school holidays.

o On the coast, high season is summer, particularly August.

o Hotels in inland cities often charge low-season rates in summer.

o Rates often drop outside the high season – in some cases by as much as 50%.

o In business-oriented hotels in cities, rooms are most expensive from Monday to Thursday and cheaper over the weekend.

o In the Alps, hotels usually close between seasons, from around May to mid-June and from mid-September to early December.

B&Bs

For charm, a heartfelt *bienvenue* (welcome) and solid home cooking, it's hard to beat France's privately run *chambres d'hôte* (B&Bs) – urban rarities but as common as muck in rural areas. By law a *chambre d'hôte* must have no more than five rooms and breakfast must be included in the price; some hosts prepare a meal (*table d'hôte*) for

an extra charge of around €30 including wine. Pick up lists of *chambres d'hôte* at tourist offices, or find one to suit online.

Bienvenue à la Ferme (www.bienvenue-a-la-ferme.com)

Chambres d'Hôtes France (www.chambresdhotesfrance.com)

Fleurs de Soleil (www.fleurs-desoleil.fr) Selective collection of 550 stylish *maisons d'hôte*, mainly in rural France.

Gîtes de France (www.gites-de-france.com) France's primary umbrella organisation for B&Bs and self-catering properties (*gîtes*); search by region, theme (charm, with kids, by the sea, gourmet, great garden etc), activity (fishing, wine tasting etc) or facilities (pool, dishwasher, fireplace, baby equipment etc).

iGuide (www.iguide-hotels.com) Gorgeous presentation of France's most charming and upmarket B&Bs, organised by region and/or theme (romantic, gastronomic, green, oenological and so forth).

Price Ranges

The following price ranges refer to a double room in high season, with private bathroom (any combination of toilet, bathtub, shower and washbasin), excluding breakfast unless otherwise noted. Breakfast is assumed to be included at a B&B. Where half board (breakfast and dinner) and full board (breakfast, lunch and dinner) is included, this is mentioned with the price.

CATEGORY	COST
€	less than €90 (less than €130 in Paris)
€€	€90–190 (€130–250 in Paris)
€€€	more than €190 (more than €250 in Paris)

Samedi Midi Éditions (www.samedimidi.com) Country, mountain, seaside...choose your *chambre d'hôte* by location or theme (romance, golf, design, cooking courses).

Camping

Be it a Mongolian yurt, boutique treehouse or simple canvas beneath stars, camping in France is in vogue. Thousands of well-equipped campgrounds dot the country, many considerately placed by rivers, lakes and the sea.

○ Most campgrounds open March or April to late September or October; popular spots fill up fast in summer so it is wise to call ahead.

○ 'Sites' refer to fixed-price deals for two people including a tent and a car. Otherwise the price is broken down per adult/tent/car. Factor in a few extra euro per night for *taxe de séjour* (holiday tax) and electricity.

○ Pitching up 'wild' in non-designated spots (*camping sauvage*) is illegal in France.

Websites with campground listings searchable by location, theme and facilities:

Bienvenue à la Ferme (www.bienvenue-a-la-ferme.com)

Camping en France (www.camping.fr)

Camping France (www.campingfrance.com)

Gîtes de France (www.gites-de-france.com)

HPA Guide (http://camping.hpaguide.com)

Climate

Bordeaux

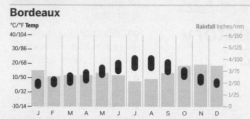

Monaco

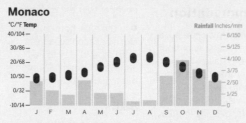

Paris

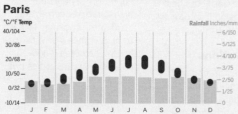

Hostels

Hostels in France range from funky to threadbare, although with a wave of design-driven, up-to-the-minute hostels opening in Paris, Marseille and other big cities, hip hang-outs with perks aplenty seem to easily outweigh the threadbare these days.

○ A dorm bed in an *auberge de jeunesse* (youth hostel) costs €20 to €50 in Paris, and anything from €15 to €40 in the provinces, depending on location, amenities and facilities; sheets are always included, breakfast more often than not.

○ To prevent outbreaks of bed bugs, sleeping bags are not permitted.

○ Hostels by the sea or in the mountains sometimes offer seasonal outdoor activities.

Hotels

Hotels in France are rated with one to five stars, although the ratings are based on highly objective criteria (eg the size of the entry hall), not the quality of the service, the decor or cleanliness.

○ French hotels almost never include breakfast in their rates. Unless specified otherwise, prices quoted don't include breakfast, which costs around €8/12/25 in a budget/midrange/top-end hotel.

○ When you book, hotels usually ask for a credit card number; some require a deposit.

○ A double room generally has one double bed (sometimes two singles pushed together!); a room with twin beds (*deux lits*) is usually more expensive, as is a room with a bathtub instead of a shower.

○ Feather pillows are practically nonexistent in France, even in top-end hotels.

○ All hotel restaurant terraces allow smoking; if you are sensitive to smoke, you may need to sit inside.

Customs Regulations

Goods brought in and out of countries within the EU incur no additional taxes provided duty has been paid somewhere within the EU and the goods are for personal consumption. Duty-free shopping is available only if you are leaving the EU.

Duty-free allowances (for adults) coming from non-EU

countries (including the Channel Islands):

○ 200 cigarettes or 50 cigars or 250g tobacco

○ 1L spirits or 2L of sparkling wine/other alcoholic drinks less than 22% alcohol

○ 4L still wine

○ 16L beer

○ other goods up to the value of €300/430 when entering by land/air or sea (€150 for under 15-year-olds)

Higher limits apply if you are coming from Andorra; anything over these limits must be declared. For further details, see www.douane.gouv.fr (partly in English).

Electricity

230V/50Hz

Book Your Stay Online

For more accommodation reviews by Lonely Planet authors, check out http://hotels.lonelyplanet.com/france. You'll find independent reviews, as well as recommendations on the best places to stay. Best of all, you can book online.

Health

France is a healthy place, so your main risks are likely to be sunburn, foot blisters, insect bites and mild stomach problems from eating and drinking with too much gusto.

Before You Go

○ Bring your medications in their original, clearly labelled, containers.

○ A signed and dated letter from your physician describing your medical conditions and medications, including generic names (French medicine names are often completely different from those in other countries), is also a good idea.

○ Dental care in France is usually good; however, it is sensible to have a dental check-up before a long trip.

In France

Visitors to France can get excellent healthcare from

Which Floor?

In France, as elsewhere in Europe, 'ground floor' refers to the floor at street level; the 1st floor – what would be called the 2nd floor in the US – is the floor above that.

hospital (*hôpital*) emergency rooms/casualty wards (*salles des urgences*) and at a doctor's office (*cabinet médical*).

◦ For minor illnesses, trained staff in pharmacies – in every village and town with a green-cross sign outside that flashes when open – give valuable advice, sell medications, can tell you when more specialised help is needed and will point you in the right direction.

◦ You will need to pay upfront for any healthcare you receive, be it at a doctor's surgery, pharmacy or hospital, unless your insurance plan makes payments directly to providers.

◦ The standard rate for a consultation with a GP/specialist is €30 to €50.

◦ Emergency contraception is available with a doctor's prescription. Condoms (*les préservatifs*) are readily available.

Insurance

◦ Comprehensive travel insurance to cover theft,

loss and medical problems is highly recommended.

◦ Some policies specifically exclude dangerous activities such as scuba diving, motorcycling, skiing and even trekking: read the fine print.

◦ Check that the policy covers ambulances or an emergency flight home.

◦ Find out in advance if your insurance plan will make payments directly to providers or reimburse you later for overseas health expenditures.

◦ If you have to claim later, make sure you keep all documentation.

◦ Paying for your airline ticket with a credit card often provides limited travel accident insurance – ask your credit card company what it is prepared to cover.

◦ Worldwide travel insurance is available at www.lonelyplanet.com/travel-insurance. You can buy, extend and claim online anytime – even if you're already on the road.

Internet Access

◦ Wi-fi (pronounced 'wee-fee' in French) is available at major airports, in most hotels, and at many cafes, restaurants, museums and tourist offices.

◦ Free public wi-fi hotspots are available in cities and many towns: Paris alone has 400 public hotspots

in 26 different locations citywide (www.paris.fr/wifi), including parks, libraries and municipal buildings. In parks look for a purple 'Zone Wi-Fi' sign near the entrance and select the 'PARIS_WI-FI_' network to connect.

◦ To search for free wi-fi hot spots in France, visit www.hotspot-locations.com.

◦ Tourist offices in some larger cities, including Lyon and Bordeaux, rent out pocket-sized mobile wi-fi devices that you carry around with you, ensuring a fast wi-fi connection while roaming the city.

◦ Alternatively, rent a mobile wi-fi device online before leaving home and arrange for it to be delivered by post to your hotel in France through HipPocketWifi (http://hippocketwifi.com), Travel WiFi (http://travel-wifi.com) or My Webspot (http://my-webspot.com).

◦ Internet cafes: at least one can usually be tracked down in cities. Prices range from €2 to €6 per hour.

Legal Matters

Police

◦ French police have wide powers of search and seizure, and can ask you to prove your identity at any time – whether or not there is 'probable cause'.

• Foreigners must be able to prove their legal status in France (eg with a passport, visa or residency permit) without delay.

• If the police stop you for any reason, be polite and remain calm. Verbally (and of course physically) abusing a police officer can lead to a hefty fine, and even imprisonment.

• You may refuse to sign a police statement, and have the right to ask for a copy.

• People who are arrested are considered innocent until proven guilty, but can be held in custody until trial.

Drugs & Alcohol

• French law does not distinguish between 'hard' and 'soft' drugs.

• The penalty for any personal use of *stupéfiants* (including cannabis, amphetamines, ecstasy and heroin) can be a one-year jail sentence and a €3750 fine but, depending on the circumstances, it might be anything from a stern word to a compulsory rehab program.

• Importing, possessing, selling or buying drugs can get you up to 10 years in prison and a fine of up to €500,000.

• Police have been known to search chartered coaches, cars and train passengers for drugs just because they're coming from Amsterdam.

• *Ivresse* (drunkenness) in public is punishable by a fine.

LGBT Travellers

The rainbow flag flies high in France, a country that left its closet long before many of its European neighbours. *Laissez-faire* perfectly sums up France's liberal attitude towards homosexuality and people's private lives in general; in part because of a long tradition of public tolerance towards unconventional lifestyles.

• Paris has been a thriving gay and lesbian centre since the late 1970s, and most major organisations are based there today.

• Attitudes towards homosexuality tend to be more conservative in the countryside and villages.

• France's lesbian scene is less public than its gay male counterpart and is centred mainly on women's cafes and bars.

• Same-sex marriage has been legal in France since May 2013.

• Gay Pride marches are held in major French cities mid-May to early July.

Money

You always get a better exchange rate in-country but it is a good idea to arrive in France with enough euros to take a taxi to a hotel if you have to.

ATMs

Automated Teller Machines (ATMs) – known as *distributeurs automatiques de billets* (DAB) or *points d'argent* in French – are the cheapest and most convenient way to get money. ATMs connected to international networks are situated in all cities and towns, and usually offer an excellent exchange rate.

Credit & Debit Cards

• Credit and debit cards, accepted almost everywhere in France, are convenient, relatively secure and usually offer a better exchange rate than travellers cheques or cash exchanges.

• Credit cards issued in France have embedded chips – you have to type in a PIN to make a purchase.

North Americans, Take Note!

Travellers with credit cards issued in the US, be aware that you might well find yourself occasionally stuck when it comes to paying with your card: certain places in France – notably, Vélib in Paris and bike-share schemes in other cities, self-service toll booths on the autoroute (highway) and garages with self-service petrol (gas) pumps – only accept credit cards with chips and PINs. There is no solution to this bar ensuring you always have an emergency stash of cash on you.

Lost Cards

For lost cards, these numbers operate 24 hours:

Amex (☎01 47 77 72 00)

MasterCard (☎08 00 90 13 87)

Visa (Carte Bleue; ☎08 00 90 11 79)

○ Visa, MasterCard and Amex can be used in shops and supermarkets, and for train travel, car hire and motorway tolls.

○ Don't assume that you can pay for a meal or a budget hotel with a credit card – enquire first.

○ Cash advances are a supremely convenient way to stay stocked up with euros but getting cash with a credit card involves both fees (sometimes US$10 or more) and interest – ask your credit-card issuer for details. Debit-card fees are usually much less.

Exchange Rates

Australia	A$1	€0.70
Canada	C$1	€0.69
Japan	¥100	€0.72
NZ	NZ$1	€0.64
UK	UK£1	€1.26
US	US$1	€0.76

For current exchange rates see www.xe.com.

Money Changers

○ Commercial banks charge up to €5 per foreign-currency transaction – if they even bother to offer exchange services any more.

○ In Paris and major cities, *bureaux de change* (exchange bureaus) are faster and easier, open longer hours and often give better rates than banks.

○ Some post-office branches exchange travellers cheques and banknotes in a variety of currencies but charge a commission for cash; most won't take US$100 bills.

Tipping

By law, restaurant and bar prices are *service compris* (ie they include a 15% service charge), so there is no need to leave a *pourboire* (tip). If you were extremely satisfied with the service, however, you can – as many locals do – show your appreciation by leaving a small 'extra' tip for your waiter.

Bars No tips for drinks served at bar; round to nearest euro for drinks served at table

Cafe 5–10%

Hotel Porter €1–2 per bag

Restaurant 10%

Taxi 10–15%

Toilet Attendant €0.50

Tour Guide €1–2 per person

Opening Hours

Opening hours vary throughout the year. We list high-season opening hours, but remember that longer summer hours often decrease in shoulder and low seasons.

Banks 9am to noon and 2pm to 5pm Monday to Friday or Tuesday to Saturday

Restaurants Noon to 2.30pm and 7pm to 11pm six days a week

Cafes 7am to 11pm

Bars 7pm to 1am

Clubs 10pm to 3am, 4am or 5am Thursday to Saturday

Shops 10am to noon and 2pm to 7pm Monday to Saturday

Public Holidays

The following *jours fériés* (public holidays) are observed in France:

New Year's Day (Jour de l'An) 1 January

Easter Sunday & Monday (Pâques & Lundi de Pâques) Late March/April

May Day (Fête du Travail) 1 May

Victoire 1945 8 May

Ascension Thursday (Ascension) May; on the 40th day after Easter

Pentecost/Whit Sunday & Whit Monday (Pentecôte & Lundi de Pentecôte) Mid-May to mid-June; on the seventh Sunday after Easter

Bastille Day/National Day (Fête Nationale) 14 July

Assumption Day (Assomption) 15 August

All Saints' Day (Toussaint) 1 November

Remembrance Day (L'onze Novembre) 11 November

Christmas (Noël) 25 December

The following are *not* public holidays in France: Shrove Tuesday (Mardi Gras; the first day of Lent); Maundy (or Holy) Thursday and Good Friday, just before Easter; and Boxing Day (26 December).

Telephone

Mobile Phones

● French mobile phone numbers begin with 06 or 07.

● France uses GSM 900/1800, which is compatible with the rest of Europe and Australia but not with the North American GSM 1900 or the totally different system in Japan (though some North Americans have tri-band phones that work here).

● Check with your service provider about roaming charges – dialling a mobile phone from a fixed-line phone or another mobile can be incredibly expensive.

● It is usually cheaper to buy a local SIM card from a French provider such as Orange, SFR, Bouygues and Free Mobile, which gives you a local phone number. To do this, ensure your phone is unlocked.

● If you already have a compatible phone, you can slip in a SIM card (from €3.90) and rev it up with prepaid credit, though this is likely to run out fast as domestic prepaid calls cost about €0.50 per minute.

● Recharge cards are sold at most *tabacs* (tobacconist-newsagents), supermarkets and online through websites such as Topengo (www.topengo.fr) or Sim-OK (https://recharge.sim-ok.com).

Phone Codes

Calling France from abroad Dial your country's international access code, then 33 (France's country code), then the 10-digit local number *without* the initial zero.

Calling internationally from France Dial 00 (the international access code), the *indicatif* (country code), the area code (without the initial zero if there is one) and the local number.

Some country codes are posted in public telephones.

Directory inquiries For national *service des renseignements* (directory inquiries), dial 11 87 12 or use the service for free online at www.118712.fr.

International directory inquiries For numbers outside France, dial 11 87 00.

Time

France uses the 24-hour clock and is on Central European Time, which is one hour ahead of GMT/UTC. During daylight saving time, which runs from the last Sunday in March to the last Sunday in October, France

---

Practicalities

Laundry Virtually all French cities and towns have at least one *laverie libre-service* (self-service laundrette). Machines run on coins.

Smoking Illegal in all indoor public spaces, including restaurants and pubs (though, of course, smokers still light up on the terraces outside).

Newspapers & Magazines Locals read their news in centre-left *Le Monde* (www.lemonde.fr), right-leaning *Le Figaro* (www.lefigaro.fr) or left-leaning *Libération* (www.liberation.fr).

Radio For news, tune in to the French-language France Info (105.5MHz; www.franceinfo.fr), multilanguage RFI (738kHz or 89MHz in Paris; www.rfi.fr) or, in northern France, the BBC World Service (648kHz) and BBC Radio 4 (198kHz). Popular national FM music stations include NRJ (www.nrj.fr), Virgin (www.virginradio.fr), La Radio Plus (www.laradioplus.com) and Nostalgie (www.nostalgie.fr).

TV & Video TV is Secam; videos work on the PAL system.

Weights & Measures France uses the metric system.

is two hours ahead of GMT/ UTC.

Toilets

Public toilets, signposted WC or *toilettes,* are not always plentiful in France, especially outside the big cities.

Love them (as a sci-fi geek) or loathe them (as a claustrophobe), France's 24-hour self-cleaning toilets are here to stay. Outside Paris these mechanical WCs are free, but in Paris they cost around €0.50 a go. Don't even think about nipping in after someone else to avoid paying unless you fancy a *douche* (shower) with disinfectant.

Some older establishments and motorway stops still have the hole-in-the-floor *toilettes à la turque* (squat toilets).

The French are completely blasé about unisex toilets, so save your blushes when tiptoeing past the urinals to reach the ladies' loo.

Tourist Information

Almost every city, town and village has an *office de tourisme* (a tourist office run by some unit of local government) or *syndicat d'initiative* (a tourist office run by an organisation of local merchants). Both are

excellent resources and can supply you with local maps as well as details on accommodation, restaurants and activities.

Useful websites:

French Government Tourist Office (www.france.fr) The lowdown on sights, activities, transport and special-interest holidays in all of France's regions. Brochures can be downloaded online.

French Tourist Offices (www.tourisme.fr) Website of tourist offices in France, with mountains of inspirational information organised by theme and region.

Travellers with Disabilities

While France presents evident challenges for *visiteurs handicapés* (disabled visitors) – cobblestones, cafe-lined streets that are a nightmare to navigate in a wheelchair *(fauteuil roulant),* a lack of kerb ramps, older public facilities and many budget hotels without lifts – don't let that stop you from visiting. Efforts are being made to improve the situation and with a little careful planning, a hassle-free accessible stay is possible. Download Lonely Planet's free Accessible Travel guide from http://lp-travel.to/AccessibleTravel.

○ Paris tourist office runs the excellent 'Tourisme & Handicap' initiative whereby museums, cultural

attractions, hotels and restaurants that provide access or special assistance or facilities for those with physical, mental, visual and/or hearing disabilities display a special logo at their entrances. For a list of qualifying places, go to www.parisinfo.com and click on 'Practical Paris'.

○ Paris metro, most of it built decades ago, is hopeless. Line 14 of the metro was built to be wheelchair-accessible, although in reality it remains extremely challenging to navigate in a wheelchair – unlike Paris buses which are 100% accessible.

○ Parisian taxi company Horizon, part of Taxis G7 (www.taxisg7.fr), has cars especially adapted to carry wheelchairs and drivers trained in helping passengers with disabilities.

○ Countrywide, many SNCF train carriages are accessible to people with disabilities. A traveller in a wheelchair can travel in both the TGV and in the 1st-class carriage with a 2nd-class ticket on mainline trains provided they make a reservation by phone or at a train station at least a few hours before departure. Details are available in the SNCF booklet *Le Mémento du Voyageur Handicapé (Handicapped Traveller Summary)* available at all train stations.

Accès Plus (☑09 69 32 26 26, 08 90 64 06 50; www. accessibilite.sncf.com) The

SNCF assistance service for rail travellers with disabilities. Can advise on station accessibility and arrange a *fauteuil roulant* or help getting on or off a train.

Access Travel (in UK 01942-888 844; www.access-travel.co.uk) Specialised UK-based agency for accessible travel.

Infomobi.com (09 70 81 83 85; www.infomobi.com) Has comprehensive information on accessible travel in Paris and the surrounding Île de France area.

Mobile en ville (09 52 29 60 51; www.mobile-en-ville.asso.fr; 8 rue des Mariniers, 14e, Paris) Association that works hard to make independent travel within Paris easier for people in wheelchairs. Among other things it organises some great family *randonnées* (walks) in and around Paris.

Tourisme et Handicaps (01 44 11 10 41; www.tourisme-hand-icaps.org; 43 rue Marx Dormoy, 18e, Paris) Issues the 'Tourisme et Handicap' label to tourist sites, restaurants and hotels that comply with strict accessibility and usability standards. Different symbols indicate the sort of access afforded to people with physical, mental, hearing and/or visual disabilities.

Visas

○ For up-to-date details on visa requirements, see the website of the **Ministère des Affaires Étrangères** (Ministry of Foreign Affairs; www.diplomatie.gouv.fr; 37 quai d'Orsay, 7e, Paris; Assemblée Nationale) and click 'Coming to France'.

○ EU nationals and citizens of Iceland, Norway and Switzerland need only a passport or a national identity card to enter France and stay in the country, even for stays of over 90 days. However, citizens of new EU member states may be subject to various limitations on living and working in France.

○ Citizens of Australia, the USA, Canada, Hong Kong, Israel, Japan, Malaysia, New Zealand, Singapore, South Korea and many Latin American countries do not need visas to visit France as tourists for up to 90 days. For long stays of over 90 days, contact your nearest French embassy or consulate and begin your application well in advance, as it can take months.

○ Other people wishing to come to France as tourists have to apply for a Schengen Visa, named after the agreements that have abolished passport controls between 26 European countries. It allows unlimited travel throughout the entire zone for a 90-day period. Apply to the consulate of the country you are entering first, or your main destination. Among other things, you need travel and repatriation insurance, and to be able to show that you have sufficient funds to support yourself.

○ Tourist visas cannot be changed into student visas after arrival. However, short-term visas are available for students sitting university-entrance exams in France.

○ Tourist visas cannot be extended except in emergencies (such as medical problems). When your visa expires you'll need to leave and reapply from outside France.

Transport

Getting There & Away

Flights, cars and tours can be booked online at www.lonelyplanet.com/bookings.

Air

Air France (www.airfrance.com) is the national carrier, with plenty of both domestic and international flights in and out of major French airports.

Bicycle

Transporting a bicycle to France is a breeze.

On **Eurotunnel Le Shuttle** (in France 08 10 63 03 04, in UK 08443 35 35 35; www.eurotunnel.com) trains through the Channel Tunnel, the fee for a bicycle, including its rider, is from UK£20 one way.

A bike that's been dismantled to the size of

Climate Change & Travel

Every form of transport that relies on carbon-based fuel generates CO_2, the main cause of human-induced climate change. Modern travel is dependent on aeroplanes, which might use less fuel per kilometre per person than most cars but travel much greater distances. The altitude at which aircraft emit gases (including CO_2) and particles also contributes to their climate change impact. Many websites offer 'carbon calculators' that allow people to estimate the carbon emissions generated by their journey and, for those who wish to do so, to offset the impact of the greenhouse gases emitted with contributions to portfolios of climate-friendly initiatives throughout the world. Lonely Planet offsets the carbon footprint of all staff and author travel.

a suitcase can be carried on board a **Eurostar** (🖉in France 08 92 35 35 39, in UK 08432 186 186; www.eurostar. com) train from London or Brussels just like any other luggage. Otherwise, there's a UK£30 charge and you'll need advance reservations. For links relevant to taking your bike on other international trains to France, see RailPassenger Info (www. railpassenger.info).

On ferries, foot passengers – where allowed – can usually (but not always) bring along a bicycle for no charge.

European Bike Express (🖉in UK 01430 422 111; www. bike-express.co.uk) transports cyclists and their bikes from the UK to places around France.

Bus

Eurolines (🖉08 92 89 90 91; www.eurolines.eu), a grouping of 32 long-haul coach operators (including the UK's National Express),

links France with cities all across Europe, Morocco and Russia. Discounts are available to people under 26 and over 60. Make advance reservations, especially in July and August.

A single Paris–London fare is between €18 and €40, including a Channel crossing by ferry or the Channel Tunnel. Book as far ahead as possible to bag the cheapest ticket.

Car & Motorcycle

A right-hand-drive vehicle brought to France from the UK or Ireland must have deflectors affixed to the headlights to avoid dazzling oncoming traffic. In the UK, information on driving in France is available from the RAC (www.rac.co.uk/driving-abroad/france) and the AA (www.theaa.com).

A foreign motor vehicle entering France must display a sticker or licence plate identifying its country of registration.

Eurotunnel

The Channel Tunnel (Chunnel), inaugurated in 1994, is the first dry-land link between England and France since the last ice age.

High-speed **Eurotunnel Le Shuttle** (🖉in France 08 10 63 03 04, in UK 08443 35 35 35; www.eurotunnel.com) trains whisk bicycles, motorcycles, cars and coaches in 35 minutes from Folkestone through the Channel Tunnel to Coquelles, 5km southwest of Calais. Shuttles run 24 hours a day, with up to three departures an hour during peak periods. LPG and CNG tanks are not permitted, meaning gas-powered cars and many campers and caravans have to travel by ferry.

Eurotunnel sets its fares the way budget airlines do: the further in advance you book and the lower the demand for a particular crossing, the less you pay; same-day fares can cost a small fortune. Fares for a car, including up to nine passengers, start at UK£23/€32.

Train

Rail services link France with virtually every country in Europe.

⊙ Book tickets and get train information from Rail Europe (www.raileurope.com). In the UK contact Railteam (www.railteam.co.uk).

⊙ A very useful train-travel resource is the information-packed website The

Man in Seat 61 (www.seat61.com).

Eurostar

The **Eurostar** (☎in France 08 92 35 35 39, in UK 08432 186 186; www.eurostar.com) whisks you from London to Paris in 2¼ hours.

Except late at night, trains link London (St Pancras International) with Paris (Gare du Nord; hourly), Calais (Calais-Fréthun; one hour, three daily), Lille (Gare Lille Europe, 1½ hours, eight daily), Disneyland Resort Paris (2½ hours, one direct daily), Lyon (4¾ hours, one to five per week), Avignon (5¾ hours, one to five per week) and Marseille (6½ hours, one to five per week), with less frequent services departing from Ebbsfleet and Ashford in Kent. Weekend ski trains connect England with the French Alps late December to mid-April. Potential future new routes include a direct London–Bordeaux service.

Eurostar offers a bewildering array of fares. A semi-flexible 2nd-class one-way ticket from Paris to London costs €66.50; super-discount fares start at €39.

For the best deals buy a return ticket, stay over a Saturday night, book up to 120 days in advance and don't mind nonexchangeability and nonrefundability. Discount fares are available for under 26s or over 60s.

Sea

Some ferry companies have started setting fares the way budget airlines do: the longer in advance you book and the lower the demand for a particular sailing, the less you pay. Seasonal demand is a crucial factor (Christmas, Easter, UK and French school holidays, July and August are especially busy), as is the time of day (an early-evening ferry can cost much more than one at 4am). People under 25 and over 60 may qualify for discounts.

To get the best fares, check **Ferry Savers** (☎in UK 0844 371 8021; www.ferrysavers.com).

Foot passengers are not allowed on Dover–Boulogne, Dover–Dunkirk or Dover–Calais car ferries except for daytime (and, from Calais to Dover, evening) crossings run by P&O Ferries. On ferries that do allow foot passengers, taking a bicycle is usually free.

Getting Around

Driving is the simplest way to get around France but a car is a liability in traffic-plagued, parking-starved city centres, and petrol bills and *autoroute* (dual carriageway/divided highway) tolls add up.

France is famous for its excellent public-transport network, which serves everywhere bar some very rural areas. The state-owned Société Nationale des Chemins de Fer Français (SNCF) takes care of almost all land transport between *départements* (counties). Transport within *départements* is handled by a combination of short-haul trains, SNCF buses and local bus companies.

Bicycle

France is great for cycling. Much of the countryside is drop-dead gorgeous and the country has a growing number of urban and rural *pistes cyclables* (bike paths and lanes; see Voies Vertes online at www.voievertes.com) and an extensive network of secondary and tertiary roads with relatively light traffic.

French law requires that bicycles must have two functioning brakes, a bell, a red reflector on the back and yellow reflectors on the pedals. After sunset and when visibility is poor, cyclists must turn on a white headlamp and a red tail lamp. When being overtaken by a vehicle, cyclists must ride in single file. Towing children in a bike trailer is permitted.

Never leave your bicycle locked up outside overnight if you want to see it – or at least most of its parts – again. Some hotels offer enclosed bicycle parking.

Bicycle Rental

Most French cities and towns have at least one bike shop that rents out *vélos tout terrains* (mountain bikes; around €15 a day), known as VTTs, as well as more road-oriented *vélos tout chemin* (VTCs), or cheaper city bikes. You usually have to leave ID and/or a deposit (often a credit-card slip of €250) that you forfeit if the bike is damaged or stolen.

A growing number of cities – including Paris, Lyon, Aix-en-Provence, Bordeaux, Caen, Marseille, Nice, Rouen and Vannes – have automatic bike-rental systems, intended to encourage cycling as a form of urban transport, with computerised pick-up and drop-off sites all over town. In general, you have to sign up either short term or long term, providing credit-card details, and can then use the bikes for no charge for the first half-hour; after that, hourly charges rise quickly.

Car & Motorcycle

Having your own wheels gives you exceptional freedom and makes it easy to visit more remote parts of France. Depending on the number of passengers, it can also work out cheaper than the train. For example, by autoroute, the 930km drive from Paris to Nice (9½ hours of driving) in a small car costs about €75 for petrol and another €75 in tolls – by comparison, a one-way, 2nd-class TGV ticket for the 5½-hour Paris to Nice run costs anything from €45 to €140 per person.

In the cities, traffic and finding a place to park can be a major headache. During holiday periods and bank-holiday weekends, roads throughout France also get backed up with traffic jams *(bouchons)*.

Motorcyclists will find France great for touring, with winding roads of good quality and lots of stunning scenery. Just make sure your wet-weather gear is up to scratch.

France (along with Belgium) has the densest highway network in Europe. There are four types of intercity roads:

Autoroutes (highway names beginning with A) Multilane divided highways, usually (except near Calais and Lille) with tolls *(péages)*. Generously outfitted with rest stops.

Routes Nationales (N, RN) National highways. Some sections have divider strips.

Routes Départementales (D) Local highways and roads.

Routes Communales (C, V) Minor rural roads.

For information on autoroute tolls, rest areas, traffic and weather, go to the Sociétés d'Autoroutes website (www. autoroutes.fr).

Bison Futé (www.bison-fute.equipement.gouv.fr) is also a good source of information about traffic conditions. Plot itineraries between your departure and arrival points, and calculate toll costs with an online mapper like Via Michelin (www.viamichelin.com) or Mappy (www.mappy.fr).

Theft from cars is a major problem in France, especially in the south.

Car Hire

To hire a car in France, you'll generally need to be over 21 years old, have had a driving licence for at least a year, and have an international credit card. Drivers under 25 usually have to pay a surcharge *(frais jeune conducteur)* of €25 to €35 per day.

Car-hire companies provide mandatory third-party liability insurance but things such as collision-damage waivers (CDW, or *assurance tous risques*) vary greatly from company to company. When comparing rates and conditions (ie the fine print), the most important thing to check is the *franchise* (deductible/excess), which for a small car is usually around €600 for damage and €800 for theft. With many companies, you can reduce the excess by half, and perhaps to zero, by paying a daily insurance supplement of up to €20. Your credit card may cover CDW if you use it to pay for the rental but the car-hire company won't know anything about this – verify conditions and details with your credit-card issuer to be sure.

Arranging your car hire or fly/drive package before you leave home is usually considerably cheaper than a walk-in rental, but beware of website offers that don't include a CDW or you may be liable for up to 100% of the car's value.

International car-hire companies:

Avis (☑08 21 23 07 60, from abroad 01 70 99 47 35; www. avis.com)

Budget (☑08 25 00 35 64; www.budget.fr)

EasyCar (☑in France 08 26 10 73 23, in the UK 0800 640 7000; www.easycar.com)

Europcar (☑08 25 35 83 58; www.europcar.com)

Hertz (☑01 41 91 95 25, 08 25 86 18 61; www.hertz.com)

Sixt (☑08 20 00 74 98; www. sixt.fr)

French car-hire companies:

ADA (☑08 99 46 46 36; www. ada.fr)

DLM (www.dlm.fr)

France Cars (www.trancecars.tr)

Locauto (☑04 93 07 72 62; www.locauto.fr)

Renault Rent (☑08 25 10 11 12; www.renault-rent.com)

Rent a Car (☑08 91 700 200; www.rentacar.fr)

Deals can be found on the internet and through such companies as:

Auto Europe (☑in USA 888-223-5555; www.autoeurope. com)

DriveAway Holidays (☑in Australia 1300 363 500; www. driveaway.com.au)

Holiday Autos (☑in UK 020 3740 9859; www.holidayautos. co.uk)

Rental cars with automatic transmission are very much the exception in France; they usually need to be ordered well in advance and are more expensive than manual cars.

For insurance reasons, it is usually forbidden to take rental cars on ferries; eg to Corsica.

All rental cars registered in France have a distinctive number on the licence plate, making them easily identifiable – including to thieves. *Never* leave anything of value in a parked car, even in the boot (trunk).

Driving Licence & Documents

An International Driving Permit (IDP), valid only if accompanied by your original licence, is good for a year and can be issued by your local automobile association before you leave home.

Drivers must carry the following at all times:

○ passport or an EU national ID card

○ valid driving licence (*permis de conduire;* most foreign licences can be used in France for up to a year)

○ car-ownership papers, known as a *carte grise* (grey card)

○ proof of third-party liability *assurance* (insurance)

Fuel

Essence (petrol), also known as *carburant* (fuel), costs around €1.28 per litre for 95 unleaded (Sans Plomb 95 or SP95, usually available from a green pump) and €1 to €1.30 for diesel (*diesel, gazole* or *gasoil,* usually available from a yellow pump). Check and compare current prices countrywide at www.prix-carburants. gouv.fr.

Filling up *(faire le plein)* is most expensive at autoroute rest stops, and usually cheapest at hypermarkets.

Many small petrol stations close on Sunday

Speed Fiends, Take Note

When it comes to catching and punishing speed fiends, France has upped its act in recent years. Automatic speed cameras, not necessarily visible, are widespread and the chances are you'll get 'flashed' at least once during your trip. Should this occur, a letter from the French government (stamped 'Liberté, Egalité, Fraternité – Liberty, Equality, Fraternity') will land on your doormat informing you of your *amende* (fine) and, should you hold a French licence, how many points you have lost. Motorists driving up to 20km/h over the limit in a 50km/h zone are fined €68 and one point; driving up to 20km/h over the limit in a zone with a speed limit of more than 50km/h costs €135 and one point.

There is no room for complacency. Moreover should you be driving a rental car, the rental company will charge you an additional fee for the time they spent sharing your contact details with the French government.

afternoons and, even in cities, it can be hard to find a staffed station open late at night. In general, after-hours purchases (eg at hypermarkets' fully automatic, 24-hour stations) can only be made with a credit card that has an embedded PIN chip, so if all you've got is cash or a magnetic-strip credit card, you could be stuck.

Insurance

Third-party liability insurance (assurance au tiers) is compulsory for all vehicles in France, including cars brought in from abroad. Normally, cars registered and insured in other European countries can circulate freely in France, but it's a good idea to contact your insurance company before you leave home to make sure you have coverage – and to check who to contact in case of a breakdown or accident.

If you get into a minor accident with no injuries, the easiest way for drivers to sort things out with their insurance companies is to fill out a Constat Aimable d'Accident Automobile (European Accident Statement), a standardised way of recording important details about what happened.

Travel Conditions

In many areas, Autoroute Info (107.7MHz; www. autorouteinfo.fr) has round-the-clock traffic information for motorists.

In rental cars it's usually in the packet of documents in the glove compartment. Make sure the report includes any information that will help you prove that the accident was not your fault. Remember, if it *was* your fault you may be liable for a hefty insurance deductible/ excess. Don't sign anything you don't fully understand. If problems crop up, call the police (☎17).

French-registered cars have details of their insurance company printed on a little green square affixed to the windscreen.

Parking

In city centres, most on-the-street parking places are *payant* (metered) from about 9am to 7pm (sometimes with a break from noon to 2pm) Monday to Saturday, except bank holidays.

Road Rules

Enforcement of French traffic laws (see www.securiteroutiere.gouv.fr) has been stepped up considerably in recent years. Speed cameras are common, as are radar traps and unmarked police vehicles. Fines for many infractions are given on the spot, and serious violations can lead to the confiscation of your driving licence and car.

Speed limits outside built-up areas (except where signposted otherwise):

Undivided N & D highways 90km/h (80km/h when raining)

Non-autoroute divided highways 110km/h (100km/h when raining)

Autoroutes 130km/h (110km/h when raining, 60km/h in icy conditions)

To reduce carbon emissions, autoroute speed limits have recently been reduced to 110km/h in some areas.

Unless otherwise signposted, a limit of 50km/h applies in *all* areas designated as built up, no matter how rural they may appear. You must slow to 50km/h the moment you come to a white sign with a red border and a place name written on it; the speed limit applies until you pass an identical sign with a horizontal bar through it.

Other important driving rules:

● Blood-alcohol limit is 0.05% (0.5g per litre of blood) – the equivalent of two glasses of wine for a 75kg adult. Police often conduct random breathalyser tests and penalties can be severe, including imprisonment.

● All passengers, including those in the back seat, must wear seat belts.

● Mobile phones may be used only if they are equipped with a hands-free kit or speakerphone.

● Turning right on a red light is illegal.

● Cars from the UK and Ireland must have deflectors affixed to their headlights to avoid dazzling oncoming motorists.

Priority to the Right

Under the *priorité à droite* ('priority to the right') rule, any car entering an intersection (including a T-junction) from a road (including a tiny village backstreet) on your right has the right of way. Locals assume every driver knows this, so don't be surprised if they courteously cede the right of way when you're about to turn from an alley onto a highway – and boldly assert their rights when you're the one zipping down a main road.

Priorité à droite is suspended (eg on arterial roads) when you pass a sign showing an upended yellow square with a black square in the middle. The same sign with a horizontal bar through the square lozenge reinstates the *priorité à droite* rule.

When you arrive at a roundabout at which you do not have the right of way (ie the cars already in the roundabout do), you'll often see signs reading *vous n'avez pas la priorité* (you do not have right of way) or *cédez le passage* (give way).

 • Radar detectors, even if they're switched off, are illegal; fines are hefty.

 • Children under 10 are not permitted to ride in the front seat (unless the back is already occupied by other children under 10).

 • A child under 13kg must travel in a backward-facing child seat (permitted in the front seat only for babies under 9kg and if the airbag is deactivated).

 • Up to age 10 and/or a minimum height of 140cm, children must use a size-appropriate type of front-facing child seat or booster.

 • All vehicles driven in France must carry a high-visibility reflective safety vest (stored inside the vehicle, not in the trunk/boot), a reflective triangle and a portable, single-use breathalyser kit.

 • If you'll be driving on snowy roads, make sure you have snow chains (*chaînes neige*), required by law whenever and wherever the police post signs.

 • Riders of any type of two-wheeled vehicle with a motor (except motor-assisted bicycles) must wear a helmet. No special licence is required to ride a motorbike whose engine is smaller than 50cc, which is why rental scooters are often rated at 49.9cc.

Hitching

Hitching is never entirely safe in any country in the world, and we don't recommend it. Travellers who decide to hitch should understand that they are taking a small but potentially serious risk. Remember that it's safer to travel in pairs and be sure to inform someone of your intended destination. Hitching is not really part of French culture.

Hitching from city centres is pretty much hopeless, so your best bet is to take public transport to the outskirts. It is illegal to hitch on autoroutes, but you can stand near an entrance ramp as long as you don't block traffic. Hitching in remote rural areas is better, but once you

get off the *routes nationales* traffic can be light and local. If your itinerary includes a ferry crossing, it's worth trying to score a ride before the ferry since vehicle tickets usually include a number of passengers free of charge. At dusk, give up and think about finding somewhere to stay.

Ride Share

A number of organisations around France arrange *covoiturage* (car sharing); ie putting people looking for rides in touch with drivers going to the same destination. The best known is Allo Stop (www.allostop.net) where you pay €3/5/8/10 for a single journey up to 50/100/150/200km. You might also try Covoiturage (www.covoiturage.fr), Bla Bla Car (www.blablacar.fr) or, for international journeys, Karzoo (www.karzoo.eu).

Local Transport

France's cities and larger towns have world-class public-transport systems.

There are *métros* (underground subway systems) in Paris, Lyon, Marseille, Lille and Toulouse, and ultramodern light-rail lines (*tramways*) in cities such as Bordeaux, Grenoble, Lille, Lyon, Nancy, Nantes, Nice, Reims, Rouen and Strasbourg, as well as parts of greater Paris.

In addition to a *billet à l'unité* (single ticket), you can purchase a *carnet* (booklet or bunch) of 10 tickets or a *pass journée* (all-day pass).

Train

Travelling by train in France is a comfortable and environmentally sustainable way to see the country. Since many train stations have car-hire agencies, it's easy to combine rail travel with rural exploration by car.

The jewel in the crown of France's public-transport system – alongside the Paris *métro* – is its extensive rail network, almost all of it run by **SNCF** (Société Nationale des Chemins de fer Français, French National Railway Company; ☑from abroad +33 8 92 35 35 35, in France 36 35; http://en.voyages-sncf.com). Although it employs the most advanced rail technology, the network's layout reflects the country's centuries-old Paris-centric nature: most of the principal rail lines radiate out from Paris like the spokes of a wheel, the result being that services between provincial towns situated on different spokes can be infrequent and slow.

Up-to-the-minute information on *perturbations* (service disruptions), eg because of strikes, can be found on www.infolignes. com.

Since its inauguration in the 1980s, the pride and joy of SNCF is the TGV (Train à Grande Vitesse; www.tgv. com), pronounced 'teh zheh veh', which zips passengers along at speeds of up to 320km/h (198mph).

The main TGV lines (or LGVs, short for *lignes à grande vitesse;* ie high-speed rail lines) head north, east, southeast and southwest from Paris (trains use slower local tracks to get to destinations off the main line):

TGV Nord, Thalys & Eurostar Link Paris Gare du Nord with Arras, Lille, Calais, Brussels (Bruxelles-Midi), Amsterdam, Cologne and, via the Channel Tunnel, Ashford, Ebbsfleet and London St Pancras.

LGV Est Européene (www. lgv-est.com) Connects Paris Gare de l'Est with Reims, Nancy, Metz, Strasbourg, Zurich and Germany, including Frankfurt and Stuttgart. The super-high-speed track stretching as far east as Strasbourg opened in July 2016.

TGV Sud-Est & TGV Midi-Méditerranée Link Paris Gare de Lyon with the southeast, including Dijon, Lyon, Geneva, the Alps, Avignon, Marseille, Nice and Montpellier.

TGV Atlantique Sud-Ouest & TGV Atlantique Ouest Link Paris Gare Montparnasse with western and southwestern France, including Brittany

(Rennes, Brest, Quimper), Tours, Nantes, Poitiers, La Rochelle, Bordeaux, Biarritz and Toulouse.

LGV Rhin-Rhône High-speed rail route bypasses Paris altogether in its bid to better link the provinces. Six services a day speed between Strasbourg and Lyon, with most continuing south to Marseille or Montpellier on the Mediterranean.

TGV tracks are interconnected, making it possible to go directly from, say, Lyon to Nantes or Bordeaux to Lille without having to switch trains in Paris or transfer from one of Paris' six main train stations to another. Stops on the link-up, which runs east and south of Paris, include Charles de Gaulle airport and Disneyland Resort Paris.

Long-distance trains sometimes split at a station – that is, each half of the train heads off for a different destination. Check the destination panel on your car as you board or you could wind up very far from where you intended to go.

Other types of trains:

Téoz (www.corailteoz.com) Especially comfortable trains that run southward from Paris Gare d'Austerlitz to Clermont-Ferrand, Limoges, Cahors, Toulouse, Montpellier, Perpignan, Marseille and Nice.

TER (Train Express Régional; www.ter-sncf.com) A train that is not a TGV is often referred to as a *corail*, a *classique* or, for intraregional services, a TER.

Transilien (www.transilien. com) SNCF services in the Île de France area in and around Paris.

SNCF Fares & Discounts

Full-fare tickets can be quite expensive. Fortunately, a dizzying array of discounts are available and station staff are very good about helping travellers find the very best fare. But first, the basics:

º 1st-class travel, where available, costs 20% to 30% extra

º Ticket prices for some trains, including most TGVs, are pricier during peak periods.

º The further in advance you reserve, the lower the fares.

º Children under four travel for free, or €9 with a *forfait bambin* to any destination if they need a seat.

º Children aged four to 11 travel for half price.

Ouigo & iDTGV

Ouigo (www.ouigo.com) is a low-cost TGV service whereby you can travel on high-speed TGVs for a snip of the usual price. Ouigo trains only serve a handful of TGV stations, including Aix-en-Provence, Avignon, Marseille, Nîmes and Paris Disneyland's Marne-La Vallée-Chessy.

º Tickets can only be purchased online from three weeks until four hours

before departure; tickets are emailed four days before departure and must be printed out or readable on a smartphone with the Ouigo app (iPhone and Android).

º The minimum single fare is €10. Children under 12 pay a flat €5 single fare.

º To plug in while aboard, reserve a seat with electric plug socket for an additional €2.

Not to be confused with Ouigo is **IDTGV** (www. idtgv.com), another SNCF subsidiary that sells tickets (online only) for as little as €19 for advance-purchase TGV travel between 30-odd cities.

Discount Tickets

The SNCF's most heavily discounted tickets are called **Prem's**, available online, at ticket windows and from ticket machines: 100% Prem's are available from Thursday evening to Monday night, for last-minute travel that weekend; Saturday-return Prem's are valid for return travel on a Saturday; and three-month Prem's can be booked a maximum of 90 days in advance. Prem's are nonrefundable and nonchangeable.

Bons Plans (Special Deals) fares, a grab bag of really cheap options, are advertised on the SNCF website under 'Fares & Cards/Special Deals'.

On regional trains, discount fares requiring neither a discount card nor advance purchase include:

Loisir Week-End rates Good for return travel that includes a Saturday night at your destination or involves travel on a Saturday or Sunday.

Découverte fares Available for low-demand 'blue-period' trains to people aged 12 to 25, seniors and the adult travel companions of children under 12.

Mini-Groupe tickets In some regions, these bring big savings for three to six people travelling together, provided you spend a Saturday night at your destination.

Discount Cards

Reductions of at least 25% (for last-minute bookings), and of 40%, 50% or even 60% (if you reserve well ahead or travel during low-volume 'blue' periods), are available with several discount cards (valid for one year):

Carte Jeune (€50) Available to travellers aged 12 to 27.

Carte Enfant+ (€75) For one to four adults travelling with a child aged four to 11.

Carte Weekend (€75) For people aged 26 to 59. Discounts on return journeys of at least 200km that either include a Saturday night away or only involve travel on a Saturday or Sunday.

Carte Sénior+ (€60) For travellers over 60.

Language

The sounds used in spoken French can almost all be found in English. There are a couple of exceptions: nasal vowels (represented in our pronunciation guides by 'o' or 'u' followed by an almost inaudible nasal consonant sound 'm', 'n' or 'ng'), the 'funny' *u* sound ('ew' in our guides) and the deep-in-the-throat *r*. Bearing these few points in mind and reading our pronunciation guides below as if they were English, you'll be understood just fine. The markers (m) and (f) indicate the forms for male and female speakers respectively.

To enhance your trip with a phrasebook, visit **lonelyplanet.com**. Lonely Planet iPhone phrasebooks are available through the Apple App store.

Basics

Hello.
Bonjour. — bon·zhoor

Goodbye.
Au revoir. — o·rer·vwa

How are you?
Comment allez-vous? — ko·mon ta·lay·voo

I'm fine, thanks.
Bien, merci. — byun mair·see

Please.
S'il vous plaît. — seel voo play

Thank you.
Merci. — mair·see

Excuse me.
Excusez-moi. — ek·skew·zay·mwa

Sorry.
Pardon. — par·don

Yes./No.
Oui./Non. — wee/non

I don't understand.
Je ne comprends pas. — zher ner kom·pron pa

Do you speak English?
Parlez-vous anglais? — par·lay·voo ong·glay

Shopping

I'd like to buy ...
Je voudrais acheter ... — zher voo·dray ash·tay ...

I'm just looking.
Je regarde. — zher rer·gard

How much is it?
C'est combien? — say kom·byun

It's too expensive.
C'est trop cher. — say tro shair

Can you lower the price?
Vous pouvez baisser le prix? — voo poo·vay bay·say ler pree

Eating & Drinking

..., please.
..., s'il vous plaît. — ... seel voo play

A coffee	*un café*	un ka·fay
A table	*une table*	ewn ta·bler
for two	*pour deux*	poor der
Two beers	*deux bières*	der bee·yair

I'm a vegetarian.
Je suis végétarien/végétarienne. (m/f) — zher swee vay·zhay·ta·ryun/vay·zhay·ta·ryen

Cheers!
Santé! — son·tay

That was delicious!
C'était délicieux! — say·tay day·lee·syer

The bill, please.
L'addition, s'il vous plaît. — la·dee·syon seel voo play

Emergencies

Help!
Au secours! — o skoor

Call the police!
Appelez la police! — a·play la po·lees

Call a doctor!
Appelez un médecin! — a·play un mayd·sun

I'm sick.
Je suis malade. — zher swee ma·lad

I'm lost.
Je suis perdu/perdue. (m/f) — zhe swee pair·dew

Where are the toilets?
Où sont les toilettes? — oo son lay twa·let

Transport & Directions

Where's ...?
Où est ...? — oo ay ...

What's the address?
Quelle est l'adresse? — kel ay la·dres

Behind the Scenes

Acknowledgements

Climate map data adapted from Peel MC, Finlayson BL & McMahon TA (2007) 'Updated World Map of the Köppen-Geiger Climate Classification', *Hydrology and Earth System Sciences*, 11, 163344.

This Book

This guidebook was curated by Nicola Williams, who also researched and wrote for it along with Alexis Averbuck, Oliver Berry, Jean-Bernard Carrillet, Kerry Christiani, Catherine Le Nevez, Hugh McNaughtan, Christopher Pitts, Daniel Robinson and Regis St Louis. This guidebook was produced by the following:

Destination Editors Helen Elfer, Daniel Fahey

Product Editors Kathryn Rowan, Elizabeth Jones

Senior Cartographer Mark Griffiths

Book Designers Jessica Rose, Wibowo Rusli

Assisting Editors Janet Austin, Katie Connolly, Victoria Harrison

Cartographer Gabe Lindquist

Assisting Book Designers Fergal Condon, Lauren Egan

Cover Researcher Naomi Parker

Thanks to Liz Heynes, Corey Hutchison, Kate Mathews, Kirsten Rawlings, Tony Wheeler

Send Us Your Feedback

We love to hear from travellers – your comments keep us on our toes and help make our books better. Our well-travelled team reads every word on what you loved or loathed about this book. Although we cannot reply individually to postal submissions, we always guarantee that your feedback goes straight to the appropriate authors, in time for the next edition. Each person who sends us information is thanked in the next edition, the most useful submissions are rewarded with a selection of digital PDF chapters.

Visit lonelyplanet.com/contact to submit your updates and suggestions or to ask for help. Our award-winning website also features inspirational travel stories, news and discussions.

Note: We may edit, reproduce and incorporate your comments in Lonely Planet products such as guidebooks, websites and digital products, so let us know if you don't want your comments reproduced or your name acknowledged. For a copy of our privacy policy visit lonelyplanet.com/privacy.

000 Map pages

Symbols & Map Key

Look for these symbols to quickly identify listings:

- ◉ Sights
- ✦ Activities
- ❸ Courses
- ◉ Tours
- ✪ Festivals & Events
- ✕ Eating
- ☕ Drinking
- ✪ Entertainment
- 🔒 Shopping
- ❶ Information & Transport

These symbols and abbreviations give vital information for each listing:

- ✐ Sustainable or green recommendation
- **FREE** No payment required

- ☏ Telephone number
- ☺ Opening hours
- P Parking
- ☺ Nonsmoking
- ❄ Air-conditioning
- @ Internet access
- ☎ Wi-fi access
- ☰ Swimming pool

- ▣ Bus
- ⛴ Ferry
- ▣ Tram
- ▣ Train
- ⬚ English-language menu
- ✐ Vegetarian selection
- ✚ Family-friendly

Find your best experiences with these Great For... icons.

- Art & Culture
- Beaches
- Budget
- Cafe/Coffee
- Cycling
- Detour
- Drinking
- Entertainment
- Events
- Family Travel
- Food & Drink
- History
- Local Life
- Nature & Wildlife
- Photo Op
- Scenery
- Shopping
- Short Trip
- Sport
- Walking
- Winter Travel

Sights
- ☺ Beach
- ☺ Bird Sanctuary
- ☺ Buddhist
- ☺ Castle/Palace
- ☺ Christian
- ☺ Confucian
- ☺ Hindu
- ☺ Islamic
- ☺ Jain
- ☺ Jewish
- ☺ Monument
- ☺ Museum/Gallery/ Historic Building
- ☺ Ruin
- ☺ Shinto
- ☺ Sikh
- ☺ Taoist
- ☺ Winery/Vineyard
- ☺ Zoo/Wildlife Sanctuary
- ☺ Other Sight

Points of Interest
- ☺ Bodysurfing
- ☺ Camping
- ☺ Cafe
- ☺ Canoeing/Kayaking
- ☺ Course/Tour
- ☺ Diving
- ☺ Drinking & Nightlife
- ☺ Eating
- ☺ Entertainment
- ☺ Sento Hot Baths/ Onsen
- ☺ Shopping
- ☺ Skiing
- ☺ Sleeping
- ☺ Snorkelling
- ☺ Surfing
- ☺ Swimming/Pool
- ☺ Walking
- ☺ Windsurfing
- ☺ Other Activity

Information
- ☺ Bank
- ☺ Embassy/Consulate
- ☺ Hospital/Medical
- @ Internet
- ☺ Police
- ☺ Post Office
- ☺ Telephone
- ☺ Toilet
- ❶ Tourist Information
- ● Other Information

Geographic
- ☺ Beach
- ☺ Gate
- ☺ Hut/Shelter
- ☺ Lighthouse
- ☺ Lookout
- ▲ Mountain/Volcano
- ☺ Oasis
- ☺ Park
-)(Pass
- ☺ Picnic Area
- ☺ Waterfall

Transport
- ☺ Airport
- ☺ BART station
- ☺ Border crossing
- ☺ Boston T station
- ☺ Bus
- ☺ Cable car/Funicular
- ☺ Cycling
- ☺ Ferry
- Ⓜ Metro/MRT station
- ☺ Monorail
- P Parking
- ☺ Petrol station
- ☺ Subway/S-Bahn/ Skytrain station
- ☺ Taxi
- ☺ Train station/Railway
- ☺ Tram
- ☺ Tube Station
- ☺ Underground/ U-Bahn station
- ● Other Transport

Jean-Bernard Carrillet

Paris-based (and Metz-born) journalist and photographer Jean-Bernard has clocked up countless trips to all French regions and is a passionate ambassador of his own country. As a hopeless French gourmand and *amateur de bon vins* (wine lover), he was all too happy to research Lyon (pike dumplings, anyone?), La Dombes (that yummy frog pie), Beaujolais (oh, that St-Amour lingers long on the palate) and the Rhône Valley down to the Gorges de l'Ardèche.

Kerry Christiani

France was *le coup de foudre* (love at first sight) for Kerry, and she's been travelling there since her school days to brush up her *français*, which she went on to study to MA level. Touring the cellars of Champagne, (over)indulging on Alsatian food and wine on the storybook Route des Vins and striking out into the forested peaks of the Vosges made writing this edition memorable. Kerry authors a number of Lonely Planet's central and southern European titles and tweets @kerrychristiani.

Catherine Le Nevez

An award-winning, Paris-based travel writer, Catherine first lived in the French capital aged four and has been hitting the road at every opportunity, completing her Doctorate of Creative Arts in Writing, Masters in Professional Writing, and postgrad qualifications in Editing and Publishing along the way. Over the last dozen-plus years she's written scores of Lonely Planet guides, along with numerous print and online articles, covering Paris, France, Europe and far beyond. Wanderlust aside, Paris remains her favourite city on earth.

Hugh McNaughtan

A former English lecturer, Hugh swapped grant applications for visa applications, and turned his love of travel intro a full-time thing. Having done a bit of restaurant-reviewing in his home town (Melbourne) he's now eaten his way across the Alps and Jura, working up an appetite on the slopes at any opportunity. He's never happier than when on the road with his two daughters. Except perhaps on the cricket field.

Christopher Pitts

Christopher Pitts first moved to Paris in 2001. He initially began writing about the city as a means to buy baguettes – and to impress a certain Parisian (it worked, they're now married with two kids). Over the past decade, he has written for various publications, in addition to working as a translator and editor. Visit him online at www.christopherpitts.net.

Daniel Robinson

Co-author (with Tony Wheeler) of Lonely Planet's first Paris guide, Daniel has been writing about France for over 25 years. Passionate about history, he is always moved by the grand châteaux of the Loire, the sombre cemeteries of the Somme, and the dramatic and tragic events that both embody Daniel's travel writing has appeared in the *New York Times*, *National Geographic Traveler* and many other publications and has been translated into 10 languages. He holds degrees in history from Princeton and Tel Aviv University.

Regis St Louis

Regis' French ancestry fuelled an early interest in all things francophone, which led to Serge Gainsbourg records, François Truffaut films and extensive travels around France. For his latest journey, Regis walked the drizzly beaches of Normandy, explored Joan of Arc lore in Rouen and idled behind sheep-powered roadblocks in the Pyrenees. A full-time travel writer since 2003, Regis has covered numerous destinations for Lonely Planet, including Montreal, Senegal and New York City. Follow his latest posts on Twitter at @regisstlouis.

Our Story

A beat-up old car, a few dollars in the pocket and a sense of adventure. In 1972 that's all Tony and Maureen Wheeler needed for the trip of a lifetime – across Europe and Asia overland to Australia. It took several months, and at the end – broke but inspired – they sat at their kitchen table writing and stapling together their first travel guide, *Across Asia on the Cheap*. Within a week they'd sold 1500 copies. Lonely Planet was born.

Today, Lonely Planet has offices in Franklin, London, Melbourne, Oakland, Dublin, Beijing, and Delhi, with more than 600 staff and writers. We share Tony's belief that 'a great guidebook should do three things: inform, educate and amuse'.

Our Writers

Nicola Williams

British writer Nicola Williams has lived in France and written about it for more than a decade. From her hillside house on the southern shore of Lake Geneva, road trips beckon to Provence, Paris, to the Dordogne and onwards to the Atlantic Coast where she has spent endless years revelling in its extraordinary landscapes, architecture and seafaring cuisine. Nicola has worked on numerous Lonely Planet titles, including *France* and *Paris*. Find her on Twitter and Instagram at @Tripalong.

Alexis Averbuck

Alexis Averbuck first came to France when she was four and now visits every chance she gets. Whether browsing markets in the Dordogne, sampling oysters in Brittany, or careening through hilltop villages in Provence (she also contributes to the *Provence & Côte d'Azur* book), she immerses herself in all things French. A travel writer for two decades, Alexis has lived in Antarctica for a year, crossed the Pacific by sailboat, and is also a painter – see her work at www.alexisaverbuck.com.

Oliver Berry

Oliver Berry has explored nearly every corner of France for Lonely Planet, travelling all the way from the mountains of Corsica to the beaches of Normandy. He has also photographed and written about France for many newspapers, magazines and online publications. For this trip he returned to the beaches and hilltop villages of the South of France, and practised his pelota skills in the French Basque Country. His latest work is published at www.oliverberry.com.

More Writers

STAY IN TOUCH LONELYPLANET.COM/CONTACT

AUSTRALIA The Malt Store, Level 3, 551 Swanston St, Carlton, Victoria 3053 ☎03 8379 8000, fax 03 8379 8111

IRELAND Unit E, Digital Court. The Digital Hub, Rainsford St, Dublin 8, Ireland

USA 124 Linden Street, Oakland, CA 94607 ☎510 250 6400, toll free 800 275 8555, fax 510 893 8572

UK 240 Blackfriars Road, London SE1 8NW ☎020 3771 5100, fax 020 3771 5101

 twitter.com/ lonelyplanet
 facebook.com/ lonelyplanet
 instagram.com/ lonelyplanet
 youtube.com/ lonelyplanet
 lonelyplanet.com/ newsletter